S0-BMW-974

For same area on 4 inch scale, see sheets
22
Adjoining 8 Sheet
23
24
J
K
L
M
N
Adjoining 15 Sheet
ST LUKES
CITY ROAD
OLD STREET
GOSWELL ROAD
NEW NORTH ROAD
OLD STREET
GREAT EASTERN
HIGH STREET
SHOREDITCH
Bunhill Fields
Burl. Ground
ARTILLERY GROUND
FINSBURY SQUARE
FINSBURY CIRCUS
MOORGATE STREET
ALDERSGATE STREET
SAINT JOHN STREET
FARRINGDON STREET
HOLBORN VIADUCT
NEWGATE STREET
CHEAPSIDE
CANNON STREET
BISHOPSGATE STREET WITHOUT
LIVERPOOL STREET
OLD STREET
GREAT EASTERN RAILWAY STATION
FENCHURCH STREET RAILWAY TERMINUS
BLACKFRIARS BRIDGE
NEW BRIDGE STREET
SOUTHWARK BRIDGE ROAD
LONDON BRIDGE
CUSTOM HOUSE QUAY
SOUTHWARK
Barclay's Brewery
HOTEL
L O N D O N
T H A M E S
G.W. Bacon, F.R.G.S. 127 Strand, London. Copyright
22
Adjoining 24 Sheet
SCALE
1 Mile

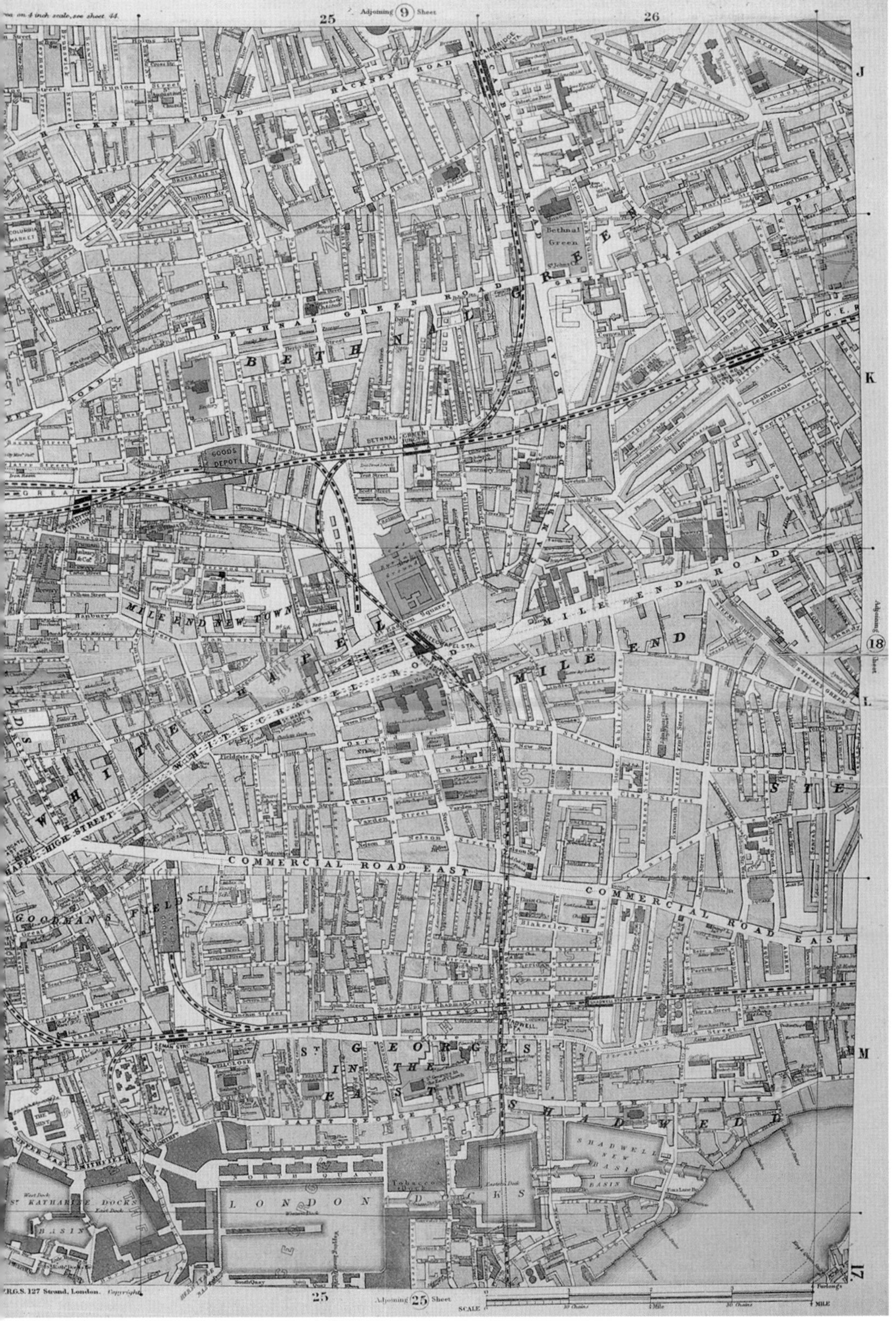

Adjoining 9 Sheet
25
26
J
K
L
M
17
HACKNEY ROAD
CAMBRIDGE ROAD
COLUMBIA MARKET
BETHNAL GREEN ROAD
BETHNAL GREEN
Bethnal Green
GOODS DEPOT
GREAT
MILE END NEW TOWN
WHITECHAPEL STA.
WHITECHAPEL ROAD
WHITECHAPEL HIGH STREET
MILE END ROAD
MILE END
STEPNEY GREEN
Adjoining 18 Sheet
COMMERCIAL ROAD EAST
GOODMAN'S FIELDS
ST GEORGES IN THE EAST
SAINT GEORGE STREET
SHADWELL
SHADWELL NEW BASIN
THE MINT
UPPER EAST SMITHFIELD
ST KATHARINE DOCKS
BASIN
LONDON DOCKS
Tobacco
NORTH QUAY
South Quay
R.G.S. 127 Strand, London. Copyright
Adjoining 25 Sheet
SCALE
MILE
Furlongs

PORTRAIT *of a* KILLER

Also by Patricia Cornwell

THE DR KAY SCARPETTA NOVELS

Postmortem (1990)

Body of Evidence (1991)

All That Remains (1992)

Cruel and Unusual (1993)

The Body Farm (1994)

From Potter's Field (1995)

Cause of Death (1996)

Unnatural Exposure (1997)

Point of Origin (1998)

Black Notice (1999)

The Last Precinct (2000)

OTHER FICTION

Hornet's Nest

Southern Cross

SHORT FICTION

Scarpetta's Winter Table

NON-FICTION

Ruth, A Portrait: The Story of Ruth Bell Graham

Food to Die For: Secrets from Kay Scarpetta's Kitchen

Beware Jack the Ripper
is going to commit
another murder on the
[illegible] December 188[illegible]
Farewell
Jack the Ripper

PORTRAIT *of a* KILLER

JACK THE RIPPER
CASE CLOSED

PATRICIA CORNWELL

A *Little, Brown* Book

First published in the United States in 2002 by G.P. Putnam's Sons,
a member of Penguin Putnam Inc.

First published in Great Britain in 2002 by Little, Brown

A CIP catalogue record for this book
is available from the British Library.

HARDBACK ISBN 0 316 86159 6
C FORMAT ISBN 0 316 72508 0

Typeset by M Rules
Printed and bound in Great Britain by
Clays Ltd, St Ives plc

Little, Brown
An imprint of
Time Warner Books UK
Brettenham House
Lancaster Place
London WC2E 7EN

www.TimeWarnerBooks.co.uk

To Scotland Yard's John Grieve

You would have caught him.

CONTENTS

There was a general panic, a great many excitable people declaring that the evil one was revisiting the earth.

—H.M., Anonymous East End Missionary, 1888

CHAPTER ONE

MR. NOBODY

Monday, August 6, 1888, was a Bank Holiday in London. The city was a carnival of wondrous things to do for as little as pennies if one could spare a few.

The bells of Windsor's Parish Church and St. George's Chapel rang throughout the day. Ships were dressed in flags, and royal salutes boomed from cannons to celebrate the Duke of Edinburgh's forty-fourth birthday.

The Crystal Palace offered a dazzling spectrum of special programs: organ recitals, military band concerts, a "monster display of fireworks," a grand fairy ballet, ventriloquists, and "world famous minstrel performances." Madame Tussaud's featured a special wax model of Frederick II lying in state and, of course, the ever-popular Chamber of Horrors. Other delicious horrors awaited those who could afford theater tickets and were in the mood for a morality play or just a good old-fashioned fright. *Dr. Jekyll and Mr. Hyde* was playing to sold-out houses. The famous American actor Richard Mansfield was brilliant as Jekyll and Hyde at Henry Irving's Lyceum, and the Opera Comique had its version, too, although poorly reviewed and in the midst of a scandal because the theater had adapted Robert Louis Stevenson's novel without permission.

On this Bank Holiday there were horse and cattle shows; special "cheap rates" on trains; and the bazaars in Covent Garden overflowing with Sheffield plates, gold, jewelry, used military uniforms. If one wanted to pretend to be a soldier on this relaxed but rowdy day, he could do so with little expense and no questions asked. Or one could impersonate a copper by renting an authentic Metropolitan Police uniform from Angel's Theatrical Costumes in Camden Town, scarcely a two-mile stroll from where the handsome Walter Richard Sickert lived.

Twenty-eight-year-old Sickert had given up his obscure acting career for the higher calling of art. He was a painter, an etcher, a student of James McNeill Whistler, and a disciple of Edgar Degas. Young Sickert was himself a work of art: slender, with a strong upper body from swimming, a perfectly angled nose and jaw, thick wavy blond hair, and blue eyes that were as inscrutable and penetrating as his secret thoughts and piercing mind. One might almost have called him pretty, except for his mouth, which could narrow into a hard, cruel line. His precise height is unknown, but a friend of his described him as a little above average. Photographs and several items of clothing donated to the Tate Gallery Archive in the 1980s suggest he was probably five foot eight or nine.

Sickert was fluent in German, English, French, and Italian. He knew Latin well enough to teach it to friends, and he was well acquainted with Danish and Greek and possibly knew a smattering of Spanish and Portuguese. He was said to read the classics in their original languages, but he didn't always finish a book once he started it. It wasn't uncommon to find dozens of novels strewn about, opened to the last page that had snagged his interest. Mostly, Sickert was addicted to newspapers, magazines, and journals.

Until his death in 1942, his studios and studies looked like a recycling center for just about every bit of newsprint to roll off the European presses. One might ask how any hard-working person could find time to go through four, five, six, ten newspapers a day, but Sickert had a method. He didn't bother with what didn't interest him, whether it was politics, economics, world affairs, wars, or people. Nothing mattered to Sickert unless it somehow affected Sickert.

He usually preferred to read about the latest entertainment to come to town, to scrutinize art critiques, to turn quickly to any story about crime, and to search for his own name if there was any reason it might be in print on a given day. He was fond of letters to the editor, especially ones he wrote and signed with a pseudonym. Sickert relished knowing what other people were doing, especially in the privacy of their own not-always-so-tidy Victorian lives. "Write, write, write!" he would beg his friends. "Tell me in detail all *sorts* of things, things that have amused you and *how* and *when* and *where,* and all sorts of gossip about every one."

Sickert despised the upper class, but he was a star stalker. He somehow managed to hobnob with the major celebrities of the day: Henry Irving and Ellen Terry, Aubrey Beardsley, Henry James, Max Beerbohm, Oscar Wilde, Monet, Renoir, Pissarro, Rodin, André Gide, Édouard Dujardin, Proust, Members of Parliament. But he did not necessarily know many of them, and no one—famous or otherwise—ever really knew him. Not even his first wife, Ellen, who would turn forty in less than two weeks. Sickert may not have given much thought to his wife's birthday on this Bank Holiday, but it was extremely unlikely he had forgotten it.

He was much admired for his amazing memory. Throughout his life he would amuse dinner guests by performing long passages of musicals and plays, dressed for the parts, his recitations flawless. Sickert would not have forgotten that Ellen's birthday was August 18th and a very easy occasion to ruin. Maybe he would "forget." Maybe he would vanish into one of his secret rented hovels that he called studios. Maybe he would take Ellen to a romantic café in Soho and leave her alone at the table while he dashed off to a music hall and then stayed out the rest of the night. Ellen loved Sickert all her sad life, despite his cold heart, his pathological lying, his self-centeredness, and his habit of disappearing for days—even weeks—without warning or explanation.

Walter Sickert was an actor by nature more than by virtue of employment. He lived on the center stage of his secret, fantasy-driven life and was just as comfortable moving about unnoticed in the deep shadows of isolated streets as he was in the midst of throbbing crowds. He had a great range of voice and was a master of greasepaint and wardrobe. So gifted at disguise was he that as a boy he often went about unrecognized by his neighbors and family.

Throughout his long and celebrated life, he was notorious for constantly changing his appearance with a variety of beards and mustaches, for his bizarre dress that in some cases constituted costumes, for his hairstyles—including shaving his head. He was, wrote French artist and friend Jacques-Emile Blanche, a "Proteus." Sickert's "genius for camouflage in dress, in the fashion of wearing his hair, and in his manner of speaking rival Fregoli's," Blanche recalled. In a portrait Wilson Steer painted of Sickert in 1890, Sickert sports a phony-looking mustache that resembles a squirrel's tail pasted above his mouth.

He also had a penchant for changing his name. His acting career, paintings, etchings, drawings, and prolific letters to colleagues, friends, and newspapers reveal many personas: Mr. Nemo (Latin for "Mr. Nobody"), An Enthusiast, A Whistlerite, Your Art Critic, An Outsider, Walter Sickert, Sickert, Walter R. Sickert, Richard Sickert, W. R. Sickert, W.S., R.S., S., Dick, W. St., Rd. Sickert LL.D., R.St. A.R.A., and RDSt A.R.A.

Sickert did not write his memoirs, keep a diary or calendar, or date most of his letters or works of art, so it is difficult to know where he was or what he was doing on or during any given day, week, month, or even year. I could find no record of his whereabouts or activities on August 6, 1888, but there is no reason to suspect he was not in London. Based on notes he scribbled on music-hall sketches, he was in London just two days earlier, on August 4th.

Whistler would be getting married in London five days later, on August 11th. Although Sickert hadn't been invited to the small, intimate wedding, he wasn't the sort to miss it—even if he had to spy on it.

The great painter James McNeill Whistler had fallen deeply in love with the "remarkably pretty" Beatrice Godwin, who was to occupy the most prominent position in his life and entirely change the course of it. Likewise, Whistler occupied one of the most prominent positions in Sickert's life and had entirely changed the course of it. "Nice boy, Walter," Whistler used to say in the early 1880s when he was still fond of the aspiring and extraordinarily gifted young man. By the time of Whistler's engagement their friendship had cooled, but Sickert could not have been prepared for what must have seemed a shockingly unexpected and complete abandonment by the Master he idolized, envied, and hated. Whistler and his new bride planned to honeymoon and travel the rest of the year in France, where they hoped to reside permanently.

The anticipated connubial bliss of the flamboyant artistic genius and egocentric James McNeill Whistler must have been disconcerting to his former errand boy–apprentice. One of Sickert's many roles was the irresistible womanizer, but offstage he was nothing of the sort. Sickert was dependent on women and loathed them. They were intellectually inferior and useless except as caretakers or objects to manipulate, especially for art or money. Women were a dangerous reminder of an infuriating and humiliating secret that Sickert carried not only to the grave but beyond it, because cremated bodies reveal no tales of the flesh, even if they are exhumed. Sickert was born with a deformity of his penis requiring operations when he was a toddler that would have left him disfigured if not mutilated. He probably was incapable of an erection. He may not have had enough of a penis left for penetration, and it is quite possible he had to squat like a woman to urinate.

"My theory of the crimes is that the criminal has been badly disfigured," says an October 4, 1888, letter filed with the Whitechapel Murders papers at the Corporation of London Records Office, "*—possibly* *had* his privy member destroyed—& he is now revenging himself on the sex by these atrocities." The letter is written in purple pencil and enigmatically signed "Scotus," which could be the Latin for Scotsman. "Scotch" can mean a shallow incision or to cut. Scotus could also be a strange and erudite reference to Johannes Scotus Eriugena, a ninth-century theologian and teacher of grammar and dialectics.

For Walter Sickert to imagine Whistler in love and enjoying a sexual relationship with a woman might well have been the catalyst that made Sickert one of the most dangerous and confounding killers of all time. He began to act out what he had scripted most of his life, not only in thought but in boyhood sketches that depicted women being abducted, tied up, and stabbed.

The psychology of a violent, remorseless murderer is not defined by connecting dots. There are no facile explanations or infallible sequences of cause and effect. But the compass of human nature can point a certain way, and Sickert's feelings could only have been inflamed by Whistler's marrying the widow of architect and archaeologist Edward Godwin, the man who had lived with actress Ellen Terry and fathered her children.

The sensuously beautiful Ellen Terry was one of the most famous actresses of the Victorian era, and Sickert was fixated on her. As a teenager, he had stalked her and her acting partner, Henry Irving. Now Whistler had links to not one but both objects of Sickert's obsessions, and these three stars in Sickert's universe formed a constellation that did not include him. The stars cared nothing about him. He was truly Mr. Nemo.

But in the late summer of 1888 he gave himself a new stage name that during his life would never be linked to him, a name that soon enough would be far better known than those of Whistler, Irving, and Terry.

The actualization of Jack the Ripper's violent fantasies began on the carefree Bank Holiday of August 6, 1888, when he slipped out of the wings to make his debut in a series of ghastly performances that were destined to become the most celebrated so-called murder mystery in history.

It is widely and incorrectly believed that his violent spree ended as abruptly as it began, that he struck out of nowhere and then vanished from the scene.

Decades passed, then fifty years, then a hundred, and his bloody sexual crimes have become anemic and impotent. They are puzzles, mystery weekends, games, and "Ripper Walks" that end with pints in the Ten Bells pub. Saucy Jack, as the Ripper sometimes called himself, has starred in moody movies featuring famous actors and special effects and spates of what the Ripper said he craved: blood, blood, blood. His butcheries no longer inspire fright, rage, or even pity as his victims moulder quietly, some of them in unmarked graves.

CHAPTER TWO

THE TOUR

Not long before Christmas, 2001, I was walking to my apartment in New York's Upper East Side, and I knew I seemed downcast and agitated, despite my efforts to appear composed and in a fine mood.

I don't remember much about that night, not even the restaurant where a group of us ate. I vaguely recall that Lesley Stahl told a scary story about her latest investigation for *60 Minutes,* and everyone at the table was talking politics and economics. I offered another writer encouragement, citing my usual empowerment spiels and do-what-you-love lines, because I did not want to talk about myself or the work that I worried was ruining my life. My heart felt squeezed, as if grief would burst in my chest any moment.

My literary agent, Esther Newberg, and I set out on foot for our part of town. I had little to say on the dark sidewalk as we passed the usual suspects out walking their dogs and the endless stream of loud people talking on mobile phones. I barely noticed yellow cabs or horns. I began to imagine some thug trying to grab our briefcases or us. I would chase him and dive for his ankles and knock him to the ground. I am five foot five and weigh 120 pounds, and I can run fast, and I'd show him, yes I would. I fantasized about what I would do if some psychopathic piece of garbage came up from behind us in the dark and suddenly . . .

"How's it going?" Esther asked.

"To tell you the truth . . ." I began, because I rarely told Esther the truth.

It was not my habit to admit to my agent or my publisher, Phyllis Grann, that I was ever frightened or uneasy about what I was doing. The two women were the big shots in my professional existence and had faith in me. If I said I had been investigating Jack the Ripper and knew who he was, they didn't doubt me for a moment.

"I'm miserable," I confessed, and I was so dismayed that I felt like crying.

"You are?" Esther's stop-for-nothing stride hesitated for a moment on Lexington Avenue. "You're miserable? Really? Why?"

"I hate this book, Esther. I don't know how the hell . . . All I did was look at his paintings and his life, and one thing led to another. . . ."

She didn't say a word.

It has always been easier for me to get angry than to show fear or loss, and I was losing my life to Walter Richard Sickert. He was taking it away from me. "I want to write my novels," I said. "I don't want to write about him. There's no joy in this. None."

"Well, you know," she said very calmly as she resumed her pace, "you don't have to do it. I can get you out of it."

She could have gotten me out of it, but I could never have gotten myself out of it. I knew the identity of a murderer and I couldn't possibly avert my gaze. "I am suddenly in a position of judgment," I told Esther. "It doesn't matter if he's dead. Every now and then this small voice asks me, what if you're wrong? I would never forgive myself for saying such a thing about somebody, and then finding out I'm wrong."

"But you don't believe you're wrong. . . ."

"No. Because I'm not," I said.

It all began innocently enough, like setting out to cross a lovely country lane and suddenly being hit by a cement truck. I was in London in May 2001, promoting the archaeological excavation of Jamestown. My friend Linda Fairstein, head of the sex crimes unit for the New York District Attorney's Office, was in London, too, and asked if I'd like to drop by Scotland Yard for a tour.

"Not right now," I said, and even as the words left my mouth, I imagined how little my readers would respect me if they knew that sometimes I just don't feel like touring one more police department, laboratory, morgue, firing range, cemetery, penitentiary, crime scene, law-enforcement agency, or anatomical museum.

When I travel, especially abroad, my key to the city is often an invitation to visit its violent, sad sights. In Buenos Aires, I was given a proud tour of that city's crime museum, a room of decapitated heads preserved in formalin inside glass boxes. Only the most notorious criminals made it into this gruesome gallery, and they had gotten what was coming to them, I supposed, as they stared back at me with milky eyes. In Salta, in northwestern Argentina, I was shown five-hundred-year-old mummies of Inca children who had been buried alive to please the gods. A few years ago in London, I was given VIP treatment in a plague pit where one could scarcely move in the mud without stepping on human bones.

I worked in the Office of the Chief Medical Examiner in Richmond, Virginia, for six years, programming computers, compiling statistical analyses, and helping out in the morgue. I scribed for the forensic pathologists, weighed organs, wrote down trajectories and the sizes of wounds, inventoried the prescription drugs of suicide victims who would not take their antidepressants, helped undress fully rigorous people who rigidly resisted our removing their clothes, labeled test tubes, wiped up blood, and saw, touched, smelled, and even tasted death because the stench of it clings to the back of one's throat.

I don't forget the faces of or the smallest details about people who are murdered. I've seen so many. I couldn't possibly count how many, and I wish I could fill a huge room with them before *it* happened and beg them to lock their doors or install an alarm system—or at least get a dog—or not park there or stay away from drugs. I feel the prick of pain when I envision the dented aerosol can of Brut deodorant in the pocket of the teenaged boy showing off and deciding to stand up in the back of a pickup truck. He didn't notice it was about to drive under a bridge. I still can't comprehend the randomness of the death of the man struck by lightning after he was handed a metal-tipped umbrella as he got off a plane.

My intense curiosity about violence hardened long ago into a suit of clinical armor that is protective but so heavy sometimes I can barely walk after visits with the dead. It seems the dead want my energy and desperately try to suck it out of me as they lie in their own blood on the street or on top of a stainless-steel table. The dead stay dead and I stay drained. Murder is not a mystery, and it is my mission to fight it with my pen.

It would have been a betrayal of what I am and an insult to Scotland Yard and every law enforcer in Christendom for me to be "tired" the day Linda Fairstein said she could arrange a tour.

"That's very kind of Scotland Yard," I told her. "I've never been there."

The next morning, I met with Deputy Assistant Commissioner John Grieve, one of the most respected investigators in Britain, and, as it turned out, an expert in Jack the Ripper's crimes. The fabled Victorian killer interested me mildly. I had never read a Ripper book in my life. I knew nothing about his murders. I did not know his victims were prostitutes or how they died. I asked a few questions. Perhaps I could use Scotland Yard in my next Scarpetta novel, I thought. If so, I would need to know factual details about the Ripper cases, and perhaps Scarpetta would have new insights to offer about them.

John Grieve offered to take me on a retrospective tour of the Ripper crime scenes—what was left of them after 113 years. I cancelled a trip to Ireland to spend a rainy, freezing morning with the famous Mr. Grieve and Detective Inspector Howard Gosling, walking about Whitechapel and Spitalfields, to Mitre Square, and to Miller's Court where Mary Kelly was flayed to the bone by this serial murderer people call the Ripper.

"Has anyone ever tried to use modern forensic science to solve these crimes?" I asked.

"No," John Grieve said, and he gave me a very short list of very weak suspects. "There's one other interesting chap you might want to check out, as long as you're going to look into it. An artist named Walter Sickert. He painted some murder pictures. In one of them in particular, a clothed man is sitting on the edge of a bed with the body of the nude prostitute he just murdered. It's called *The Camden Town Murder.* I've always wondered about him."

It wasn't the first time Sickert had been connected with Jack the Ripper's crimes. Most people have always found the notion laughable.

I began to wonder about Sickert when I was flipping through a book of his art. The first plate I landed on was an 1887 painting of the well-known Victorian performer Ada Lundberg at the Marylebone Music Hall. She is supposed to be singing but looks as if she is screaming as the leering, menacing men look on. I am sure there are artistic explanations for all of Sickert's works. But what I see when I look at them is morbidity, violence, and a hatred of women. As I continued to follow Sickert and the Ripper, I began to see unsettling parallels. Some of his paintings bear a chilling resemblance to mortuary and scene photographs of Jack the Ripper's victims.

I noticed murky images of clothed men reflected in mirrors inside gloomy bedrooms where nude women sit on iron bedsteads. I saw impending violence and death. I saw a victim who had no reason to fear the charming, handsome man who had just coaxed her into a place and state of utter vulnerability. I saw a diabolically creative mind, and I saw evil.

I began adding layer after layer of circumstantial evidence to the physical evidence discovered by modern forensic science and expert minds.

All along, forensic scientists and I have hoped for DNA. But it would be a year and more than a hundred tests later before we would begin to see the first shadows of the 75- to 114-year-old genetic evidence that Walter Sickert and Jack the Ripper left when they touched and licked postage stamps and envelope flaps. Cells from the inside of their mouths sloughed off into their saliva and were sealed in adhesive until DNA scientists apprehended the genetic markers with tweezers, sterile water, and cotton swabs.

The best result came from a Ripper letter that yielded a single-donor mitochondrial DNA sequence, specific enough to eliminate 99% of the population as the person who licked and touched the adhesive backing of that stamp. This same DNA sequence profile turned up as a component of another Ripper letter, and two Walter Sickert letters.

Genetic locations from this DNA sequence were found on other Sickert items, such as overalls he wore when he painted. The DNA in all but the single-donor Ripper stamp is mixed with other genetic sequence profiles from other people. (This is neither surprising nor damning.) The DNA evidence is the oldest ever tested in a criminal case.

This is only the beginning. We aren't finished with our DNA testing and other types of forensic analyses. These could go on for years as the technology advances at an exponential rate.

There is other physical evidence as well. Forensic scientists as well as art, paper, and lettering experts found the following: a Ripper letter written on artists' paper; watermarks on paper used in Ripper letters that match watermarks on paper used by Walter Sickert; Ripper letters written with the waxy-soft crayonlike ground used in lithography; Ripper letters with paint or ink applied with a paintbrush. A microscopic exam revealed that the "dried blood" on Ripper letters is consistent with the oil-and-wax mixtures used in etching ground, and under ultraviolet light it fluoresced milky white, which is also consistent with etching ground. Art experts say that sketches in Ripper letters are professional and are consistent with Walter Sickert's art works and technique.

As an interesting aside, a blood-detection test conducted on the blood-like etching ground smeared and painted on Ripper letters came up as inconclusive—which is very unusual. Two possible explanations are as follows: It could be a reaction to microscopic particles of copper, since in this type of testing copper could cause inconclusive results or a false positive; or it could be the presence of blood mixed with the brown etching ground.

Handwriting quirks and the position of the Ripper's hand when he wrote his taunting, violent letters lurk in other Ripper writings that are disguised. These same quirks and hand positions lurk in Sickert's erratic handwriting as well.

Paper of letters the Ripper sent to the Metropolitan Police precisely matches paper of a letter the Ripper sent to the City of London Police—even though the handwriting is different. It is evident that Sickert was right-handed, but video footage taken of him when he was in his 70s shows he was quite adept at using his left hand. Lettering expert Sally Bower believes that in some Ripper letters the writing was disguised by a right-handed person writing with his left hand. It is obvious that the actual Ripper wrote far more of the Ripper letters than he has ever been credited with. In fact, I believe he wrote most of them. In fact, Walter Sickert wrote most of them. Even when his skilled artistic hands altered his writing, his arrogance and characteristic language cannot help but assert themselves.

No doubt there will always be skeptics and critics tainted by self-interest who will refuse to accept that Sickert was a serial killer, a damaged, diabolical man driven by megalomania and hate. There will be those who will argue that it's all coincidence.

As FBI profiler Ed Sulzbach says, "There really aren't many coincidences in life. And to call coincidence after coincidence after coincidence a coincidence is just plain stupid."

Fifteen months after my first meeting with Scotland Yard's John Grieve, I returned to him and presented the case.

"What would you do had you known all this and been the detective back then?" I asked him.

"I would immediately put Sickert under surveillance to try to find where his bolt holes [secret rooms] were, and if we found any, we would get search warrants," he replied as we drank coffee in an East End Indian restaurant.

"If we didn't get any more evidence than what we've now got," he went on, "we'd be happy to put the case before the crown prosecutor."

CHAPTER THREE

THE UNFORTUNATES

It is hard to imagine that Walter Sickert did not engage in London's festive activities on the much-anticipated Bank Holiday of August 6th. For the art lover on a budget, a penny would buy admission into all sorts of exhibits in the squalid East End; for the better off, a shilling would pay for a peek at the masterpieces of Corot, Diaz, and Rousseau in the high-priced galleries on New Bond Street.

Trams were free—at least those running to Whitechapel, the city's crowded clothing district where costermongers, merchants, and money changers loudly hawked their goods and services seven days a week while ragged children prowled the fetid streets for food and a chance to trick a stranger out of a coin. Whitechapel was home to "the people of the dustbin," as many good Victorians called the desperate wretches who lived there. For a few farthings, a visitor could watch street acrobatics, performing dogs, and freak shows, or get drunk. Or he could solicit sex from a prostitute—or "unfortunate"—of whom there were thousands.

One of them was Martha Tabran. She was about forty and separated from a furniture warehouse packer named Henry Samuel Tabran, who had walked out of her life because of her heavy drinking. He was decent enough to give her a weekly allowance of twelve shillings until he heard she was living with another man, a carpenter named Henry Turner. But Turner eventually lost patience with Martha's drinking habits and had left her two or three weeks ago. The last time he saw her alive was two nights earlier, on Saturday, August 4th—the same night Sickert was making sketches at Gatti's music hall near the Strand. Turner handed Martha a few coins, which she wasted on drink.

For centuries, many people believed women turned to prostitution because they suffered from a genetic defect that caused them to enjoy sex for the sake of sex. There were several types of immoral or wanton women, some worse than others. Although concubines, mistresses, and good wenches were not to be praised, the greatest sinner was the whore. A whore was a whore by choice and was not about to retire from her "wicked and abominable course of life," Thomas Heywoode lamented in his 1624 history of women. "I am altogether discouraged when I remember the position of one of the most notorious in the trade," who said, " 'For once a whore and ever a whore, I know it by my self.' "

Sexual activity was to be confined to the institution of marriage and had been ordained by God for the sole purpose of the continuation of the species. The solar center of a woman's universe was her uterus, and monthly menstrual cycles precipitated great storms of disorders—throbbing lust, hysteria, and insanity. Women were a lower order and incapable of rational, abstract thought, a view with which Walter Sickert concurred. He was quite eager to assert that women were incapable of understanding art, that they were interested in it only when it "ministers to their vanity" or elevates them "in those social classifications they study so anxiously." Women of genius, the rare few there were, Sickert said, "count as men."

His beliefs were not unusual for the era. Women were a different "race." Contraception was a blasphemy against God and society, and poverty flourished as women gave birth at an alarming rate. Sex was to be enjoyed by women for the sole reason that physiologically, an orgasm was thought to be essential for the secretion of the fluids necessary for conception. To experience the "thrill" while unmarried or by oneself was perverse and a serious threat to sanity, salvation, and health. Some nineteenth-century English physicians cured masturbation with clitorectomy. The "thrill" for the sake of the "thrill," especially among females, was socially abhorrent. It was wicked. It was barbaric.

Christian men and women had heard the stories. Way back in the days of Herodotus, Egyptian females were so aberrant and blasphemous, they dared to mock God by giving themselves up to raging lust and flaunting the pleasures of the flesh. In those primitive days, satisfying lust for money was desirable, not shameful. A voracious sexual appetite was good, not evil. When a beautiful young woman died, there was nothing wrong with hot-blooded males enjoying her body until it was getting a bit ripe and ready for the embalmer. Such stories were not repeated in polite company, but the decent nineteenth-century families of Sickert's day knew that the Bible had not a single nice thing to say about strumpets.

The notion that only guiltless people cast the first stone was forgotten. That was plain enough when crowds swelled to watch a public beheading or hanging. Somewhere along the way the belief that the sins of the father will be visited on the children got translated into the belief that the sins of the mother will be revisited among the children. Thomas Heywoode wrote that a woman's "vertue once violated brings infamy and dishonour." The poisons of the offending woman's sin, Heywoode promised, will extend to the "posteritie which shall arise from so corrupt a seed, generated from unlawful and adulterate copulation."

Two hundred and fifty years later, the English language was a bit easier to understand, but Victorian beliefs about women and immorality were the same: Sexual intercourse was for the purposes of procreation, and the "thrill" was the catalyst to conception. Quackery perpetuated by physicians stated as medical fact that the "thrill" was essential to a woman's becoming pregnant. If a raped woman got pregnant, then she had experienced an orgasm during the sexual encounter, and intercourse could not have been against her will. If a raped woman did not become pregnant, she could not have had an orgasm, indicating her claims of violation might be the truth.

Men of the nineteenth century were very much preoccupied with the female orgasm. The "thrill" was so important, one has to wonder how often it was faked. That would be a good trick to learn—then barrenness could be blamed on the male. If a woman could not have an orgasm and was honest about it, her condition might be diagnosed as female impotence. A thorough examination by a doctor was needed, and the simple treatment of digital manipulation of the clitoris and breasts was often sufficient in determining whether the patient was impotent. If the nipples hardened during the examination, the prognosis was promising. If the patient experienced the "thrill," the husband would be most pleased to know that his wife was healthy.

London's Unfortunates, as prostitutes were called by the press, police, and the public, did not drift along the cold, dirty, dark streets in search of the "thrill," despite the belief of many Victorians that prostitutes wanted to be prostitutes because of their insatiable sexual appetites. If they would give up their evil ways and turn to God, they would be blessed with bread and shelter. God took care of His own, so the Salvation Army said when its women volunteers braved the East End slums and handed out little cakes and promises from the Lord. Unfortunates such as Martha Tabran would gratefully take the cake and then take to the streets.

Without a man to support her, a woman had scant means of keeping herself or her children alive. Employment—if a woman could find it—

meant working six twelve-hour days making coats in sweatshops for the equivalent of twenty-five cents a week. If she was lucky, it meant earning seventy-five cents a week for seven fourteen-hour days gluing together match boxes. Most of the wages went to greedy slumlords, and sometimes the only food came from mother and children searching the streets or picking through garbage for festering fruit and vegetables.

Sailors from foreign ships anchored at the nearby docks, military men, and the upper-class male clandestinely on the prowl made it all too easy for a desperate woman to rent out her body for a few coins until it became as dilapidated as the vermin-infested ruins where the people of the East End dwelled. Malnutrition, alcoholism, and physical abuse reduced a woman to shambles quickly, and the Unfortunate slid lower in the pecking order. She sought out the darkest, most remote streets, stairwells, and courtyards, both she and her client usually falling-down drunk.

Alcohol was the easiest way to not be present, and a disproportionate number of people of "The Abyss," as writer Jack London called the East End, were alcoholics. Probably all Unfortunates were. They were diseased and old beyond their years, cast out by husbands and children, and unable to accept Christian charity because it did not include drink. These pitiful women frequented pubs and asked men to treat them to drinks. Business usually followed.

No matter the weather, Unfortunates haunted the night like nocturnal animals, in wait for any man, no matter how rough or disgusting, who might be enticed into parting with pennies for pleasure. Preferably, sex was performed standing up, with the prostitute gathering her many layers of clothing and lifting them out of the way, her back to her client. If she was lucky, he was too drunk to know that his penis was being inserted between her thighs and not into any orifice.

Martha Tabran fell behind in her rent after Henry Turner walked out on her. Her whereabouts since aren't clear, but one might guess she was in and out of common lodging houses, or if she had a choice between a bed and a drink, she most likely took the drink and dozed in doorways, in parks, and on the street, continually chased off by the police. Martha spent the nights of August 4th and 5th in a common lodging house on Dorset Street, just south of a music hall on Commercial Street.

At eleven o'clock this Bank Holiday night of August 6th, Martha met up with Mary Ann Connolly, who went by the alias of Pearly Poll. The weather had been unpleasant all day, overcast and unsettled as the temperature continued to drop to an unseasonable fifty-two degrees. Afternoon fog was followed by a thick mist that obscured the new moon and was forecast to last until seven o'clock the next morning. But the two women were used to unpleasant conditions and might have been miserably uncomfortable but rarely vulnerable to hypothermia. It was the habit of Unfortunates to walk about in everything they owned. If one did not have a permanent residence, to leave belongings in a lodging house was to lose them to a thief.

The late hour was lively and alcohol flowed freely as Londoners stretched out what was left of their day off from labor. Most plays and musicals had begun at 8:15 and would have let out by now, and many theatergoers and other adventurers in horse-drawn cabs and on foot braved the mist-shrouded streets in search of refreshment and other entertainment. Visibility in the East End was poor under the best conditions. Gaslights were few and spaced far apart. They gave out smudges of illumination, and shadows were impenetrable. It was the world of the Unfortunate, a continuum of sleeping away days and getting up to drink before venturing out into another numbing night of sordid and dangerous employment.

Fog made no difference unless the pollution was especially high and the acrid air stung the eyes and lungs. At least when it was foggy, one didn't have to notice whether a client was pleasant in appearance or even see his face. Nothing about the client mattered anyway, unless he was inclined to take a personal interest in an Unfortunate and supply her with room and food. Then he was of consequence, but virtually no client was of consequence when one was past her prime, dirty, dressed like a pauper, and scarred or missing teeth. Martha Tabran preferred to dissolve into the mist and get it over with for a farthing, another drink, and maybe another farthing and a bed.

The events leading to her murder are well documented and considered reliable unless one is inclined to feel, as I do, that the recollections of a hard-drinking prostitute named Pearly Poll might lack a certain clarity and veracity. If she didn't outright lie when she was interviewed by the police and later when she testified at the coroner's inquest on August 23rd, she was probably confused and suffering from alcohol-induced amnesia. Pearly Poll was frightened. She told police she was so upset that she might just drown herself in the Thames.

During the inquest, Pearly Poll was reminded several times that she was under oath as she testified that on August 6th, at 10:00 P.M., she and Martha Tabran began drinking with two soldiers in Whitechapel. The couples went their separate ways at 11:45. Pearly Poll told the coroner and jurors that she went up Angel Court with the "corporal," while Martha headed toward George Yard with the "private," and that both soldiers wore white bands around their caps. The last time Pearly Poll saw Martha and the private, they were walking toward the dilapidated tenement block of George Yard Buildings on Commercial Street, in the dark heart of the East End slums. Pearly Poll claimed nothing out of the ordinary happened while she had been with Martha that night. Their encounter with the soldiers had been pleasant enough. There had been no fighting or arguments, nothing at all that might have set off even the faintest alarm in either Pearly Poll or Martha, who certainly had seen it all and had survived the streets a long time for good reason.

Pearly Poll claimed to know nothing about what happened to Martha after 11:45 P.M., nor is there any record of what Pearly Poll herself was up to after she slipped away with her corporal for "immoral purposes."

When she learned that Martha had been murdered, Pearly Poll might have had cause to worry about her own welfare and to think twice about giving too much information to the coppers. She wouldn't put it past those boys in blue to listen to her story and then send her to prison as "a scapegoat for five thousand of her class." Pearly Poll was to stick to her story: She had ended up in Angel Court, a good mile's walk from where she left Martha, and inside the City of London. The City was not under the jurisdiction of the Metropolitan Police.

For a wily, street-smart prostitute to place herself outside the legal reach of the Metropolitan Police was to encourage the constables and detectives to avoid turning the case into a complicated, competitive multi-jurisdictional investigation. The City of London—better known as "the Square Mile"—is an ornery oddity that can be traced back to 1 A.D. when the Romans founded the city on the banks of the Thames. The City remains a city unto itself with its own municipal services and government, including its own police force, which today serves a resident population of 6,000—a number that swells to more than a quarter of a million during business hours.

Historically, the City has never been interested in the concerns of the greater London area unless one of its problems somehow impacts on the City's autonomy or quality of life; it has always been a stubborn, wealthy oasis in the midst of a spreading metropolis. The existence of the City remains unknown to many a tourist. I don't know if Pearly Poll really took her client into the deserted City to avoid the Metropolitan Police or for any other reason. She might not have gone near the City, but instead conducted her business quickly, collected her meager fee, and went off to the nearest public house or returned to Dorset Street to find a bed.

Two hours and fifteen minutes after Pearly Poll said she saw Martha last, Police Constable 226 Barrett of Metropolitan Police Division H was on routine patrol on Wentworth Street, which intersected with Commercial Street and ran along the north side of George Yard Buildings. At 2:00

A.M., Barrett noticed a soldier out alone. He appeared to belong to one of the regiments of footguards who wore white bands around their caps. Barrett estimated that the soldier, a private, was between the ages of twenty-two and twenty-six, and five foot nine or ten. The young man in his neat uniform had a fair complexion and a small, dark-brown mustache turned up at the ends, and wore no medals on his uniform except a good-conduct badge. The soldier told P.C. Barrett that he was "waiting for a chum who had gone with a girl."

At the same time this brief exchange was taking place, a Mr. and Mrs. Mahoney of George Yard Buildings passed the landing where Martha's body was later found and heard nothing of note and saw no sign of anyone. Martha had not been murdered yet. Perhaps she was nearby in the shadows, waiting for the constable to resume his patrol so she could resume business with the soldier. Perhaps the soldier had nothing to do with Martha at all and is simply a source of confusion. Whatever the truth, it is evident that P.C. Barrett's attention was piqued by a soldier alone in the street at 2:00 A.M. outside George Yard Buildings, and whether he questioned this soldier or not, the soldier felt compelled to offer an explanation as to why he was there.

The identities of that soldier and any other soldiers associated with Pearly Poll and Martha the night of August 6th and early morning of the 7th remain unknown. Pearly Poll, Barrett, and other witnesses who had noticed Martha on the street were never able to positively identify any soldiers in the guard room at the Tower of London or in Wellington Barracks. Every man who seemed even remotely familiar had a believable alibi. A search through the belongings of soldiers produced no evidence, including blood. Martha Tabran's killer would have been bloody.

Chief Inspector Donald Swanson of Scotland Yard's Criminal Investigation Department (CID) acknowledged in his special report that there was no reason to think that Martha Tabran had been with anybody but the soldier she had walked off with before midnight, although it was possible, due to the "lapse of time," that she might have been with another client. She might have been with several. The puzzle of the "private" seen with Martha at 11:45 and the "private" seen by P. C. Barrett at 2:00 A.M. nagged at Scotland Yard because he was seen so close to when and where Martha was murdered. Maybe he did it. Maybe he really was a soldier.

Or maybe he was a killer disguised as a soldier. What a brilliant bit of trickery that would have been. There were plenty of soldiers out on Bank Holiday night, and cruising for prostitutes was not an uncommon activity among military men. It may seem a stretch to consider that Jack the Ripper might have donned a soldier's uniform and pasted on a fake mustache to commit his first murder, but this would not be the last time a mysterious man in uniform would be connected with a murder in London's East End.

Walter Sickert was familiar with uniforms. Later, during World War I when he was painting battle scenes, he would admit to being especially "enchanted" by French ones. "I have got my Belgian uniforms today," he wrote in 1914. "The artillery man's forage cap with a little gold tassel is the sauciest thing in the world." As a boy, Sickert frequently sketched men in uniforms and armor. As Mr. Nemo, the actor, his most critically acclaimed performance was in 1880, when he played a French soldier in Shakespeare's *Henry V.* At some point between 1887 and 1889, Sickert completed a painting he titled *It All Comes from Sticking to a Soldier*—the painting that depicts music-hall performer Ada Lundberg singing as she is surrounded by leering men.

Sickert's interest in things military never waned throughout his life, and it was his habit to ask the Red Cross for the uniforms of soldiers who were disabled or dying. His motive, he said, was to outfit models for his military sketches and paintings. At one time, an acquaintance recalled, Sickert's studio was piled with uniforms and rifles.

"I am doing a portrait of a dear dead man, a Colonel," he wrote. He asked a friend to help him "borrow some uniforms from Belgians in hospital. One has a kind of distaste for using misfortunes to further one's own ends." He didn't really. He admitted more than once to his "purely selfish practice of life." As he himself said, "I live entirely for my work— or as some people put it, for myself."

It is surprising that the possibility of a Ripper who wore disguises hasn't been emphasized more or explored as a likely scenario, one that would surely help explain why he seemed to vanish without a trace after his crimes. A Ripper using disguises would also explain the variety of descriptions witnesses gave of the men supposedly last seen with the victims. The use of disguises by violent offenders is not uncommon. Men who dressed as police, soldiers, maintenance workers, deliverymen, servicemen, paramedics, and even clowns have been convicted of violent serial crimes, including sexual murders. A disguise is a simple and effective way to gain access and lure the victim without resistance or suspicion, and to get away with robbery, rape, or murder. Disguises allow the perpetrator to return to the scene of the crime and watch the investigative drama or to attend the victim's funeral.

A psychopath intent on murder uses any means to con a victim out of life. Eliciting trust before the kill is part of the psychopath's script, and this requires acting, whether the person has ever stepped foot on a stage or not. When one has seen a psychopath's victims, alive or dead, it is hard to call such an offender a *person.* To begin to understand Jack the Ripper one must understand psychopaths, and to understand is not necessarily to accept. What these people do is foreign to every fantasy and feeling most of us have ever experienced. All people have the capacity for evil, but psychopaths are not like all of us.

The psychiatric community defines psychopathy as an antisocial behavioral disorder, more dominant in males than females and statistically five times more likely to occur in the male offspring of a father suffering from the disorder. Symptoms of psychopathy, according to the *Diag-*

nostic and Statistical Manual of Mental Disorders, include stealing, lying, substance abuse, financial irresponsibility, an inability to deal with boredom, cruelty, running away from home, promiscuity, fighting, lack of remorse.

Psychopaths are uniquely different from one another in very much the same way that individuals differ from one another. A psychopath might be promiscuous and lie but be financially responsible. A psychopath might fight and be promiscuous but not steal, might torture animals but not abuse alcohol or drugs, might torture people and not animals. A psychopath might commit multiple murders but not be promiscuous. The combinations of antisocial behaviors are countless, but the most distinctive and profound characteristic of *all* psychopaths is that they do not feel remorse. They have no concept of guilt. They do not have a conscience.

I had heard and read about a vicious killer named John Royster months before I actually saw him in person during his murder trial in New York City in the winter of 1997. I was shocked by how polite and gentle he seemed. His pleasant looks, neat clothes, slight build, and the braces on his teeth jolted me as his handcuffs were removed and he was seated at his defense counsel's table. Had I met Royster in Central Park and seen him flash his silver smile at me as I jogged by, I would not have felt the slightest breath of fear.

From June 4 through June 11, 1996, John Royster destroyed the lives of four women by grabbing them from behind, throwing them to the ground, and repeatedly smashing their heads against pavement, concrete, and cobblestone until he thought they were dead. He was cool and calculating enough to put down his knapsack and take off his coat before each assault. As his victims lay bleeding on the ground, battered beyond recognition, he raped them if he could. Then he calmly gathered up his belongings and left the scene. Bashing a woman's head to mush was sexually exciting to him, and he admitted to the police that he felt no remorse.

In the late 1880s, this sort of antisocial behavioral disorder—an insipid phrase—was diagnosed as "moral insanity," which ironically is a defense that recently has been tried in court. In his 1893 book on criminology, Arthur MacDonald defined what we would call a psychopath as a "pure murderer." These people are "honest," MacDonald writes, because they are not thieves "by nature" and many are "chaste in character." But all are "unconscious" of feeling "any repulsion" over their violent acts. As a rule, pure murderers begin to show "traces of a murderous tendency" when they are children.

Psychopaths can be male or female, child or adult. They are not always violent but they are always dangerous, because they have no respect for rules and no regard for any life but their own. Psychopaths have an x-factor unfamiliar if not incomprehensible to most of us, and at the time of writing no one is certain whether this x-factor is genetic, pathological (due to a head injury, for example), or caused by a spiritual depravity beyond our limited understanding. Ongoing research into the criminal brain is beginning to suggest that a psychopath's gray matter is not necessarily normal. In the general prison population of murderers in America, it has been shown that more than 80% of them were abused as children, and 50% of these offenders have frontal lobe abnormalities.

The frontal lobe is the master control for civilized human behavior and is located, as its name implies, in the frontal part of the brain. Lesions, such as tumors or damage from a head injury, can turn a well-behaved person into a stranger with poor self-control and aggressive or violent tendencies. In the mid-1900s, severe antisocial behavior was remedied by the notorious prefrontal lobotomy, a procedure accomplished by surgery or by hammering an ice pick through the roof of an eye orbit to shear the wiring that connects the frontal part of the brain to the rest of it.

The psychopathic brain, however, cannot be wholly accounted for by traumatic childhoods and brain lesions. Studies using PET scans (positron emission tomography), which show images of the living brain at work, reveal that there is noticeably less neural activity in a psychopath's frontal lobe than there is in a "normal" person's. This suggests that the inhibitions and constraints that keep most of us from engaging in violent acts or giving in to murderous impulses do not register in the frontal lobe of the psychopathic brain. Thoughts and situations that would give most of us pause, cause distress or fear, and inhibit cruel, violent, or illegal impulses don't register in the psychopath's frontal lobe. That it is wrong to steal, rape, assault, lie, or do anything else that degrades, cheats, and dehumanizes others does not compute with the psychopath.

As much as 25% of the criminal population and as much as 4% of the entire population is psychopathic. The World Health Organization (WHO) now classifies "dissocial personality disorder" or antisocial personality disorder or sociopathy as a disease. Call it what you will, but psychopaths do not exhibit normal human feelings and are a small percentage of the population who are responsible for a large percentage of crime. These people are extraordinarily cunning and lead double lives. Those closest to them usually have no idea that behind the charming mask there is a monster who does not reveal himself until—as the Ripper did—right before he attacks.

Psychopaths are incapable of love. When they show what appears to be regret, sadness, or sorrow, these expressions are manipulative and originate from their own needs and not out of any genuine consideration for another creature. Psychopaths are often attractive, charismatic, and above average in intelligence. While they are given to impulse, they are organized in the planning and execution of their crimes. There is no cure. They cannot be rehabilitated or "preserved from criminal misadventure," as Francis Galton, the father of fingerprint classification, wrote in 1883.

A psychopath often stalks his victims before contact, all the while engaging in violent fantasies. Psychopaths may go through dry runs to practice their modus operandi (MO) as they meticulously plan their actions in a manner that will insure success and evasion. Rehearsals can go on for years before the violent opening night, but no amount of practice or attention to strategy can guarantee that the performance will be flawless. Mistakes happen, especially on opening night, and when Jack the Ripper committed his first murder, he made an amateurish mistake.

CHAPTER FOUR

BY SOME PERSON UNKNOWN

When Martha Tabran took her killer to the dark first-floor landing at 37 George Yard Buildings, he relinquished control to her and inadvertently introduced the risk that something could go wrong with his plan.

Her turf may not have been the killing ground he had in mind. Maybe something else happened that he did not anticipate, such as an insult, a taunt. Prostitutes, especially intoxicated old veterans, were not the sort to be sensitive, and all Martha had to do was reach between his legs and say, "Where is it, love?" Sickert used the term "impotent fury" in a letter. More than a century after the event, I can't re-create what actually happened in that pitch-black, fetid stairwell, but the killer got enraged. He lost control.

To stab someone thirty-nine times is overkill, and a frenzied overkill is usually prompted by an event or a word that sets off the killer in an unanticipated way. This observation neither suggests nor assumes that

Martha's killer did not premeditate murder and fully intend to commit one, whether it was Martha Tabran's or whoever else happened to come along that night or early morning. When he accompanied Martha to the stairwell, he intended to stab her to death. He brought a strong, sharp knife or dagger to the scene, and he left with it. He may have been disguised as a soldier. He knew how to come and go undetected and to be careful about leaving obvious evidence—a lost button, a cap, a pencil. The two most personal forms of murder are stabbing and strangulation. Both require the assailant to have physical contact with the victim. Shootings are less personal. Bashing in a person's head, especially from behind, is less personal.

Stabbing someone dozens of times is very personal. When cases like that come into the morgue, the police and the medical examiner routinely assume that the victim and assailant knew each other. It is unlikely that Martha knew her killer, but she elicited a very personal reaction from him when she did or said something that didn't follow his script. She may have resisted him. Martha was known for having fits and being quite difficult when she was drunk, and she had been drinking rum and ale earlier with Pearly Poll. Residents of George Yard Buildings later stated that they heard "nothing" at the early hour of Martha's death, but their testimony doesn't count for much when one considers the exhausted, inebriated condition of impoverished people who were accustomed to drunken behavior, scuffles, and violent domestic fights. It was best not to get involved. One could get hurt or in trouble with the police.

At 3:30 A.M., an hour and a half after P.C. Barrett spotted the loitering soldier outside George Yard Buildings, a resident named Alfred Crow was returning home from work. He was a cab driver, and Bank Holidays were always busy and kept him out late. He must have been tired. He may even have unwound with a few pints after dropping off his last fare. As he passed the first-floor landing, he noticed "something" on the ground that might have been a body, but he didn't examine it and went to bed. The creed of the East End, as Victorian economist and social reformer Beatrice Webb put it, was don't "meddle" with the neighbors. Crow later explained in his testimony at the inquest that it was not uncommon to see drunks unconscious in the East End. No doubt he saw them all the time.

It seems no one realized that the "something" on the landing was a dead body until 4:50 A.M., when a waterside laborer named John S. Reeves was heading out of the building and noticed a woman lying on her back in a pool of blood. Her clothes were disarrayed, as if she had been in a struggle, Reeves recalled, but he saw no footprints on the staircase, nor did he find a knife or any other type of weapon. He said he did not touch the body but immediately located P.C. Barrett, who sent for Dr. T. R. Killeen. The time of the doctor's arrival wasn't given, but when he looked at the body, the lighting could not have been good.

He deduced at the scene that the victim, whose identity would remain unknown for days, had been dead for approximately three hours. She was "36 years old," the doctor divined, and "very well nourished," meaning she was overweight. This detail is significant, because virtually all of the Ripper's victims, including other murdered women the police discounted as having been slain by him, were either very thin or fat. With rare exceptions, they were in their late thirties or early forties.

Walter Sickert preferred female studio models obese or emaciated, and the lower their social class and the uglier they were, the better. This is evident from his frequent references to women as "skeletal" or "the thinnest of the thin like a little eel" and in the big women with wide hips and grotesquely pendulous breasts that he repeatedly depicts in his art. Other people could have the "chorus girls," Sickert once wrote, but leave him the "hags."

He did not have any artistic interest in females who had attractive bodies. He often remarked that any woman who wasn't too fat or too thin was boring, and in a letter he wrote to his American friends Ethel Sands and Ann Hudson, he voiced delight over his latest models and how "thrilled" he was by the "sumptuous poverty of their class." He loved their "every day dirty, old, worn clothes." He added in another letter that were he twenty, he "wouldn't look at any woman under 40."

Martha Tabran was short, overweight, homely, and middle-aged. When she was murdered, she was wearing a green skirt, a brown petticoat, a long black jacket, a black bonnet, and elastic-sided boots—"all old," according to the police. Martha would have been suited to Sickert's taste, but victimology is an indicator, not a science. Although victims of serial murder often share some trait that is significant to the killer, this does not imply that a violent psychopath is unbending in what sort of person he targets. Why Jack the Ripper focused on Martha Tabran instead of some other prostitute of similar description can't be known, unless the explanation is as pedestrian as opportunity.

Whatever his reason, he should have learned a valuable lesson from his frenzied murder of Martha Tabran: To lose control and stab a victim thirty-nine times was to cause a bloody mess. Even if he didn't track blood on the landing or elsewhere—assuming witnesses were accurate in their description of the crime scene—he would have had blood on his hands, his clothes, and the tops of his boots or shoes, making evasion more difficult. And for an educated man like Sickert, who knew that diseases were not caused by miasma but by germs, finding himself spattered and soaked with a prostitute's blood was likely to have been disgusting.

Martha Tabran's cause of death should have been exsanguination due to multiple stab wounds. There was no suitable mortuary in the East End, and Dr. Killeen performed the postmortem examination at a nearby dead house or shed. He attributed a single wound to the heart as "sufficient to cause death." A stab wound to the heart that does not nick or sever an artery can certainly cause death if it is not treated immediately by surgery in a trauma unit. But people have been known to survive after being stabbed in the heart with knives, ice picks, and other instruments. What causes the heart to stop pumping is not the wound, but the leakage of blood that fills the pericardium or sac that surrounds the heart.

Knowing whether Martha's pericardial sac was filled with blood would not only assuage a medical curiosity, it might also give a hint as to how long she survived as she bled from other stab wounds. Every detail helps the dead speak, and Dr. Killeen's descriptions tell us so little that we don't know if the weapon was double- or single-edged. We don't know what the angle of trajectory was, which would help position the killer in relation to Martha at the time of each injury. Was she standing or lying down? Were any of the wounds large or irregular, which would be consistent with the weapon twisting as it was withdrawn because the victim was still moving? Did the weapon have a guard—often mistakenly called a hilt (swords have hilts)? Knife guards leave contusions—bruises—or abrasions on the skin.

Reconstructing how a victim died and determining the type of weapon used begin to paint a portrait of the killer. Details hint at his intent, emotions, activity, fantasies, and even his occupation or profession. The height of the killer can also be conjectured. Martha was five foot three. If the killer was taller than she and the two of them were standing when he began stabbing her, then one would expect her initial wounds to be high up on her body and angled down. If both of them were standing, it would have been difficult for him to stab her in the stomach and genitals, unless he was very short. Most likely, those injuries would have been inflicted when she was on the ground.

Dr. Killeen assumed the killer was very strong. Adrenaline and rage are terrifically energizing and can produce a great deal of strength. But the Ripper didn't need superhuman strength. If his weapon was pointed, strong, and sharp, he didn't need much power to penetrate skin, organs, and even bone. Dr. Killeen also mistakenly assumed that a wound penetrating the sternum or "chest bone" could not have been inflicted by a "knife." He jumped from that conclusion to his next one: that two weapons were involved, possibly a "dagger" and a "knife," leading to an early theory that the killer might be ambidextrous.

Even if he was, the image of a man simultaneously stabbing Martha with a dagger in one hand and a knife in the other in darkness is bizarre and absurd, and chances are good he would have stabbed himself a few times. What is known of the medical evidence does not point to an ambidextrous assault. Martha's left lung was penetrated in five places. The heart, which is on the left side of the body, was stabbed once. A right-handed person is more likely to inflict injuries to the left side of the body if the victim is facing him.

A penetration of the sternum does not merit the emphasis Dr. Killeen gave it. A sharp-pointed knife can penetrate bone, including the skull. In a case that occurred in Germany decades before the Ripper began his spree, a man murdered his wife by stabbing her through the sternum, and later confided to the forensic examiner that the "table knife" penetrated the bone as easily as if it were "butter." The edges of the wound indicated that the table knife cleanly penetrated the bone once and went through the right lung, the pericardium, and the aorta.

Dr. Killeen's belief that two weapons were used in Martha Tabran's murder was buttressed by a difference in the size of the stab wounds. However, this discrepancy can be accounted for if the blade was wider at the guard than it was at the tip. Stab wounds can be different widths depending on their depth, the twisting of the blade, and the elasticity of the tissue or the part of the body being penetrated. It is hard to ascertain what Dr. Killeen meant by a knife or a dagger, but a knife usually refers to a single-edged blade while a dagger is narrow and double-edged and has a pointed tip. The terms *knife* and *dagger* are often used as synonyms, as are the terms *revolver* and *pistol.*

As I was researching the Ripper cases, I explored the types of cutting instruments that might have been available to him. The variety and availability is bewildering, if not depressing. British travelers to Asia returned home with all sorts of souvenirs, some better suited than others for stabbing or cutting. The Indian *pesh kabz* is a fine example of a weapon that could leave wounds of several different widths, depending on their depth.

The strong steel blade of this "dagger," as it was called, could create an array of wounds that would perplex any medical examiner, even now.

The curved blade is almost an inch and a half wide at the ivory handle, and becomes double-edged two-thirds of the way up when it begins to taper off to a point as thin as a needle. The one I bought from an antiques dealer was made in 1830 and (including its sheath) would easily fit in one's waistband, boot, or deep coat pocket—or up a sleeve. The curved blade of the Oriental dagger called a *djambia* (circa 1840) would also leave wounds of different widths, although the entire blade is double-edged.

The Victorians enjoyed an abundance of beautiful weapons that were made for killing human beings and were cavalierly collected during travels abroad or bought for a bargain at bazaars. In one day, I discovered the following Victorian weapons at a London antiques fair and at the homes of two antiques dealers in Sussex: daggers, kukris, a dagger stick disguised to look like a polished tree branch, daggers disguised to look like canes, tiny six-shot revolvers designed to fit neatly into a gentleman's vest pocket or a lady's purse, "cut-throat razors," Bowie-type knives, swords, rifles, and beautifully decorated truncheons, including a "Life Preserver" that is weighted with lead. When Jack the Ripper cruised for weapons, he was blessed with an embarrassment of riches.

No weapon was ever recovered in Martha Tabran's murder, and since Dr. Killeen's postmortem report seems to be missing—as are many records related to the Jack the Ripper case—all I had to go on were the sketchy details of the inquest. Of course I cannot determine with absolute certainty the weapon that took Martha's life, but I can speculate: Based on the frenzied attack and subsequent wounds, it may very well have been what the Victorians called a dagger—or a weapon with a strong blade, a sharp point, and a substantial handle designed to stab without the risk of the perpetrator's losing his grip and cutting himself.

If it is true that there were no defense injuries, such as cuts or bruises on Martha's hands or arms, their absence suggests she did not put up much of a struggle, even if her clothing was "disarrayed." Without more detail about exactly how her clothing was "disarrayed," I can't surmise whether she had begun to undress when she was attacked; whether the killer rearranged, undid, cut, or ripped her clothing; whether he did so before or after her death. In criminal cases of that era, clothing was important mainly for purposes of identifying the victim. It wasn't necessarily examined for tears, cuts, seminal fluid, or any other type of evidence. After the victim was identified, the clothing was usually tossed out the mortuary door into an alleyway. As the Ripper's victim count went up, some socially minded people thought it might be a good idea to collect the clothing of the dead and donate it to paupers.

In 1888, little was known about the behavior of blood. It has a character all its own and a behavior that dutifully abides by the laws of physics. It isn't like any other liquid, and when it is pumping at a high pressure through a person's arteries, it is not going to simply drip or slowly drain when one of those arteries is cut. At Martha's crime scene inside the stairwell, a high arterial spatter pattern on a wall would indicate that the stab wound to her neck severed an artery and occurred while she was standing and still had a blood pressure. An arterial pattern peaks and dips in rhythm with the heart and would also indicate whether a victim was on the ground when an artery was cut. The examination of the pattern helps establish the sequence of events during the attack. If a major artery is severed and there is no arterial spatter, in all likelihood other injuries have already just about extinguished the victim's life.

The stabbing and cutting wounds to Martha Tabran's genitals indicate a sexual component to the crime. Yet if it is true—as it seems to have been in all of the alleged Ripper murders—that there was no indication of "connection," as the Victorians called intercourse, then this is a pattern that should have been treated very seriously, but wasn't. I am not sure how a "connection" was determined. The problem with a prostitute is she may have "connected" numerous times in one night, and rarely if ever cleaned off the many levels of civilization she carried on her body.

Furthermore, body fluids could not be tested for blood type or DNA, nor was there any attempt to distinguish between human and animal blood in criminal investigations. Had there been evidence of recent sexual activity, the seminal fluid would have been of no forensic value. However, a consistent absence of seminal fluid or evidence of attempted intercourse—as is true in every Ripper murder—suggests that the killer did not engage in sexual activity with the victim before or after death. This pattern is not unheard of but it is uncommon with violent psychopaths, who may rape as they kill, climax as their victims die, or masturbate over the bodies after death. The lack of seminal fluid in the Ripper lust-murders is consistent with the supposition that Sickert was incapable of sex.

By modern standards, Martha Tabran's murder was investigated so poorly that it could hardly be called an investigation at all. Her murder did not excite the police or the press. There was virtually no public mention of her brutal slaying until the first inquest hearing on August 10th. There was little follow-up as time passed. Martha Tabran wasn't important to anyone in particular. It was assumed, as we used to say when I worked in the morgue, that she simply died the way she lived.

Her murder was savage, but it was not seen as the initial attack of an evil force that had invaded the city. Martha was a filthy worn-out whore and deliberately placed herself at great risk by the life she chose to live. She willingly plied a trade that required her to elude the police as much as her murderer did, it was pointed out in the press. It was hard to feel much pity for the likes of her, and public sentiment then was really no different from what it is now: The victim is to blame. Excuses in modern courtrooms are just as disheartening and infuriating. If she hadn't dressed that way; if he hadn't driven into that part of town; if she didn't go to bars looking for a man; I told her not to go jogging in that area of the park; what do you expect when you let your child walk home alone from the bus stop? As my mentor Dr. Marcella Fierro, chief medical examiner of Virginia, says, "A woman has a right to walk around naked and not be raped or murdered." Martha Tabran had a right to live.

"The inquiry," Chief Inspector Donald Swanson summarized in his report, "was confined amongst persons of deceased's class in the East End, but without any success."

CHAPTER FIVE

A GLORIOUS BOY

Walter Richard Sickert was born May 31, 1860, in Munich, Germany.

One of England's most important artists wasn't English. The "thoroughly English" Walter, as he was often described, was the son of a thoroughly Danish artist named Oswald Adalbert Sickert and a not-so-thoroughly English-Irish beauty named Eleanor Louisa Moravia Henry. As a child, Walter was thoroughly German.

Sickert's mother was called "Nelly"; his younger sister, Helena, was called "Nellie"; and Sickert's first wife, Ellen Cobden, was called "Nelly." Ellen Terry was called "Nelly." For purposes of clarity, I will not use the name "Nelly" except when referring to Sickert's mother, and I will resist giving in to the temptation to resort to Oedipal psychobabble because the four strongest women in Sickert's life had the same nickname.

Walter was the firstborn of six children—five boys and one girl. Remarkably, it appears that not one of them would ever have children.

Each child apparently had a curdled chemistry, except, perhaps, Oswald Valentine, a successful salesman about whom, it seems, nothing else is known. Robert would become a recluse and die from injuries sustained when he was hit by a lorry. Leonard always seemed strangely detached from reality and would die after a long battle with substance abuse. Bernhard was a failed painter and suffered from depression and alcoholism. A poetic observation their father, Oswald, wrote seems tragically prophetic:

> Where there is freedom, there, of course,
> the bad thing has to be free, too, but it dies,
> since it carries the germ of destruction within
> itself and dies of its own consequence/logicality.

The Sickerts' only daughter, Helena, had a brilliant mind and a fiery spirit, but a body that failed her all of her life. She was the only member of the family who seemed interested in humanitarian causes and other people. She would explain in her autobiography that early suffering made her compassionate and gave her sensitivity toward others. She was sent off to a harsh boarding school where she ate terrible food and was humiliated by the other girls because she was sickly and clumsy. The males in her home made her believe she was ugly. She was inferior because she wasn't a boy.

Walter was the third generation of artists. His grandfather, Johann Jurgen Sickert, was so gifted as a painter that he earned the patronage of Denmark's King Christian VIII. Walter's father, Oswald, was a talented painter and graphic artist who could make neither a name for himself nor a living. An old photograph shows him with a long bushy beard and cold eyes that glint of anger. Along with most of the Sickert family, details about him have faded like a poorly made daguerreotype. A search of records came up with a small collection of his writings and art that are included with his son's papers at Islington Public Libraries. Oswald's handwritten high German had to be translated into low German and then English, a process that took about six months and produced only sixty fragments of pages because most of what he wrote was impossible to read and could not be deciphered at all.

But what could be made out gave me a glimpse of an extraordinarily strong-willed, complex, and talented man who wrote music, plays, and poetry. His gift of words and his theatrical flair made him a favorite for giving speeches at weddings, carnivals, and other social events. He was active politically during the Danish-German War of 1864 and traveled quite a lot to different cities, encouraging the working men to pull together for a united Germany.

"I want your help," he said in one undated speech. "Everyone of you needs to do his share. . . . It is also up to those of you who deal with the workers, to the larger tradesmen, factory owners, among you, it is up to you to care for the honest worker." Oswald could rouse the spirits of the oppressed. He could also compose beautiful music and poetic verses full of tenderness and love. He could create cartoonlike artwork that reveals a cruel and fiendish sense of fun. Pages of his diaries show that when Oswald wasn't sketching, he was wandering, a practice imitated by his eldest son.

Oswald was always on the move, so much so that one wonders when he got his work done. His walks might consume the better part of the day, or perhaps he was on a train somewhere until late at night. A cursory sampling of his activities reveals a man who could scarcely sit still and constantly did what he pleased. The diary pages are incomplete and undated, but his words portray him as a self-absorbed, moody, restless man.

During one week, on Wednesday, Oswald Sickert traveled by train from Echkenförde to Schleswig to Echen to Flensburg in northern Germany. On Thursday, he took a look "at the new road along the railroad" and walked "along the harbor to the Nordertor [North Gate]" and across a field "to the ditch and home." He ate lunch and spent the afternoon at

"Notke's beergarden." From there he visited a farm and then went home. On Friday: "Went by myself" to visit Allenslob, Nobbe, Jantz, Stropatil, and Möller. He met up with a group of people, ate dinner with them, and at 10:00 P.M. returned home. On Saturday: "Went for a walk by myself through the city."

On Sunday he was out of the house all day, then he had dinner, and afterward there was music and singing at home until 10:00 P.M. On Monday, he walked to Gottorf, then "back across over the property/estates and the peat bog. . . ." On Tuesday, he went by horse to Mugner's, fished until 3:00 P.M. and caught "30 perch." He met acquaintances at a pub. "Ate and drank" lunch. "Return at 11:00 P.M."

Oswald's writings make it clear he hated authority, particularly the police, and his angry, mocking words eerily portend Jack the Ripper's own taunts to the police: "Catch me if you can," the Ripper repeatedly wrote.

"—Hooray! The watchman is asleep!" wrote Walter Sickert's father. "When you see him like that, you wouldn't believe that he is a watchman. Shall I nudge him out of love for humanity and tell him what the bell has tolled [or what trouble he is in for]. . . . O no, let him slumber. Maybe he dreams that he has me, let him hold on to this illusion."

Oswald's sentiments about authority must have been voiced within the walls of his home, and Walter could not have been oblivious to them. Nor could he or his mother have been unaware of Oswald's frequent visits to beer gardens and pubs—to his being "plied with punch."

"I have boozed away the money," Oswald wrote. "I owed that much to my stomach. I sleep during my leisure hours, of which I have plenty."

Whatever prompted his obsessive walks, frequent journeys, and regular patronage of pubs and beer gardens, they cost money. And Oswald could not earn a living. Without his wife's money the family would not have survived. Perhaps it is no coincidence that in a Punch and Judy script Oswald wrote (probably in the early 1860s), the sadistic puppet-husband Punch is spending the family money on booze and cares nothing for his wife and infant son:

PUNCH APPEARS IN THE BOX:

. . . Ah yes, I believe you don't know me . . . my name is Punch. This also used to be my father's name, and my grandfather's, too.
. . . I like nice clothes. I am married by the way. I have a wife and a child. But that doesn't mean anything . . .

WIFE (JUDY): No, I can't stand this anymore! Even this early in the morning, this awful man has drunk brandy!
. . . Oh, what an unhappy woman I am. All earnings are spent on spirits. I have no bread for the children—

If Walter Sickert got his carelessness with money and his restlessness from his father, he got his charm and good looks from his mother. He may have been handed a few of her less attractive attributes as well. The story of Mrs. Sickert's bizarre childhood has an uncanny resemblance to Charles Dickens's *Bleak House*—Walter's favorite novel. In that book, an orphan girl named Esther is mysteriously sent to live in the mansion of the kind and wealthy Mr. Jarndyce, who later wants to marry her.

Born in 1830, Nelly was the illegitimate daughter of a beautiful Irish dancer who had no interest in being a mother. She neglected Nelly, she was a heavy drinker, and finally she ran off to Australia to get married when Nelly was twelve. It was at this juncture in Nelly's life that she suddenly found herself in the guardianship of a wealthy anonymous bachelor who sent her to a school in Neuville-les-Dieppe, on the English Channel in northern France. Over the next six years, he wrote her affectionate letters he cryptically signed "R."

When Nelly turned eighteen and at last met her guardian, he revealed himself as Richard Sheepshanks, a former ordained priest turned much-acclaimed astronomer. He was witty and dashing—everything a young woman might conjure up in her dreams—and she was intelligent and very pretty. Sheepshanks spoiled Nelly and adored her even more than she adored him. He introduced her to the right people and placed her in the proper settings. Soon she found herself going to parties, the theater, and the opera, and traveling abroad. She learned several foreign languages, and developed into a cultured young woman, all under the watchful eye of her fairy-tale, doting benefactor, who at some point finally confessed to her that he was her biological father.

Sheepshanks made Nelly promise to destroy all of his letters to her, and it isn't possible to determine whether his love as a father skirted the passion of a lover. Perhaps she knew very well what he was feeling and chose to deny it, or she could have been trusting and naive. But it must have been a shocking moment for him when Nelly joyfully announced in Paris that she was in love and was engaged to be married to an art student named Oswald Sickert.

Her father's reaction was an outburst of rage. He wildly accused her of being ungrateful, dishonest, and unfaithful, and he demanded that she break off the engagement immediately. Nelly refused. Her father withdrew his generosity and returned to England. He wrote several bitter letters to her and then died suddenly after a stroke. Nelly never got over his death and blamed herself for it. She destroyed all of his letters except one that she hid inside an old chronometer of his. "Love me, Nelly, love me dearly, as I love you," he had written.

Richard Sheepshanks left nothing to Nelly. Fortunately, his kind sister, Anne Sheepshanks, came to Nelly's rescue and gave her a generous allowance that made it possible for her to support a husband and six children. Nelly's desolate childhood and ultimate betrayal and abandonment by her father would surely have left their scars. Although there is no record of how she felt about her irresponsible dance-hall mother or the seemingly incestuous love of a father who had been little more than a romantic secret most of her young life, one assumes that Nelly would have suffered from deeply felt grief, anger, and shame.

Had Helena Sickert not grown up to be a famous suffragette and political figure who wrote her memoirs, it is safe to say that there would be very little to tell us about the Sickert family and what Walter was like as a boy. Almost every published reference to Walter's early life can be traced back to Helena's memoirs. If any other family member left a record, either it no longer exists or it is safely locked up somewhere.

Helena's description of her mother reveals an intelligent, complex woman who could be fun, charming, and independent and at other times strict, emotionally absent, manipulative, and submissive.

The home Nelly made for her family was an inconsistent one—severe and harsh, then suddenly blooming into games and song. In the evenings, Nelly often sang while Oswald accompanied her on the piano. She sang when she was at her needlework and when she took her children for romps in the woods or to swim. She taught them delightful nonsense songs such as "The Mistletoe Bough" and "She Wore a Wreath of Roses" and the children's favorite:

> I am Jack Jumper the youngest but one
> I can play nick-nacks upon my own thumb . . .

From an early age, Walter was a fearless swimmer with a head full of pictures and music. He was blue-eyed with long blond curls, and his mother used to dress him in "Little Lord Fauntleroy velvet suits," recalled a family friend. Helena, four years younger than Walter, remembers her mother's endless praises of his "beauty" and "perfect behavior," the latter of which did not quite mirror his sister's view. Walter may have been lovely to look at, but he was anything but gentle or sweet. Helena recollected that he was a charming, energetic, and quarrelsome little boy who made friends on command but was indifferent to them once they no longer amused him or served a useful purpose. His mother often found herself having to console Walter's abandoned playmates and make feeble excuses for her son's suddenly vanishing from their lives.

Walter's coldness and self-absorption were obvious at a young age, and one suspects that his mother never considered that her relationship with him might have been a contributing factor to the darkening shades of his character. Nelly may have adored her angelic-looking son, but not necessarily for healthy reasons. It's possible that he was nothing more than an extension of her own ego, and that her doting behavior was a projection of her own deeply rooted and unrequited needs. She probably treated him the only way she knew how, which was to disconnect from him emotionally the way her mother had from her, and to feel for him the selfish and inappropriate intensity that she had experienced from her father. When Walter was a toddler, an artist named Fuseli insisted on painting the "glorious" little boy. Nelly kept the life-size portrait hanging in her sitting room until the day she died at the age of ninety-two.

Oswald Sickert's pretense that he was head of the household was a fraud, and Walter must have known it. A ritual the children witnessed all too often was "Mummy" begging her husband for money while he dug in his purse and demanded, "How much must I give you, extravagant woman?"

"Will fifteen shillings be too much?" she would ask after going down the list of all their household needs.

Oswald would then magnanimously give her money that was hers to begin with, for she diligently turned over her yearly allowance to him. His scripted generosity was always rewarded with his wife's kisses and expressions of delight, their playacting weirdly re-creating the relationship between her and her omnipotent, controlling father, Richard Sheepshanks. Walter learned his parents' drama by heart. He would adopt the worst traits of his father and forever seek out women who would pander to his megalomania and every need.

Oswald Sickert was an artist for the humorous German journal *Die Fliegende Blätter,* but there was nothing funny about him at home. He had no patience with children and bonded with none of his own. His daughter, Helena, recalls that he talked only to Walter, who would later claim that he remembered "everything" his father ever told him. There wasn't much that Walter didn't learn quickly and remember precisely. As a child in Germany, he taught himself to read and write, and throughout his life his acquaintances would marvel at his photographic recall.

Legend has it that Walter was taking a walk with his father one day and passed by a church where Oswald directed his young son's attention to a memorial. "There's a name you will never remember," Oswald commented as he kept walking. Walter paused to read

MAHARAJA MEERZARAM
GUAHAHAPAJE RAZ
PAREA MANERAMAPAM
MUCHER

L.C.S.K.

When he was eighty years old, Walter Sickert could still recall the inscription and write it without error.

Oswald did not encourage any of his children to pursue art, but from an early age, Walter could not resist drawing, painting, and making models out of wax. Sickert would claim that what he knew of art theory he had learned from his father, who in the 1870s used to take him to the Royal Academy at Burlington House to study the paintings of the "Old Masters." Searches through collections of Sickert archives suggest that Oswald may have had a hand in Walter's development as a draftsman as well. In Islington Public Libraries in north London, there is a collection of sketches that have been attributed to Oswald but are now believed by historians and art experts to include sketches made by the father's talented son, Walter. It is possible that Oswald critiqued Walter's early artistic efforts.

Many of the drawings are clearly the efforts of the tentative but gifted hand of someone learning to sketch street scenes, buildings, and figures. But the creative mind guiding the hand is disturbed, violent, and morbid, a mind that takes delight in conjuring up a cauldron of men being boiled alive and demonic characters with long, pointed faces, tails, and evil smiles. A favorite theme is that of soldiers storming castles and battling one another. A knight abducts a buxom maiden and rides off with her as she pleads not to be raped or murdered or both. Sickert could have been describing his own juvenilia when he described an etching made by Karel du Jardin in 1652: It is, he said, a ghastly scene of a "cavalier" on horseback pausing to look at a "stripped" and "hacked" up "corpse," while troops "with spears and pennants" ride off in the distance.

The most violent amateurish drawing in this collection depicts a bosomy woman in a low-cut dress sitting in a chair, her hands bound behind her, her head thrown back as a right-handed man plunges a knife into the center of her chest at the level of her sternum. She has additional wounds on the left side of her chest, a wound on the left side of her neck—where the carotid artery would be—and possibly a wound below her left eye. Her killer's only facial feature is a slight smile, and he is dressed in a suit. Opposite this sketch, on the same scrap of rectangular paper, there is a crouching, frightening-looking man who is about to spring on a woman dressed in long skirt, shawl, and bonnet.

While I have found no hint that Oswald Sickert was sexually violent, he could be mean-spirited and stony. His favorite target was his daughter. Helena's fear of him was so great that she would tremble in his presence. He showed not a whit of sympathy for her while she was bedridden with rheumatic fever for two years. When she recovered at the age of seven, she was very weak and had poor control of her legs. She dreaded it when her father began forcing her to take walks with him. During these outings, he never spoke. To her, his silence was more frightening than his harsh words.

When she awkwardly ran to keep up with his relentless pace, or if she clumsily bumped into him, "he would," Helena wrote, "then silently take me by the shoulder and silently turn me into the opposite direction, where I was apt to run into the wall or gutter." Her mother never intervened on her behalf. Nelly preferred her "pretty little fellows" with their fair hair and sailor suits to her homely, red-headed daughter.

Walter was by far the prettiest of the fair little fellows and the "cleverest." He usually got his way through manipulation, deception, or charm. He was the leader, and other children did what he demanded, even if Walter's "games" were unfair or unpleasant. When playing chess, he thought nothing of changing the rules as it suited him, such as making it possible to check the king without consequences. When Walter was a bit older, after the family had moved to England in 1868, he began recruiting friends and siblings to play scenes from Shakespeare, and some of his stage direction was nasty and degrading. In an unpublished draft of Helena's memoirs, she recalled:

> I must have been a child when [Walter] roped us in to rehearse the three witches to his Macbeth in a disused quarry near Newquay, which innocently I thought was really called "The Pit of Achaeron." Here he drilled us very severely. I was made (being appropriately thin and red-haired) to discard my dress & shoes & stockings, in order to brood over the witches cauldron, or stride around it, regardless of thorns and sharp stones, in my eyes the acrid smoke of scorching seaweed.

This account as well as other telling ones were softened or deleted by the time Helena's memoirs were published, and were it not for a six-page handwritten remnant that was donated to the National Art Library of the Victoria & Albert Museum, there would be little known about Walter's youthful tendencies. I suspect that much has been censored.

In the Victorian era and the early 1900s it was unheard of to tell all, especially about family. Queen Victoria herself could have burned down one of her palaces with the conflagration she made of her private papers. By the time Helena published her memoirs in 1935, her brother Walter was seventy-five years old and a British icon hailed by young artists as the *roi,* or king. His sister might have had second thoughts about lacerating him in her book. She was one of the few people he was never able to dominate, and the two of them were never close.

It isn't clear that she even knew quite what to make of him. He was "... at once the most fickle and the most constant of creatures ... unreasonable, but always rationalizing. Utterly neglectful of his friends and relations in normal times and capable of the utmost kindness, generosity and resourcefulness in crises—never bored, except by people."

Sickert scholars agree that he was a "handful." He was "brilliant" with a "volatile temperament," and when he was three, his mother told a family friend that he was "perverse and wayward"—a physically strong boy whose "tenderness" easily turns to "temper." He was a master of persuasion and, like his father, disdainful of religion. Authority did not exist any more than God did. In school, Walter was energetic and intellectually keen, but he did not abide by rules. Those who have written about his life are vague and elusive about his "irregularities," as his biographer Denys Sutton put it.

When Sickert was ten, he was "removed" from a boarding school in Reading, where, he would later say, he found the "horrible old schoolmistress" intolerable. He was expelled from University College School for reasons unknown. Around 1870, he attended Bayswater Collegiate School, and for two years, he was a student at Kings College School. In 1878, he was awarded first class honors in his London Matriculation (the exam all schoolchildren took in their last year), but he did not attend a university.

Sickert's arrogance, his lack of feeling, and his extraordinary power of manipulation are typical of psychopaths. What is not so apparent—although it betrays itself in Walter's fits of temper and sadistic games—is the anger that simmered beneath his bewitching surface. Add rage to emotional detachment and a total lack of compassion or remorse, and the resulting alchemy turns Dr. Jekyll into Mr. Hyde. The precise chemistry of this transformation is a mixture of the physical and spiritual that we may never fully understand. Does an abnormal frontal lobe cause a person to become a psychopath? Or does the frontal lobe become abnormal because the person is a psychopath? We don't yet know the cause.

We do know the behavior, and we know that psychopaths act without fear of consequences. They do not care about the suffering left in the aftermath of their violent storms. It doesn't bother a violent psychopath if his assassination of a president might damage the entire nation, if his killing spree might break the hearts of women who have lost their husbands and children who have lost their fathers. Sirhan Sirhan has been heard to boast in prison that he has become as famous as Bobby Kennedy. John Hinckley, Jr.'s failed attempt on Reagan's life catapulted the pudgy, unpopular loser onto the cover of every major magazine.

The psychopath's only palpable fear is that he will be caught. The rapist aborts his sexual assault when he hears someone unlocking the front door. Or maybe violence escalates and he kills both his victim and whoever is entering the house. There can be no witnesses. No matter how much violent psychopaths might taunt the police, the thought of captivity fills them with terror, and they will go to any length to avoid it. It is ironic that people who have such contempt for human life will desperately hold on to their own. They continue to thrive on their games, even on death row. They are determined to live and to the bitter end believe they can dodge death by lethal injection or cheat the electric chair.

The Ripper was the gamesman of all gamesmen. His murders, his clues and taunts to the press and the police, his antics—all were such fun. His greatest disillusionment must have come from realizing early on that his opponents were unskilled dolts. For the most part, Jack the Ripper played his games alone. He had no worthy contenders, and he boasted and taunted almost to the point of giving himself away. The Ripper wrote hundreds of letters to the police and the press. One of his favorite words was *Fools*—a word that was also a favorite of Oswald Sickert's. The

Ripper letters contain dozens of *Ha Ha's*—the same annoying American laugh of James McNeill Whistler that Sickert must have heard hour after hour when he was working for the great Master.

From 1888 to the present day, the millions of people who have associated Jack the Ripper with mystery and murder undoubtedly have no clue that more than anything else, this infamous killer was a mocking, arrogant, spiteful, and sarcastic man who believed virtually everyone on earth was an "idiot" or a "fool." The Ripper hated the police, he loathed "filthy whores," and he was maniacal in his sarcastic, "funny little" communications with those desperate to catch him.

The Ripper's mockeries and utter indifference to his destruction of human life are evident in his letters, which begin in 1888 and end, as far as we know, in 1896. As I read and reread—more times than I can count—the some 250 Ripper letters that survive at the Public Record Office and the Corporation of London Records Office, I began to form a rather horrifying image of a furious, spiteful, and cunning child who was the master controller of a brilliant and talented adult. Jack the Ripper felt empowered only when he savaged people and tormented the authorities, and he got away with all of it for more than 114 years.

When I first began to go through the Ripper letters, I concurred with what the police and most people believe: Almost all of the letters are hoaxes or the communications of mentally unbalanced people. However, during my intensive research of Sickert and the way he expressed himself—and the way the Ripper expressed himself in so many of his alleged letters—my opinion changed. I now believe that the majority of the letters were written by the murderer. The Ripper's childish and hateful teases and mocking comments and taunts in his letters include:

"Ha Ha Ha"
"Catch me if you can"
"It's a jolly nice lark"
"What a dance I am leading"

"Love, Jack the Ripper"

"Just to give you a little clue"

"I told her I was Jack the Ripper and I took my hat off"

"Hold on tight you cunning lot of coppers"

"good bye for the present From the Ripper and the dodger"

"Won't it be nice dear old Boss to have the good ole times once again"

"You might remember me if you try and think a little Ha Ha."

"I take great pleasure in giving you my whereabouts for the benefit of the Scotland Yard boys"

"The police alias po-lice, think themselves devilish clever"

"you donkeys, you double-faced asses"

"Be good enough to send a few of your clever policemen down here"

"The police pass me close every day, and I shall pass one going to post this."

"Ha! Ha!"

"you made a mistake, if you thought I dident see you . . ."

"the good old times once again"

"I really wanted to play a little joke on you all but I haven't got enough time left to let you play cat and mouse with me."

"Au revoir, Boss."

"a good Joke I played on them"

"ta ta"

"Just a line to let you know that I love my work."

"They look so clever and talk about being on the right track"

"P.S. You can't trace me by this writing so its no use"

"I think you all are asleep in Scotland Yard"

"I am Jack the ripper catch me if you can"

"I am now going to make my way to Paris and try my little games"

"Oh, it was such a jolly job the last one."

"Kisses"

"I am still at liberty . . . Ha, ha, ha!"

"don't I laugh"

"I think I have been very good up to now"

"Yours truly, Mathematicus"

"Dear Boss . . . I was conversing with two or three of your men last night"

"What fools the police are."

"But they didnt search the one I was in I was looking at the police all the Time."

"why I passed a policeman yestaday & he didnd take no notice of me."

"The police now reckon my work a practical *joke, well well Jacky's a very practical joker ha ha ha"*

"I am very much amused"

"I'm considered a very *handsome Gentleman"*

"You see I am still knocking about. Ha. Ha"

"you will have a job to catch me"

"No use you're tryin to catch me because it wont do"

"You never caught me and you never will Ha Ha"

My father the lawyer used to say that you can tell a lot by what makes a person angry. A review of the 211 Ripper letters in the Public Record Office at Kew reveals that Jack the Ripper was intellectually arrogant. Even when he disguised his writing to look ignorant, illiterate, or crazy, he did not like to hear that he was. He couldn't resist reminding people he was literate by an occasional letter with perfect spelling, neat or beautiful script, and excellent vocabulary. As the Ripper protested more than once in communications that were increasingly ignored by the police and the press, "I ain't a maniac as you say I am to dam [sic] clever for you" and "Do you think I am mad? What a mistake you make."

In all likelihood, an illiterate cockney would not use the word "conundrum" or sign his letter "Mathematicus." In all likelihood, an ignorant brute would not refer to the people he has murdered as "victims" or describe mutilating a woman as giving her a "Caesarian." The Ripper also used vulgarities, such as "cunt," and worked hard to misspell, mangle, or write in snarls. Then he mailed his trashy letters—"I have not got a stamp"—from Whitechapel, as if to imply that Jack the Ripper was a low-life resident of the slums. Few Whitechapel paupers could either read or write, and a large percentage of the population was foreign and did not speak English. Most people who misspell do so phonetically and consistently, and in some letters, the Ripper misspells the same word several different ways.

The repeated word "games" and much-used "ha ha"s were favorites of the American-born James McNeill Whistler, whose "ha! ha!" or "cackle," as Sickert called it, was infamous and was often described as a much-dreaded laugh that grated against the ear of the English. Whistler's "ha ha" could stop a dinner party conversation. It was enough of an announcement of his presence to make his enemies freeze or get up and leave. "Ha ha" was much more American than English, and one can only imagine how many times a day Sickert heard that irritating "ha ha" when he was with Whistler or in the Master's studio. One can read hundreds of letters written by Victorians and not see a single "ha ha," but the Ripper letters are filled with them.

Generations have been misled to think the Ripper letters are pranks, or the work of a journalist bent on creating a sensational story, or the drivel of lunatics, because that was what the press and the police thought. Investigators and most students of the Ripper crimes have focused on the handwriting more than the language. Handwriting is easy to disguise, especially if one is a brilliant artist, but the unique and repeated use of linguistic combinations in multiple texts is the fingerprint of a person's mind.

One of Walter Sickert's favorite insults was to call people "fools." The Ripper was very fond of this word. To Jack the Ripper, everybody was a fool except him. Psychopaths tend to think they are more cunning and more intelligent than everyone else. Psychopaths tend to believe they can outsmart those out to catch them. The psychopath loves to play games, to harass and taunt. What fun to set so much chaos in motion and sit back and watch. Walter Sickert wasn't the first psychopath to play games, to taunt, to mock, to think he was smarter than anyone else, and to get away with murder. But he may be the most original and creative killer of all time.

Sickert was a learned man who may have had the I.Q. of a genius. He was a talented artist whose work is respected but not necessarily enjoyed. His art shows no whimsy, no tender touches, no dreams. He never pretended to paint "beauty," and as a draftsman he was better than most of his peers. Sickert "Mathematicus" was a technician. "All lines in nature . . . are located somewhere in radiants within the 360 degrees of four right angles," he wrote. "All straight lines . . . and all curves can be considered as tangents to such lines."

He would teach his students that "the basis of drawing is a highly cultivated sensibility to the exact direction of lines . . . within the 180 degrees of right angles." Allow him to simplify: "Art may be said to be . . . the individual co-efficient of error . . . in [the craftsman's] effort to attain the expression of form." Whistler and Degas did not define their art in such terms. I'm not sure they would have understood a word of what Sickert said.

Sickert's precise way of thinking and calculating was evident not only in his own description of his work, but also in the way he executed it. His method in painting was to "square up" his sketches, enlarging them geometrically to preserve the exact perspectives and proportions. In some of his pictures, the grid of his mathematical method is faintly visible behind the paint. In Jack the Ripper's games and violent crimes, the grid of who he was is faintly visible behind his machinations.

CHAPTER SIX

WALTER AND THE BOYS

By the age of five, Sickert had undergone three horrific operations for a fistula.

In every Sickert biography I have read, there is no more than a brief mention of these operations, and I am not aware that anyone has ever gone on record to say what this fistula was or why three life-threatening operations were required to repair it. Furthermore, there is to date no scholarly, objective book that sets forth in detail his eighty-one years on this earth.

While much is to be learned from Denys Sutton's 1976 biography of Sickert because the author was a thorough researcher and relied on conversations with people who had known the "old master," Sutton was somewhat compromised since he had to obtain permission from the Sickert Trust in order to use copyrighted materials such as letters. The legal restrictions on the reproduction of Sickert materials, including his art, are the foreboding mountains one must scale to view the entire panorama of the man's intensely conflicted and complicated personality. In a research note in Sutton's archives at the University of Glasgow, there appears to be a reference to a "Ripper" painting Sickert may have done in the 1930s. If there is such a painting, I have found no mention of it anywhere else.

There are other references to Sickert's peculiar behavior that should have aroused at least a bit of curiosity in anyone who studied him carefully. In a letter from Paris, November 16, 1968, André Dunoyer de Segonzac, a well-known artist with connections to the Bloomsbury group, wrote Sutton that he had known Walter Sickert around 1930 and had very clear memories of Sickert claiming to have "lived" in Whitechapel in the same house where Jack the Ripper had lived, and that Sickert had told him "spiritedly about the discreet and edifying life of this monstrous assassin."

The art historian and Sickert scholar Dr. Anna Gruetzner Robins of the University of Reading says that she does not see how it is possible for one to study Sickert extensively and not begin to suspect that he was Jack the Ripper. Some of her published studies on his art have included observations that are a bit too insightful for the proper Sickert palate. It seems that truths about him are as cloaked in fog as the Ripper was, and bringing to light any detail that might portend anything ignoble about the man is blasphemous.

In early 2002, Howard Smith, the curator of the Manchester City Art Gallery, contacted me to ask if I was aware that in 1908 Walter Sickert painted a very dark, gloomy painting titled *Jack the Ripper's Bedroom*. The work was donated in 1980, and the curator at the time notified Dr. Wendy Baron—who did her doctoral dissertation on Sickert and has written more on the artist than anyone else—to let her know of this remarkable find. "We have just received a bequest of two oil paintings by Sickert," curator Julian Treuherz wrote to Dr. Baron on September 2, 1980. One of them, he said, was "Jack the Ripper's Bedroom, oil on canvas, 20 × 16"."

Dr. Baron replied to Mr. Treuherz on October 12th and verified that the bedroom in the painting was indeed the bedroom in a Camden Town residence (at 6 Mornington Crescent) where Sickert rented the top two floors when he moved back to London from France in 1906. Dr. Baron further observed that this Camden Town residence was where "Sickert believed Jack the Ripper had lodged" in the 1880s. Although I have not found any references to the Mornington Crescent address as the place where Sickert thought the Ripper once lived, Sickert could have had a secret room there during the 1888 serial murders. And in letters the Ripper wrote, he said he was moving into a lodging house, which could have been the one at 6 Mornington Crescent—where Sickert was living in 1907 when yet another prostitute's throat was slashed barely a mile from his rooms.

Sickert used to tell friends the story that he once had stayed in a house whose landlady claimed that Jack the Ripper had lived there during the crimes and that she knew his identity: The Ripper was a sickly veterinary student who was eventually whisked off to an asylum. She told Sickert the sickly serial killer's name, which Sickert said he wrote down in a copy of Casanova's memoirs he happened to be reading at the time. But alas, despite Sickert's photographic memory, he could not recall the name, and his copy of the book was destroyed in World War II.

The painting *Jack the Ripper's Bedroom* was ignored and remained in storage for twenty-two years. It seems the painting is one of the few Dr. Baron has left out of her writings. Certainly I had never heard of it. Nor had Dr. Robins or the Tate Gallery or anyone else I met during my research. Apparently, not everyone is eager to publicize this painting. The idea of Sickert being Jack the Ripper is "rubbish," said Sickert's nephew John Lessore, who is not related to Sickert by blood but through Sickert's third wife, Thérèse Lessore.

While writing this book, I had no contact with the Sickert Trust. Neither the people who control it nor anyone else has dissuaded me from publishing what I believe to be the naked truth. I have drawn upon the recollections of people who were Walter Sickert's contemporaries—such as Whistler and Sickert's first two wives—who were under no legal obligation to a Sickert Trust.

I have avoided the recycled inaccuracies that have metastasized from one book to another. I have concluded that information cited since Sickert's death consistently says nothing intentionally damning or humiliating about his life or character. The fistula was not considered important because apparently those who have mentioned it did not fully realize what it was or that it could have caused devastating repercussions in Sickert's psyche. I must admit I was shocked when I asked John Lessore about his uncle's fistula and he told me—as if it were common knowledge—that the fistula was a "hole in [Sickert's] penis."

I don't think Lessore had a clue as to the significance of what he was saying, and I would be surprised if Denys Sutton knew much about Sickert's fistula, either. Sutton's reference to the problem says no more than that Sickert underwent two failed operations "for fistula in Munich," and in 1865, while the Sickert family was in Dieppe, his great-aunt Anne Sheepshanks suggested a third attempt by a prominent London surgeon.

Helena does not mention her elder brother's medical problem in her memoirs, but one wonders how much she knew. It's unlikely that her eldest brother's genitalia were a topic of family conversation. Helena was an infant when Sickert suffered through his operations, and chances are that by the time she was old enough to give much thought to the organs of reproduction, Sickert was not inclined to run around naked in front of her—or anyone else. He obliquely alluded to his fistula when he used to joke that he came to London to be "circumcised."

In the nineteenth century, fistulas of the anus, rectum, and vagina were so common that St. Mark's Hospital in London was dedicated to treating them. There are no references to fistulas of the penis in the medical literature I consulted, but the term may have been loosely used to describe penile anomalies such as the one Sickert suffered from. The word "fistula"—Latin for reed or pipe—is generally used to describe an abnormal opening or sinus that can cause such atrocities as a rectum connected to the bladder or to the urethra or to the vagina.

A fistula can be congenital but is often caused by an abscess that takes the path of least resistance, and burrows through tissue or the skin surface, forming a new opening for urine, feces, and pus to escape. Fistulas could be extremely uncomfortable, embarrassing, and even fatal. Early medical journals cite harrowing cases such as miserably painful ulcers, bowels emptying into bladders, bowels or bladders emptying into vaginas or uteri, and menstruation through the rectum.

During the mid-1800s, doctors attributed the cause of fistulas to all sorts of things: sitting on damp seats, sitting outside on omnibuses after physical exertion, swallowing small bones or pins, the "wrong" food, alcohol, improper clothing, the "luxurious" use of cushions, or sedentary habits associated with certain professions. Dr. Frederick Salmon, the founder of St. Mark's Hospital, treated Charles Dickens for a fistula caused by, he said, the great writer's sitting at his desk too much.

St. Mark's was established in 1835 to relieve the poor of rectal diseases and their "baneful varieties" and in 1864 moved to City Road in Islington. In 1865, it suffered financial devastation when the hospital secretary fled from London after embezzling £400, or one quarter of the hospital's annual income. A fund-raising dinner to be hosted by the fistula-free Dickens was proposed, but he declined the honor. In the same year, Walter Sickert arrived at St. Mark's in the autumn to be "cured" by its recently appointed surgeon, Dr. Alfred Duff Cooper, who later married the daughter of the Duke of Fife and was knighted by King Edward VII.

Dr. Cooper was a twenty-seven-year-old medical star rapidly on the rise in his profession. His specialties were the treatment of rectal and venereal diseases, but no search of his published writings or other literature unearthed any mention of his treating so-called fistulas of the penis. Explanations of Sickert's fistula range from fair to awful. Nature may have slighted him with a genetically inherited malformation of the genitals called hypospadias, in which the urethra terminates just below the tip of the penis. German medical literature published at the time of Sickert's birth indicates that a case of simple hypospadias was "trifling" and more common than generally known. A "trifling" case meant the fistula would not interfere with procreation and was not worth the risk of a surgical procedure that could cause infection and death.

Since Sickert's malformation required three operations, his problem must not have been "trifling." In 1864, Dr. Johann Ludwig Casper, professor of forensic medicine at the University of Berlin, published a description of a more serious form of hypospadias: In this malformation, there is an opening in the urethra at the "root" or base of the penis. Even worse is epispadias, which occurs when the urethra is divided and runs like a "shallow gutter" along the back of a rudimentary or incompletely developed penis. In mid–nineteenth century Germany, such cases were considered a type of hermaphroditism or "doubtful sex."

When Sickert was born, his gender may have been ambiguous, meaning his penis was small, possibly misshapen, and imperforate (lacking a urethra). The bladder would have been connected to a canal that opened at the base of the penis—or near the anus—and there may have been a cleft in the scrotum that resembled the female clitoris, vagina, and labia. It is possible that Sickert's gender wasn't clearly established until his testicles were discovered in the folds of the so-called labia and it was determined that he had no uterus. In cases of ambiguous genitalia, if the afflicted child's gender turns out to be male, he is usually masculine and healthy in all respects as he matures except for his penis, which may be acceptably functional but is certainly not normal. In the early days of surgery, attempts to repair seriously deformed genitalia generally resulted in mutilation.

Without medical records, I can't say exactly what Sickert's penile anomaly was, but if his problem was only "trifling" hypospadias, why did his parents resort to risky surgery? Why did his mother and father wait so long before attempting to correct what must have been a very unpleasant affliction? Sickert was five when he underwent surgery the third time, and one wonders how soon this occurred following the first two operations. We know that his great-aunt interceded to bring him to London, suggesting that his disability was acute and that possibly the two previous operations had been recent and may have resulted in complications. If indeed he was three or four when this nightmarish medical ordeal began, it could be that his parents delayed corrective procedures until they were certain of his gender. I do not know when Sickert was named Walter Richard. To date, no birth certificate or record of a christening has turned up.

In Helena's memoirs she writes that when she was a child "we" always referred to Walter and his brothers as "Walter and the boys." Who are *we*? I doubt his brothers referred to themselves as *Walter and the boys,* nor would I imagine that little Helena came up with the phrase on her own. I am inclined to suspect that the reference to *Walter and the boys* came from one or both parents.

Given Helena's picture of a young Walter who was precocious and dominant, such a law unto himself that he wasn't placed in the same category as the other sons, it may be that the phrase *Walter and the boys* was a way of acknowledging his precocity. It may also be that he was physically different from his brothers—or maybe from all boys. If the latter is the explanation, the repeated use of the phrase could have been humiliating and emasculating for the young Walter.

Sickert's early boyhood was traumatized by medical violence. When corrective surgery for hypospadias occurs after the age of eighteen months, it can create fears of castration. Sickert's operations would have resulted in strictures and scarring that could have made erections painful or impossible. He may have suffered partial amputation. His art does not include nude males, with the exception of two sketches I found that appear to have been done when he was in his teens or in art school. In each, the nude male figure has a vague stub of a penis that looks anything but normal.

One of the most distinctive features of the Ripper letters is that so many of them were written with drawing pens and daubed or smeared with bright inks and paints. They show the skilled hand of a highly trained or professional artist. More than a dozen include phallic drawings of knives—all long, daggerlike instruments—except for two strange, short, truncated blades in brazenly taunting letters. One of the stubby-knife letters, mailed on July 22, 1889, was penned in black ink on two pages of cheap paper that bear no watermarks.

London West

Dear Boss

Back again & up to the old tricks. Would you like to catch me? I guess you would well look here—I leave my diggings—close to Conduit St to night at about 10:30 watch Conduit St & close round there—Ha—Har I dare you 4 more lives four more cunts to add to my little collection & I shall rest content Do what you will you will never nap . . . Not a big blade but sharp [Jack the Ripper jotted beside his drawing of the knife]

Following the signature is a postscript that trails off in the very clear letters "R. St. w." At first glance this abbreviation might appear to be an address, especially since "St" is used twice in the letter to indicate Street, and "W" might mean West. There is no such London address as *R Street West,* but I suppose one might interpret the "R. St." as an odd abbreviation of Regent Street, which runs into Conduit Street. It is possible, however, that the cryptic initials are a double entendre—another "catch me if you can." They could hint of the killer's identity and where he spent some of his time.

On a number of Sickert's paintings, etchings, and sketches, he abbreviates Sickert as St. In later years he puzzled the art world by deciding that he was no longer Walter but Richard Sickert, and signed his work R. S. or R. St. In another letter the Ripper wrote to the police on

September 30, 1889—only two months after the one I just described—there is another similarly drawn truncated knife blade and what appears to be a scalpel or cut-throat razor with the initials R (possibly W) S faintly scratched on the blade. I'm not aware that the elusive initials on these 1889 letters have ever been noticed, and Sickert might have been amused by that. He did not want to be caught, but he must have found it exhilarating when the police missed his cryptic clues entirely.

Regent Street and New Bond Street would have been familiar to Walter Sickert. In 1881, he tagged along with Ellen Terry as she hit the shops of Regent Street in search of gowns for her role as Ophelia at the Lyceum. At 148 New Bond Street was the Fine Art Society, where James McNeill Whistler's paintings were exhibited and sold. In the July 1889 letter, the Ripper uses the word "diggings," which is American slang for a house or residence, and can also refer to a person's office. Sickert's professional business would have included the Fine Art Society, which was "close round" Conduit Street.

Speculations about what the Ripper meant in this letter are enticing. However, they are by no means a reliable account of what was going through Sickert's mind. But there are many reasons to think that Sickert would have read Robert Louis Stevenson's *The Strange Case of Dr. Jekyll and Mr. Hyde,* which was published in 1885. Sickert wouldn't have missed its theatrical performances that began in the summer of 1888. Stevenson's work might have helped Sickert to define his own duality.

There are many parallels between Jack the Ripper and Mr. Hyde: inexplicable disappearances; different styles of handwriting; fog; disguises; secret dwellings where changes of clothing were kept; disguised build, height, and walk. Through the symbolism in his novel, Stevenson gives us a remarkable description of psychopathy. Dr. Jekyll, the good man, is in "bondage" to the mysterious Mr. Hyde, who is "a spirit of enduring evil." After Hyde commits murder, he escapes through the dark streets, euphoric from his bloody deed. He is already fantasizing about the next one.

Dr. Jekyll's evil side is the "animal" that lives within him and feels no fear and relishes danger. It is in the "second character" of Hyde that Dr. Jekyll's mind becomes most nimble, his faculties "sharpened to a point." When the beloved doctor transforms himself into Hyde, he is overwhelmed by rage and a lust to torture and murder whoever he comes upon and can overpower. "That child of hell had nothing human," Stevenson wrote. Neither did Sickert when his "From Hell" other self replaced his ruined manhood with a blade.

As if Sickert's childhood operations and subsequent dysfunctions weren't misfortune enough, he suffered from what in the nineteenth century was called "depraved conditions of the blood." Letters written by Sickert in later life indicate that he periodically suffered from abscesses and boils that would send him to bed. He would refuse to seek out a doctor. An exact diagnosis of Sickert's congenital deformity and any other health problems associated with it may always remain elusive, although in 1899, he refers to his "organs of generation" having "suffered all his life," and to his "Physical misery." St. Mark's patient records do not exist prior to 1900, nor does it appear that Sir Alfred Duff Cooper kept any papers that might reveal information about Sickert's surgery in 1865. Cooper's records were not passed down in the family, according to his grandson, the historian and author John Julius Norwich.

Surgery in the early to mid-1800s was not a pleasant experience, especially surgery to the penis. The anesthetics ether, nitrous oxide (laughing gas), and chloroform had been discovered some thirty years earlier, but it wasn't until 1847 that British surgeons began using chloroform, which may not have helped young Walter much. Dr. Salmon, the head of St. Mark's, did not believe in anesthesia and did not allow the use of chloroform in his hospital because it was prone to cause death if the dose wasn't just right.

Whether Walter was chloroformed during his two surgeries in Germany is not known, although he mentions in a letter to Jacques-Emile Blanche that he remembered being chloroformed while his father, Oswald

Sickert, looked on. It is hard to know exactly what Sickert was referring to or when or how many times—or even if he was telling the truth. Sickert may or may not have been given anesthesia in London when Dr. Cooper operated on him in 1865. What is most amazing is that the little boy did not die.

Only a year earlier, in 1864, Louis Pasteur had concluded that germs cause disease. Three years later, in 1867, Joseph Lister would argue that germs could be combated by using carbolic acid as an antiseptic. Infection was such a common cause of hospital deaths that many people refused to be operated on, preferring to take their chances with cancer, gangrene, fulminating infections caused by injuries such as burns and fractures, or other potentially fatal maladies. Walter survived, but it is unlikely that he relished recollecting his hospital experience.

One can only imagine his terror when at the age of five he was whisked away by his father to the foreign city of London. The boy left behind mother and siblings and was in the care of a parent not known for compassion or warmth. Oswald Sickert wasn't the sort to hold little Walter's hand and offer words of love and comfort when he helped his son into the horse-drawn cab that would take them to St. Mark's Hospital. The father may have said nothing at all.

At the hospital, Walter and his small bag of belongings were left with the matron, most likely Mrs. Elizabeth Wilson, a seventy-two-year-old widow who believed in cleanliness and discipline. She would have assigned him a bed, placed his belongings in a locker, deloused and bathed him, then read him the hospital rules. At this time, Mrs. Wilson had one assistant nurse, and there was no nurse on duty at night.

How long Walter was in the hospital before Dr. Cooper performed the surgical procedure, I don't know, and I can't state as fact whether chloroform or an injection of a 5% solution of cocaine or any other type of anesthesia or pain reliever was used. Since it didn't become standard practice at St. Mark's to anesthetize patients until 1882, one might suspect the worst.

Inside the operating theater, an open coal fire blazed to warm the room and heat the irons used to cauterize bleeding. Only steel instruments were sterilized. Dressing gowns and towels were not. Most surgeons wore black frock coats not unlike the ones butchers wore in slaughterhouses. The stiffer and filthier with blood, the more the coat boasted of a surgeon's experience and rank. Cleanliness was considered to be finicking and affected, and a London Hospital surgeon of that time compared washing a frock coat to an executioner manicuring his nails before chopping off a person's head.

St. Mark's operating table was a bedstead—most certainly an iron one—with head- and footboards removed. What a ghastly impression a little boy must have had of an iron bedstead. On his ward he was confined to an iron bedstead, and he had an operation on one. It would be understandable if he associated an iron bedstead with bloody, painful terror—and rage. Walter was alone. His father may not have been very reassuring and might have viewed his son's disfigurement with shame or disgust. Walter was German. This was his first time in London. He was abandoned and powerless in an English-speaking prison where he was surrounded by suffering and subjected to the orders, probing, scrubbings, and bitter medicines of an old, no-nonsense nurse.

Mrs. Wilson—assuming she was on duty at the time of Walter's operation—would have assisted in the procedure by placing Walter on his back and separating his thighs. Typically, in operations on the rectum or the genitals, the patient was virtually hog-tied, with arms straightened, legs arched, wrists bound to ankles. Walter may have been restrained with cloth ligatures, and as an extra precaution, the nurse may have firmly held his legs in place while Dr. Cooper took a scalpel and cut along the fistula's entire track, according to the hospital's standard procedure.

If Walter was a lucky little boy, his ordeal began by his feeling suffocated as his nose and mouth were covered with a chloroform-soaked rag that was guaranteed to make him violently sick later. If he was an unlucky little fellow, he was wide awake and experienced every horror happening to him. It is no wonder Sickert would go through life with no love for "those terrible hospital nurses, their cuffs, their enemas & their razors," as he wrote more than fifty years later.

Dr. Cooper may have used a blunt knife for separating tissue, or a "curved director" (steel probe) to pass through the opening in the penis, or a trocar to puncture tender flesh. He may have passed a section of "stout thread" through the track of the new opening and tied a "firm knot" at the end, to strangulate the tissue over time in much the same way a thread or post keeps the hole in a newly pierced ear from closing. It all depends on what was really wrong with Walter's penis, but Dr. Cooper's corrective procedures would by necessity have been made only more extensive and painful after Walter's two earlier operations in Germany. There would have been scar tissue. There could have been other disastrous sequelae, such as strictures and partial—or almost complete—amputation.

Dr. Cooper's published medical procedures do not mention fistulas of the penis—or hypospadias—but his method when performing typical fistula operations on a child was to operate as quickly as possible to prevent shock and insure that the "little patient," Dr. Cooper wrote, wasn't "exposed" or left with open wounds "more than absolutely necessary." At the end of this ordeal, Dr. Cooper would close any incisions with silk sutures called "ligatures" and pack cotton wool into the wounds. While Walter was going through all this and who knows what else, the elderly Mrs. Wilson in her starchy uniform would have assisted as needed, doing her best to quiet straining limbs and screams if Walter had not been anesthetized. Or if he had, her face may have been the last one he saw as the sickly-sweet chloroform knocked him out. She may have been the first person he saw when he woke up throbbing with pain and retching.

In 1841, Charles Dickens was operated on without anesthesia. "I suffered agonies, as they related all to me, and did violence to myself in keeping to my seat," Dickens wrote in a letter to a friend. "I could scarcely bear it." Surgery on the penis must have been more painful than any rectal or anal procedure, especially when a patient was a five-year-old foreigner who could not have possessed the coping skills, the insight, or perhaps fluency enough in English to understand what was happening to him when Mrs. Wilson changed his dressings, administered his medicines, or appeared at his bedside with a supply of leeches if he had an inflammation believed to be due to an excess of blood.

Mrs. Wilson may have had a sweet bedside manner. Or she may have been strict and humorless. A typical requirement of a nurse in those days was that she be single or widowed so that all her time could be devoted to the hospital. Nurses were underpaid, worked long, grueling hours, and were exposed to extraordinarily unpleasant conditions and risks. It was not uncommon for nurses to "get into drink" a bit too much, to run home for a nip, to show up at work a bit mellow. I don't know about Mrs. Wilson. She could have been a teetotaler.

Walter's hospital stay must have seemed to him an endless stretch of bleak, scary days, with breakfast at eight, followed by milk and soup at 11:30, then a late-afternoon meal and lights out at 9:30 P.M. There he lay, day in and day out, in pain, no one on duty at night to hear him cry or comfort him in his native tongue or hold his hand. Had he secretly hated Nurse Wilson, no one could really blame him. Had he imagined she was the one who destroyed his penis and caused him so much anguish, that would be understandable. Had he hated his mother, who was far away from him during his ordeal, that would come as no surprise.

In the nineteenth century, to be born illegitimate or to be the child of an illegitimate parent was a terrible stigma. When Sickert's maternal grandmother had sex out of wedlock, according to Victorian standards, she enjoyed it, which implied that she suffered from the same genetic disorder that prostitutes did. The common belief was that this congenital defect was passed down the bloodline and was a "contagious blood poison" routinely described in the newspapers as a "disease that has been the curse of mankind from an early period in the history of the race, leaving its baneful effects on posterity to the third and fourth generations."

Sickert might have blamed his boyhood agonies, his humiliations, and his maimed masculinity on a genetic defect or "blood poison" that he inherited from his immoral dance-hall grandmother and his illegitimate mother. The psychological overlays to young Walter's physical curse are tragic to contemplate. He was damaged, and his language as an adult reveals a significant preoccupation with "things medical" when he was writing about things that were not.

Throughout his letters and art reviews there are metaphors such as operating table, operation, diagnosis, dissection, laying bare, surgeon, doctors, fateful theater, castrated, eviscerated, *all* your organs taken out, anesthetized, anatomy, ossify, deformation, inoculated, vaccinating. Some of these images are quite shocking, even revolting, when they suddenly uncoil and strike in the middle of a paragraph about art or daily life, just as Sickert's use of violent metaphors strikes unexpectedly, too. When he is discussing art, one doesn't expect to run into morbid horror, horrors, deadly, dead, death, dead ladies' hearts, hacking himself to pieces, terrify, fear, violent, violence, prey, cannibalism, nightmare, stillborn, dead work, dead drawings, blood, putting a razor to his throat, nailing up coffins, putrefied, razor, knife, cutting.

In a 1912 article for the *English Review* he wrote, "Enlarged photographs of the naked corpse should be in every art school as a standard of drawing from the nude."

CHAPTER SEVEN

THE GENTLEMAN SLUMMER

The heaviest rain of the year fell during the last week of August 1888. On average, the sun burned through the mist no more than an hour each day.

Temperatures remained unseasonably cool, and coal fires burned inside dwellings, gushing black smoke into the air and adding to the worst pollution in the city's history. In the Victorian era, there was no such thing as pollution monitoring and the word "smog" had not been coined. But the problems created by coal were nothing new.

It had been known since the English stopped using wood for fuel in the seventeenth century that smoke from burning coal damaged life and all of its edifices, but this did not dissuade people from using it. In the 1700s, it is estimated that there were 40,000 houses with 360,000 chimneys in the metropolis. By the late 1800s, coal consumption had gone up, especially among the poor. The approaching visitor smelled London many miles before he saw it.

Skies were sodden and blotchy, streets were paved with soot, and limestone buildings and ironworks were being eaten away. The polluted thick mist lingered longer and became denser as it took on a different hue than it had in the past. Watercourses dating from Roman times became so foul that they were filled in. A public health report written in 1889 declared that at the rate London was polluting itself, engineers would soon be forced to fill in the Thames, which was fouled with the excrement of millions every time the tide seeped in. There was good reason to wear dark clothing, and on some days the sulfurous, smoky air was so hellish and the stench of raw sewage so disgusting that Londoners walked about with burning eyes and lungs, handkerchiefs held over their faces.

The Salvation Army reported in 1890 that out of a population of approximately 5.6 million in the city, 30,000 were prostitutes, and 32,000 men, women, and juveniles were in prison. A year earlier, in 1889, 160,000 people were convicted of drunkenness, 2,297 committed suicide, and 2,157 were found dead on streets, in parks, and in hovels. Slightly less than one-fifth of the population was homeless, in workhouses or asylums, in hospitals, or ravaged by poverty and near starvation. Most of the "raging sea" of misery, to quote the founder of the Salvation Army, General William Booth, was located in London's East End, where a cunning predator like Jack the Ripper could easily butcher drunken, homeless prostitutes.

When the Ripper was terrorizing the East End, the population of his hunting ground was estimated at a million. If one includes the overcrowded nearby hamlets, the population doubles. East London, which included the London docks and run-down areas of Whitechapel, Spitalfields, and Bethnal Green, was bordered on the south by the River Thames, to the west by the City of London, to the north by Hackney and Shoreditch, with the River Lea to the east. The growth of the East End had been heavy because the road that led from Aldgate to Whitechapel to Mile End was a major artery for leaving the city, and the earth was level and easy to build upon.

The anchor of the East End was the London Hospital for the poor, which is still located on Whitechapel Road but is now called the Royal London Hospital. When Scotland Yard's John Grieve took me on one of several retrospective visits to what is left of the Ripper crime scenes, our meeting place was the Royal London Hospital, a grim Victorian brick building that doesn't seem to have been modernized much. The depressing nature of the place is but a faint imprint of what a pitiful pit it must have been in the late 1800s, when Joseph Carey Merrick—mistakenly called John Merrick by the showman who "owned" him last—was granted shelter in two of the hospital's first-floor back rooms.

Merrick—doomed to be known as the "Elephant Man"—was rescued from torment and certain death by Sir Frederick Treves, a courageous, kind physician. Dr. Treves was on the London Hospital's staff in November 1884 when Merrick was a slave to the carnival trade across the street inside a deserted greengrocer's shop. In front was a huge sheet of canvas advertising a life-size "frightful creature that could only have been possible in a nightmare," as Dr. Treves described it years later when he was Sergeant-Surgeon to King Edward VII.

For twopence, one could gain admittance to this barbaric spectacle. Children and adults would file inside the cold, vacant building and crowd around a red tablecloth hanging from the ceiling. The showman would yank back the curtain to "ooh!"s and "aah!"s and cries of shock as the hunched figure of Merrick cowered on his stool, dressed in nothing but an oversized pair of filthy, threadbare trousers. Dr. Treves lectured on anatomy and had seen just about every conceivable form of disfigurement and filth, but he had never encountered or smelled any creature quite so disgusting.

Merrick suffered from von Recklinghausen's disease, caused by mutations in genes that promote and inhibit cell growth. His physical aberrations included bony deformations so grotesque that his head was almost three feet in circumference with a mass that projected from his brow like a "loaf" and occluded one eye. The upper jaw was similar to a tusk, with the upper lip curled inside out, making it very difficult for Merrick to speak. "Sack-like masses of flesh covered by . . . loathsome cauliflower skin" draped from his back, his right arm, and other parts of his body, his face frozen in an inhuman mask incapable of expression. Until Dr. Treves intervened it was believed that Merrick was obtuse and mentally impaired. In fact, he was an extremely intelligent, imaginative, and loving human being.

Dr. Treves noted that one would have expected Merrick to be a bitter, hateful man because of the abominable way he had been treated all of his life. How could he be kind and sensitive when he had known nothing but mockery and cruel abuse? How could anyone be born with more against him? As Dr. Treves pointed out, Merrick would have been better off insensible and unaware of his hideous appearance. In a world that worships beauty, what greater anguish can there be than to suffer from such revolting ugliness? I don't think anyone would argue with the notion that Merrick's deformity was more tragic than Walter Sickert's.

It is quite possible that at some point Sickert paid his twopence and took a peek at Merrick. Sickert was living in London in 1884 and engaged to be married. He was an apprentice to Whistler, who knew the East End rag-shop scenes in the slums of Shoreditch and Petticoat Lane and would etch them in 1887. Sickert went where the Master went. They wandered together. Sometimes Sickert wandered about the sordid squalor on his own. The "Elephant Man" was just the sort of cruel, degrading exhibition that Sickert would have found amusing, and perhaps, for an instant, Merrick and Sickert were eye to eye. It would have been a scene replete with symbolism, for each was the other inside out.

In 1888, Joseph Merrick and Walter Sickert were simultaneously living secret lives in the East End. Merrick was a voracious reader and keenly curious. He would have been all too aware of the horrible murders beyond his hospital walls. A rumor began to circulate that it was Merrick who went out in his black cloak and hood at night and slaughtered Unfortunates. It was the monster Merrick who butchered women because they would not have him. To be deprived of sex would drive any man mad, especially such a beast as that carnival freak who ventured out into the hospital garden only after dark. Fortunately, no rational person took such nonsense seriously.

Merrick's head was so heavy he could scarcely move it, and the stalk of his neck would snap if his head ever fell back. He did not know what it was like to settle into a pillow at night, and in his fantasies he lay himself down to sleep and prayed the Lord would one day bless him with the sweet caresses and kisses of a woman—best of all, a blind one. Dr. Treves thought it a tragic irony that Merrick's organs of generation were nothing like the rest of him, but unfortunately, he was perfectly capable of the sexual love he would never have. Merrick slept sitting up with his huge head hung low, and he could not walk without a cane.

It is not known whether the baseless rumors that he was the Whitechapel killer ever reached his safe little rooms crammed with signed photographs of celebrities and royalty, some of whom had come to see him. What a great act of benevolence and tolerance to visit the likes of him and not outwardly register horror. What a story to relate to one's friends, to dukes and duchesses, to lords and ladies, or to Queen Victoria herself. Her Majesty was fascinated by life's mysteries and curiosities and had been quite fond of Tom Thumb, an American midget named Charles Sherwood Stratton who was only forty inches tall. It was easier to enter the cloistered world of harmless and amusing mutants than to wade through the "bottomless pit of decaying life," as Beatrice Webb described the East End, where rents were steep because overcrowding gave slumlords the upper hand.

The equivalent of a dollar to a dollar-fifty a week in rent was sometimes a fifth of a worker's salary, and when one of these Ebenezer Scrooge slumlords decided to raise the rent, sometimes a large family found itself homeless with nothing but a handcart to carry away all its worldly goods. A decade later Jack London went undercover in the East End to see for himself what it was like, and he related terrible stories of poverty and filth. He described an elderly woman found dead inside a room so infested with vermin that her clothing was "gray with insects." She was skin and bones, covered with sores, her hair matted with "filth" and a "nest of vermin," London wrote. In the East End, he reported, an attempt at cleanliness was a "howling farce," and when rain fell it was "more like grease than water."

This greasy rain fell in drips and drizzles in the East End most of Thursday, August 30th. Horse-drawn wagons and barrows splashed through the muddy rubbish-filled water in narrow, crowded streets, where flies droned in clouds and people scratched for the next penny. Most inhabitants of this wretched part of London had never tasted real coffee, tea, or chocolate. Fruit or meat never touched their lips unless it was overripe or rotten. There was no such thing as a bookshop or a decent tearoom. There were no hotels, at least not the sort that civilized people might visit. An Unfortunate could not get out of the weather and find a bit of food unless she could convince a man to take her in or give her small change so she could rent a bed for the night in a common lodging house called a doss-house.

"Doss" was slang for bed, and a typical doss-house was a hellish, decaying dwelling where men and women paid four or five pence to sleep in communal rooms filled with small iron bedsteads covered with gray blankets. Supposedly, the bedclothes were washed once a week. The casual poor, as the guests were called, sat around in crowded dormitories, smoking, mending, sometimes talking, joking if the lodger was still an optimist who believed life might get better, or telling a morose tale if the threadbare soul had been worn into a numb hopelessness. In the kitchen, men and women gathered to cook whatever they had been able to find or steal during the day. Drunks wandered in and held out palsied hands, grateful for a bone or scrap that might sail their way on the cruel winds of laughter as lodgers watched them grab and gnaw like animals. Children begged, and were beaten for getting too close to the fire.

Inside these inhuman establishments, one abided by strict, degrading rules posted on walls and enforced by the doorkeeper or warden. Misbehavior was rewarded by banishment to the mean streets, and early in the morning lodgers were herded out the door unless they paid in advance for another night. Doss-houses were usually owned by a better class of people who lived elsewhere and did not oversee their properties and may never even have seen them. For a little capital, one could own a piece of a poorhouse and have no idea—perhaps by choice—that one's "Model Lodgings" investment was an abomination overseen by "keepers" who often used dishonest and abusive means to maintain control over the desperate residents.

Many of these doss-houses catered to the criminal element, including the Unfortunates who might, on a good night, have pennies for lodging. Perhaps the Unfortunate might persuade a client to take her to bed, which was certainly preferable to sex on the street when one was exhausted, drunk, and hungry. Another breed of lodger was the "gentleman slummer," who, like thrill-seeking men of every era, would leave his respectable home and family to enter a forbidden world of low-life pub-crawling and music halls and cheap, anonymous sex. Some men from the better parts of the city became addicted to this secret entertainment, and Walter Sickert was one of them.

His best-known artistic leitmotif is an iron bedstead, and on it is a nude prostitute with a man aggressively leaning over her. Sometimes both the man and the nude woman are sitting, but the man is always clothed. It was Sickert's habit to keep an iron bedstead in any studio he was using at the time, and on it he arranged many a model. Occasionally he posed himself on the bed with a wooden lay figure—mannikin—that supposedly had belonged to one of Sickert's artistic idols, William Hogarth.

Sickert enjoyed shocking guests he had invited over for tea and cake, and on one occasion, not long after the 1907 slaying of a prostitute in Camden Town, Sickert's guests arrived at his dimly lit Camden Town studio to discover the lewdly positioned lay figure in bed with Sickert, who was making jests about the recent murder. No one seemed to think much about that display or anything else bizarre Walter Sickert did. After all, he was Sickert. None of his contemporaries—nor many of the critics and academics who study him today—wondered why he acted out violence and was obsessed with notorious crimes, including those of Jack the Ripper.

Sickert was in a superior and untouchable position if he wanted to get away with murdering Unfortunates. He was of a class that was above suspicion, and he was a genius at becoming any number of different characters in every sense of the word. It would have been easy and exciting for him to disguise himself as either an East Ender or a gentleman slummer and voyeuristically prowl the pubs and doss-houses of Whitechapel and its nearby hellholes. He was an artist capable of changing his handwriting and designing taunting letters that are the mark of a brilliant draftsman. But nobody noticed the remarkable nature of these documents until art historian Dr. Anna Gruetzner Robins and paper conservator Anne Kennett examined the originals at the Public Record Office (PRO) in June 2002.

What had always been assumed to be human or animal blood on the Ripper letters turns out to be sticky brown etching ground—or perhaps a mixture of inks that remarkably resembles old blood. These bloody-looking smears, drips, and splotches were applied with an artist's brush, or are imprints left by fabrics or fingers. Some of the Ripper's stationery is "vellum" or other paper with watermarks. Apparently the police never noticed feathering brush strokes or types of paper when investigating the Ripper murders. Apparently no one has ever paid any attention to the thirty or so different watermarks found on letters thought to be hoaxes written by some illiterate or deranged prankster. Apparently no one has asked whether such a prankster was likely to have possessed drawing pens, colorful inks, lithographic or Chinagraph crayons, etching ground, and artist's paints and paper.

If any part of Sickert's anatomy symbolized his entire being, it wasn't his disfigured penis. It was his eyes. He watched. Watching—spying, stalking with the eyes and the feet—is a dominant trait of psychopathic killers, unlike the disorganized offenders who are given to impulse or messages from outer space or God. Psychopaths watch people. They watch pornography, especially violent pornography. They are very scary voyeurs.

Modern technology has made it possible for them to watch videotapes of themselves raping, torturing, and killing their victims. They relive their horrific crimes over and over again, and masturbate. For some psychopaths, the only way they can reach orgasm is to watch, stalk, fantasize, and replay their last rampages. Ted Bundy, says former FBI profiler Bill Hagmaier, strangled and raped his victims from behind, his excitement mounting as her tongue protruded and her eyes bulged. He reached climax as she reached death.

Then come the fantasies, the reliving, and the violent-erotic tension is unbearable and these killers strike again. The denouement is the dying or dead body. The cooling-off period is the safe haven that allows relief and the reliving of the crime. And the fantasies begin. And the tension builds again. And they find another victim. And they introduce another scene into their script to add more daring and excitement: bondage, torture, mutilation, dismemberment, grotesque displays of the carnage, and cannibalism.

As former FBI Academy instructor and profiler Edward Sulzbach has reminded me over the years, "The actual murder is incidental to the fantasies." The first time I heard him say this in 1984 I was baffled and didn't believe him. In my naive way of thinking I assumed that the big thrill was the kill. I had been a police reporter for the *Charlotte Observer* in North Carolina and was no coward when it came to dashing off to crime scenes. Everything centered on the terrible *event*, I thought. Without the event, there was no story. It shames me now to realize how naive I was. I thought I understood evil, but I didn't.

I thought I was a veteran investigator of horrors, and I knew nothing.

I didn't understand that psychopaths follow the same human patterns "normal" people do, but the violent psychopath strays off track in ways that would never register on the average person's navigational system. Many of us have erotic fantasies that are more exciting than the actualization of them, and looking forward to an event often gives us more delight than the experience of it. So it is for violent psychopaths as they anticipate their crimes.

Sulzbach also likes to say, "Never look for unicorns until you run out of ponies."

Violent crimes are often mundane. A jealous lover kills a rival or partner who has betrayed him or her. A card game turns ugly and someone is shot. A street thug wants cash for drugs and stabs his victim. A drug dealer is gunned down because he sold bad drugs. These are the ponies. Jack the Ripper wasn't a pony. He was a unicorn. In the 1880s and 1890s, Sickert was far too clever to paint pictures of murders and entertain his friends by reenacting a real killing that had happened just beyond his door. The behavior that casts suspicion on him now was not apparent in 1888, when he was young and secretive and afraid of getting caught. Only his Ripper letters to the newspapers and the police offered evidence, but they were met with a blind eye, if not utter indifference and perhaps a chuckle or two.

There were two vices Sickert hated, or so he told his acquaintances. One was stealing. The other was alcoholism, which ran in his family. There is no reason to suspect that Sickert drank, at least not to excess until much later in life. By all accounts, he stayed away from drugs, even for therapeutic purposes. Whatever his cracked facets or emotional twists, Sickert was clear-headed and calculating. He had an intense curiosity about anything that might catch his artist's eye or appear on his radar for violence. There was much to appeal to him on the Thursday night of August 30, 1888, when a brandy warehouse in the London docks caught fire around 9:00 P.M. and illuminated the entire East End.

People came from miles around and peered through locked iron gates at an inferno that defied the gallons of water dumped on it by the fire brigade. Unfortunates drifted toward the blaze, both curious and eager to take advantage of an unplanned opportunity for sexual commerce. In the finer parts of London, other entertainment lit up the night as the famous Richard Mansfield thrilled theatergoers with his brilliant performance as Dr. Jekyll and Mr. Hyde at the Lyceum. The comedy *Uncles and Aunts* had just opened to a grand review in *The Times*, and *The Paper Chase* and *The Union Jack* were going full tilt. The plays had begun at 8:15, 8:30, or 9:00, and by the time they ended, the fire at the docks still roared. Warehouses and ships along the Thames were backlit by an orange glow visible for many miles. Whether Sickert was at his home or at one of the theaters or music halls, he was unlikely to miss the drama at South and Spirit quays that was attracting such an excited crowd.

Of course, it is purely speculative to say that Sickert wandered toward the water to watch. He might not have been in London on this night, although there is nothing on record to prove he wasn't. There are no letters, no documents, no news accounts, no works of art that might so much as hint that Sickert was not in London. Divining what he was doing often means discovering what he wasn't doing.

Sickert wasn't interested in people knowing where he was. He was notorious for his lifelong habit of renting at least three secret "studios" at a time. These hovels were scattered about in locations so private and so unexpected and so unpredictable that his wife, colleagues, and friends had no idea where they were. His known studios, which numbered close to twenty during his life, were often slovenly "small rooms" filled with chaos that "inspired" him. Sickert worked alone behind locked doors. It was rare that he would see anyone, and if he did, a visit to these rat holes required a telegram or a special knock. In his older years, he erected tall black gates in front of his door and chained a guard dog to one of the iron bars.

As is true of any good actor, Sickert knew how to make an entrance

Frau Sickert, Walter Sickert's great-grandmother. *Tate Gallery Archive, Photograph Collection.*

Eleanor Louisa Moravia Sickert, Walter Sickert's mother, in 1911. *Tate Gallery Archive, Photograph Collection.*

Oswald Adalbert Sickert, Walter Sickert's father. *Tate Gallery Archive, Photograph Collection.*

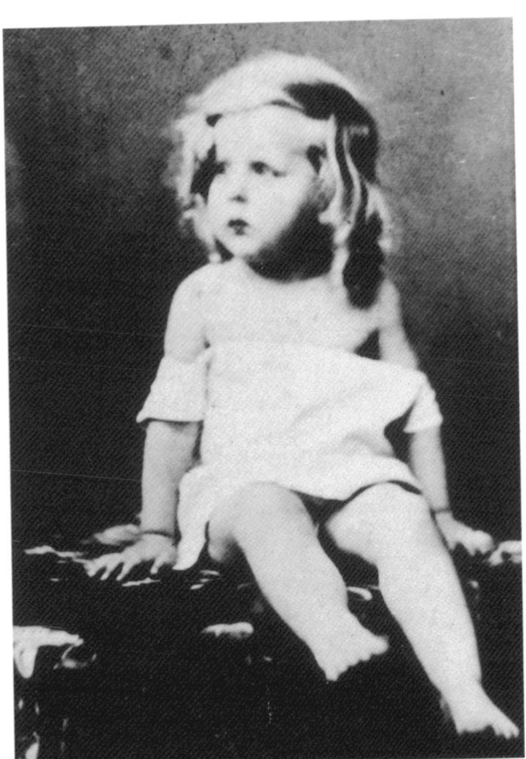

Walter Sickert with his flaxen curls, age two, about 1862. *Tate Gallery Archive, Photograph Collection.*

Walter, age nine, after his three surgeries, about 1869.
Tate Gallery Archive, Photograph Collection.

Walter the actor, on tour in Liverpool at age twenty.
Tate Gallery Archive, Photograph Collection.

Ellen Cobden, the daughter of a famous politician and first wife of Jack the Ripper. She divorced Sickert in 1899. *By courtesy of the trustees of the Cobden Estate, with acknowledgements to West Sussex Record Office.*

Walter at age twenty-four, James McNeill Whistler's apprentice, about 1884. *Tate Gallery Archive, Photograph Collection.*

One of Sickert's self-portraits, one of Sickert's many looks. *Ashmolean Museum, Oxford.*

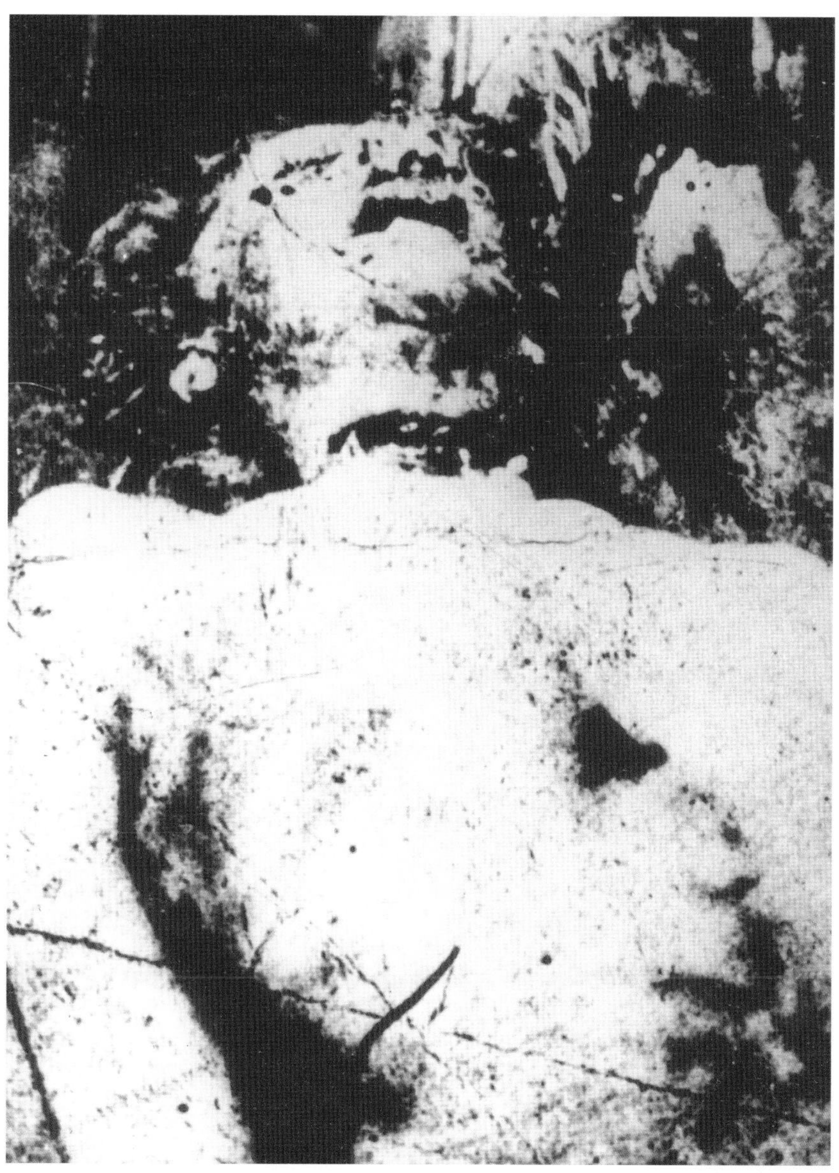

Catherine Eddows's facial mutilations included cuts through her lower eyelids, her nose almost severed from her face, and an ear lobe slashed off. *© Public Record Office, London.*

Sickert's sketch *He Killed His Father in a Fight* displays a violent imagination and a similarity to the Mary Kelly murder scene, especially with its wooden bed frame. *The Whitworth Art Gallery, The University of Manchester.*

and an exit. He had a habit of vanishing for days or weeks without telling Ellen or his second or third wives or his acquaintances where he was or why. He might invite friends to dinner and not show up. He would reappear as he pleased, usually with no explanation offered. Outings often turned into his going missing, for he liked to go to the theater and music halls alone and afterward wander during the late night and misty early morning hours.

Sickert's routes were peculiar and illogical, especially if he was returning home from the theaters and music halls in central London along the Strand. Denys Sutton writes that Sickert often walked north to Hoxton, then retraced his steps to end up in Shoreditch on the western border of Whitechapel. From there he would have to walk west and north to return to 54 Broadhurst Gardens in northwest London, where he lived. According to Sutton, the reason for these strange peregrinations and detours into a dangerous part of East London is that Sickert needed "a long silent tramp to meditate on what he had just seen" in a music hall or theater. The artist pondering. The artist observing a dark, foreboding world and the people who lived in it. The artist who liked his women ugly.

CHAPTER EIGHT

A BIT OF BROKEN LOOKING GLASS

Mary Ann Nichols was approximately forty-two years old and missing five teeth.

She was five foot two or three and plump, with a fleshy, plain face, brown eyes, and graying dark brown hair. During her marriage to a printer's machinist named William Nichols, she had given birth to five children, the oldest twenty-one, the youngest eight or nine at the time of her murder.

For the past seven years or so, she and William had been separated because of her drinking and quarrelsome ways. His support of five shillings each week ceased, he later told the police, when he learned she was living the life of a prostitute. Mary Ann had nothing left, not even her children. Years ago she had lost custody of them when her ex-husband informed the courts that she was living in sin with a blacksmith named Drew, who soon enough left her, too. The last time her former husband saw Mary Ann alive was in June of 1886 at the funeral of a son who had burned to death when a paraffin lamp exploded.

During her desolate times, Mary Ann had been an inmate at numerous workhouses, which were huge, dreaded barracks packed with as many as a thousand men and women who had nowhere else to go. The poor despised the workhouses, yet there were always long queues on cold mornings as the penniless waited in hopes of admission into what were called "casual wards." If the workhouse wasn't full, and a person was taken in by the porter, he or she was carefully interrogated and searched for money. The discovery of even a penny sent the person back out on the street. Tobacco was confiscated; knives and matches were not allowed. Every inmate was stripped and washed in the same tub of water and dried off with communal towels. They were issued with workhouse clothing and directed to stinking, rat-infested wards where canvas beds stretched out between poles like hammocks.

Breakfast at 6:00 A.M. might be bread and a gruel called "skilly" made with oatmeal or moldy meat. Then the inmate was put to work, performing the same cruel tasks that had been used to punish criminals for hundreds of years: pounding stones, scrubbing, picking oakum (untwisting old rope to reuse the hemp), or sent to the infirmary or mortuary to clean the sick ward or tend to the dead. It was rumored among inmates that the incurably sick in the infirmary were "polished off" with poison. Dinner was at 8:00 P.M., and the inmates got leftovers from the infirmary's patients. Filthy fingers attacked mounds of table scraps and stuffed them into ravenous mouths. Sometimes there was suet soup.

Guests of the casual wards were required to stay at least two nights and one day, and to refuse to work was to end up homeless again. Rosier accounts of these degrading places can be found in gilded publications that tend to mention only "shelters" for the poor that provided uncomfortable but clean beds and "good meat soup" and bread. Such civilized charity was not to be found in London's East End unless it was at

Salvation Army shelters, which were generally avoided by the street-smart who had grown cynical about their purpose. Ladies of the Salvation Army regularly visited doss-houses to preach God's generosity to paupers who knew better. Hope was not for a fallen woman like Mary Ann Nichols. The Bible could not save her.

She had been in and out of the Lambeth Workhouse several times between the previous Christmas and April 1888. In May she vowed to change her ways and took a coveted job as a domestic servant in a respectable family home. Her vows did not last, and in July she left in shame after stealing clothing valued at £3 10 shillings. Mary Ann sank deeper into her drunken ways and returned to the life of an Unfortunate. For a while she and another prostitute named Nelly Holland shared a bed in a doss-house in the maze of decaying buildings in Thrawl Street, which ran from east to west between Commercial Street and Brick Lane in Whitechapel.

After a while, Mary Ann moved on to White House in nearby Flower and Dean Street and stayed there until she ran out of money and was evicted on August 29th. The following night, she walked the streets wearing everything she owned: a brown ulster fastened with big brass buttons engraved with the figures of a man and a horse; a brown linsey frock; two gray woolen petticoats with the stenciled marks of the Lambeth Workhouse; two brown stays (stiff bodices made of whalebone); flannel underclothing; ribbed black woolen stockings; men's elastic-sided boots that had been cut on the uppers, toes, and heels for a better fit; and a black straw bonnet trimmed in black velvet. In a pocket she had tucked a white handkerchief, a comb, and a bit of broken looking glass.

Mary Ann was spotted several times between 11:00 P.M. and 2:30 the following morning, and in each instance, she was alone. She was seen in Whitechapel Road, and then at the Frying Pan pub. At around 1:40 A.M., she was in the kitchen of her former lodging house at 18 Thrawl Street, where she said she was penniless and asked that her bed be kept for her, promising to return soon with money for payment. She was intoxicated, witnesses said, and on her way out of the door she promised to be back soon and bragged about her "jolly" bonnet, which appeared to have been recently acquired.

Mary Ann was last seen alive at 2:30 A.M. when her friend Nelly Holland came upon her at the corner of Osborn Street and Whitechapel Road, opposite the parish church. Mary Ann was drunk and staggering along a wall. She told Nelly that so far this night she had earned three times what she needed for her bed at the lodging house but had spent it. Despite her friend's pleas that she come with her and go to bed, Mary Ann insisted on trying one last time to earn a few pennies. The parish church clock chimed as Mary Ann wove her way along the unlit Whitechapel Road, dissolving into darkness.

Approximately an hour and fifteen minutes later and half a mile away in a street called Buck's Row that bordered the Jews' Cemetery in Whitechapel, Charles Cross, a carman, was walking along on his way to work and passed a dark shape against some gates on a footpath near a stableyard. At first he thought the shape was a tarpaulin, but he realized it was a woman lying motionless, her head to the east, her bonnet on the ground by her right side, her left hand up against the closed gateway. As Cross was trying to get a better look to see what was wrong with her, he heard footsteps and turned around as another carman named Robert Paul appeared in the street.

"Take a look," Cross called out as he touched the woman's hand. "I believe she is dead." Robert Paul crouched down and put a hand on her breast. He thought he felt a slight movement and said, "I believe she is still breathing."

Her clothing was disarrayed, and her skirt was raised above her hips, so the men decided she had been "outraged" or raped. They chastely rearranged her clothing to cover her, not noticing any blood because it was too dark. Paul and Cross rushed off to find the nearest constable and happened upon G. Mizen 55 Division H, who was making his rounds at the nearby corner of Hanbury Street and Old Montague Street, on the west side of the Jews' Cemetery. The men informed the constable that there was a woman on the pavement either dead or "dead drunk."

When Mizen and the two men reached the stable yard in Buck's Row, Constable John Neil had come across the body and was alerting other police in the area by calling out and flashing his bull's-eye lantern. The woman's throat had been severely cut, and Dr. Rees Ralph Llewellyn, who lived nearby at 152 Whitechapel Road, was immediately roused from bed and summoned to the scene. Mary Ann Nichols's identity was unknown at this time, and according to Dr. Llewellyn, she was "quite dead." Her wrists were cold, her body and lower extremities were still very warm. He was certain she had been dead less than half an hour and that her injuries were "not self-inflicted." He also observed that there was little blood around her neck or on the ground.

He ordered the body moved to the nearby Whitechapel Workhouse mortuary, a private "dead house" for workhouse inmates and not intended for any sort of proper forensic postmortem examination. Llewellyn said he would be there shortly to take a better look, and Constable Mizen sent a man to fetch an ambulance from the Bethnal Green police station. Victorian London hospitals did not have horse-drawn or motorized ambulances and there was no such thing as the London Ambulance Service.

The usual means of rushing a desperately sick or injured person to the nearest hospital was for friends or Good Samaritan passersby to carry the patient by the arms and legs. Sometimes the cry "Send for a shutter!" rang out, and the patient would be conveyed on a window shutter carried like a stretcher. Ambulances were used by police, and most police stations had one of these unwieldy wooden-sided handcarts with its lashed-in sturdy black leather bottom that was equipped with thick leather straps. A tan leather convertible top could be unfolded, but probably did little more than offer partial protection from prying eyes or bad weather.

In most cases, an ambulance was used to remove a drunk from a public place, but occasionally the cargo was the dead. It must have been quite a chore for a constable to navigate a handcart at night along unlit, narrow, rutted streets. Such an ambulance is extremely heavy, even without a patient, and is very difficult to turn. Based on the one I found in Metropolitan Police storage, I would guess that the cart weighs several hundred pounds and would have been extremely difficult to pull up the gentlest hill, unless the constable at the handles was strong and had a good grip.

This morbid means of transportation was one that Walter Sickert would have seen had he lingered in the dark and watched his victims being carted away. It must have been thrilling to spy on a constable huffing and straining as Mary Ann Nichols's almost severed head lolled from side to side while the big wheels bounced and her dripping blood speckled the street.

Sickert is known to have drawn, etched, and painted only what he saw. Without exception, this is true. He painted a handcart that is almost identical to the one I saw in police storage. His picture is unsigned, undated, and titled *The Hand Cart, Rue St Jean, Dieppe*. Some catalogues refer to it as *The Basket Shop*, and in the painting the view is from the rear of a handcart that has what looks very much like a folded-down tan convertible top. Stacked in front of a shop across the narrow, deserted street are what appear to be large, long baskets, similar to what the French used as stretchers for the dead. A barely visible figure, possibly a man wearing some sort of hat, is walking on the pavement, looking over to see what is inside the cart. At his feet is an inexplicable black square shape that might be a piece of luggage, but could be part of the pavement, rather like a raised cast-iron manhole cover or sewer trapdoor. In Mary Ann Nichols's murder case, the newspapers reported that the police did not believe the "trap" in the street had been opened, implying that the killer had not escaped through the labyrinth of vaulted brick sewers that ran beneath London's streets.

A trap is also an opening in stage floors that gives actors quick and easy access to a scene in progress, usually to the surprise and delight of the unsuspecting audience. In most productions of Shakespeare's *Hamlet,* the ghost enters and exits through the trap. Sickert probably knew far more about stage traps than sewer traps. In 1881, he played the ghost in Henry Irving's *Hamlet* at the Lyceum Theater. The dark shape at the figure's feet in Sickert's painting could be a theater trap. It could be a sewer trap. Or it could be a detail Sickert created to tease viewers.

Mary Ann Nichols's body was lifted off the street and placed inside a wooden shell that was strapped into the ambulance. Two constables accompanied the body to the mortuary, where it was left in the ambulance outside in the yard. By now, it was after 4:30 A.M., and while the constables waited at the mortuary for Inspector John Spratling, a boy who lived in George Yard Buildings helped the police clean up the crime scene. Pails of water were splashed on the ground, and blood flowed into the gutter, leaving only a trace between the stones.

P.C. John Phail later testified that as he watched the washing of the pavement he noticed a "mass of congealed" blood about six inches in diameter that had been under the body. It was his observation that contrary to what Dr. Llewellyn had said, there was quite a lot of blood, and it appeared to Phail that it had flowed from the murdered woman's neck under her back and as far down as her waist. Dr. Llewellyn might have noticed the same details had he turned over the body.

Inspector Spratling arrived at the mortuary and impatiently waited in the dark for the keeper to arrive with the keys. By the time Mary Ann Nichols's body was carried inside, it must have been after 5:00 A.M., and she had been dead for at least two hours. Her body, still inside the shell, was placed on a wooden bench that was typical of those used in mortuaries then. Sometimes these benches or tables were acquired secondhand from butchers at the local slaughterhouses. Inspector Spratling pulled up Mary Ann's dress for a closer inspection in the gas lamp's gloom and discovered that her abdomen had been slashed open, exposing the intestines. The next morning, Saturday, September 1st, Dr. Llewellyn performed the postmortem and Wynne Edwin Baxter, the coroner for the South-Eastern Division of Middlesex, opened the inquest into Mary Ann Nichols's death.

Unlike grand jury proceedings in the United States, which are closed to everyone except those subpoenaed, death inquests in Britain are open to the public. In an 1854 treatise on the office and duties of coroners, it was noted that while it may be illegal to publish evidence that could prove important in the trial, these facts were routinely published anyway and benefitted the public. Details might serve as a deterrent, and by knowing the facts—especially when there are no suspects—the public becomes part of the investigative team. Someone might read about the case and realize that he or she has helpful information to add.

Whether this reasoning is valid or not, coroners' inquisitions and even ex parte proceedings were usually fair game to journalists in 1888, as long as their reporting was truthful and balanced. As appalling as this may seem to anyone unaccustomed to the publication of evidence and testimony before the actual trial, were it not for Britain's open policy there would be virtually no detailed death investigation records of Jack the Ripper's crimes. With the exception of a few pages here and there, the postmortem reports have not survived. Many of them were lost during World War II, and others may have disappeared in a clerical, or careless, or dishonest Bermuda Triangle.

It is regrettable that so many documents are missing, because much more could be learned if we had access to the original police reports, photographs, memoranda, and whatever else is gone. But I doubt there was a cover-up. There was no "Rippergate" instigated by police authorities and politicians who were trying to shield the public from a shocking truth. Yet the doubters continue to champion their theories: Scotland Yard has always known who the Ripper was but protected him; Scotland

Yard accidentally let him go or tucked him into an asylum and didn't inform the public; the royal family was involved; Scotland Yard didn't care about butchered prostitutes and wanted to hide how little the police did to solve the murders.

Untrue. No matter how badly the Metropolitan Police may have botched the Ripper investigation, there was no deliberate mendacity or disinformation that I could find. The boring fact is that most of what went wrong was due to sheer ignorance. Jack the Ripper was a modern killer born a hundred years too soon to be caught, and over the decades, records, including the original postmortem report of Mary Ann Nichols, have been lost, misplaced, or spirited away. Some ended up in the hands of collectors. I myself bought an alleged original Ripper letter for $1,500.

I suspect the document is authentic and possibly even written by Sickert. If a Ripper letter was available in 2001 through a search by a rare-documents dealer, then that letter at some point must have disappeared from the case files. How many others disappeared? I was told by officials at Scotland Yard that the overriding reason they finally turned over all Ripper files to the Public Record Office in Kew is that so much had vanished. Police officials feared that eventually there would be nothing left except reference numbers linked to empty folders.

The fact that the Home Office sealed the Ripper case records for a hundred years only increased the suspicion of conspiracy enthusiasts. Maggie Bird, the archivist in Scotland Yard's Records Management Branch, offers a historical perspective on the subject. She explains that in the late nineteenth century it was routine to destroy all police personnel files once the officer turned sixty-one, which accounts for the absence of significant information about the police involved in the Ripper cases. Personnel files on Inspector Frederick Abberline, who headed the investigation, and his supervisor, Chief Inspector Donald Swanson, are gone.

As a matter of routine, Ms. Bird says, even now high-profile murder cases are sealed for twenty-five, fifty, or seventy-five years, depending on the nature of the crime and whether there remains a privacy issue for the family of the victim or victims. If the Ripper case records had not been sealed for a century, there might not be anything left of them at all. It took two short years after the records were unsealed for "half of them" to vanish or be stolen, according to Ms. Bird.

At present, all Scotland Yard files are stored in a huge warehouse, the boxes labeled, numbered, and logged into a computer system. Ms. Bird claims "with hand on heart" that there are no Ripper files lurking about or lost in those boxes. As far as she knows, all have been turned over to the Public Record Office, and she attributes any gaps in the records to "bad handling, human nature or pinching, and the bombings of World War II," when the headquarters—where the records were then stored—were partially destroyed during a blitzkrieg.

While it may have been appropriate to prevent the publication of the graphic details and morgue photographs of nude, mutilated bodies for a period of time, I suspect discretion and sensitivity were not the only motives behind locking up files and hiding the key. No good could come from reminding the world that the Yard never caught its man, and there was no point in dwelling on an ugly chapter in English history when the Metropolitan Police was disgraced by one of its worst commissioners.

Her Majesty the Queen must have been suffering a spell of some sort when she decided to drag a tyrannical general out of Africa and put him in charge of the civilian police in a city that already hated "blue bottles" and "coppers."

Charles Warren was a brusque, arrogant man who wore elaborate uniforms. When the Ripper crimes began in 1888, Warren had been commissioner for two years, and his answer to everything was political subterfuge and force, as he had proven the year before on Bloody Sunday, November 13th, when he forbade a peaceful socialist demonstration in Trafalgar Square. Warren's order was illegal, and it was ignored by socialist reformers such as Annie Besant and MP Charles Bradlaugh, and the peaceful demonstration was to go on as planned.

Following Warren's orders, the police attacked the unsuspecting and unarmed protesters. Mounted police charged in, "rolling men and women over like ninepins," wrote Annie Besant. Soldiers arrived, ready to fire and swinging truncheons, and peace-loving, law-abiding working men and women were left with shattered limbs. Two were dead, many were wounded, people were imprisoned without representation, and the Law and Liberty League was formed to defend all victims of police brutality.

To add to Warren's abuse of power, when the funeral for one of those slain was scheduled, he forbade the hearse to travel along any of the main roads west of Waterloo Bridge. The massive procession moved slowly along Aldgate, through Whitechapel, and ended at a cemetery in Bow Road, passing through the very section of the city where a year later the Ripper began murdering the Unfortunates whom Annie Besant, Charles Bradlaugh, and others were trying to help. Sickert's brother-in-law, T. Fisher Unwin, published Annie Besant's autobiography, and Sickert painted Charles Bradlaugh's portrait twice. Neither was a coincidence. Sickert knew these people because Ellen and her family were active Liberals and moved in those political circles. In the early days of Sickert's career, Ellen helped him professionally by introducing him to well-known figures whose portraits he might paint.

Annie Besant and Charles Bradlaugh gave their lives to the poor. Walter Sickert took the lives of the poor, and it was disgraceful that some newspapers began to suggest that the Ripper's crimes were a socialist statement directed at graphically exposing the underside of the class system and the dirty secrets of the greatest city in the world. Sickert murdered sick and miserable prostitutes who were old long before their time. He murdered them because it was easy.

He was motivated by his lust for sexual violence, his hatred, and his insatiable need for attention. His murders had nothing to do with making socialist political statements. He killed to satisfy his uncontrollable violent psychopathic needs. No doubt when the papers and public hinted at motive—especially a social or ethical one—Sickert enjoyed a secret delight and rush of power. "[H]a! ha! ha!" the Ripper wrote. "To tell you the truth you ought to be obliged to me for killing such a deuced lot of vermin, why they are ten times worse than men."

CHAPTER NINE

THE DARK LANTERN

During the reign of George III, robbers ruled the highways and by-ways, and most villains could buy their way out of trouble with a bribe.

London was protected by night watchmen armed with staves, lanterns, and wooden rattles that made a startling clack-clack-clack sound when the head was spun. It wasn't until 1750 that times began to change. Henry Fielding, better known as an author than a magistrate, gathered a faithful group of constables under his command. With £400 allotted by the government, Fielding formed the first squadron of "thief-takers."

They broke up gangs and other scoundrels who terrorized the lives of Londoners. When Henry Fielding was ready to move on, he was followed by his brother John, in whose case justice was truly blind. Sir John Fielding had lost his eyesight and was famous for wearing a bandage over his eyes when he confronted prisoners. He was said to recognize criminals by voice.

Under Sir John Fielding's supervision, the thief-takers had their headquarters in Bow Street and became known as the Bow Street Patrol and then as the Bow Street Runners. At this stage, policing was somewhat privatized, and a Bow Street Runner might investigate the burglary of a resident's town house for a fee or simply find the perpetrator and coax him to agree on a settlement with the victim. In an odd way, criminal and civil law were combined, because while it was unlawful to commit bad deeds, order could be restored and a lot of fuss and bother could be avoided by striking a deal.

Better to have half of one's belongings returned than none at all. Better to give back half of what one had stolen than to lose it all and end up in prison. Some Bow Street Runners retired as wealthy men. Nothing much could be done about riots and murders, which were rampant, as were other evil deeds. Dogs were stolen and killed for their hides. Cattle were tortured by "bullock-baiting," and sporting mobs chased the pain-crazed animals until they collapsed and died. From the late 1700s until 1868, executions were public and drew tremendous crowds.

Hanging days were holidays, and the gruesome spectacle was considered a deterrent to crime. During the days of thief-takers and Bow Street Runners, violations of the law punishable by death included horse stealing, forging, and shoplifting. In 1788, thousands gathered at Newgate to watch thirty-year-old Phoebe Harris burned at the stake for counterfeiting coins. Highwaymen were heroes, and admirers cheered them on as they dangled, but the convicted upper class were ridiculed no matter their crime.

When Governor Joseph Wall was hanged in 1802, onlookers fought over the executioner's rope, buying it for a shilling per inch. In 1807, a crowd of 40,000 gathered to watch the execution of two convicted murderers, and men, women, and children were trampled to death. Not every prisoner died quickly or according to plan, and some of the agonal scenes were ghastly. The knot slipped or didn't catch properly and instead of compression of the carotid causing unconsciousness fast, the strangling prisoner flailed violently as men grabbed his kicking legs and pulled down hard to hasten death along. Usually the condemned man lost his trousers and twisted and writhed naked in front of the screaming mob. In the old days of the axe, a refusal to place a few coins into an executioner's hand could result in bad aim that required a few extra chops.

In 1829, Sir Robert Peel convinced government and the public that they had a right to sleep safely within their own homes and walk the streets without worry. The Metropolitan Police was established with its headquarters at 4 Whitehall Place, its back door opening onto Scotland Yard, the former site of a Saxon palace that had served as a residence for visiting Scottish kings. By the late seventeenth century, most of the palace had fallen into ruin and was demolished, and what remained was used as offices by the government. Many well-known figures once served the crown from Scotland Yard, including the architects Inigo Jones and Christopher Wren and the great poet John Milton, who at one time was the Latin secretary to Oliver Cromwell. Architect and comic writer Sir John Vanbrugh built a house on the old palace grounds that Jonathan Swift compared to a "goose pie."

Few people outside Britain realize that Scotland Yard has always been a place and not a police organization. Since 1829, "Scotland Yard" has referred to the headquarters of the Metropolitan Police, and that remains true today, although the official name now is "New Scotland Yard." I suspect some people will continue to hold to the belief that Scotland Yard is a group of sleuths like Sherlock Holmes and that a uniformed London officer is a bobby. Perhaps there will always be books and movies with provincial police who are stumped by a murder and deliver that delightfully hackneyed line, "I think this is a job for Scotland Yard."

From its earliest days, Scotland Yard and its uniformed divisions were resented by the public. Policing was viewed as an affront to an Englishman's civil rights and associated with martial law and the government's way of spying and bullying. When the Metropolitan Police were first organized, they did their best to avoid a military appearance by dressing themselves in blue coats and trousers and topped themselves off with rabbit-skin stovepipe hats reinforced with steel frames just in case an apprehended criminal decided to knock an officer on the head. The hats also came in handy as footstools for climbing over fences and walls or getting into windows.

At first, the Metropolitan Police had no detectives. It was bad enough having bobbies in blue, but the idea of men in ordinary garb sneaking about to collar people was violently opposed by citizens and even by the uniformed police, who resented the fact that detectives would get better pay and worried that the real purpose of these plainclothesmen was to tattle on the rank and file. Developing a solid detective division by 1842 and introducing plainclothes officers in the mid-1840s entailed a few fumbles, including the unenlightened decision to hire educated gentlemen who had no police training. One can only imagine such a person interviewing a drunk East End husband who has just smashed his wife in the head with a hammer or taken a cut-throat razor to her throat.

The Criminal Investigation Department (CID) was not formally organized until 1878, or a mere ten years before Jack the Ripper began terrorizing London. By 1888, public sentiment about detectives had not changed much. There remained misgivings about police wearing plainclothes or arresting people by artifice. The police were not supposed to trap citizens, and Scotland Yard strictly enforced the rule that plainclothes policing could take place only when there was ample evidence that crimes in a certain area were being committed repeatedly. This approach was enforcement, not prevention. It delayed Scotland Yard's decision to order undercover measures when the Ripper began his slaughters in the East End.

Scotland Yard was completely unprepared for a serial killer like the Ripper, and after Mary Ann Nichols's murder, the public began to cast its eye on the police more than ever, and to criticize, belittle, and blame. Mary Ann's murder and inquest hearings were obsessively covered by every major English newspaper. Her case made the covers of tabloids such as *The Illustrated Police News* and the budget editions of *Famous Crimes,* which one could pick up for a penny. Artists rendered sensational, salacious depictions of the murders, and no one—neither the officials of the Home Office nor the policemen nor the detectives and brass at Scotland Yard nor even Queen Victoria—had the slightest comprehension of either the problem or its solution.

When the Ripper began making his rounds there were only uniformed men walking their beats, all of them overworked and underpaid. They were issued the standard equipment of a whistle, a truncheon, perhaps a rattle, and a bull's-eye lantern, nicknamed a *dark lantern* because all it really did was vaguely illuminate the person holding it. A bull's-eye lantern was a dangerous, cumbersome device comprised of a steel cylinder ten inches high, including a chimney shaped like a ruffled dust cap. The magnifying lens was three inches in diameter and made of thick, rounded, ground glass, and inside the lamp were a small oil pan and wick.

The brightness of the flame could be controlled by turning the chimney. The inner metal tube would rotate and block out as much of the flame as needed, allowing a policeman to flash his lantern and signal another officer out on the street. I suppose that *flash* is a bit of an exaggeration if one has ever seen a bull's-eye lantern lit up. I found several rusty but authentic Hiatt & Co., Birmingham, bull's-eye lanterns that were manufactured in the mid-1800s, precisely the sort used by the police during the Ripper investigation. One night I carried a lantern out to the patio and lit a small fire in the oil pan. The lens turned into a reddish-orange wavering eye. But the convexity of the glass causes the light to vanish when viewed from certain other angles.

I held my hand in front of the lantern and at a distance of six inches could barely see a trace of my palm. Smoke wisped out of the chimney and the cylinder got hot—hot enough, according to police lore, to brew tea. I imagined a poor constable walking his beat and holding such a thing by its two metal handles or clipping the lantern to his leather snake-clasp belt. It's a wonder he didn't set himself on fire.

The typical Victorian may not have had a clue about the inadequacy of bull's-eye lanterns. Magazines and penny tabloids showed constables shining intense beams into the darkest corners and alleyways while frightened suspects reel back from the blinding glare. Unless these cartoonlike depictions were deliberately exaggerated, they lead me to suspect that most people had never seen a bull's-eye lantern in use. But that shouldn't come as a surprise. Police patrolling the safer, less crime-ridden areas of London would have little or no need to light their lanterns. It was in the forbidden places that the lanterns shone their bloodshot eyes as they blearily probed the constables' beats, and most Londoners traveling by foot or in horse-drawn cabs did not frequent those parts.

Walter Sickert was a man of the night and the slums. He would have had good reason to know exactly what a bull's-eye lantern looked like because it was his habit to wander the forbidden places after his visits to the music halls. During his Camden Town period, when he was producing some of his most blatantly violent works, he used to paint murder scenes by the spooky glow of a bull's-eye lantern. Fellow artist Marjorie Lilly, who shared his house and one of his studios, observed him doing this on more than one occasion, and later described it as "Dr. Jekyll" assuming the "mantle of Mr. Hyde."

The dark blue woolen uniforms and capes the police wore could not keep them warm and dry in bad weather, and when days were warm, a constable's discomfort must have been palpable. He could not loosen the belt or tunic or take off his military-shaped helmet with its shiny Brunswick star. If the ill-fitting leather boots he had been issued maimed his feet, he could either buy a new pair with his own pay or suffer in silence.

In 1887, a Metropolitan policeman gave the public a glimpse of what the average constable's life was like. In an anonymous article in the *Police Review and Parade Gossip,* he told the story of his wife and their dying four-year-old son having to live in two rooms in a lodging house in Bow Street. Of the policeman's twenty-four-shillings-a-week salary, ten went to pay the rent. It was a time of great civil unrest, he wrote, and animosity toward the police ran hot.

With nothing more than a small truncheon tucked into a special pocket of a trouser leg, these officers went out day after day and night after night, "well nigh exhausted with [our] constant contact with passionate wretches who had been made mad with want and cupidity." Angry citizens screamed vile insults and accused the police of being "against the people and the poor," read the unsigned article. Other better-off Londoners sometimes waited from four to six hours before calling the police after a robbery or burglary and then publicly complained that the police were unable to bring offenders to justice.

Policing was not only a thankless job but also an impossible one, with one sixth of the 15,000-member force off sick, on leave, or suspended on any given day. The supposed ratio of one policeman to 450 citizens was misleading. The number of men actually on the street depended on which shift was on duty. Since the number of policemen on duty always doubled during the night shift (10:00 P.M. to 6:00 A.M.), this meant that during the day shift (6:00 A.M. to 2:00 P.M.) and the late shift (2:00 P.M. to 10:00 P.M.) there were only some 2,000 beat officers working. That is a ratio of one policeman to every 4,000 citizens, or one policeman to cover every six miles of street. In August, the ratio got even worse when as many as 2,000 men took holiday leave.

During the night shift a constable was expected to walk his beat in 10 to 15 minutes at an average pace of two and a half miles per hour. By the time the Ripper began his crimes, this requirement was no longer enforced, but the habit was deeply ingrained. Criminals, in particular, could tell a constable's regular leathery walk quite a ways off.

The Greater London area was seven hundred square miles, and even if the police ranks doubled during the early morning hours, the Ripper could have prowled East End passageways, alleys, courtyards, and back streets without seeing a single Brunswick star. If a constable was drawing near, the Ripper was forewarned by the unmistakable walk. After the kill, he could slip into the shadows and wait for the body to be discovered. He could eavesdrop on the excited conversations of witnesses, the doctor, and the police. Jack the Ripper could have seen the moving orange eyes of the bull's-eye lanterns without any threat of being seen.

Psychopaths love to watch the drama they script. It is common for serial killers to return to the crime scene or insert themselves in the investigation. A murderer showing up at his victim's funeral is so common that today's police often have plainclothes officers clandestinely videotape the mourners. Serial arsonists love to watch their fires burn. Rapists love to work for social services. Ted Bundy worked as a volunteer for a crisis clinic.

When Robert Chambers strangled Jennifer Levin to death in New York's Central Park, he sat on a wall across the street from his staged crime scene and waited two hours to watch the body discovered, the police arrive, and the morgue attendants finally zip up the pouch and load it into an ambulance. "He found it amusing," recalled Linda Fairstein, the prosecutor who sent Chambers to prison.

Sickert was an entertainer. He was also a violent psychopath. He would have been obsessed with watching the police and doctors examining the bodies at the murder scenes, and he might have lingered in the dark long enough to see the hand ambulance wheel his victims away. He might have followed at a distance to catch a glimpse of the bodies being locked inside the mortuaries, and he might even have attended the funerals. In the early 1900s he painted a picture of two women gazing out of a window, and inexplicably titled the work *A Passing Funeral*. Several Ripper letters make taunting references to his watching the police at the scene or being present at the victim's burial.

"I see them and they cant see me," the Ripper wrote.

The Metropolitan Police Commissioner Sir Charles Warren did not care much about crime, and he didn't know much about it, either. He was an easy target for a psychopath with the brilliance and creativity of Walter Sickert, who would have enjoyed making a fool of Warren and ruining his career. And in the end Warren's failure to capture the Ripper, among his other blunders, brought about his resignation on November 8, 1888.

Drawing public attention to the deplorable conditions of the East End and ridding London of Warren may be the only good deeds Jack the Ripper did, even if his motivation was somewhat less than altruistic.

CHAPTER TEN

MEDICINE OF THE COURTS

Dr. Llewellyn testified at the Mary Ann Nichols inquest that she had a slight laceration of the tongue and a bruise on the lower right jaw from the blow of a fist or the "pressure of a thumb." She had a circular bruise on the left side of her face that may have been from the pressure of a finger.

Her neck had been cut in two places. One incision was four inches long, beginning an inch below the left jaw, just below the left ear. A second incision also began on the left side, but about an inch lower than the first incision and a little forward of the ear. The second incision was "circular," Dr. Llewellyn stated. I don't know what he meant by "circular" unless he was trying to say that the incision was curved instead of straight—or simply that it encircled her neck. It was eight inches long, severed all blood vessels, muscle tissue, and cartilage, and nicked the vertebrae before terminating three inches below her right jaw.

Dr. Llewellyn's recital of the injuries to Mary Ann's abdomen was as unspecific as his other determinations. On the left side were one jagged incision "just about at the lower part of the abdomen" and "three or four" similar cuts that ran in a downward direction on the right side of the abdomen. In addition, there were "several" cuts running across the abdomen and small stabs to her "private parts." In his conclusion, Dr. Llewellyn said that the abdominal wounds were sufficient to cause death, and he believed they had been inflicted before her throat was cut. He based his conclusion on the lack of blood around her neck at the scene, but he failed to tell the coroner or the jurors that he had neglected to turn over the body. It is possible that he still didn't know that he had overlooked—or failed to see—a large quantity of blood and a six-inch clot.

All injuries were from left to right, Dr. Llewellyn testified, and this led him to the conclusion that the killer was "left handed." The weapon—and there was only one this time, he stated—was a long-bladed, "moderately" sharp knife used with "great violence." The bruises on her jaw and face, he said, were also consistent with a left-handed assailant, and he theorized that the killer placed his right hand over Mary Ann's mouth to stop her from screaming as he used his left hand to repeatedly slash her abdomen. In the scenario Dr. Llewellyn describes, the killer was facing Mary Ann when he suddenly attacked her. Either they were standing or the killer already had her on the ground, and he somehow managed to keep her from shrieking and thrashing about as he shoved up her clothes and started cutting through skin, fat, right down to her bowels.

It makes no sense for a calculating, logical, and intelligent killer like Jack the Ripper to slash open a victim's abdomen first, leaving her ample opportunity to put up a ferocious struggle as she suffered unimaginable terror, panic, and pain. Had the coroner carefully questioned Dr. Llewellyn about the relevant medical details, a very different reconstruction of Mary Ann Nichols's murder might have emerged. Maybe the killer did not approach her from the front. Maybe he never said a word to her. Maybe she never saw him.

A prevailing theory is that Jack the Ripper approached his victims and talked to them before they walked off together to an isolated, dark area where he suddenly and swiftly killed them. For quite some time, I assumed that this was the Ripper's modus operandi (MO) in all cases. As countless other people have done, I envisioned the Ripper using the ruse of soliciting sex to get the woman to go with him. Since sex with prostitutes was often performed while the woman's back was turned to her client, this seemed like the perfect opportunity for the Ripper to cut her throat before she had any idea what was happening.

I don't discount the possibility that this MO might have been the Ripper's—at least in some of the murders. It really never occurred to me that it might be incorrect in any of them until I had a moment of enlightenment during the Christmas holiday of 2001 when I was in Aspen with my family. I was spending an evening alone in a condo at the base of Ajax Mountain, and as usual, I had several suitcases of research materials with me. I happened to be going through a Sickert art book for what must have been the twentieth time and stopped flipping pages when I got to his celebrated painting *Ennui.* What a strange thing, I thought, that this particular work of his was considered so extraordinary that Queen Elizabeth The Queen Mother bought one of its five versions and hung it in Clarence House. Other versions are privately owned or hang in various prestigious museums, such as Tate Britain.

In all five versions of *Ennui,* a bored older man sits at a table, his cigar lit, a tall glass of what I assume to be beer in front of him. He stares into space, deep in thought and completely uninterested in the woman behind him, who is leaning against a dresser, her head resting on her hand as she gazes unhappily at stuffed doves inside a glass dome. Central to the picture is a painting of a woman, a diva, on the wall behind the bored couple's heads. Having seen several versions of *Ennui,* I was aware that the diva in each has a slightly different appearance.

In three of them, she has what appears to be a thick feather boa thrown around her naked shoulders. But in the late Queen Mother's version and the one in Tate Britain there is no feather boa, just some indistinguishable reddish-brown shape that envelopes her left shoulder and extends across her upper arm and left breast. It wasn't until I was feeling ennui myself as I sat in the Aspen condo that I noticed a vertical crescent, rather fleshy-white, above the diva's left shoulder. The fleshy-white shape has what appears to be a slight bump on the left side that looks very much like an ear.

Upon closer inspection, the shape becomes a man's face half in the shadows. He is coming up behind the woman. She is barely turning her face as if she senses his approach. Under the low magnification of a lens, the half-shadowed face of the man is more apparent, and the woman's face begins to look like a skull. But at a higher magnification, the painting dissolves into the individual touches of Sickert's brushes. I went to London and looked at the original painting at Tate Britain, and I did not change my mind. I sent a transparency of the painting to the Virginia Institute of Forensic Science and Medicine to see if we could get a sharper look through technology.

Computerized image enhancement detects hundreds of gray shades that the human eye can't see and makes it possible for a fuzzy photograph or erased writing to become visible or discernible. While forensic image enhancement might work with bank security videos or bad photographs, it does not work on paintings. All our efforts accomplished with *Ennui* was to separate Sickert's brush strokes until we ended up with the reverse of what he was doing when he put the strokes together. I was reminded, as I would be repeatedly in the Ripper case, that forensic science does not and will not ever take the place of human detection, deduction, experience, and common sense—and very hard work.

Sickert's *Ennui* was mentioned in the Ripper investigation long before I gave the matter a thought, but in a very different way from what I have just described. In one version of the painting, the feather-boa-enveloped diva has a white blob on her left shoulder that is slightly reminiscent of one of the stuffed doves under the glass dome on top of the dresser. Some Ripper enthusiasts insist that the "bird" is a "sea gull" and that Sickert cleverly introduced the "gull" into his painting to drop the clue that Jack the Ripper was Sir William Gull, who was Queen Victoria's surgeon. The advocates of this interpretation usually subscribe to the so-called royal conspiracy that implicates Dr. Gull and the Duke of Clarence in five Ripper murders.

The theory was advanced in the 1970s. Although my intention in this work is not to focus on who the Ripper was not, I will state categorically that he was not Dr. Gull or the Duke of Clarence. In 1888, Dr. Gull was seventy-one years old and had already suffered a stroke. The Duke of Clarence no more used a sharp blade than he was one. Eddy, as he was called, was born two months prematurely after his mother went out to watch her husband on ice skates and apparently spent too much time being "whirled" about in a sledge. Not feeling well, she was taken back to Frogmore, where there was only a local practitioner to oversee Eddy's unexpected birth.

His developmental difficulties probably had less to do with his premature birth than they did with the small royal gene pool that spawned him. Eddy was sweet but obtuse. He was sensitive and gentle but a dismal student. He could barely ride a horse, was unimpressive during his military training, and was far too fond of clothes. The only cure his frustrated father, the Prince of Wales, and his grandmother the Queen could come up with was from time to time to launch Eddy on long voyages to distant lands.

Rumors about his sexual preferences and indiscretions continue to this day. It may be that he engaged in homosexual activity, as some books claim, but he was also involved with women. Perhaps Eddy was sexually immature and experimented with both sexes. He would not have been the first member of a royal family to play both sides of the net. Eddy's emotional attachments were to women, especially to his beautiful, doting mother, who did not seem unduly concerned that he cared more about clothes than the crown.

On July 12, 1884, Eddy's frustrated father, the Prince of Wales and future king, wrote to Eddy's German tutor, "It is with sincere regret that we learn from you that our son dawdles so dreadfully in the morning. . . . He will have to make up the lost time by additional study." In this unhappy seven-page missive written from Marlborough House, the Prince of Wales is emphatic—if not desperate—that his son, who was in direct line to the throne, "must put his shoulder to the wheel."

Eddy had neither the energy nor the interest to go about preying on prostitutes, and to suggest otherwise is farcical. On the nights of at least three of the murders, he allegedly was not in London or even close by (not that he needs an alibi), and the murders continued after his untimely death on January 14, 1892. Even if the royal family's surgeon, Dr. Gull, had not been elderly and infirm, he was far too consumed by fussing over the health of Queen Victoria and that of the rather frail Eddy to have had interest or time to run about Whitechapel in a royal carriage at all hours of the night, hacking up prostitutes who were blackmailing Eddy because of his scandalous "secret marriage" to one of them. Or something like that.

It is true, however, that Eddy had been blackmailed before, as shown by two letters he wrote to George Lewis, the formidable barrister who would later represent Whistler in a lawsuit involving Walter Sickert. Eddy wrote to Lewis in 1890 and 1891 because he had gotten himself into a compromising situation with two ladies of low standing, one of them a Miss Richardson. He was trying to disengage himself by paying for the return of letters he imprudently had written to her and another lady friend.

"I am very pleased to hear you are able to settle with Miss Richardson," Eddy wrote Lewis in November of 1890, "although £200 is rather expensive for letters." He goes on to say he heard from Miss Richardson "the other day" and that she was demanding yet another £100. Eddy promises he will "do all I can to get back" the letters he wrote to the "other lady," as well.

Two months later, Eddy writes, in "November" [crossed out] "December," 1891 from his "Cavelry [sic] Barracks" and sends Lewis a gift "in acknowledgement for the kindness you showed me the other day in getting me out of that trouble I was foolish enough to get into." But apparently "the other lady" wasn't so easily appeased because Eddy tells Lewis he had to send a friend to see her "and ask her to give up the two or three letters I had written to her . . . you may be certain that I shall be careful in the future not to get into any more trouble of the sort."

Whatever was in the letters the Duke of Clarence wrote to Miss Richardson and "the other lady" isn't known, but one might infer that he acted in a manner bound to cause the royal family trouble. He was well aware that news of his involvement with the sort of woman who would blackmail him would not have been well received by the public and certainly not by his grandmother. What this attempted extortion does show is that Eddy's inclination in such situations was not to have the offending parties murdered and mutilated, but to pay them off.

Sickert's works of art may contain "clues," but they are about himself and what he felt and did. His art is about what he saw, and it was filtered through an imagination that was sometimes childlike and at other times savage. The point of view in most of his works indicates that he watched people from behind. He could see them, but they could not see him. He could see his victims, but they could not see him. He would have watched Mary Ann Nichols for a while before he struck. He would have determined her degree of drunkenness and worked out his best approach.

He may have drifted up to her in the dark and showed her a coin and given her a line before going around behind her. Or he may have come out of the damp dark and suddenly was upon her. Her injuries, if they were accurately described, are consistent with her killer yoking her and jerking her head back as he slashed his knife across her exposed throat. She may have bitten her tongue, explaining the abrasion Dr. Llewellyn found. If she tried to twist away, that could explain why the first incision was incomplete and basically a failed attempt. The bruising of her jaw and face may have come about as her killer tightened his restraint of her and cut her throat a second time, this incision so violent that in one stroke he almost decapitated her.

His position behind her would have prevented him from being splashed by the arterial blood that would have spurted out of her severed left carotid artery. Few murderers would choose to have blood spattering their faces, especially the blood of a victim who probably had diseases—at the very least, sexually transmitted ones. When Mary Ann was on her back, her killer moved to the lower part of her body and shoved up her clothes. She could not scream. She may have made no sound except the wet choking rushes and gurgles of air and blood sucking in and out of her severed windpipe. She may have aspirated her own blood and drowned in it as virtually all of her blood bled out from her body. All of this takes minutes.

Coroners' reports, including Dr. Llewellyn's, tend to assure us that the person "died instantly." There is no such thing. One might be disabled instantly by a gunshot wound to the head, but it takes minutes for someone to bleed to death, suffocate, drown, or cease all bodily functions due to a stroke or cardiac arrest. It is possible that Mary Ann was still conscious and aware of what was happening when her murderer began cutting up her abdomen. She may have been barely alive when he left her body in the courtyard.

Robert Mann was the Whitechapel Workhouse inmate in charge of the mortuary on the morning her body was brought in. During the inquest inquiry of September 17th, Mann testified that at some point after 4:00 A.M., the police arrived at the workhouse and ordered him out of bed. They said there was a body parked outside the mortuary and to hurry along, so he accompanied them to the ambulance parked in the yard. They carried the body inside the mortuary, and Inspector Spratling and Dr. Llewellyn appeared briefly to take a look. Then the police left, and Mann recalled that it must have been around 5:00 A.M. when he locked the mortuary door and went to breakfast.

An hour or so later, Mann and another inmate named James Hatfield returned to the mortuary and began to undress the body without police or anyone else present. Mann swore to Coroner Baxter that no one had instructed him not to touch the body, and he was sure the police weren't present. You're absolutely certain of that? He was, well, maybe not. He could be mistaken. He couldn't remember. If the police said they were there, then maybe they were. Mann got increasingly confused during his testimony, and "was subject to fits . . . his statements hardly reliable," *The Times* reported.

Wynne Baxter was a solicitor and an experienced coroner who would preside over the inquest of Joseph Merrick two years later. Baxter would not tolerate lying in his courtroom or the abuse of proper protocol in a case. He was more than a little irked that inmates had removed Mary Ann Nichols's clothing. He rigorously questioned the confused, fitful Mann, who steadfastly maintained that the clothing was neither torn nor cut when the body arrived. All he and Hatfield had done was strip the dead woman naked and wash her before the doctor showed up so he wouldn't have to waste his time doing it.

They cut and tore clothing to speed things along and make their chore a bit easier. Mary Ann was wearing a lot of layers, some of them stiff with dried blood, and it is very difficult to pull clothing over the arms and legs of a body that is as rigid as a statue. When Hatfield took the stand, he agreed with everything Mann had said. The two inmates unlocked the mortuary after breakfast. They were by themselves when they cut and tore off the dead woman's clothing.

They washed her, they were alone with her body, and they had no reason to think there was anything inappropriate about that. Transcripts of their testimonies at the inquest give the impression that the men were frightened and bewildered because they didn't think they had done anything wrong. They really didn't understand what the fuss was about. The workhouse mortuary wasn't supposed to handle police cases, anyway. It was just a whistle-stop for dead inmates on their way to a pauper's grave.

In Latin, *forensic* means "forum," or a public place where Roman lawyers and orators presented their cases before judges. Forensic or legal medicine is the medicine of the courts, and in 1888, it hardly existed in practice. The sad truth is, there wasn't much physical evidence that could have been either utilized or ruined in Mary Ann Nichols's murder. But not knowing with certainty whether Mary Ann's clothing was already cut or torn when her body arrived at the mortuary is a significant loss. Whatever the killer did would reveal more about him and his emotions at the time of the murder.

On the basis of the descriptions of Mary Ann's body at the crime scene, I suspect her clothing was disarrayed but not cut or torn off, and it was on the early morning of August 31st when the Ripper advanced to his next level of violence. He shoved up her ulster, woolen petticoats, flannel underclothing, and skirts. He made one jagged, then "three or four" quick slashes downward, and "several" across, almost in the pattern of a grid. A few small stabs to the genitals and he was gone, vanished in the dark.

Without reviewing postmortem diagrams or photographs, it is very difficult to reconstruct injuries and re-create what a killer did and what he might have been feeling. Wounds can be fierce or they can be tentative. They can show hesitation or rage. Three or four shallow incisions on a wrist in addition to the deep one that severed veins tell a different story about a person's suicide than one decisive cut does.

Psychiatrists interpret mental states and emotional needs through a patient's demeanor and confessions of feelings and behavior. The physicians of the dead have to make those same interpretations through the braille of injuries old and new and debris on the body and the way the person was dressed and where he or she died. Listening to the dead speak is a unique gift and demands highly specialized training. The language of silence is hard to read, but the dead do not lie. They may be difficult to understand, and we might misinterpret them or fail to find them before their communications have begun to fade. But if they still have something to say, their veracity is unimpeachable. Sometimes they continue to talk long after they have been reduced to bone.

If people have a great deal to drink and get into their cars or into fights, their dead bodies admit it through alcohol levels. If a man was a heroin and cocaine addict, his dead body displays the needle tracks, and the metabolites morphine and benzoylecgonine show up in urine, the vitreous fluid of the eye, and the blood. If one frequently engaged in anal sex or was into genital tattoos and body piercing, or if a woman shaved off her pubic hair because her lover's fantasy was to have sex with a child—these people speak openly after they are dead. If a teenage boy tried for a more intense orgasm by masturbating while dressed in leather and partially compressing the blood vessels in his neck with a noose—but he didn't mean to slip off the chair he was standing on and hang himself—he'll confess. Shame and lies are for those left behind.

It is startling what the dead have to say. I never cease to be amazed and pained. One young man was so determined to end his life that when he shot himself in the chest with his crossbow and didn't die, he pulled out the arrow and shot himself again. Anger. Desperation. Hopelessness. No turning back. I want to die, but I'll go ahead and book a family holiday and write down the details of my funeral so I don't inconvenience my family. I want to die, but I want to look nice, so I'll put on makeup and fix my hair and shoot myself in the heart because I don't want to ruin my face, the wife decides after her husband has run off with a younger woman.

I'll shoot you in the mouth, bitch, because I'm tired of hearing you nag. I'll throw your body in the bath and dump acid all over it, you cunt. That's what you get for screwing around on me. I'll stab you in the eyes because I'm tired of you staring at me. I'll drain your blood and drink it because aliens are taking all of mine. I'll dismember you and boil you piece by piece so I can flush you down the toilet and no one will ever know. Hop on the back of my Harley, you slut, and I'll take you to a motel and cut you hundreds of times with a razor and scissors and watch you slowly die, because that's the initiation I gotta do before I can be a member of the gang.

Mary Ann Nichols's wounds tell us that the Ripper did not want her to struggle or scream, and that he was ready for the next step of moving his knife below her throat and destroying her naked body. But he wasn't a master of this move yet and could go only so far. He did not remove her bowels or organs. His cuts were only so deep. He took no body part with him as a trophy or a talisman that might bring him sexual fantasy and wonder when he was alone in one of his secret rooms. For the first time, I believe, the Ripper had ripped, and he needed to think about that for a while and feel what it was like and whether he wanted more.

"I like the work some more blood," the Ripper wrote on October 5th.

"I must have some more," the Ripper wrote on November 2nd.

It was scarcely a week later when Jack the Ripper would publicly call himself by that infernal name. Perhaps it makes sense. Before his murder of Mary Ann Nichols, he had not "ripped". Sickert came up with the stage name "Mr. Nemo" for a reason, and it wasn't one driven by modesty. Sickert would have picked the name "Jack the Ripper" for a good reason, too. We can only guess what it was.

"Jack" was street slang for a sailor or a man, and "Ripper" is someone who "rips." But Walter Sickert was never obvious. I scanned through a dozen dictionaries and encyclopedias dating from 1755 to 1906, checking definitions. Sickert could have come up with the name "Jack the Ripper" by reading Shakespeare. As Helena Sickert said in her memoirs, when she and her brothers were growing up, they were all "Shakespeare mad," and Sickert was known to quote long passages of Shakespeare as an actor. Throughout his life he loved to stand up at dinner parties and deliver Shakespearean soliloquies. The word "Jack" is found in *Coriolanus, The Merchant of Venice,* and *Cymbeline.* Shakespeare doesn't use the word "ripper," but there are variations of it in *King John* and *Macbeth.*

Definitions of "Jack" include: boots; a diminutive of "John" used contemptuously to mean a saucy fellow; a footboy who pulls off his master's boots; a scream; a male; American slang for a stranger; American slang for a jackass; a cunning fellow who can do anything—such as a "Jack of all trades." Definitions of "Ripper" include: one who rips; one who tears; one who cuts; a fine fellow who dresses well; a good fast horse; a good play or part.

Jack the Ripper was the stranger, the cunning fellow who could do anything. He "hath his belly-full of fighting." He was a "cock that nobody can match." He ripped "up the womb of your dear mother England." Sickert, in the deep crevices of his psyche, might have felt that from his own mother's womb he had been "ripp'd." What happened inside his mother's womb was unjust and not his fault. He would repay.

CHAPTER ELEVEN

SUMMER NIGHT

Mary Ann Nichols's eyes were wide open when her body was discovered on the pavement. She stared blindly into the dark, her face a wan yellow in the weak flame of a bull's-eye lantern.

In Charles Darwin's *Expression of the Emotions,* wide staring eyes are the accompaniment to "horror," which Darwin associates with "extreme terror" or the "horrible pain of torture." It is a centuries-old fallacy that a person dies with the last emotion frozen on his or her face. But symbolically, Mary Ann's expression seemed to capture the last thing she saw in her life—the dark silhouette of her murderer cutting her up. The fact that the police made note in their reports of her wide, staring eyes may reflect what the men in blue on the street were beginning to feel about the Whitechapel murderer: He was a monster, a phantom who, in Inspector Abberline's words, did not leave "the slightest clue."

The image of a woman with her throat slashed and her wide eyes staring up blindly from the pavement would not easily be forgotten by those who saw it. Sickert would not have forgotten it. More than anyone else, he would have remembered her stare as life fled from her. In 1903, if his dates are reliable, he drew a sketch of a woman whose eyes are wide open and staring. She looks dead and has an inexplicable dark line around her throat. The sketch is rather innocuously titled *Two Studies of a Venetian Woman's Head.* Three years later he followed it with a painting of a nude grotesquely sprawled on an iron bedstead and titled that picture *Nuit d'Été,* or *Summer Night.* One recalls that Mary Ann Nichols was murdered on a summer night. The woman in the sketch and the woman in the painting look alike. Their faces resemble the face of Mary Ann Nichols, based on a photograph taken of her when she was inside her shell at the mortuary and had already been "cleaned up" by workhouse inmates Mann and Hatfield.

Mortuary photographs were made with a big wooden box camera that could shoot only directly ahead. Bodies the police needed to photograph had to be stood up or propped upright against the dead-house wall because the camera could not be pointed down or at an angle. Sometimes the nude dead body was hung on the wall with a hook, nail, or peg at the nape of the neck. A close inspection of the photograph of a later victim, Catherine Eddows, shows her nude body suspended, one foot barely touching the floor.

These grim, degrading photographs were for purposes of identification and were not made public. The only way a person could know what Mary Ann Nichols's dead body looked like was to have viewed it at the mortuary or at the murder scene. If Sickert's sketch of the so-called Venetian woman is indeed a representation of Mary Ann Nichols's staring dead face, then he might well have been at the scene or somehow got hold of the police reports—unless the detail was in a news story I somehow missed. Even if Sickert had seen Mary Ann at the mortuary, her eyes would have been shut by then, just as they are in her photograph. By the time she was photographed and viewed by those who might identify her and by the inquest jurors, her wounds had been sutured, and her body had been covered to the chin to hide the gaping cuts to the throat.

Unfortunately, few morgue photographs of the Ripper's victims exist, and the ones preserved at the Public Record Office are small and have poor resolution, which worsens with enlargement. Forensic image enhancement helps a little, but not much. Other cases that were not linked to the Ripper at the time—or ever—may not have been photographed at all. If they were, those photographs seem to have vanished. Crime-scene photographs usually weren't taken unless the victim's body was indoors. Even then the case had to be unusual for the police to fetch their heavy box camera.

In today's forensic cases, bodies are photographed many times and from many angles with a variety of photographic equipment, but during the Ripper's violent spree, it was rare to call for a camera. It would have been even rarer for a mortuary or a dead house to be equipped with one. Technology had not advanced enough for photographs to be taken at night. These limitations mean that there is only a scant visual record of Jack the Ripper's crimes, unless one browses through a Walter Sickert art book or takes a look at his "murder" pictures and nudes that hang in fine museums and private collections. Artistic and scholarly analysis aside, most of Sickert's sprawling nudes look mutilated and dead.

Many of the nudes and other female subjects have bare necks with black lines around them, as if to suggest a cut throat or decapitation. Some dark areas around a figure's throat are intended to be shadows and shading, but the dark, solid, black lines I refer to are puzzling. They are not jewelry, so if Sickert drew and painted what he saw, what are these lines? The mystery grows with a picture titled *Patrol,* dated 1921—a painting of a policewoman with bulging eyes and an open-neck tunic that reveals a solid, black line around her throat.

What is known about *Patrol* is vague. Sickert most likely painted it from a photograph of a policewoman, possibly Dorothy Peto of the Birmingham police. Apparently, she acquired the painting and moved to London, where she signed on with the Metropolitan Police, to which she eventually donated the life-size Sickert portrait of herself. The intimation of at least one Metropolitan Police archivist is that the painting may be valuable, but it is disliked, especially by women. When I saw *Patrol,* it was hanging behind a locked door and chained to a wall. No one seems quite sure what to do with it. I suppose it's another Ripper "ha ha"—albeit an accidental one—that Scotland Yard owns a painting by the most notorious murderer the Yard never caught.

Patrol isn't exactly a tribute to women or policing, nor would it appear that Sickert intended it to be anything other than another one of his subtle, scary fantasies. The frightened expression on the policewoman's face belies the power of her profession, and in typical Sickert fashion, the painting has the patina of morbidity and of something very bad about to happen. The wooden-framed 74¼-by-46¼-inch canvas *Patrol* is a dark mirror in the bright galleries of the art world, and references to it and reproductions of it are not easily found.

Certain of his paintings do seem as secret as Sickert's many hidden rooms, but the decision to keep them under cover may not have been made solely by their owners. Sickert himself had a great deal to say about which of his works were to be exhibited. Even if he gave a painting to a friend—as is the case with *Jack the Ripper's Bedroom*—he could have asked the person to lend it to various exhibitions, or keep it private. Some of his work was probably part of his catch-me-if-you-can fun. He was brazen enough to paint or draw Ripperish scenes, but not always reckless enough to exhibit them. And these unseemly works continue to surface, now that the search is on.

Most recently, an uncatalogued Sickert sketch was discovered that seems to be a flashback to his music-hall days of 1888. Sickert made the sketch in 1920, and it depicts a bearded male figure talking to a prostitute. The man's back is partially toward us, but we get the impression that his penis is exposed and that he is holding a knife in his right hand. At the bottom of the sketch is what appears to be a disemboweled woman whose arms have been dismembered—as if Sickert is showing the before and after of one of his kills. Art historian Dr. Robins believes the sketch went unnoticed because, in the past, the notion of looking for this sort of violence in Sickert's works was not foremost on the minds of people such as herself, and archival curators, and Sickert experts.

But when one works hard and begins to know what to look for, the unusual turns up, including news stories. Most people interested in news accounts of Jack the Ripper's murders rely on facsimiles from public records or microfilm. When I began this investigation, I chose *The Times* as the newspaper of record and was fortunate to find copies of the originals for 1888–91. In that era, newsprint had such a high cotton fiber content that *The Times* papers I own could be ironed, sewn together, and bound, good as new.

I have continued to be surprised by the number of news publications that have survived for over a hundred years and are still supple enough for one to turn their pages without fear of damaging them. Having begun my career as a journalist, I know full well that there are many stories to a story and that without looking at as many bits and pieces of reportage as I can find I can't begin to approach the whole truth. Ripper journalism in the major papers of the day is not scarce, but what is often overlooked are the quiet witnesses of lesser-known publications, such as the *Sunday Dispatch*.

One day, my dealer at an antiquarian bookshop in Chelsea, London, called to tell me he had found at auction a ledger book filled with, quite possibly, every *Sunday Dispatch* article written about the Ripper murders and others that might be related. The clippings, rather sloppily cut out and crookedly pasted into the ledger, were dated from August 12, 1888, through September 29, 1889. The story of the book continues to mystify me. Dozens of pages throughout the ledger were slashed out with a razor, enormously piquing my curiosity about their contents. Alongside the clippings are fascinating annotations written either in blue and black ink or with gray, blue, and purple pencils. Who went to all this trouble and why? Where has the ledger been for more than a century?

The annotations themselves suggest that most likely they were written by someone quite familiar with the crimes and most interested in how they were being handled by the police. When I first acquired the ledger, I fantasized that it might have been kept by Jack the Ripper himself. It seems that whoever cut out the clippings was focused on reports of what the police knew, and he agrees or disagrees with them in his notes. Some details are crossed out as inaccurate. Comments such as "Yes! Believe me" or "unsatisfactory" or "unsatisfactory—very" or "important. Find the woman"—and most peculiar of all, "7 women 4 men"—are scribbled next to certain details in the articles. Sentences are underlined, especially if they relate to descriptions witnesses gave of the men the victims were last seen with.

I doubt I will ever know whether an amateur sleuth kept this ledger or whether a policeman or a reporter did, but the handwriting is inconsistent with that of Scotland Yard's leading men, such as Abberline, Swanson, and other officers whose reports I have read. The penmanship in the ledger is small and very sloppy, especially for a period when script was consistently well formed, if not elegant. Most police officers, for example, wrote with a very good and in some instances beautiful hand. In fact, the handwriting in the clippings book reminds me of the rather wild and sometimes completely illegible way Walter Sickert wrote. His handwriting is markedly different from the average Englishman's. Since the precocious Sickert taught himself to read and write, he was not schooled in traditional calligraphy, although his sister Helena said he was capable of a "beautiful hand" when it suited him.

Was the ledger Sickert's? Probably not. I have no idea who kept it, but the *Sunday Dispatch* articles add another dimension to the reportage of the time. The journalist who covered crime for the *Sunday Dispatch* is anonymous—bylines then were as rare as female reporters—but had an excellent eye and a very inquisitive mind. His deductions, questions, and perceptions add new facets to cases such as the murder of Mary Ann Nichols. The *Sunday Dispatch* reported that the police suspected she was the victim of a gang. In London, at that time, roving packs of violent young men preyed upon the weak and poor. These hooligans were vindictive when they attempted to rob an Unfortunate who turned out to have no money.

The police maintained that Mary Ann had not been killed where her body was found, nor had Martha Tabran. The two slain women had been left in the "gutter of the street in the early hours of the morning," and no screams were heard. So they must have been murdered elsewhere, possibly by a gang, and their bodies dumped. The anonymous *Sunday Dispatch* reporter must have asked Dr. Llewellyn if it was possible that the killer had attacked Mary Ann Nichols from the rear and not the front, which would have made the killer right-handed—not left-handed, as Dr. Llewellyn claimed.

If the killer had been standing behind the victim when he cut her throat, the reporter explains, and the deepest wounds were on the left side and trailed off to the right, which was the case, then the killer must have held the knife in his right hand. Dr. Llewellyn made a bad deduction. The reporter made an excellent one. Walter Sickert's dominant hand was his right one. In one of his self-portraits he appears to be holding a paintbrush in his left hand, but it is an optical illusion created by his painting his reflection in a mirror.

Dr. Llewellyn might not have been very interested in a reporter's point of view, but perhaps he should have been. If the *Sunday Dispatch* journalist's beat was crime, he had probably seen more cut throats than Dr. Llewellyn had. Cutting a person's throat was not an uncommon way to murder someone, especially in cases of domestic violence. It was not an unusual way to commit suicide, but people who cut their own throats used cut-throat razors, rarely knives, and they almost never sliced their necks all the way through to the vertebra.

The Royal London Hospital still has its admission and discharge record books for the nineteenth century, and a survey of entries shows the illnesses and injuries typical of the 1880s and 1890s. It must be kept in mind that the patients were presumed alive when they arrived at the hospital, which covered only the East End. Most people who cut their throats, assuming they severed a major blood vessel, would never have made it to a hospital but would have gone straight to the mortuary. They would not be listed in the admission and discharge record books.

Only one of the murders cited during the period of 1884 to 1890 was eventually considered a possible Ripper case, and that is the murder of Emma Smith, aged forty-five, of Thrawl Street. On April 2, 1888, she was attacked by what she described as a gang of young men who beat her, almost ripped off an ear, and shoved an object, possibly a stick, up her vagina. She was intoxicated at the time, but she managed to walk home, and friends helped her to the London Hospital, where she was admitted and died two days later of peritonitis.

In Ripperology, there is considerable speculation about when Jack the Ripper began killing and when he stopped. Since his favorite killing field seems to have been the East End, the records of the London Hospital are important, not because the Ripper's dead-at-the-scene victims would be listed in the books, but because patterns of how and why people were hurting themselves and others can be instructive. I was worried that "cut throats" might have been miscalled suicides when they were really murders that might be additional ones committed by the Ripper.

Unfortunately, the hospital records don't include much more detail than the patient's name, age, address, in some cases the occupation, the illness or injury, and if and when he or she was discharged. Another one of my purposes in scanning the London Hospital books was to see if there were any statistical changes in the number and types of violent deaths before, during, and after the so-called Ripper rampage of late 1888. The answer is, not really. But the records reveal something about the period, especially the deplorable conditions of the East End and the prevailing misery and hopelessness of those who lived and died there by unnatural causes.

During some years, poisoning was the favored form of taking one's life, and there were plenty of toxic substances to choose from, all of them easily acquired. Substances that East End men and women used to poison themselves from 1884 to 1890 include oxalic acid, laudanum, opium, hydrochloric acid, belladonna, ammonia carbonate, nitric acid, carbolic acid, lead, alcohol, turpentine, camphorated chloroform, zinc, and strychnine. People also tried to kill themselves by drowning, gunshot, hanging, and jumping out of windows. Some leaps out of upper-story windows were actually accidental deaths when fire engulfed a rooming or common lodging house.

It is impossible to know how many deaths or near-deaths were poorly investigated—or not investigated at all. I also suspect that some deaths thought to be suicides might have been murders. On September 12, 1886, twenty-three-year-old Esther Goldstein of Mulberry Street, Whitechapel, was admitted to the London Hospital as a suicide by cut throat. The basis of this determination is unknown, but it is hard to imagine that she cut her neck through her "thyroid cartilage." A slice through a major blood vessel close to the skin surface is quite sufficient to end one's life, and cutting through the muscles and cartilage of the neck is more typical of murder because more force is required.

If Esther Goldstein was murdered, that doesn't mean she was a victim of Jack the Ripper, and I doubt she was. It is unlikely that he killed an East End woman or two every now and then. When he started, he made a dramatic entrance and continued his performance for many years. He wanted the world to know about his crimes. But I can't say with certainty when he made his first kill.

In the same year that the Ripper crimes began, 1888, four other East End women died from cut throats—all supposed to be suicides. When I first went through the musty old pages of the Royal London Hospital record books and noticed the numerous women admitted with cut throats, I anticipated that these deaths might have been Ripper murders assumed to be suicides. But more time and research revealed that cut throats were not unusual in a day when most impoverished people did not have access to guns.

CHAPTER TWELVE

THE YOUNG AND BEAUTIFUL

People of the East End were put out of their misery by infections and diseases such as tuberculosis, pleurisy, emphysema, and pneumoconiosis. Men, women, and children were burned and scalded to death by accidents at home and at work.

Starvation killed, as did cholera, whooping cough, and cancer. Parents and their children, weakened by malnutrition and surrounded by filth and vermin, did not have immune systems that could fight off non-lethal illnesses. Colds and flu became bronchitis and pneumonia and death. Many infants weren't long for the world of the East End, and the people who lived and suffered there hated the London Hospital and avoided it if they could. To go there was to get worse. To let a doctor touch them was to die. Often this was true. An abscessed toe requiring amputation could lead to osteomyelitis—a bone infection—and death. A cut requiring sutures could lead to a staphlyoccus infection—and death.

A sampling of hospital admissions for alleged suicides shows that in

1884, five men tried to kill themselves by cutting their throat, while four women cut their throat and two slit their wrists. In 1885, five women are listed as suicides or attempted suicides by poisoning and one by drowning. Eight men slashed their throat, one used a gun, and another a noose. In 1886, five women attempted suicide by cutting their throat. Twelve women and seven men tried to poison themselves, and another twelve men cut their throat or stabbed or shot themselves.

It simply isn't possible to sort out who really committed suicide and who might have been murdered. If the individual was a person of the dustbin in the East End, and the death or attempted death was witnessed, then police tended to accept what witnesses said. When a woman's abusive, drunken husband hurled two lit oil lamps at her, setting her on fire, she told police with her dying breath that it was entirely her fault. Her husband wasn't charged. Her death was listed as an accident.

Unless a case was obvious, there was no certainty that the manner or even cause of death would be accurate. If a woman's throat was cut indoors and the weapon was nearby, the police assumed she had killed herself. Such assumptions, including those made by the well-meaning Dr. Llewellyn, not only sent police down a false trail—if they bothered following them up at all—but bad diagnoses and determinations of injury and death could destroy a case in court. Forensic medicine was not sophisticated in Dr. Llewellyn's day, and this rather than carelessness is the most likely explanation for his hasty, baseless conclusions.

Had he examined the pavement after Mary Ann's body was picked up and loaded into the ambulance, he would have noticed the blood and the blood clot that Constable Phail observed. Dr. Llewellyn might have noticed blood or a bloody fluid trickling into the gutter. Visibility was bad, so maybe he should have thought to wipe up some of this fluid to determine first whether it was blood, and second whether the serum was separating from the blood as it does during coagulation, which would have offered another clue about the time of death.

Although taking the ambient temperature at the crime scene and the temperature of the body wasn't standard in death investigation, Dr. Llewellyn should have noted the stage of rigor mortis or stiffness, which occurs when the body no longer produces the adenosine triphosphate (ATP) needed for muscles to contract. Dr. Llewellyn should have checked for livor mortis, which occurs when the blood no longer circulates and accumulates in certain parts of the body due to gravity. In a hanging, for example, the lower body will turn purplish-red if the victim has been suspended by his or her neck for as little as half an hour. Livor mortis becomes fixed after about eight hours. Not only could livor mortis have suggested the time of Mary Ann Nichols's death, it could have told Dr. Llewellyn if her body had been moved at some point after her murder.

I remember a case from years ago when the police arrived at the scene to discover a body as stiff as an ironing board propped against an armchair. The people in the house didn't want anyone to know the man had died in bed during the middle of the night, so they tried to move him to a chair. Rigor mortis replied, "Lie." In another instance from my early days of working in the medical examiner's office, the fully dressed body of a man came into the morgue accompanied by the story that he had been found dead on the floor. Livor mortis replied, "Lie." The blood had settled to his lower body, and on his buttocks was the perfect shape of the toilet seat he was still sitting on hours after his heart went into arrhythmia.

To determine time of death from any single postmortem artifact is like diagnosing a disease from one symptom. Time of death is a symphony of many details, and one plays on another. Rigor mortis is hastened along by the victim's muscle mass, the temperature of the air, the loss of blood, and even the activity preceding death. The nude body of a thin woman who has hemorrhaged to death outside in fifty-degree weather will cool faster and stiffen more slowly than the same woman clothed in a warm room and dead from strangulation.

Ambient temperature, body size, clothing, location, cause of death, and many more postmortem minutiae can be naughty little talebearers that fool even an expert and completely confuse him or her as to what really happened. Livor mortis—especially in Dr. Llewellyn's day—can be mistaken for fresh bruises. An object pressing against the body, such as part of an overturned chair wedged beneath the victim's wrist, will leave a pale area—or blanching—in the shape of that object. If this is misinterpreted as "pressure marks," then a case of nonviolent death can suddenly turn criminal.

There is no telling how much was hopelessly garbled in the Ripper murders and what evidence might have been lost, but one can be sure that the killer left traces of his identity and daily life. They would have adhered to the blood on the body and the ground. He also carried away evidence such as hairs, fibers, and his victim's blood. In 1888, it wasn't standard practice for police or doctors to look for hairs, fibers, or other minuscule amounts of evidence that might have required microscopic examination. Fingerprints were called "finger marks" and simply meant that a human being had touched an object such as a glass windowpane. Even if a patent (visible) fingerprint with well-defined ridge detail was discovered, it didn't matter. It wouldn't be until 1901 that Scotland Yard would establish its first Central Finger Print Bureau.

Five years earlier, in 1896, two patent fingerprints in red ink were left on a Ripper letter the police received October 14th. The letter is written in red ink, and the red ink fingerprints appear to have been made by the first and second fingers of the left hand. The ridge detail is good enough for comparison. Perhaps the prints were left deliberately—Sickert was the sort to know the latest criminal investigative technology, and leaving prints would be another "ha ha."

The police would not have linked them to him. They never noticed the prints, as far as I can tell, and some sixty years after his death, it is still unlikely a comparison between those prints and Sickert's will ever be made. At present, we don't have his fingerprints. They were burned up when he was cremated. The best I have been able to do so far is to find a barely visible print left in ink on the back of one of his copper etching plates. The print has yet to reveal sufficient ridge detail for a match, and one has to consider the possibility that the print wasn't left by Sickert but by a printer.

Fingerprints were known about long before the Ripper began his murders. Ridge detail on human finger pads gives us a better grip and is unique to every individual, including identical twins. It is believed that the Chinese used fingerprints some three thousand years ago to "sign" legal documents, but whether this was ceremonial or for purposes of identification is unknown. In India, fingerprints were used as a means of "signing contracts" as early as 1870. Seven years later, an American microscopist published a journal article suggesting that fingerprints should be used for identification, and this was echoed in 1880 by a Scottish physician working in a hospital in Japan. But as is true with every major scientific breakthrough—including DNA—fingerprints weren't instantly understood, immediately utilized, or readily accepted in court.

During the Victorian era, the primary means of identifying a person and linking him or her to a crime was a "science" called anthropometry, which was developed in 1879 by the French criminologist Alphonse Bertillon. He believed that people could be identified and classified through a detailed description of facial characteristics and a series of eleven body measurements including height, reach, head width, and length of the left foot. Bertillon maintained that skeletons were highly individualized, and anthropometry continued to be used to classify criminals and suspects until the turn of the century.

Anthropometry was not only flawed, it was dangerous. It was contingent on physical attributes that aren't as individual as is believed. This pseudoscience placed far too much emphasis on what a person looked like and seduced the police into consciously or subconsciously accepting as facts the superstitions of yet another pseudoscience—physiognomy, which asserts that criminality, morality, and intellect are reflected in a person's body and face. Thieves are usually "frail," while violent men are usually "strong" and "in good health." All criminals have superior "finger reach," and almost all female offenders are "homely, if not repulsive." Rapists tend to be "blond," and pedophiles often are "delicate" and look "childish."

If people in the twenty-first century have difficulty accepting the fact that a psychopathic killer can be attractive, likeable, and intelligent, imagine the difficulty in the Victorian era, when standard criminology books included long descriptions of anthropometry and physiognomy. Victorian police officers were trained to identify suspects by their skeletal structure and facial features and to assume that a certain "look" could be linked to a certain type of behavior.

Walter Sickert would not have been tagged as a suspect during the time of the Ripper murders. The "young and beautiful Sickert" with "his well known charm," as Degas once described him, couldn't possibly be capable of cutting a woman's throat and slashing open her abdomen. I have even heard it suggested in recent years that if an artist such as Sickert had violent proclivities, he would have sublimated them through his creative work and not acted them out.

When the police were looking for Jack the Ripper, a great deal of importance was placed on witness descriptions of men last seen with the victims. Investigative reports reveal that much attention was paid to hair color, complexion, and height, with the police not taking into account that all of these characteristics can be disguised. Height not only varies in an individual depending on posture, hats, and footwear, but can be altered by "trickery." Actors can wear tall hats and special lifts in their shoes. They can stoop and slightly bend their knees under voluminous coats or capes; they can wear caps low over their eyes, making themselves appear to be inches taller or shorter than they are.

Early publications on medical jurisprudence and forensic medicine reveal that much more was known than was actually applied in crime cases. But in 1888, cases continued to be made or lost on the basis of witness descriptions instead of physical evidence. Even if the police had known anything at all about forensic science, there was no practical way to get evidence tested. The Home Office—the department of government that oversees Scotland Yard—did not have forensic laboratories then.

A physician such as Dr. Llewellyn might never have touched a microscope; he might not have known that hair, bone, and blood could be identified as human. Robert Hooke had written about the microscopic properties of hairs, fibers, and even vegetable debris and bee stings more than two hundred years earlier, but to death investigators and the average doctor, microscopy was as rarified as rocket science or astronomy must have seemed.

Dr. Llewellyn attended the London Hospital Medical College and had been a licensed physician for thirteen years. His surgery was no more than three hundred yards from where Mary Ann Nichols was murdered. He was in private practice. Although the police knew him well enough to request him by name when Mary Ann Nichols's body was discovered, there is no reason to suppose that Llewellyn was a divisional surgeon for Scotland Yard; that is, he was not a physician who offered his services part-time to a particular division, which in this instance was the H Division covering Whitechapel.

The job of a divisional surgeon was to attend to the troops. Free medical care was a benefit of working for the Metropolitan Police, and a police surgeon was to be available when needed to examine prisoners, or to go to the local jail to determine if a citizen was drunk, ill, or suffering from an excess of "animal spirits," which I presume refers to excitement or hysteria. In the late 1880s, the divisional surgeon also responded to death scenes for a fee of a guinea per case; he was paid two guineas if he performed the postmortem. But by no means was he expected to be well acquainted with the microscope, the nuances of injuries and poisonings, and what the body can reveal after death.

Most likely, Dr. Llewellyn was a local doctor the police felt comfortable calling upon, and it is possible that he was practising in Whitechapel for humanitarian reasons. He was a Fellow of the British Gynecological

Society, and would have been accustomed to being called upon at all hours of the night. When the police rapped on his door on the cool, overcast early morning of August 31st, he probably got to the scene as quickly as possible. He wasn't trained to do much more than determine that the victim was really dead and offer the police an educated guess as to when death had occurred.

Unless the body was turning green around the abdomen, which would indicate the beginning stages of decomposition, it was traditional in the early days of death investigation to wait at least twenty-four hours before performing the postmortem, on the remote chance that the person might still be alive and "come to" as he or she was being cut open. For centuries, the fear prevailed that one might be mistaken for dead and buried alive. Bizarre stories of people suddenly trying to sit up inside their coffins were in circulation, prompting some who were sufficiently concerned about such a fright to have their grave rigged with a bell attached to a string that ran through the earth to the coffin. Some stories may have been veiled references to cases of necrophilia. In one instance, a woman in her coffin wasn't really dead when a man had sex with her. She was paralyzed, it turned out, but conscious enough to consent to the weakness of the flesh.

Police reports of Mary Ann Nichols's murder leave little doubt that Dr. Llewellyn did not seem particularly interested in a victim's clothing, especially the filthy rags of a prostitute. Clothing was not a source of evidence but of identification. Perhaps someone recognized a victim by what he or she was wearing. People did not carry around forms of identification in the late 1800s, unless it was a passport or visa. But that would have been rare. Neither one was required for British citizens to travel to the Continent. A body was unidentified when it was collected from the street and taken to the mortuary unless he or she was known by the locals or the police.

I have often wondered how many poor souls went to their graves unidentified or misnamed. It would not have been a difficult task to murder someone and conceal the victim's identity, or to fake one's own death. During the investigations of the Ripper murders, no attempt was made to distinguish human blood from that of birds or fish or mammals. Unless the blood was on the body or near it, or on a weapon at the scene, the police could not say that the blood was related to the crime or came from a horse or a sheep or a cow. In the 1880s, the streets of Whitechapel near slaughterhouses were putrid with blood and entrails, and men walked about with blood on their clothing and hands.

Dr. Llewellyn misinterpreted just about every detail in Mary Ann Nichols's murder. But he probably did the best he could with his limited training and what was available at the time. It might be interesting to imagine how the murder of Mary Ann Nichols would be investigated today. I'll place the scene in Virginia—not because it is where I once worked and have continued to be mentored, but because it has one of the best statewide medical examiner systems in America.

In Virginia, each of the four district offices has forensic pathologists who are medical doctors trained in pathology and the subspecialty of forensic pathology, training that involves ten years of postgraduate education, not counting three additional years if the forensic pathologist also wants a law degree. Forensic pathologists perform the postmortems, but it is the medical examiner—a physician of any specialty working part-time to assist the pathologist and the police—who is called to the scene of a sudden, unexpected, or violent death.

If Dr. Rees Ralph Llewellyn were employed in Virginia, he would have a private practice and serve part-time as a medical examiner for one of the four districts, depending on where he lived. If Mary Ann Nichols were murdered today, the local police would call Dr. Llewellyn to the scene, which would be cordoned off and protected from the public and bad weather. A tent would be set up, if need be, and there would be a perimeter of strong lights and spitting flares. Officers would be on the street to keep away the curious and divert traffic.

Dr. Llewellyn would use a clean chemical thermometer and insert it into the rectum—providing there was no injury to it—and take the temperature of the body; then he would take the temperature of the air. A quick calculation could give him a very rough idea of when Mary Ann was killed because a body under relatively normal circumstances, assuming an ambient temperature of about seventy-two degrees, would cool one and a half degrees Fahrenheit per hour for the first twelve hours. Dr. Llewellyn would check the stages of livor mortis and rigor mortis and carefully perform an external examination of the body and what is around and under it. He would take photographs, and collect any obvious evidence on the body that might be dislodged or contaminated during transportation. He would ask the police many questions and make notes. He would then send the body to his district medical examiner's office or morgue, where a forensic pathologist would perform the postmortem. All other scene evidence collected and photography would be handled by police detectives or a police forensic squad.

Fundamentally, this is not so different from the way a murder is handled in England today, except that a coroner's court would hold an inquest at the conclusion of the scene investigation and examination of the body. Information and witnesses would be marshalled before the coroner and a jury, and a decision would be rendered by verdict as to whether the death was natural, an accident, a suicide, or a murder. In Virginia, the manner of death would be the sole decision of the forensic pathologist who performed the postmortem. In England, the decision would rely on jurors, which can be unfortunate if a majority of them don't comprehend the medico-legal facts of the case, especially if those facts are weak.

However, jurors can go a step further than the forensic pathologist and commit an "undetermined" case to trial. I think of the case of a "drowned" woman whose husband has just taken out a large life insurance policy on her. The medical expert's job is not to make deductions, no matter what he or she privately believes. But jurors can. Jurors could convene in their private room and suspect the woman was murdered by her greedy husband and send the case to court.

The American way of investigating death was imported from England. But over the decades, individual U.S. states, counties, and cities have slowly been withdrawing from the notion of the "coroner," who is usually a nonmedical person elected and invested with the power to decide how someone died and whether a crime was committed. When I first began working at the Office of the Chief Medical Examiner in Richmond, I assumed that other jurisdictions had the same medical examiner system that Virginia did. I was dismayed to learn this wasn't true. Many elected coroners in other states were funeral home directors, which at best is a conflict of interest. At worst, it is an occasion for medico-legal incompetence and the financial abuse of people who are grieving.

The U.S. has never had a national standard of death investigation, and we are far from it now. Some cities or states continue to have elected coroners who go to the scenes but do not perform the postmortems because they are not forensic pathologists or even physicians. There are offices—such as the one in Los Angeles—in which the chief medical examiner is called a coroner, even though he isn't elected and is a forensic pathologist.

Then there are states that have medical examiners in some cities and coroners in others. Some locales have neither, and local government begrudgingly pays a small fee for what I call a "circuit forensic pathologist" to ride in and handle a medico-legal case, usually in an inadequate—if not appalling—location such as a funeral home. The worst facility I remember was one in Pennsylvania. The postmortem was performed in a hospital "morgue" used as a temporary storage room for stillborn infants and amputated body parts.

CHAPTER THIRTEEN

HUE AND CRY

The English system of investigating death can be traced back some eight hundred years to the reign of Richard I, when it was decreed that in every county of His Majesty's realm, officers would insure the "pleas of the crown." These men were called "crowners," a name that eventually evolved into "coroner."

Coroners were elected by the freeholders of the county and were required to be a knight, assuring they were financially secure, of good standing, and, of course, objective and honest in their collection of revenues due to the crown. A sudden death was a potential source of income for the king if there was a finding of wrongdoing in murders and suicides, or even if there was an inappropriate response by the one who discovered the dead body—such as not responding at all and looking the other way.

It is human nature to make a hue and cry when one stumbles upon a dead body, but during the medieval era, not to do so was to risk punishment and financial penalty. When a person died suddenly, the coroner was to be notified immediately. He would respond as quickly as he could and assemble a jury for what would later be called an inquest. It is frightening to consider how many deaths were labeled evil deeds when the truth may have been that the poor soul simply choked on his mutton, had a stroke, or dropped dead at a young age from a congenitally bad heart or an aneurysm. Suicide and murder were sins against God and the King. If a person took his or her own life or someone else did, the coroner and jury determined wrongdoing by the deceased or perpetrator, and the offender's entire estate could end up in the crown's coffers. This placed the coroner in a tempting position to perhaps bargain a bit and show a little compassion before riding off with coins jingling in his pockets.

Eventually, the coroner's power placed him in a seat of judgment and he became an enforcer of the law. Suspects seeking refuge in the church would soon enough find themselves face-to-face with the coroner, who would demand a confession and arrange the seizure of the man's assets in the name of the crown. Coroners were involved in the gruesome practice of trial by ordeal, requiring a person to prove innocence by showing no pain or injury after holding a hand in the fire or enduring other dreadful tortures while the coroner sat nearby and somberly watched. Before the days of medico-legal postmortems and professional police investigation, a wife's tumble down the castle steps might be murder if her husband could not endure terrible tortures and escape unscathed.

Coroners of old were the equivalent of today's forensic pathologist having no medical training and driving a morgue van to a death scene, glancing at the body, listening to witnesses, finding out how much the dead person is worth, deciding that a sudden death from a bee sting was a deliberate poisoning, testing the wife's innocence by holding her head under water, and if she didn't drown after five or ten minutes, concluding she was innocent. If she drowned, wrongdoing was the verdict and the family estate was forfeited to the Queen or the president of the United States, depending on where the death occurred. In the coroner system of days gone by, jurors could be bribed. Coroners could increase their wealth. Innocent people could lose everything they owned or be hanged. It was best not to die suddenly, if possible.

Times did change for the better. In the sixteenth century, the coroner's role narrowed its focus to the investigation of sudden deaths and stayed clear of law enforcement and trial by ordeal. In 1860—the year Walter Sickert was born—a committee recommended that the election process for coroner be treated as seriously as voting for Members of Parliament. A growing awareness of the importance of competent postmortem examinations and handling of evidence added further value and prestige to the office of coroner, and in 1888—when the Ripper murders began—a government act mandated that death investigation findings by coroners would no longer render any sort of financial benefit to the crown.

These important pieces of legislation are rarely if ever mentioned in connection with the Ripper crimes. Objective death investigation became a priority, and the possibility of material gain by the crown was removed. The change in law meant a change of mind-set that allowed and encouraged the coroner to concentrate on justice and not insidious pressure from the establishment. The crown had nothing to gain by interfering with the inquests of Martha Tabran, Mary Ann Nichols, or the Ripper's other victims—even if the women had been upper-class subjects with influence and wealth. The coroner had nothing to gain but plenty to lose if the freewheeling press depicted him as an incompetent fool, a liar, or a greedy tyrant. Men such as Wynne Baxter supported themselves through respectable legal practices. They did not add much to their incomes by presiding over inquests, but put their livelihoods at risk if their integrity and skills were impugned.

The evolution in the coroner's system had reached a new level of objectivity and seriousness in 1888, reinforcing my belief that there was no investigative or political conspiracy to "cover up" some nefarious secret during the Ripper murders or after they were believed to have ended. There were, of course, the usual bureaucratic attempts to prevent further embarrassment by discouraging the publication of police memoirs and classifying secret official memorandums that were never written for the public to see. Discretion and nondisclosure may not be popular, but they do not always imply scandal. Honest people delete personal e-mails and use shredding machines. But try as I might, for the longest time I could find no excuse for the silence of the elusive Inspector Abberline. So much is made of him. So little is known. So absent does he seem from the Ripper investigation he headed.

Frederick George Abberline was a modest, courteous man of high morals who was as reliable and methodical as the clocks he repaired before he joined the Metropolitan Police in 1863. During his thirty years of service, he earned eighty-four commendations and rewards from judges, magistrates, and the commissioner of police. As Abberline himself matter-of-factly put it, "I think [I] was considered very exceptional."

He was admired, if not cherished, by his colleagues and the public he served, and does not seem the sort to deliberately outshine anyone, but took great pride in a job well done. I find it significant that there is not a single photograph of him that anybody seems to know of, and I don't believe this is so because all of them "walked away" from Scotland Yard's archives and files. I would expect "nicked" pictures would have been recirculating for years, their prices mounting with each resale. It also seems that any existing pictures would have been published at least once somewhere.

But if there is even one photograph of Abberline, I do not know of it. The only hint of what he looked like is to be found in a few sketches published in magazines that don't always spell his name correctly. Artistic versions of the legendary inspector show an indistinct-looking man with mutton-chop whiskers, small ears, a straight nose, and a high forehead. In 1885, it appears, he was losing his hair. He may have slumped a bit and doesn't impress me as particularly tall. As was true of the mythical East End monster Abberline tracked but never caught, the detective could disappear at will and become anybody in a crowd.

His love of clocks and gardening says a great deal about him. These are solitary, gentle pursuits that require patience, concentration, tenacity, meticulousness, a light touch, and a love of life and the way things work. I can't think of many better qualities for a detective, except, of course, honesty, and I have no doubt that Frederick Abberline was as true as a tuning fork. Although he never wrote his autobiography or allowed anyone else to tell his story, he did keep a diary of sorts, a hundred-page book of press cuttings about crimes he worked on interspersed with comments written in his graceful, generous hand.

Based on the way he assembled his cuttings book, I would say that he didn't get around to it until after his retirement. When he died in 1929, this collection of newsprint remnants of his shining career remained the property of his descendants, who eventually donated the book to a person or persons unknown. I knew nothing about it until early in 2002 when I was doing further research in London and an official with the Yard showed me the eight-by-eleven book bound in black. I don't know if it had just been donated or had just turned up. I don't know if it actually belongs to Scotland Yard or perhaps to someone who works there. Exactly where this little-known cuttings book has been since Abberline pasted it together and when it turned up at Scotland Yard are questions I can't answer. Typically, Abberline remains mysterious and offers few answers even now.

His diary is neither confessional nor full of details about his life, but he does reveal his personality in the way he worked cases and in the comments he wrote. He was a brave, intelligent man who kept his word and abided by the rules, which included not divulging details about the very sorts of cases I expected and hoped to find hidden between his cuttings book's covers. Abberline's entries abruptly stop with an October 1887 case of what he called "spontaneous combustion" and do not resume until a March 1891 case of trafficking in infants.

There is not so much as a hint about Jack the Ripper. One won't find a single word about the 1889 Cleveland Street male brothel scandal that must have been a briar patch for Abberline, as accusations included the names of men close to the throne. To read Abberline's diary is to think the Ripper murders and the Cleveland Street scandal never happened, and I have no reason to suspect that someone removed any related pages from the cuttings book. It appears Abberline chose not to include what he knew would be the most sought-after and controversial details of his investigative career.

On pages 44–45 of his diary, he offers an explanation for his silence:

> I think it is just as well to record here the reason why as from the various cuttings from the newspapers as well as the many other matters that I was called upon to investigate that never became public property—it must be apparent that I could write many things that would be very interesting to read.
>
> At the time I retired from the service the authorities were very much opposed to retired officers writing anything for the press as previously some retired officers had from time to time been very indiscreet in what they had caused to be published and to my knowledge had been called upon to explain their conduct—and in fact—they had been threatened with action for libel.
>
> Apart from that there is no doubt the fact that in describing what you did in detecting certain crimes you are putting the criminal closer on their guard and in some cases you may be absolutely telling them how to commit crime.
>
> As an example in the Finger-Print detection you find now the expert thief wears gloves.

The opposition to former officers writing their memoirs did not deter everyone, whether it was the men of Scotland Yard or the City of London Police. I have three examples on my desk: Sir Melville Macnaghten's *Days of My Years,* Sir Henry Smith's *From Constable to Commissioner,* and Benjamin Leeson's *Lost London: The Memoirs of an East End*

Detective. All three include Jack the Ripper anecdotes and analyses which I think the world would be better without. It is sad that men whose lives and careers were touched by the Ripper cases would spin theories almost as baseless as some of those offered by people who weren't even born at the time of the crimes.

Henry Smith was the Acting Commissioner of the City of London Police during the murders of 1888, and he modestly writes, "There is no man living who knows as much of those murders as I do." He declares that after the "second crime"—which may have been Mary Ann Nichols, who was not murdered in Smith's jurisdiction—he "discovered" a suspect he was fairly sure was the murderer. Smith described him as a former medical student who had been in a lunatic asylum and had spent "all of this time" with prostitutes, whom he cheated by passing off polished farthings as sovereigns.

Smith conveyed this intelligence to Sir Charles Warren, who did not find the suspect, according to Smith. It was just as well. The former lunatic turned out to be the wrong man. I feel compelled to add that a sovereign would have been unusually generous payment for an Unfortunate who was more than accustomed to exchanging favors for farthings. The damage done by Smith during the Ripper investigation was to perpetuate the notion that the Ripper was a doctor or a medical student or someone involved in a field connected with medicine.

I don't know why Smith made such an assumption as early as the "second case," when no victim had been disemboweled yet and no organs had been taken. Following Mary Ann Nichols's murder, there was no suggestion that the weapon was a surgical knife or that the killer possessed even the slightest surgical skills. Unless Smith simply has the timing wrong in his recollections, there was no reason for the police to suspect a so-called medically trained individual this early in the investigation.

Smith's overtures to Charles Warren apparently evoked no response, and Smith took it upon himself to put "nearly a third" of his police force in plainclothes and instruct them to "do everything which, under ordinary circumstances, a constable should not do," he says in his memoirs. These clandestine activities included sitting on doorsteps smoking pipes and lingering in pubs, gossiping with the locals. Smith wasn't idle, either. He visited "every butcher's shop in the city," and I find this almost comical as I imagine the commissioner—perhaps in disguise or wearing a suit and tie—dropping by to quiz slaughterhouse butchers about suspicious-looking men of their profession who might be going about cutting up women. I feel quite sure the Metropolitan Police would not have appreciated his enthusiasm or violation of boundaries.

Sir Melville Macnaghten probably diverted if not derailed the Ripper investigation permanently with his certainties that were not based on firsthand information or the open-minded and experienced deductions of an Abberline. In 1889, Macnaghten joined the Metropolitan Police as assistant commissioner of the CID. He had nothing to recommend him but twelve years of work on his family's tea plantations in Bengal, where he went out each morning to shoot wild cats, foxes, alligators, or maybe have a go at a good pig sticking.

When his memoirs were published in 1914, four years after Smith published his recollections, Macnaghten restrained himself until page 55, where he began engaging in a little literary pig sticking that was followed by amateurish sleuthing and pomposity. He alluded to Henry Smith as being "on the tiptoe of expectation" and having a "prophetic soul" since Smith was in hot pursuit of the murderer weeks before the first murder had even happened—according to Macnaghten. Smith considered the August 7th slaying of Martha Tabran as the Ripper's debut, while Macnaghten was certain that the first murder was Mary Ann Nichols on August 31st.

Macnaghten goes on to recall those terrible foggy evenings and the "raucous cries" of young newspaper sellers shouting out that there had been "Another horrible murder . . . !" The scene he sets becomes more dramatic with each page until one can't help but get annoyed and wish that his autobiography had been one of those quashed by the Home Office. I suppose it is possible Macnaghten heard those raucous cries and experienced those fatal foggy nights, but I doubt he was anywhere near the East End.

He had just returned from India and was still working for his family. He did not begin at Scotland Yard until some eight months after the Ripper murders supposedly had ended and were no longer foremost on the Yard's mind, but this didn't keep him from deciding not only who Jack the Ripper probably was, but also that he was dead and had murdered five victims "& 5 victims only": Mary Ann Nichols, Annie Chapman, Elizabeth Stride, Catherine Eddows, and Mary Kelly. It was Melville Macnaghten's "rational theory" that after the "fifth" murder of November 9, 1888, the Ripper's "brain gave way altogether" and he most likely committed suicide.

When the young, depressed barrister Montague John Druitt threw himself into the Thames toward the end of 1888, he unwittingly cast himself as one of three main suspects Macnaghten named in Jack the Ripper's bloody drama. The other two, lower on Macnaghten's list, were a Polish Jew named Aaron Kosminski, who was "insane" and "had a great hatred of women," and Michael Ostrog, a Russian doctor who was committed to a "lunatic asylum."

For some reason, Macnaghten thought that Montague Druitt was a doctor. This erroneous supposition was passed down the line for quite a long time, and I suppose some people may still think Druitt was a doctor. I don't know where Macnaghten got his information, but perhaps he was confused because Montague's uncle, Robert Druitt, was a prominent physician and medical writer, and Montague's father, William, was a surgeon. I am afraid that Montague or "Monty" will always remain a bit shadowy because it does not appear there is much information available about him.

In 1876, when he was a dark, handsome, athletic nineteen-year-old, Druitt enrolled at New College, Oxford, and five years later was admitted to the Inner Temple in London to pursue a career in law. He was a good student and an exceptionally talented cricketer, and worked part-time as an assistant at Valentine's School, a boys' boarding school in Blackheath. Homosexuality or child molesting—or both—are suggested as the reasons why Druitt, a thirty-one-year-old bachelor when he died, was fired from Valentine's School in the autumn of 1888. Macnaghten claimed in his memo that Druitt was "sexually insane," which in the Victorian era could have referred to homosexuality. But Macnaghten backs up his accusation with nothing more than so-called reliable information that he supposedly destroyed.

Mental illness ran in Druitt's bloodline. His mother was committed to an asylum in the summer of 1888 and had attempted suicide at least once. One of Druitt's sisters later committed suicide as well. When Druitt drowned himself in the Thames in the early winter of 1888, he left a suicide note that indicated he feared he would end up like his mother and thought it best for him to kill himself. His family archives at the Dorset Record Office and the West Sussex Record Office turned up only one letter of his, which he wrote to his uncle Robert in September 1876. Although Druitt's handwriting and language do not resemble anything found in alleged Ripper letters, even to consider making a judgment based on this isn't meaningful or fair. In 1876, Druitt wasn't yet twenty years old. Handwriting and verbal performance can not only be disguised—they also tend to change as one ages.

Druitt became a suspect in the Ripper murders for the convenient reason that he happened to commit suicide not long after what Macnaghten considers the last Ripper killing on November 9, 1888. The young barrister was probably guilty of nothing more than a hereditary mental illness, and perhaps what fatally tipped the scales against him was acute distress over whatever he allegedly had done to be fired from Valentine's School. We can't know his mind or feelings at that point in his life, but his despair was sufficient for him to put rocks in the pockets of his overcoat and jump into the frigid, polluted Thames. Druitt's body was recovered from the water the last day of 1888, and it was supposed, based on the degree of decomposition, that he had been dead for about a month. At his inquest in Chiswick, the jury returned a verdict of "suicide whilst of unsound mind."

Doctors and lunatics seem to have been popular Ripper suspects. B. Leeson, a constable at the time of the Ripper murders, states in his memoirs that when he began his career, the training consisted of ten days' attendance at a police court and a "couple of hours" of instruction from a chief inspector. The rest one had to learn through experience. Leeson wrote, "I am afraid I cannot throw any light on the problem of the Ripper's identity." However, he added, there was a particular doctor who was never far away when the crimes were committed. I guess Leeson was never far away when the murders were committed, either, otherwise he couldn't possibly have noticed this "same" doctor.

Perhaps Frederick Abberline refrained from writing about the Ripper cases because he was smart enough not to trot out what he didn't know. In his cuttings books, every case he includes is one he personally investigated and solved. The news articles he pasted on pages and underlined (precisely, with a straight edge), and his comments are neither copious nor especially enthusiastic. He made it plain that he worked very hard and wasn't always happy about it. On January 24, 1885, when the Tower of London was bombed, for example, he found himself "especially overworked, as the then Home Secretary Sir Wm. Harcourt wished to be supplied every morning with the progress of the case and after working very hard all day I had to remain up many nights until 4 and 5 A.M. the following morning making reports for his information."

If Abberline had to do this over the Tower of London bombing case, one can be sure that during the Ripper murders he was often up all night and in the Home Secretary's office first thing in the morning for briefings. In the Tower bombing, Abberline arrived "immediately after the explosion" and suggested that all people on the scene were to remain there and be interviewed by the police. Abberline conducted many of the interviews himself, and it was during this process that he "discovered" one of the perpetrators through "the hesitation in his replies and his general manner." There was quite a lot of press about the bombing and Abberline's excellent detective work, and if four years later his presence seemed to fade, it was probably because of his supervisory position and his discretion. He was a man who worked relentlessly and without applause, the quiet clockmaker who did not want attention but was determined to fix what was wrong.

I suspect he anguished over the Ripper murders and spent much time walking the streets at night, speculating, deducing, trying to coax leads out of the foggy, filthy air. When his colleagues, friends, family, and the merchants of the East End gave him a retirement dinner in 1892, they presented him with a silver tea and coffee service and praised his honorable and extraordinary work in the detection of crime. According to the *East London Observer*'s account of the appreciation dinner, H Division's Superintendent Arnold told those who had gathered to celebrate Abberline's career that during the Ripper murders, "Abberline came down to the East End and gave the whole of his time with the object of bringing those crimes to light. Unfortunately, however, the circumstances were such that success was impossible."

It must have been painful and infuriating for Abberline when he was forced in the autumn of 1888 to confess to the press that "not the slightest clue can at present be obtained." He was used to outwitting criminals. It was reported that he worked so hard to solve the Ripper murders that he "almost broke down under the pressure." Often he did not go to bed and went for days without sleep. It wasn't uncommon for him to wear plain-clothes and mingle with the "shady folk" in doss-house kitchens until the early hours of the morning. But no matter where Abberline went, the "miscreant" was not there. I have to wonder if his path ever crossed Walter Sickert's. It would not surprise me if the two men had talked at one time or another and if Sickert had offered suggestions. What a "real jolly" that would have been.

"Theories!" Abberline would later thunder when someone brought up the Ripper murders. "We were lost almost in theories; there were so many of them." By all indications, it was not a pleasant subject to bring up with him in later years, after he had moved on to other cases. Better to let him talk about the improved sanitation in the East End or how he solved a long string of bond robberies by tracing clues that led to an unclaimed hatbox in a railway station.

For all his experience and gifts, Abberline did not solve the biggest crime of his life. It is a shame if that failure gave him pain and regret for even a moment when he worked in his garden during his retirement years. Frederick Abberline went to his grave having no idea what he had been up against. Walter Sickert was a murderer unlike any other.

CHAPTER FOURTEEN

CROCHET WORK AND FLOWERS

Mary Ann Nichols's body remained at the mortuary in Whitechapel until Thursday, September 6, when her decomposing flesh was finally allowed privacy and rest.

She was enclosed in a "solid-looking" wooden coffin and loaded into a horse-drawn hearse that carried her seven miles to Ilford Cemetery, where she was buried. The sun shone only five minutes that day, and it was misty and rainy.

The next day, Friday, the British Association's fifty-eighth annual meeting considered important topics such as the necessity of lightning rods being properly installed and inspected, and the vagaries of lightning and the great damage it and wild geese could do to telegraph wires. The hygienic qualities of electric lighting were presented, and a physicist and an engineer debated whether electricity was a form of matter or energy. It was announced that poverty and misery could be eliminated if "you could prevent weakness and sickness and laziness and stupidity." One bit of good news was that Thomas Edison had just started a factory that would begin producing 18,000 phonographs a year for £20 or £25 each.

The weather had been worse this day than yesterday, with no sunshine reported at all, and squalls roared in from the north. Heavy rain and sleet smacked down, and Londoners moved about in a cold mist, going to and from work and later to the theaters. *Dr. Jekyll and Mr. Hyde* was still drawing large audiences at the Lyceum, and a parody of it called *Hide and Seekyll* had opened at the Royalty Theater. The play *She* was reviewed in that day's paper as "a formidable experiment of dramatizing," offering a murder and cannibals at the Gaiety. At the Alhambra, one of Walter Sickert's favorite music halls, the doors opened at 10:30 P.M. with a cast of dancing women and Captain Clives and his "marvelous dog."

Annie Chapman was sleeping off her last glass of spirits while London's early night life was going on. The week had been a bad one, worse than usual. Annie was forty-seven years old and missing her two front teeth. She was five feet tall, overweight, with blue eyes and short, dark-brown, wavy hair. As the police later put it, "she had seen her better day." On the street she was known as "Dark Annie." In some accounts her estranged husband was said to be a veterinary surgeon, but in most of them he was described as a coachman employed by a gentleman who lived in the Royal Borough of Windsor.

Annie and her husband had no contact with each other after they separated, and she made no inquiries into his life until her weekly allowance of ten shillings suddenly stopped in late 1886. One day, a wretched-looking woman, having the appearance of a tramp, appeared at the Merry Wives of Windsor pub and inquired about Chapman. She said she had walked twenty miles from London, staying in a lodging house along the way, and wanted to know if her husband was ill or using that as an excuse not to send money. The woman at the door of the Merry Wives of Windsor informed the tramp that Mr. Chapman had died on

Christmas Day. He left Annie nothing but two children who wanted nothing to do with her: a boy who was an inmate of the Cripples' Home, and a well-educated daughter living in France.

Annie moved in with a sieve maker for a while, and when he left her, she borrowed small sums from her brother, who finally cut her off. She had no further contact with any members of her family, and when her health allowed, she made pennies by selling crochet work and flowers. Acquaintances described her as "clever" and industrious by nature, but the more her addiction to alcohol tightened its grip on her life, the less she cared what she did to earn her keep.

During the four months before her death, Annie had been in and out of the infirmary. She was spending her nights in Spitalfields doss-houses, the most recent one located at 35 Dorset Street, which joined Commercial Street and Crispin Street like a short rung on a ladder. There were an estimated 5,000 lodging-house beds in the hellish dens of Spitalfields, and *The Times* later observed that at Annie's inquest the "glimpse of life . . . was sufficient to make [jurors] feel there was much in the 19th century civilization of which they had small reason to be proud." In Annie Chapman's world, the poor were "herded like cattle," and were "near starvation." Violence smoldered day and night, fueled by misery, alcohol, and rage.

Four nights before her death, Annie got into an altercation with another lodger named Eliza Cooper, who confronted her in the lodging-house kitchen, demanding the return of a scrap of soap Annie had borrowed. Annie angrily threw a halfpenny on the table and told her to go buy it herself. The two women began to quarrel and carried their disagreement to the nearby Ringer public house, where Annie slapped Eliza across the face and Eliza punched Annie in the left eye and chest.

Annie's bruises were still noticeable early on the morning of Saturday September 8th, when John Donovan, the deputy of the lodging house on Dorset Street, demanded payment of eightpence for a bed if she planned to stay. She replied, "I have not got it. I am weak and ill and have been in the infirmary." Donovan reminded her that she knew the rules. She replied that she would go out and get the money and please not to let her bed to someone else. Donovan would later tell police that she "was under the influence of drink" when the night watchman escorted her off the property.

Annie took the first right into Little Paternoster Row, and when the night watchman saw her last she was in Brushfield Street, which ran east to west between what was then called Bishopsgate Without Norton Folgate and Commercial Street. Had she headed just a little further north along Commercial Street, she would have reached Shoreditch, where there were several music halls (the Shoreditch Olympia, Harwood's, and Griffin's). A little farther north was Hoxton—or the very route Walter Sickert sometimes took when he walked home to 54 Broadhurst Gardens after evenings at various music halls, theaters, or wherever it was he went on his obsessive wanderings late at night and in the early morning hours.

At 2:00 A.M., when Annie emerged onto the East End streets, it was fifty degrees and sodden out. She was dressed in a black skirt, a long black jacket hooked at the neck, an apron, wool stockings, and boots. Around her neck was a piece of a black woollen scarf tied in front with a knot, and under it she wore a handkerchief that she recently had bought from another lodger. On the wedding ring finger of her left hand she wore three base metal or "flash" rings. In a pocket on the inside of her skirt was a small comb case, a piece of coarse muslin, and a torn bit of envelope that she had been seen to pick off the lodging-house floor and use to tuck away two pills she had gotten from the infirmary. The torn envelope had a red postmark on it.

If anyone saw Annie alive over the next three and a half hours, no witness ever came forward. At quarter to five, thirty-seven-year-old John Richardson, a porter at the Spitalfields Market, headed toward 29 Hanbury Street, a lodging house for the poor that, like so many other dilapidated dwellings in Spitalfields, had once been a barnlike workplace for weavers to toil on hand looms until steam power had put them out of business. Richardson's mother rented the house and sublet half of its rooms to seventeen people. He, being the dutiful son, had dropped by, just as he always did when he was up early, to check the security of the cellar. Two months ago someone had broken into it and had stolen two saws and two hammers. His mother also ran a packing-case business, and stolen tools were no small matter.

Satisfied that the cellar was safely locked, Richardson went through a passage that led into the backyard and sat on the steps to cut a bothersome piece of leather off his boot. His knife was "an old table knife," he later testified at the inquest, "about five inches long," and he had used it earlier to cut "a bit of carrot," then absent-mindedly tucked the knife into a pocket. He estimated he was sitting out on the steps no longer than several minutes, his feet resting on flagstone that was just inches from where Annie Chapman's mutilated body would be found. He neither heard nor saw anyone. Richardson laced up his mended boot and headed to the market just as the sun began to rise.

Albert Cadosch lived next door at 25 Hanbury Street, his backyard separated from number 29 by a temporary wooden fence that was five to five and a half feet high. He later told police that at 5:25 A.M., he walked into his backyard and heard a voice say "No" from the other side of the fence. Several minutes later, something heavy fell against the palings. He did not check to see what had caused the noise or who had said "No."

Five minutes later, at 5:30 A.M., Elisabeth Long was walking along Hanbury Street, heading west to Spitalfields Market, when she noticed a man talking to a woman only a few yards from the fence around the yard at 29 Hanbury Street, where Annie Chapman's body would be found on the other side barely half an hour later. Mrs. Long testified at the inquest that she was "positive" the woman was Annie Chapman. Annie and the man were talking loudly but seemed to be getting along,

Mrs. Long recalled. The only fragment of the conversation she overheard as she made her way down the street was the man asking, "Will you?" and the woman identified as Annie replying, "Yes."

Obviously, the times given by witnesses conflict, and they never stated at the inquest how they happened to know what time it was when they walked past people or stumbled upon bodies. In that era, most people told the time by their routines, the position of the sun in the sky, and church clocks that chimed the hour or half hour. Harriet Hardiman of 29 Hanbury Street testified at the inquest she was certain it was 6:00 A.M. when she was awakened by a commotion outside her window. She was a cat meat saleswoman whose shop was inside the lodging house; she made her living by going out with a barrow full of stinking fish or slop left over from slaughterhouses to sell to cat owners while long lines of felines followed her through the streets.

Harriet was fast asleep on the ground floor when the excited voices woke her with a start. Fearing the building was on fire, she awakened her son and told him to go outside and look. When he returned, he said that a woman had been murdered in the yard. Both mother and son had slept soundly all night, and Harriet Hardiman later testified she often heard people on the stairs and in the passage that led into the yard, but all had been quiet. John Richardson's mother, Amelia, had been awake half the night and certainly she would have been aware had someone been arguing or screaming. But she claimed she had heard not a sound, either.

Residents were continually in and out of 29 Hanbury Street, and the front and back doors were always kept unlocked, as was the passage door that opened onto the enclosed yard at the rear of the house. It would have been easy for anyone to unlatch the gate and walk into the yard, which is what Annie Chapman must have done just before she was murdered. At 5:55 A.M., John Davis, a porter who lived in the lodging house, headed out to the market and had the distinct misfortune of discovering Annie Chapman's body in the yard between the house and the fence, very close to where Richardson had been sitting on the stone steps about an hour earlier mending his boot.

She was on her back, her left hand on her left breast, her right arm by her side, her legs bent. Her disarrayed clothing was pulled up to her knees, and her throat was cut so deeply that her head was barely attached to her body. Annie Chapman's killer had slashed open her abdomen and removed her bowels and a flap of her belly. They were in a puddle of blood on the ground above her left shoulder, an arrangement that may or may not be symbolic.

Quite likely, the placement of the body organs and tissue was utilitarian—to get them out of the Ripper's way. It would become apparent that he was after the kidneys, uterus, and vagina, but one can't dismiss the supposition that he also intended to shock people. He succeeded. John Davis fled upstairs to his room and drank a glass of brandy. Then he frantically rushed into his workshop for a tarpaulin to drape over the body and ran to find the nearest police constable.

Moments later, Inspector Joseph Chandler of the Commercial Street police station arrived. When he saw what he was dealing with, he sent for Dr. George Phillips, a divisional surgeon. A crowd was gathering and voices cried out, "Another woman has been murdered!" With little more than a glance, Dr. Phillips determined that the victim's throat had been cut before her "stomach" was mutilated, and that she had been dead about two hours. He noted that her face seemed swollen and that her tongue was protruding between her front teeth. She had been strangled to death, Dr. Phillips said—or at least rendered unconscious before the killer cut her throat. Rigor mortis was just beginning to set in, and the doctor noted "six patches" of blood on the back wall, about eighteen inches above Annie's head.

The droplets ranged from very small to the size of a sixpence and each "patch" was in a tight cluster. In addition, there were "marks" of blood on the fence behind the house. Neatly arranged at Annie's feet were a bit of coarse muslin, a comb, and a piece of bloody torn envelope with the Sussex Regiment coat of arms on it and a London postmark with the date August 20, 1888. Nearby were two pills. Her cheap metal rings were missing, and an abrasion on her finger indicated that they had been forcibly removed. Later, on an undated, unsigned postcard believed to have been sent by the Ripper to the City Police, the writer skillfully drew a cartoon figure with a cut throat. He wrote "poor annie" and claimed to have her rings "in my possession."

None of Annie's clothing was torn, her boots were on, and her black coat was still buttoned and hooked. The neck of the coat inside and out was stained with blood. Dr. Phillips also pointed out drops of blood on her stockings and her left sleeve. It was not mentioned in the newspaper or police reports, but Dr. Phillips must have scooped up her intestines and other body tissues and placed them back inside her abdominal cavity before covering her body with sacking. Police helped place her into the same shell that had cradled Mary Ann Nichols's body until the day before, when she had finally been taken away to be buried. Police transported Annie Chapman's body by hand ambulance to the Whitechapel mortuary.

It was daylight now. Hundreds of excited people were hurrying to the enclosed yard at 29 Hanbury Street. Neighbors on either side of the lodging house began charging admission to step inside for a better view of the bloodstained area where Annie had been slain.

HAVE YOU SEEN THE "DEVIL"

If not

Pay one Penny & Walk inside

wrote Jack the Ripper on October 10.

On the same postcard, the Ripper added, "I am waiting every evening for the coppers at Hampstead heath," the sprawling parkland famous for its healing springs, its bathing ponds, and its longtime appeal to writers, poets, and painters, including Dickens, Shelley, Pope, Keats, and Constable. On Bank Holidays, as many as 100,000 people had been known to visit the rolling farmland and dense copses. Walter Sickert's home in South Hampstead was no more than a twenty-minute walk away from Hampstead Heath.

Alleged Ripper letters not only drop hints—such as the "Have You Seen The 'Devil'" postcard, which could be an allusion to East End residents charging money for peeks at the Ripper's crime scenes—but also reveal an emerging geographical profile. Many of the locations mentioned—some of them repeatedly—are places and areas that were well known to Walter Sickert: the Bedford Music Hall in Camden Town, which he painted many times; his home at 54 Broadhurst Gardens; and theatrical, artistic, and commercial parts of London that Sickert would have frequented.

Postmarks and mentions of locations in close proximity to the Bedford Music Hall include Hampstead Road, King's Cross, Tottenham Court, Somers Town, Albany Street, St. Pancras Church.

Those that are in close proximity to 54 Broadhurst Gardens include Kilburn, Palmerston Road (a stone's throw from his house), Princess Road, Kentish Town, Alma Street, Finchley Road (which runs off Broadhurst Gardens).

Postmarks and locations in close proximity to theaters, music halls, art galleries, and places of possible business or personal interest to Sickert include Piccadilly Circus, Haymarket, Charing Cross, Battersea (near Whistler's studio), Regent Street North, Mayfair, Paddington (where Paddington Station is located), York Street (near Paddington), Islington (where St. Mark's Hospital is located), Worcester (a favorite place for painters), Greenwich, Gipsy Hill (near the Crystal Palace), Portman Square (not far from the Fine Art Society, and also the location of the Heinz Gallery collection of architectural drawings), Conduit Street (close to the Fine Art Society, and during the Victorian era the site of the 19th Century Art Society and the Royal Institute of British Architects).

Sickert's sketches are remarkably detailed, his pencil recording what his eyes were seeing so that he could later paint the picture. His mathematical formula of "squaring up" paintings, or using a geometrical formula for enlarging his drawings without losing dimension and perspective, reveals an organized and scientific mind. Sickert painted many intricate buildings during his career, especially unusually detailed paintings of churches in Dieppe and Venice. One might suppose he would have been interested in architecture and perhaps visited the Heinz Gallery, which had the largest collection of architectural drawings in the world.

Sickert's first career was acting, which he is believed to have begun in 1879. In one of the earliest existing Sickert letters, one he wrote in 1880 to historian and biographer T. E. Pemberton, he described playing an "old man" in *Henry V* while on tour in Birmingham. "It is the part I like best of all," he wrote. Despite recycled stories that Sickert gave up acting because his true ambition was to be a painter, letters collected by Denys Sutton reveal a different story. "Walter was anxious to take up a stage career," one letter said. But, wrote another Sickert acquaintance, "He was not very successful so he took up painting."

In his early twenties, Sickert was still an actor and touring with Henry Irving's company. He was acquainted with the famous architect Edward W. Godwin, a theater enthusiast, costume designer, and good friend of Whistler's. Godwin lived with Ellen Terry during Sickert's early acting days and had built Whistler's house—the White House, on Tite Street in Chelsea. Godwin's widow, Beatrice, had just married Whistler on August 11, 1888. Although I can't prove that biographical and geographical details such as these were connected in Sickert's psyche when Ripper letters were posted or purportedly written from the London locations cited, I can speculate that these areas of the city at least would have been familiar to him. They were not likely places for "homicidal lunatics" or East End "low life paupers" to have spent much time.

While it is true that many of the Ripper letters were posted in the East

End, it is also true that many of them were not. But Sickert spent a fair amount of time in the East End and probably knew that run-down part of London better than the police did. The orders of the day did not allow Metropolitan Police constables to enter pubs or mingle with the locals. Patrolling policemen were supposed to stay on their beats, and to enter lodging houses or pubs without cause or simply to stray from their measured walks around the assigned streets was to invite reprimand or suspension. Sickert, however, could mingle as he pleased. No place was off-limits to him.

The police seemed to suffer from East End myopia. No matter how much the Ripper tried to inveigle them into investigating other locales or likely haunts, he was mostly ignored. There appears to be no record that the police thoroughly investigated the postmarks or locations of Ripper letters not posted from the East End or thought twice about other letters that were allegedly written or posted from other cities in Great Britain. Not all envelopes have survived, and without a postmark one has only the location that the Ripper wrote on his letter. That may or may not have been where he really was at the time.

According to the postmarks, the alleged locations of the Ripper at various times, or where he claimed to be going, include Birmingham, Liverpool, Manchester, Leeds, Bradford, Dublin, Belfast, Limerick, Edinburgh, Plymouth, Leicester, Bristol, Clapham, Woolwich, Nottingham, Portsmouth, Croydon, Folkestone, Gloucester, Leith, Lille, Lisbon, and Philadelphia.

A number of these locations seem extremely unlikely, especially Portugal and the United States. As far as anyone seems to know, Walter Sickert never visited either country. Other letters and their alleged dates make it almost impossible to believe that, for example, he could have posted or written letters in London, Lille, Birmingham, and Dublin all on the same day, October 8. But again, what is unclear 114 years after the fact—when so many envelopes and their postmarks are missing, when evidence is cold and witnesses are dead—is whether letters really were written on a given date and where they were written from. Only postmarks and eyewitnesses could swear to that.

Of course not all the Ripper letters were written by Sickert, but he could disguise his handwriting in ways an average person could not, and no records have yet turned up to prove he wasn't in a given city on a given day. October 1888 was a busy letter-writing period for the Ripper. Some eighty letters written that month still exist, and it would make sense for the killer to be on the run after multiple, closely spaced murders. As the Ripper himself wrote in several letters, Whitechapel was getting too hot for him and he was seeking peace and quiet in distant ports.

We know from modern cases that serial killers tend to move around. Some virtually live in their cars. October would have been a convenient time for Sickert to disappear from London. His wife, Ellen, was part of a Liberal delegation that was holding meetings in Ireland to support Home Rule and Free Trade. She was away from England for almost the entire month of October. If she and Sickert had any contact at all during this separation, no letters or telegrams to each other seem to have survived.

Sickert loved to write letters and sometimes apologized to friends for writing them so often. He habitually wrote letters to newspapers. He had such a knack for stirring up news that letters by him and articles about him amounted to as many as six hundred in one year. It is daunting to go through Sickert's archives at Islington Public Libraries and look at his several reams of cuttings. He began gathering them himself around the turn of the century, and then used press agencies to keep up with his seemingly endless publicity. Yet throughout his life, he was known as a man who refused to give interviews. He managed to create the myth that he was "shy" and hated publicity.

Sickert's obsession with writing letters to the editor became an embarrassment to some newspapers. Editors squirmed when they got yet another Sickert letter about art or the aesthetic quality of telephone poles or why all Englishmen should wear kilts or the disadvantages of chlorinated water. Most editors did not wish to insult the well-known artist by ignoring him or relegating his prose to a small, inconspicuous space.

Between January 25 and May 25, 1924, Sickert delivered a series of lectures and articles that were published in the *Southport Visiter,* near Liverpool. Although these articles came to more than 130,000 words, that wasn't enough. On May 6th, 12th, 15th, 19th, and 22nd, Sickert wrote or telegraphed W. H. Stephenson of the *Southport Visiter:* "I wonder if the Visiter could bear one more article at once. . . . If so you should have it at once" and "delighted writing" and "please ask printer to express early six copies" and "Do let me send you just one more article" and "if you hear of any provincial paper that would care to carry series over the summer let me know."

Throughout Sickert's life, his literary prolificacy was astonishing. His cuttings book at Islington Public Libraries contains more than 12,000 news items about him and letters he wrote to editors in Great Britain alone, most of them written between 1911 and the late 1930s. He published some four hundred lectures and articles, and I believe these known writings do not represent the entirety of his literary output. Sickert was a compulsive writer who enjoyed persuading, manipulating, and impressing people with his words. He craved an audience. He craved seeing his name in print. It would have been in character for him to have written a startling number of the Ripper letters, including some of those sent from all over the map.

He may have written far more of them than some document examiners would be inclined to believe, because one makes a mistake to judge Walter Sickert by the usual handwriting-comparison standards. He was a multitalented artist with an amazing memory. He was multilingual. He was a voracious reader and skilled mimic. There were a number of books on graphology available at the time, and the handwriting in many Ripper letters is similar to examples of writing styles that Victorian graphologists associated with various occupations and personalities. Sickert could have opened any number of graphology books and imitated the styles he found there. For graphologists to study Ripper letters must have struck Sickert as most amusing.

Using chemicals and highly sensitive instruments to analyze inks, paints, and paper is scientific. Handwriting comparison is not. It is an investigative tool that can be powerful and convincing, especially in detecting forgeries. But if a suspect is adept in disguising his handwriting, comparison can be frustrating or impossible. The police investigating the Ripper cases were so eager to pinpoint similarity in handwriting that they did not explore the possibility that the killer might use many different styles. Other leads, such as cities the Ripper mentioned and postmarks on envelopes, were not pursued. Had they been, it may have been discovered that most of the distant cities shared points in common, including theaters and racecourses. Many of these locations would appear on a map of Sickert's travels.

Let's start with Manchester. There were at least three reasons for Sickert to visit that city and be quite familiar with it. His wife's family, the Cobdens, owned property in Manchester. Sickert's sister, Helena, lived in Manchester. Sickert had friends as well as professional connections in Manchester. Several Ripper letters mention Manchester. One of them that the Ripper claims to have written from Manchester on November 22, 1888, has a partial A Pirie & Sons watermark. Another letter the Ripper claims to have written from East London, also on November 22nd, has a partial A Pirie & Sons watermark. The stationery Walter and Ellen Sickert began using after they were married on June 10, 1885, has the A Pirie & Sons watermark.

Dr. Paul Ferrara, director of the Virginia Institute of Forensic Science and Medicine, made the first watermark connection when we were examining original Ripper and Sickert letters in London and Glasgow. Transparencies of the letters and their watermarks were submitted to the

Institute, and when the Ripper partial watermark and a Sickert complete watermark were scanned into a forensic image-enhancement computer and superimposed on the video screen, they matched identically.

In September 2001, the Virginia Institute of Forensic Science and Medicine received permission from the British government to conduct nondestructive forensic testing on the original Ripper letters at the Public Record Office. Dr. Ferrara, DNA analyst Lisa Schiermeier, forensic image enhancement expert Chuck Pruitt, and others traveled to London, and we examined the Ripper letters. Some of what seemed the most promising envelopes—ones that still had flaps and stamps intact—were moistened and painstakingly peeled back for swabbing. Photographs were taken and handwriting was compared.

From London, we went on to other archives and examined paper, and took DNA samples from the letters, envelopes, and stamps of Walter Richard Sickert; his first wife, Ellen Cobden Sickert; James McNeill Whistler; and so-called Ripper suspect Montague John Druitt. Some of these tests were for the purpose of elimination. Obviously, neither Ellen Sickert nor Whistler has ever been a suspect, but Walter Sickert worked in Whistler's studio. He posted letters for him and was in close physical contact with the Master and his belongings. It is possible that Whistler's DNA—and certainly Ellen's DNA—could have contaminated Sickert evidence.

We swabbed Whistler envelopes and stamps at the University of Glasgow, where his massive archive is kept. We swabbed envelopes and stamps at the West Sussex Record Office, where Ellen Cobden Sickert's family archives—and, coincidentally, some of Montague John Druitt's family archives—are kept. Unfortunately, the only Druitt sample available to us was the letter he wrote in 1876 while he was a student at Oxford. The DNA results from the envelope's flap and stamp are contaminated, but will be retested.

Other documents yet to be tested are two envelopes I believe were addressed and sealed by the Duke of Clarence, and an envelope of Queen Victoria's physician, Dr. William Gull. I do not believe that Druitt or any of these so-called suspects had a thing to do with murder and mutilation, and I would like to clear their names if I can. DNA testing will continue until all practical means are exhausted. The importance extends far beyond the Ripper investigation.

There is no one left to indict and convict. Jack the Ripper and all who knew him well have been dead for decades. But there is no statute of limitations on murder, and the Ripper's victims deserve justice. And whatever we can learn that furthers our knowledge of forensic science and medicine is worth the trouble and expense. I was not optimistic we would get a DNA match, but I was surprised and quite crestfallen when the first round of testing turned up not a single sign of human life in all fifty-five samples. I decided to try again, this time swabbing different areas of the same envelopes and stamps.

Still, we came up with nothing. There are a number of possible explanations for these disappointing results: The one-billionth of a gram of cells in human saliva that would have been deposited on a stamp or envelope flap did not survive the years; heat used to laminate the Ripper letters for conservation destroyed the nuclear DNA; suboptimal storage for a hundred years caused degradation and destruction of the DNA; or perhaps the adhesives were the culprit.

The "glutinous wash," as adhesives were called in the mid–nineteenth century, was derived from plant extracts, such as the bark of the acacia tree. During the Victorian era, the postal system underwent an industrial revolution, with the first Penny Black stamp posted on May 2, 1840, from Bath. The envelope folding machine was patented in 1845. Many people did not want to lick envelopes or stamps for "sanitary" reasons, and used a sponge. To add to the scientific odds against us when we swabbed envelopes and stamps, we could not possibly know who had licked their envelopes and who had not. The last genetic option left for us was to try a third round of testing, this time for mitochondrial DNA.

When one reads about DNA tests used in modern criminal or paternity cases, what is usually being referred to is the nuclear DNA that is located in virtually every cell in the body and passed down from both parents. Mitochondrial DNA is found outside the nucleus of the cell. Think of an egg: The nuclear DNA is found in the yolk, so to speak, and the mitochondrial DNA would be found in the egg white. Mitochondrial DNA is passed down only from the mother. While the mitochondrial region of a cell contains thousands more "copies" of DNA than the nucleus does, mitochondrial DNA testing is very complex and expensive, and the results can be limited because the DNA is passed down from only one parent.

The extracts of all fifty-five DNA samples were sent to The Bode Technology Group, an internationally respected private DNA laboratory, best known for assisting the Armed Forces Institute of Pathology (AFIP) in using mitochondrial DNA to determine the identity of America's Vietnam War Unknown Soldier. More recently, Bode has been using mitochondrial DNA to identify victims of the 9/11 terrorist attack on the World Trade Center. The examination of our samples took months, and while I was back in London's Public Record Office with art and paper experts, Dr. Paul Ferrara telephoned to tell me that Bode had finished the testing and had gotten mitochondrial DNA on almost every sample. Most of the genetic profiles were a mishmash of individuals. But six of the samples had the same mitochondrial DNA sequence profile component found on the Openshaw envelope.

"Markers" are locations. Markers in the Ripper/Sickert tests are where the base positions of DNA are located on the D loop sequence of the mitochondrial DNA—which is about as easy for most people to envision as it is for me to understand the mathematical equation for relativity, $E = mc^2$. An imposing challenge for DNA experts is to help the hoi polloi understand what DNA is and what test results mean. Posters showing matching fingerprints create a flurry of nods and "oh yes, I get it" looks from jurors. But the analysis of human blood—beyond its screaming fresh red or its old dark dried presence on clothing and weapons and at crime scenes—has always induced catatonia and pinpoint pupils in panicky eyes.

ABO blood-group typing was antenna-tangling enough. DNA blows mental transformers, and the hackneyed explanation that a DNA "fingerprint" or profile looks like a bar code on a soup can in the supermarket isn't helpful in the least. I can't envision my flesh and bones as billions of bar codes that can be scanned in a laboratory and come up as me. So I often use analogies, because I confess that without them I don't always comprehend the abstractions of science and medicine, even though I write about them for a living.

The swabbed samples in the Jack the Ripper case can be imagined as fifty-five sheets of white paper that are cluttered with thousands of different combinations of numbers. Most of the sheets of paper have smears, and illegible numbers, and mixtures of numbers that indicate they came from many different people. However, two sheets of paper each have a sequence of numbers that came from a single donor—or only one person: One sheet is James McNeill Whistler, and the other is a partial postage stamp on the back of a letter the Ripper wrote to Dr. Thomas Openshaw, the curator of the London Hospital Museum.

The Whistler sequence has nothing in common with any Ripper letter or any other non-Whistler item tested. But the Openshaw sequence is found in five other samples. These five samples are not single-donor, as far as we can tell at this point, and show a mixture of other base positions or "locations" in the mitochondrial region. This could mean that the sample was contaminated by the DNA of other people. A drawback in our testing is that the ever-elusive Walter Sickert has yet to offer us his DNA profile. When he was cremated, our best evidence went up in flames. Unless we eventually find a premortem sample of his blood, skin, hair, teeth, or bones, we will never resurrect Walter Richard Sickert in a laboratory. But we may have found pieces of him.

The clean single-donor sequence recovered from the partial stamp on the back of the Openshaw envelope is our best basis of comparison. Its sequence is the three markers, 16294—73—263, or the locations of DNA base positions in the mitochondrial regions—rather much as A7, G10,

D12, and so on indicate places on a map. The five samples that have this same 16294—73—263 single-donor Openshaw sequence are the front stamp from the Openshaw envelope; an Ellen Sickert envelope; an envelope from a Walter Sickert letter; a stamp from a Walter Sickert envelope; and a Ripper envelope with a stain that tests positive for blood, but which may be too degraded to determine if it is human.

The results from the Ellen Sickert letter could be explained if she moistened the envelope and stamp with the same sponge her husband, Walter, used—assuming either one of them used a sponge. Or Sickert might have touched or licked the adhesive on the flap or stamp, perhaps because he mailed the letter for her.

Other samples contained one or two markers found in the single-donor Openshaw sequence. For example, a set of white overalls that Sickert wore while painting had a mixture of markers that included 73 and 263. What is startling about this result is that there was a result. The overalls are about eighty years old and had been washed, ironed, and starched before they were donated to the Tate Archive. I saw no point in swabbing around the collar, the cuffs, the crotch, and the armpits, but we did it anyway.

The Openshaw letter that yielded the mitochondrial DNA results was written on A Pirie & Sons stationery. The letter has a London postmark dated October 29, 1888, and reads:

ENVELOPE: Dr. Openshaw
Pathological curator
London Hospital
White chapel

LETTER: *Old boss you was rite it was*
the left kidny i was goin to
hopperate agin close to your
ospitle just as i was goin

to dror mi nife along of
er bloomin throte them
cusses of coppers spoilt
the game but i guess i wil
be on the job soon and will
send you another bit of
innerds Jack the ripper

O have you seen the devle
with his mikerscope and scalpul
a lookin at a Kidney
with a slide cocked up

One reason I believe this letter is genuine is that it is so blatantly contrived. The bad handwriting looks disguised and is jarringly inconsistent with the handwriting of someone with access to pen and ink and fine-quality watermarked stationery. The address on the envelope is literate, the spelling perfect, which is vastly different from the overblown illiteracy of the letter with its inconsistent misspellings, such as "kidny" and "Kidney," "wil" and "will," "of" and "o." Steward P. Evans and Keith Skinner point out in their extremely helpful book *Jack the Ripper: Letters from Hell* that the postscript in the Dr. Openshaw letter alludes to a verse in an 1871 Cornish folktale:

Here's to the devil,
With his wooden pick and shovel,
Digging tin by the bushel,
With his tail cock'd up!

An allusion to a Cornish folktale makes no sense if we are supposed to believe this Openshaw letter was written by an uneducated homicidal maniac who ripped a kidney from a victim and sent it off in the post.

Walter Sickert visited Cornwall as a boy. He painted in Cornwall when he was Whistler's apprentice. Sickert knew Cornwall and the Cornish people. He was well read and was familiar with folk tunes and music-hall songs. It is unlikely that a poor, uneducated person from London spent time in Cornwall or sat around in the slums reading Cornish folk-tales.

One could argue—and should—that the absence of a reliable known reference source, in this instance Walter Sickert's DNA, suggests we are assuming without conclusive scientific evidence that the single-donor sequence from the Openshaw letter was deposited by Walter Sickert, alias Jack the Ripper. We can't assume any such thing.

Although statistically the single-donor sequence excludes 99% of the population, in Dr. Ferrara's words, "The matching sequences might be a coincidence. They might not be a coincidence." At best, we have a "cautious indicator" that the Sickert and Ripper mitochondrial DNA sequences may have come from the same person.

CHAPTER FIFTEEN

A PAINTED LETTER

Walter Sickert was a forensic scientist's worst adversary. He was like a tornado tearing through a lab.

He created investigative chaos with his baffling varieties of papers, pens, paints, postmarks, and disguised handwritings, and by his constant moving about without leaving a trail through diaries, calendars, or dates on most of his letters and work. His knockout punch to forensic science was to decide to be cremated. When a body is burned at 1,800 degrees Fahrenheit, that's the end of DNA. If Sickert left behind samples of blood or hair that we could be certain were his, we have yet to find them.

Not even a pedigree of Sickert's DNA can be attempted because that would require a sample from his children or siblings. Sickert had no children. His sister had no children. As far as anyone can tell, none of his four brothers had children. To exhume Sickert's mother, father, or siblings on the remote chance that their mitochondrial DNA might have something in common with what Bode laboratories miraculously managed to conjure up from the genetic fragments of past lives we gave them would be ridiculous and unthinkable.

The Ripper case is not one to be conclusively solved by DNA or fingerprints, and in a way, this is good. Society has come to expect the wizardry of forensic science to solve all crimes, but without the human element of deductive skills, teamwork, very hard investigation, and smart prosecution, evidence means nothing. Had we gotten an irrefutable DNA match of a Sickert and a Ripper letter, any sharp defense lawyer would say that Sickert's writing a letter doesn't prove he murdered anyone. Perhaps he simply composed a number of Ripper letters because he had a wacky, warped sense of humor. A good prosecutor would counter that if Sickert wrote even one of those Ripper letters, he was in trouble, because the letters are confessional. In them, the Ripper claims to have murdered and mutilated people he calls by name, and he threatens to kill government officials and policemen.

The watermarks add yet another layer. To date, three Ripper letters and eight Sickert letters have the A Pirie & Sons watermark. It seems that from 1885 to 1887, the Sickerts' 54 Broadhurst Gardens stationery was A Pirie, and was folded at the middle like a greeting card. The front of the fold was bordered in pale blue, the embossed address also pale blue. The A Pirie & Sons watermark is centered on the crease. In the three Ripper letters, the stationery was torn along the crease and only half of the A Pirie & Sons watermark remains.

Unless Jack the Ripper was incredibly stupid, he would have removed the side of folded stationery that was embossed with the address. This is not to say that criminals haven't been known to make numbskull oversights, such as leaving a driving license at a crime scene or writing a "hold-up" note on a deposit slip that includes the bank robber's address and Social Security number. But Jack the Ripper did not make fatal errors, or he would have been caught at the time of his crimes.

Jack the Ripper was also arrogant and did not believe he would ever be caught. Sickert must not have been worried about the partial watermarks on the Ripper letters he wrote. Perhaps this was another "catch me if you can" taunt. The A Pirie & Sons watermarks we found on Sickert stationery include a watermarked date of manufacturing, and the three partial dates on the Ripper letters with the A Pirie & Sons watermark are 18 and 18 and 87. The 87, obviously, is 1887.

Repeated trips to archives turned up other matching watermarks that must not have worried Sickert, either. Letters Sickert wrote to Jacques-Emile Blanche in 1887 are on stationery with the address embossed in black, and a Joynson Superfine watermark. A search through the Blanche-Sickert correspondence in the Institut Bibliotheque de L'Institut de France in Paris shows that during the late summer and autumn of 1888 and in the spring of 1889, Sickert was still using Joynson Superfine paper with the return address of 54 Broadhurst Gardens either embossed with no color or in bright red with a red border.

Letters Ellen wrote to Blanche as late as 1893 with a 10 Glebe Place, Chelsea, return address are on stationery that also has the Joynson Superfine watermark. In the Whistler collection at Glasgow, there are seven Sickert letters with the Joynson Superfine watermarks, and it would appear that Sickert was using this stationery about the same time he was using A Pirie & Sons.

In the Sir William Rothenstein collection at Harvard University's Department of Manuscripts, I found two other Sickert letters with the Joynson Superfine watermark. Rothenstein was an artist and a writer, and a trusted enough friend of Sickert's that the latter felt comfortable asking him to lie under oath. During the late 1890s, Sickert had become friendly with a Madame Villain, a fishwife in Dieppe he referred to as "Titine." Although there was no evidence he committed adultery with her, she did supply him room and board and a space in her small home that he used as a studio. Whatever the nature of their relationship, it would have been used against him in court had he contested Ellen's divorce suit, which he did not. "If subpoenaed," he wrote to Rothenstein in 1899, during the divorce, "you might truly remain as you are in ignorance of Titine's very name. You might say I always call her 'Madame.' "

Both Joynson Superfine watermarked letters that Sickert wrote to Rothenstein are undated. One of them—oddly, written in German and Italian—is on stationery that must have belonged to Sickert's mother because the return address is hers. A second Joynson Superfine watermarked letter to Rothenstein, which includes mathematical scribbles and a cartoonish face and the word "ugh," has a return address of 10 Glebe Place, Chelsea, which is the same return address on Ellen Sickert's 1893 letter to Blanche. There is a Ripper letter at the PRO with a part Joynson mark. It would appear that Sickert used Joynson Superfine watermarked paper from the late 1880s through the late 1890s. I have found no letters with this watermark that date from after his divorce in 1899, when he moved to continental Europe.

Four letters catalogued in "The Whitechapel Murders" file at the Corporation of London Records Office were written on Joynson Superfine paper: October 8, 1888; October 16, 1888; January 29, 1889; and February 16, 1889. Two of these letters are signed "Nemo." Three other letters with no watermarks are also signed "Nemo." On October 4, 1888 (four days before the first "Nemo" letter was written to the City of London Police), *The Times* published a letter to the editor that was signed "Nemo." In it the writer described "mutilations, cutting off the nose and ears, ripping up the body, and cutting out certain organs—the heart, & c.—. . ." The writer continued:

> My theory would be that some man of his class has been hocussed and then robbed of his savings (often large), or, as he considers, been in some way greatly injured by a prostitute—perhaps one of the earlier victims; and then has been led by fury and revenge to take the lives of as many of the same class as he can . . .
>
> Unless caught red-handed, such a man in ordinary life would be

harmless enough, polite, not to say obsequious, in his manners, and about the last a British policeman would suspect.

But when the villain is primed with his opium, or bang, or gin, and inspired with his lust for slaughter and blood, he would destroy his defenceless victim with the ferocity and cunning of the tiger; and past impunity and success would only have rendered him the more daring and restless.

Your obedient servant

October 2

NEMO

I have already mentioned that Sickert's stage name when he was an actor was "Mr. Nemo."

Other unusual signatories in the some fifty letters at the Corporation of London Records Office are suspiciously reminiscent of those of some PRO Ripper letters: "Justitia," "Revelation," "Ripper," "Nemesis," "A Thinker," "May-bee," "A friend," "an accessary," and "one that has had his eyes opened." Quite a number of these fifty letters were written in October 1888 and also include both art and comments similar to those found in the Jack the Ripper letters at the PRO. For example, in a PRO letter to the Editor of the Daily News Office, October 1, 1888, the Ripper says, "I've got someone to write this for me." In an undated letter at the Corporation of London Records Office, the anonymous sender says, "I've got someone to write this for me."

Other "Whitechapel Murder" letters in the Corporation of London Records Office include a postcard dated October 3rd, with the anonymous sender using many of the same threats, words, and phrases found in Ripper letters at the PRO: "send you my victims ears"; "It amuses me that you think I am mad"; "Just a card to let you know"; "I will write to you again soon"; and "My bloody ink is running out." On October 6, 1888, "Anonymous" offers a suggestion that the killer might be keeping "the victims *silent* by pressure on certain nerves in the neck," and adds that an additional benefit to subduing the victim is that the killer can "preserve his own person and clothing comparatively unstained." In October 1888, an anonymous letter written in red ink uses the terms "spanky ass" and "Saucy Jacky" and promises to "send next ears I clip to Charly Warren."

An undated letter includes a bit of newspaper attached by a rusty paperclip. When my co-worker, Irene Shulgin, removed the cutting and turned it over, she found the phrase "author of works of art." In a letter dated October 7, 1888, the writer signs his name "Homo Sum," Latin for "I am a man." On October 9, 1888, an anonymous writer takes offense, once again, at being thought of as a lunatic: "Don't you rest content on the lunacy fad." Other anonymous letters offer tips to the police, encouraging officers to disguise themselves as women and wear "chain armour" or "light steel collars" under their clothes. An anonymous letter of October 20, 1888, claims the "motive for the crimes is hatred and spite against the authorities of Scotland Yard one of whom is marked as a victim."

In a July 1889 letter a writer signs his letter "Qui Vir," Latin for "Which Man." In a letter Sickert wrote to Whistler in 1897, he rather sarcastically refers to his former "impish master" as "Ecce homo," or "behold the man." In the "Qui Vir" letter, which is at the Corporation of London Records Office, the writer suggests that the killer is "able to choose a time to do the *murder* & get *back to his hiding* place." On September 11, 1889, an anonymous writer teases the police by saying he always travels in "third class Cerage" and "I ware black wiskers all over my face." Approximately twenty percent of these Corporation of London Records Office letters have watermarks, including, as I mentioned, the Joynson Superfine. I also found a Monckton's Superfine watermark on a letter signed "one of the public." A letter Sickert wrote to Whistler in the mid to late 1880s also has a Monckton's Superfine watermark.

Certainly, I wouldn't dare claim that these letters were written by Sickert or even Jack the Ripper, but the anonymous communications fit the

THE ILLUSTRATED LONDON NEWS

No. 2454.—VOL. LXXXVIII. SATURDAY, MAY 1, 1886. WITH EXTRA SUPPLEMENT | SIXPENCE

"Dear Boss." Many of the Ripper letters were addressed to Metropolitan Police Commissioner Charles Warren. *Collection of Patricia Cornwell.*

Falsely accused: The Duke of Clarence. His response to blackmail was money, not murder. *Collection of Patricia Cornwell.*

A.
Prefix ______ Code ______
Office of Origin and Service Instructions.

POST OFFICE TELEGRAPHS.
(Inland Telegrams.)

Words. | Sent At ______ M. | Charge. | To ______ | By ______

No. of Message ______
For Postage Stamps.
The Stamps ... affixed by the Sender.
LONDON E.D. 5 NO 21 88 8
A Receipt for the Charges on this Telegram can be obtained, price Twopence.

NOTICE.—This Telegram will be accepted for transmission subject to the Regulations made pursuant to the 2nd Section of the Telegraph Act, 1885, and to the Notice printed at the back hereof.

12 words, 6D. Every additional word, ½D. Every word telegraphed is charged for, whether in addresses or text.

TO { Inspector Abberline Scotland Yard

Jack the Ripper wishes to
give himself up will Abberline
communicate with him at number
39 Cutler Street Houndsditch with
this end in view

FROM { Jack the Ripper
This is written with the "Blood of Kelly" all Long Liz's blood is used up

The Name and Address of the Sender, IF NOT TO BE TELEGRAPHED, should be written in the Space provided at the Back of the Form.

(PRINTED BY McCORQUODALE & Co. LIMITED.)

Telegram from the Ripper to Inspector Abberline. Sickert was extremely fond of sending telegraphs—and so was the Ripper. © *Public Record Office, London.*

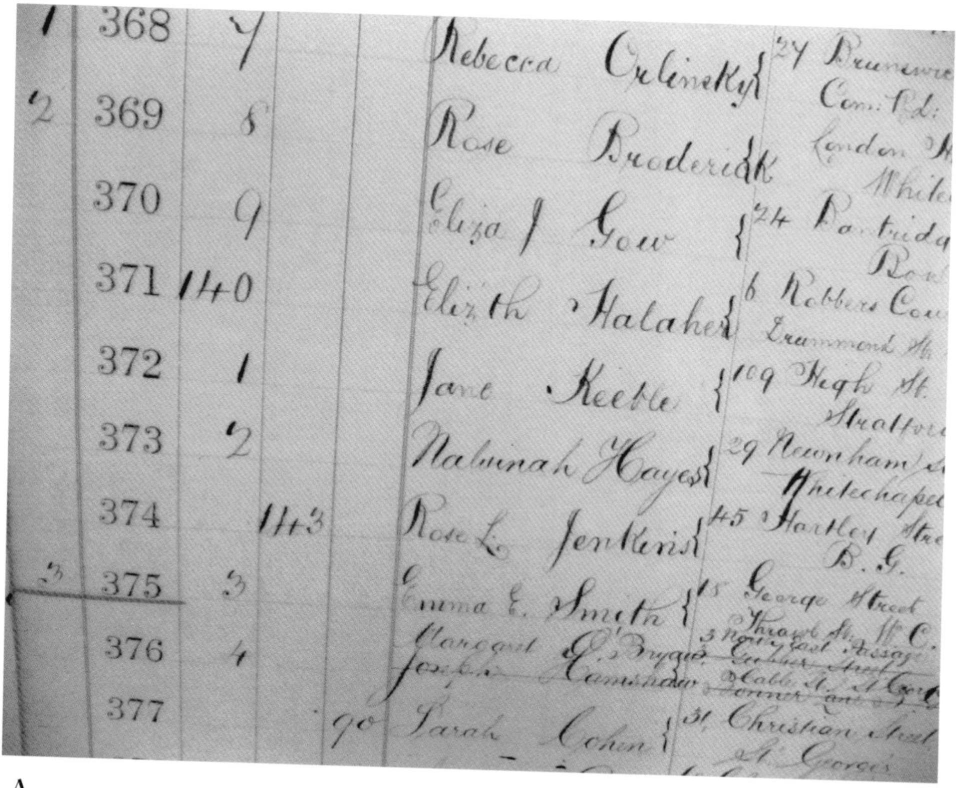

1	368	7		Rebecca Orlinsky	24 Brunswic… Com: Rd:
2	369	8		Rose Broderick	London H… White…
	370	9		Eliza J Gow	24 Partrida… Ro…
	371	140		Eliz'th Halaher	6 Robbers Cou… Drummond St
	372	1		Jane Keeble	109 High St. Stratfor…
	373	2		Malvinah Hayes	29 Newnham S… Whitechapel
	374		143	Rose L. Jenkins	45 Hartley Stre… B. G.
3	375	3		Emma E. Smith	15 George Street Thrawl St. W. C.
	376	4		Margaret O'Bryan	3 … Passage
				Joseph Hamshaw	…
	377		90	Sarah Cohen	31 Christian Street St George's

A view of the Royal London Hospital Patient Record Book. The hospital was the only one in the East End. I believe that none of the Ripper's victims survived long enough to be admitted. *Royal London Hospital Archives.*

44

Why I did not write my Reminiscences when I retired from the Metropolitan Police.

I think it is just as well to record here the reason why as from the various cuttings from the newspapers as well as the many other matters that I was called upon to investigate – that never became public property – it must be apparent that I could write many things that would be very interesting to read.

At the time I retired from the service the Authorities were very much opposed to retired Officers writing anything for the press as previously some retired Officers had from time to time been very indiscreet in what they had caused to be published and to my knowledge had been called upon

Pages 44 and 45 of Inspector Abberline's private clipping book. Abberline headed the Ripper investigation, but never revealed how he worked the cases or how he felt about failing to solve the most notorious crimes of his career. *With kind permission of the Metropolitan Police Service.*

45 (2)

upon to explain their conduct and in fact they had been threatened with actions for libel.

Apart from that there is no doubt the fact that in describing what you did in detecting certain crimes you are putting the Criminal Classes on their guard and in some cases you may be absolutely telling them how to commit crime.

As an example in the finger Print detection you find now the expert thief wears gloves.

F. G. Abberline

I am Jack the ripper

Catch me if you can

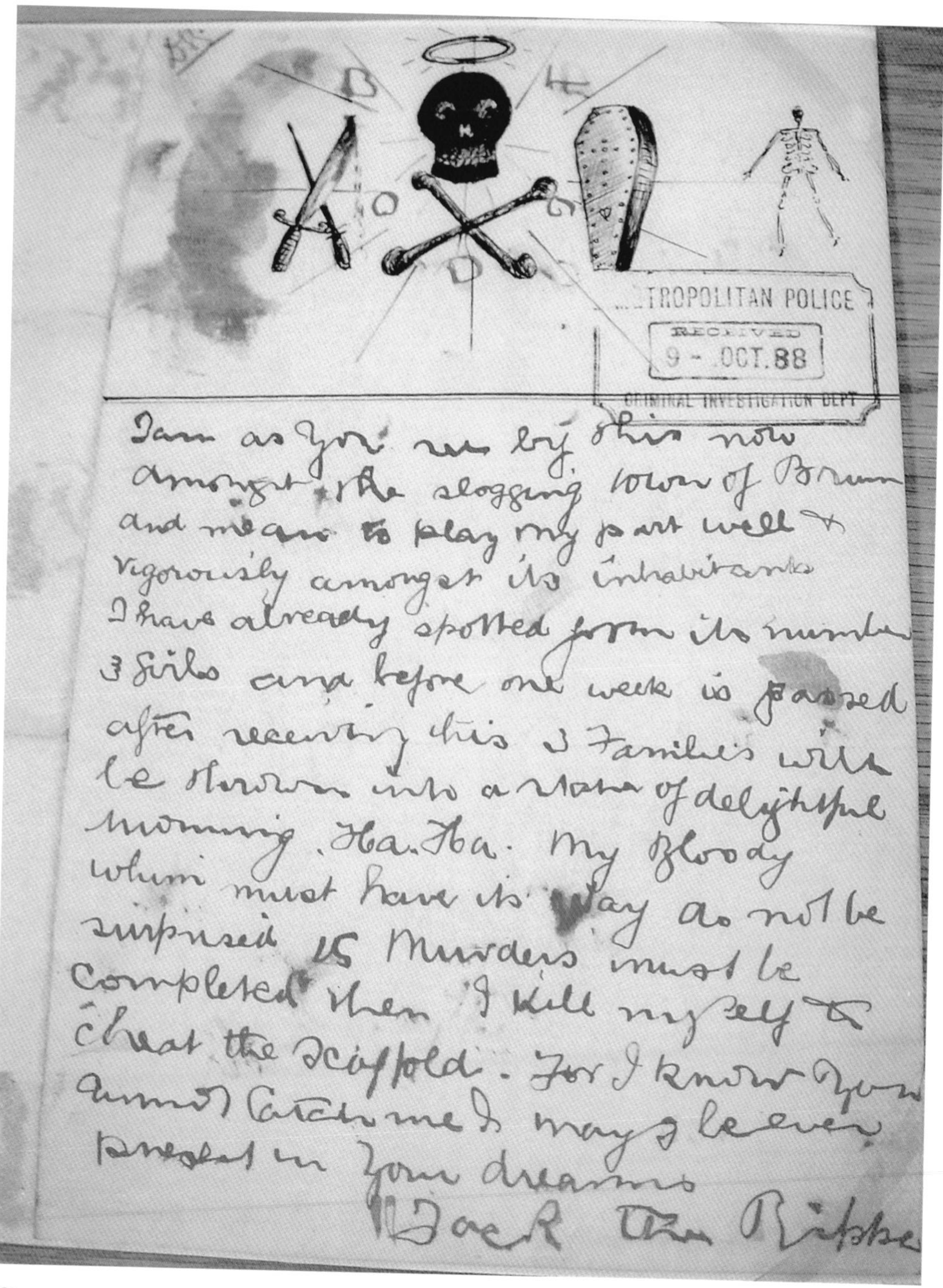

...TROPOLITAN POLICE
RECEIVED
9 - OCT.88
CRIMINAL INVESTIGATION DEPT

I am as you see by this now
amongst the slogging town of Brum
and mean to play my part well &
vigorously amongst its inhabitants
I have already spotted from its number
3 girls and before one week is passed
after receiving this 3 Familie's will
be thrown into a state of delightful
morning. Ha. Ha. My Bloody
whim must have its way as not be
surprised 15 Murders must be
completed then I kill myself to
cheat the scaffold. For I know you
cannot catch me & may be even
present in your dreams

Jack the Ripper

Some art experts recognize a professional artistic hand and Sickert's technique in what may at first glance appear to be crude drawings in these three Ripper letters. © *Public Record Office, London.*

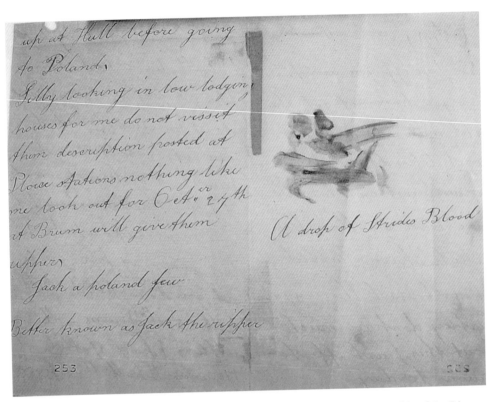

up at Hull before going
to Poland,
Lilly looking in low lodgin
houses for me do not vissit
them description posted at
Ploice stations nothing like
me look out for Oct.er 27th
at Brum will give them
ripper
Jack a poland Jew
Better known as Jack the ripper

A drop of Strides Blood

253

Art and paper experts now believe that what was once assumed to be blood in Ripper letters is actually consistent with etching ground that was finger painted or applied with a paintbrush. © *Public Record Office, London.*

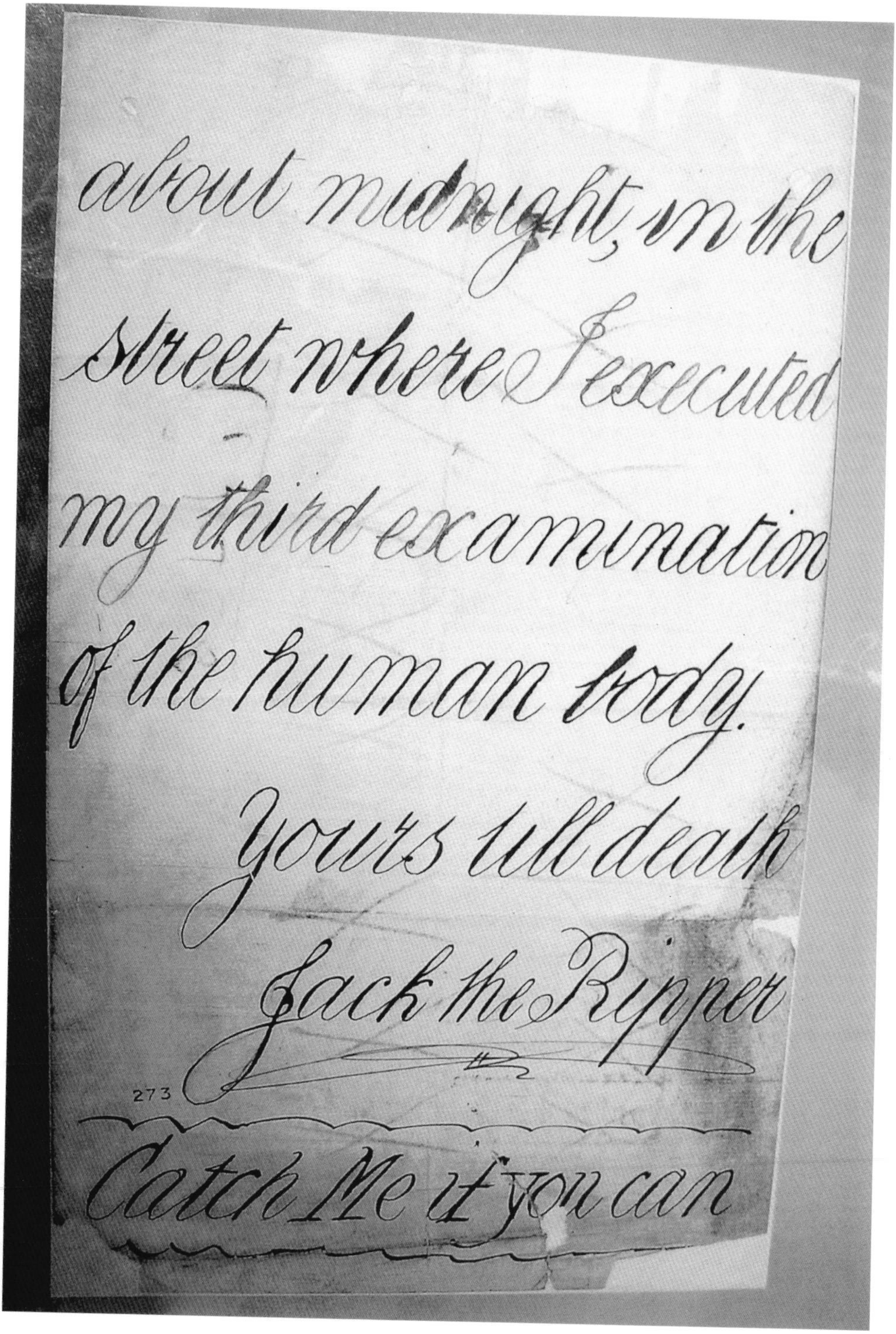

about midnight, in the street where I executed my third examination of the human body.

Yours till death

Jack the Ripper

273

Catch Me if you can

Ripper letter written with a paintbrush. © *Public Record Office, London.*

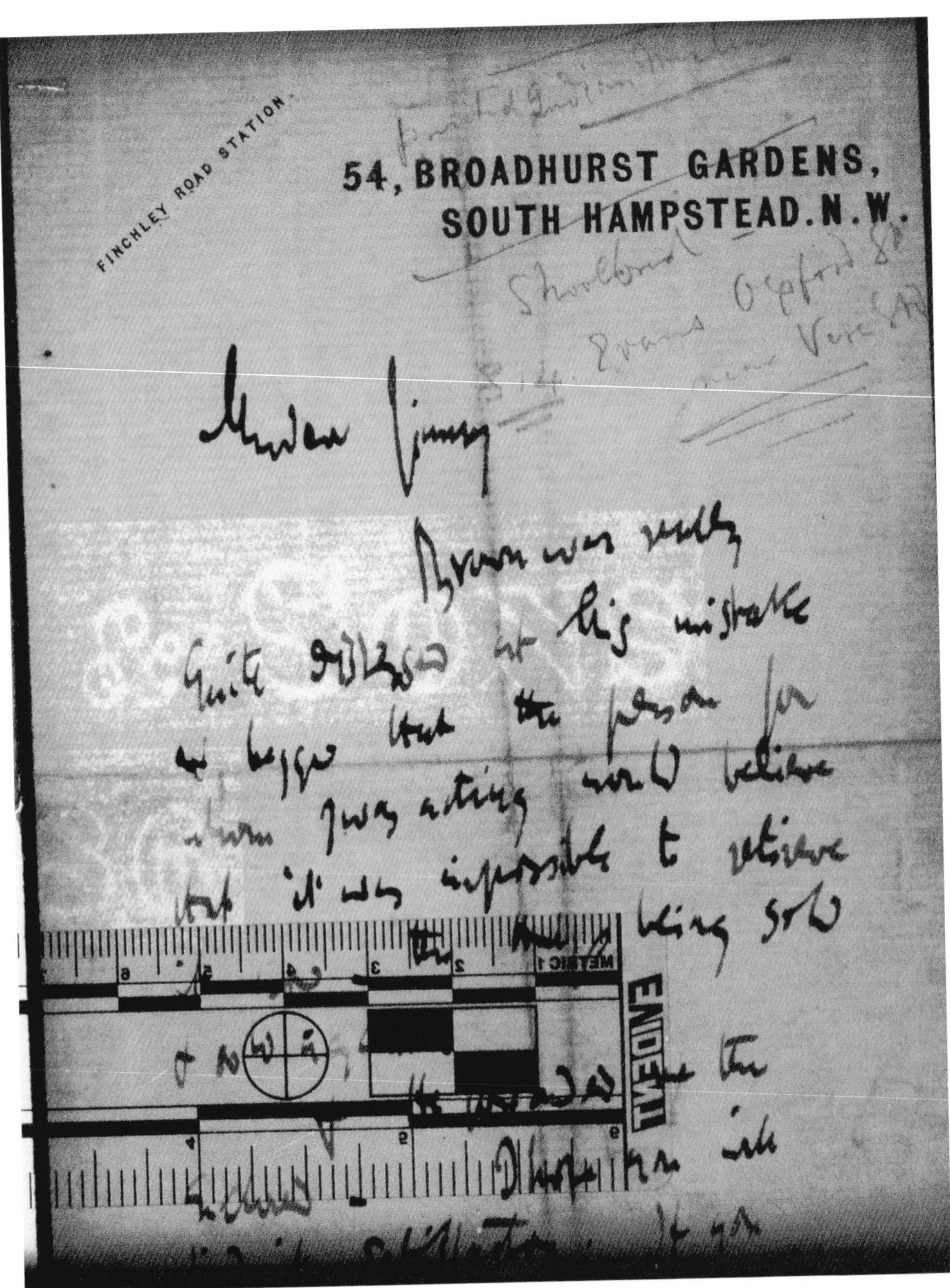

FINCHLEY ROAD STATION.

54, BROADHURST GARDENS,
SOUTH HAMPSTEAD. N.W.

My dear Jimmy

The "Dr. Openshaw" Ripper letter (right) with a watermark that matches the watermark in a "Dear Jimmy" letter Sickert wrote to Whistler (above). *Right, Royal London Hospital Archives; above, Permission of Special Collections Department, Glasgow University Library.*

Old boss you was rite it was
the left kidny i was goin to
hoperate agin close to your
ospitle just as i was going
to drop mi nife along of
bloomin throat them
cusses of coppers spoilt
the game but i guess i wil
be on the job soon and will
send you another bit of
innerds Jack the ripper

O have you seen the devle
with his mikerscope and scalpul
a lookin at a kidney
with a slide cocked up

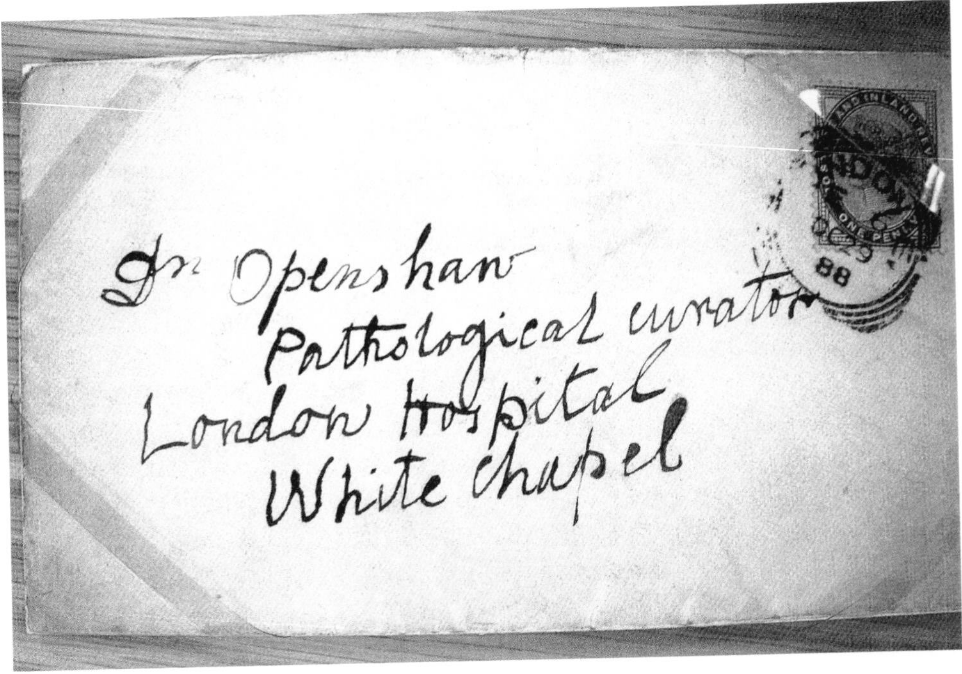

The oldest DNA ever tested in a criminal investigation yielded a mitochondrial DNA sequence from the backs of stamps on the Dr. Openshaw letter's envelope that is a component of mitochondrial DNA sequences found on another Ripper envelope and two Sickert envelopes. *Royal London Hospital Archives.*

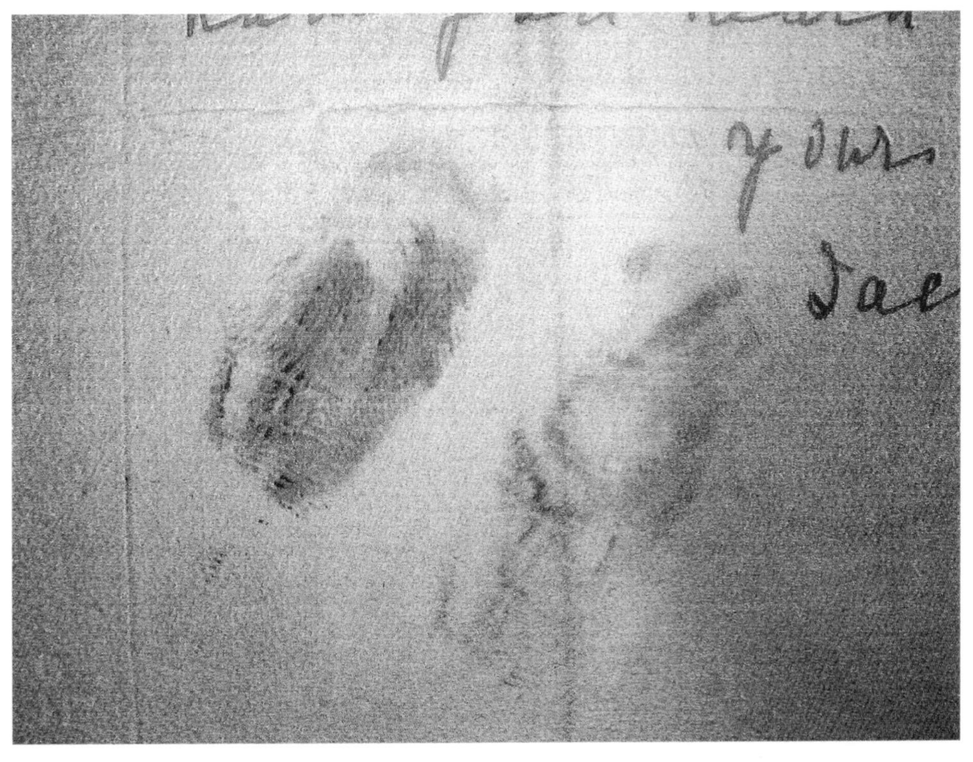

The Ripper's fingerprints, on a letter mailed to the Metropolitan Police in 1896. © *Public Record Office, London.*

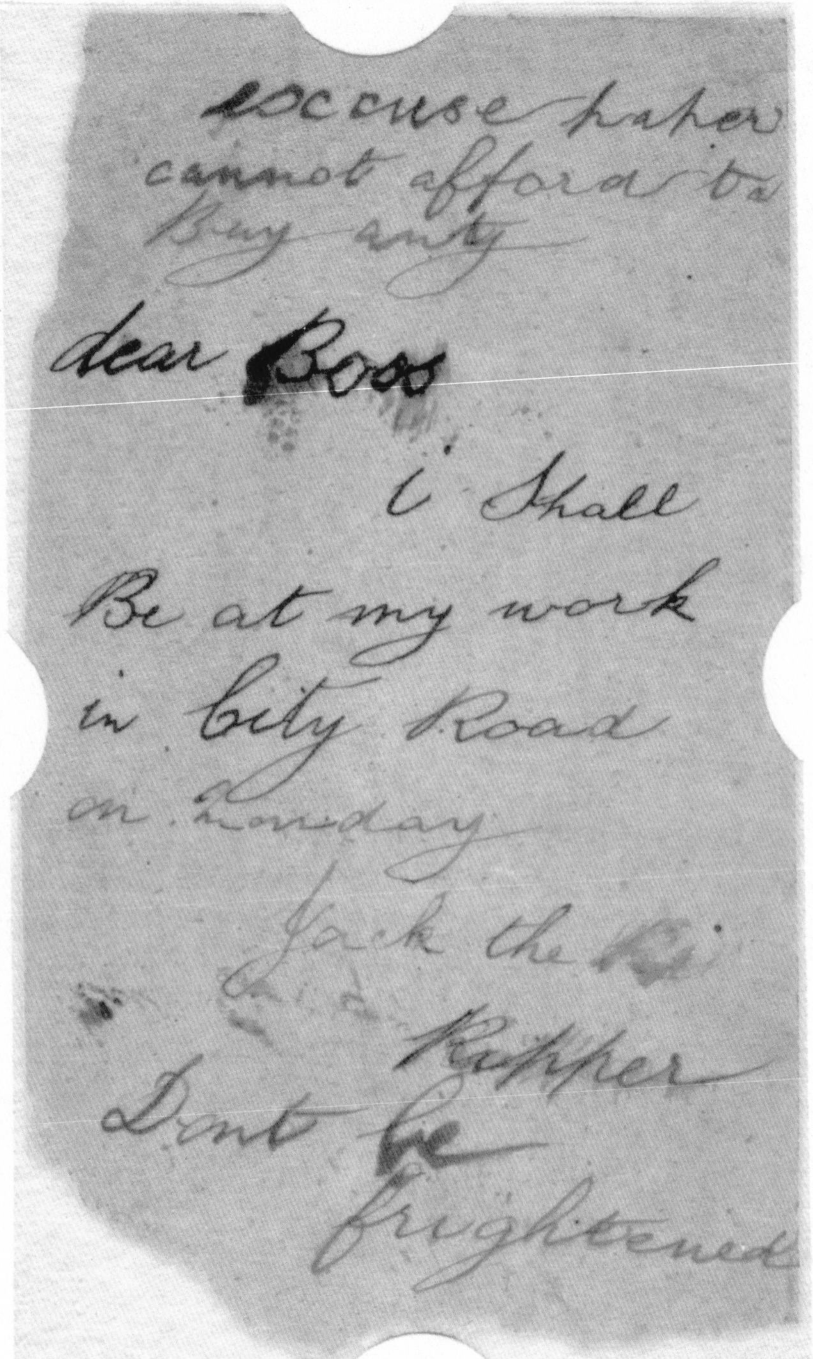

excuse paper
cannot afford to
buy any

dear Boss

i Shall
Be at my work
in City Road
on Monday
Jack the
Ripper
Dont be
frightened

A Ripper letter on a torn bit of cheap paper, with the note that he can't afford stationery. © *Public Record Office, London.*

Jack the Ripper's Bedroom, painted by Sickert in 1908. It is a view of his bedroom in the house where he was living at the time Emily Dimmock was murdered. *Original resides with Manchester City Art Gallery, Manchester.*

Ennui by Sickert. Leaning over the left shoulder of the woman in the painting on the wall appears to be the partial face of a man coming up behind her.

profile of a violent psychopath who taunts the police and tries to insert him- or herself into the investigation. Watermarks and language aside, the problem of handwriting remains. The amazing variety found in the Ripper letters has been a source of hot debate. Many people, including forensic documents examiners, have argued that it is not possible for one person to write in so many hands.

This is not necessarily true, says paper historian and forensic paper analyst Peter Bower, one of the most respected paper experts in the world, and perhaps best known for his work on the papers used by artists as various as Michelangelo, J.M.W. Turner, Constable, and others—as well as for determining that the notorious Jack the Ripper diary was a fraud. Bower has assisted in our examination of the Ripper/Sickert letters. He says he has seen "good calligraphers" who can write in an incredible number of different hands, but "it takes extraordinary skill." His wife, Sally Bower, is a much respected letterer, or person who designs and draws lettering. Although she is not a handwriting expert, she has a different perspective because she is an expert in how a person forms the letters strung together in words. When she looked through Ripper letters with her husband, she immediately connected a number of letters through quirks and how the hand made the writing. I have no doubt that Sickert had an amazing ability to write in many different hands, but his disguised writings are becoming less concealing as the investigation progresses.

Peter Bower's vast knowledge of paper obviously includes watermarks; his opinion of those we have found is that A Pirie & Sons and Joynson Superfine "would not have been the commonest paper." But the watermarks were not necessarily uncommon in the late nineteenth century. Monckton's Superfine was a rarer watermark and Monckton's also manufactured artists' drawing and watercolor paper.

Matching watermarks do not necessarily mean the paper was from the same batch, and almost none of the Sickert letters or Sickert/Ripper letters are from the same batch, says Peter Bower, who spent days going through Sickert and Ripper archives and measuring the paper using a 30×

lens to study the measurements, fiber content, and distances between chain lines. When paper is manufactured by machine, as A Pirie and Joynson and Monckton's were, the paper comes from one batch, meaning it is from the same roll. Another batch with the same watermark and a fiber content that is relatively the same may have slight differences in measurements of the sheets of paper due to the speed of drying or the way the machine cut it.

These characteristics—measurements and spacing between the wire the paper was formed on—are the paper's Y profile, and matching Y profiles mean the paper came from the same batch. Bower says it is not unusual for an individual to have stationery that comes from many batches, and that even when the paper is ordered from the stationer, there could be different batches mixed in, although the watermarks and embossing or engraving are the same. The discrepancies in the Sickert and Ripper letters pertain to their measurements. For example, the "Dear Openshaw" letter with the A Pirie watermark is from the same batch as the November 22nd A Pirie Ripper letter posted from London, but not from the same batch as the other November 22nd A Pirie letter supposedly posted from Manchester. Clearly, the Ripper had a mixture of A Pirie batches when he wrote these November 22nd letters, unless one wishes to make the case that there were two different individuals who just happened to write Ripper letters on A Pirie & Sons paper of the same type and color on November 22nd.

Differences in measurements can, in some instances, be attributed to conservation. When paper is heated by applying a protective membrane, for example, the paper shrinks slightly. More probable is that the differences in measurements can be explained by reorders from the stationer. During the late 1880s, personalized stationery was usually ordered in a quire, or twenty-four sheets, including unprinted second sheets. A reorder of the same personalized stationery on the same type of paper with the same watermark could quite easily come from a different batch. Or perhaps the stationer used a different standard size, such as *Post quarto*, which was approximately seven by nine inches, or *Commercial Note*, which was eight by five inches, or *Octavo Note*, which was nominally seven by four-and-a-half inches.

An example of a discrepancy in paper size is a Ripper letter with a Joynson Superfine watermark that was sent to the City of London Police. The torn half of the folded stationery measures $6\frac{15}{16}$ inches by $9\frac{9}{10}$ inches. Another Ripper letter on the same type of paper with the same watermark was sent to the Metropolitan Police and that stationery is *Commercial Note*, or eight by five inches. A Sickert letter written on Monckton's Superfine that we examined in Glasgow measures seven and one-eighth inches by nine inches, while a Ripper letter sent to the City of London Police on the same type of paper with a matching Monckton's Superfine watermark measures seven and one-eighth inches by eight and nine-tenths. Most likely, this suggests the Monckton's Superfine stationery is from different batches, but this by no means indicates it was from different Ripper letter-writers.

I point out these different paper batches only because a defense lawyer would. In fact, paper of the same type and watermark but from different batches doesn't necessarily mean a setback in a case and, as Bower pointed out, having studied other artists' paper, he "would expect to find variations like this." Bower also discovered paper in Ripper letters that did not have variations, and because they also had no watermarks, these letters were not really noticed by anyone else. Two Ripper letters written to the Metropolitan Police and one Ripper letter written to the City of London Police are on matching very cheap pale blue paper—and for three letters to come from the same batch of paper strongly indicates that the same person wrote them, just as matching watermarks, especially three different types of matching watermarks, are hard to dismiss as coincidence.

Our discovery of "matching" watermarks has been a source of great excitement for all of us working the Ripper case, but I must admit that a not-so-good watermark moment came early in the investigation. The head of conservation at the Public Record Office, Mario Aleppo, contacted me and said his staff had found numerous other A Pirie & Sons watermarks and I might want to have a look. I immediately returned to London and discovered to my horror that the A Pirie & Sons watermarks were not on Ripper letters but on the stationery the Metropolitan Police were using at the time. I was shocked. For a moment, I was completely unnerved and thought my life might disintegrate right before my eyes. There has always been a theory that Jack the Ripper was a cop.

The A Pirie & Sons watermark on the Metropolitan Police stationery is the only other non-Sickert/Ripper-related A Pirie watermark I have found during my research, but I am happy to report that the watermark on the Metropolitan Police stationery is quite different from the one on the Ripper and the Sickert letters. The police stationery watermark has no date and includes the words LD and Register. The paper is of a different quality and color. It is eight by eleven inches and not greeting-card size. Besides the difference in the wording and design of the watermarks, the police paper is *wove* and the Sickert/Ripper paper is *laid*.

The firm Alexander Pirie & Sons, Ltd., got its start in the paper-making business in 1770 in Aberdeen, and its rapid growth and respected reputation resulted in the acquisition of cotton mills, plants, and factories in London, Glasgow, Dublin, Paris, New York, St. Petersburg, and Bucharest. A Pirie didn't become a separate company until 1864, and from this information one might presume that there was no A Pirie & Sons watermark prior to that date. However, existing records in Aberdeen do not indicate exactly when A Pirie began using its name on watermarks. A Pirie became a limited-liability company in 1882, merged with another firm in 1922, and went out of business at some point in the 1950s.

The records of A Pirie & Sons are preserved in a strong room at the Stoneywood Mills in Aberdeen. Keenly aware of my limitations as a paper-manufacturing or stationery expert, I asked antiquarian books and documents researcher Joe Jameson if he would go to Aberdeen and look through thousands of A Pirie records. For two cold, rainy days, he dug through boxes and was able to ascertain migraine-producing details about lime waste, rag boiling, paper machines, how many tons of soda were ordered, sediment removed from river water, shareholders, sketches of trademarks, types of paper manufactured—just about anything one might want to know about how paper was made from the late 1700s until the 1950s.

Over the better part of a century, tons of Alexander Pirie & Sons paper were shipped to London and other parts of the world. This prestigious company was proprietorial and did not hesitate to sue if another manufacturer tried to delude the public into thinking its paper was made by A Pirie & Sons. The obvious question in this case is exactly what I asked Peter Bower: How common was the A Pirie watermark found on the three Ripper and eight Sickert letters?

After a thorough search of the company records, I can only say with certainty that while the paper may not be uncommon, as Bower said, it might be somewhat uncommon as personal stationery. It seems that A Pirie paper was used primarily for the printing of bankers' and other business ledgers, business stationery, and nonwatermarked printing and lithographic printing paper. I have no idea which stationers the Sickerts used when Walter or Ellen ordered the blue-bordered stationery printed on A Pirie & Sons paper. The shop may not have been in London, and its records may no longer exist. I also can't say how unique their particular watermark was, but it isn't to be found in an A Pirie & Sons list of fifty-six trademark designs that were in the Aberdeen records.

But there is a very good chance I didn't see their watermark in the examples I found because the Aberdeen records might be incomplete. I do know that in the only A Pirie & Sons catalogue I managed to get hold of, the list of their products for 1900 shows twenty-three designs, and the watermark of interest is not among them.

Walter Sickert knew about watermarks. He knew about paper. It is hard to imagine him writing Ripper letters and not being aware of the watermark. It is hard to imagine that Sickert wouldn't have been aware of the type of paper he was using, including good paper such as Monckton's Superfine and art paper. He may have used his A Pirie & Sons and Joynson Superfine personal stationery because he assumed that even if the police did notice the partial watermarks on the torn paper, they probably would not have linked a Ripper letter to the charming gentleman-artist Walter Sickert, who was not a suspect at the time. One does have to wonder, however, what might have happened had the police published the partial watermarks and printed them on posters.

Probably nothing. If Sickert's friends—or Ellen—recognized a partial watermark, they weren't likely to link Walter Sickert with Jack the Ripper. What surprises me most is that I cannot find any evidence that the police noticed the watermarks, and they should have. More than ten percent of the 211 Ripper letters at the Public Record Office have watermarks or partial ones. Not all watermarked paper is expensive, but it also isn't associated with the East End paupers who police and the press believed were writing most of the Ripper letters.

Sickert was a magpie with paper. He did not waste it. If he had run out of paper, he would paste together remnants of whatever he could find and send a note scrawled on a paper patchwork quilt. In several letters to Whistler, Sickert jotted, "No paper in the house," especially if he was approaching the Master about needing money.

"Excuse paper cannot afford to Buy any dear Boss," the Ripper wrote on November 15, 1888.

Sickert made sketches on a variety of papers, from coarse brown toilet paper to vellum. Paying attention to types of paper and watermarks in criminal and civil investigations certainly was not new technology in 1888. Why no policeman or detective observed what many of the Jack the Ripper letters were written on or with is baffling and inexcusable. Someone should have noticed that the "ink" was actually paint, and "pens" were really paintbrushes or drawing pens with large nibs. Microscopy, infrared spectrophotometry, pyrolysis-gas chromatography, mass spectrometry, x-ray fluorescence, and neutron activation analysis were not required to figure out that much.

One explanation for these oversights is that until now police and others dismissed the letters as hoaxes. Photocopies and photographs aren't the best means of seeing the delicate feathering of brushes, or the beautiful purple, blue, red, burgundy, orange, sienna, and sepia colors used to write words and make splashes and strokes on these letters from so-called illiterates and lunatics. It takes an art expert's eye to detect that smears thought to be blood are really etching ground, and if Dr. Ferrara had not used an Omnichrome alternate light source and a variety of different filters, we would not have been able to coax eradicated writing out from under its cover of heavy black ink.

In one letter, the Ripper sets the police a fill-in-the-blanks challenge for his "name" and "address," but as a "Ha Ha" he blots out the "information" with dark black rectangles and coffin shapes. Under the black ink the Omnichrome revealed *ha* and the barely legible and partial signature *Ripper.* This sort of diabolical teasing is typical of someone who believes that anything "hidden" will puzzle the hell out of the police. Another bit of Ripper fun was to take an envelope and glue a strip of paper on the front of it, implying that the envelope was recycled and the original recipient's name is under the strip.

Dr. Ferrara performed long, delicate surgery to lift that strip. There was nothing under it. But the Ripper's mean-spirited, mocking teases failed to bring him the satisfaction he craved. There is no sign, for example, that anyone cared what was under that strip before Dr. Ferrara removed it 114 years after the Ripper sent the "joke" in the post. There is no hint that the police tried to figure out what was hidden under the shapes in heavy black ink.

It is easy to forget that in 1888 Walter Sickert wasn't on investigators' minds and that Scotland Yard did not have access to the likes of Peter and Sally Bower, art historian and Sickert expert Dr. Anna Gruetzner Robins, paper conservator Anne Kennett, and curator of the Sickert archives Vada Hart. It has required intellectual sleuths such as these to discover that many of the Ripper letters contain telltale signs of Sickert's handwriting, and that in some cases, a single letter was written and drawn in several colors or mediums and with at least two different writing instruments, including colored pencils, lithographic crayons, and paintbrushes.

One Ripper communication received by the police on October 18, 1889, is on an eleven-by-fourteen-inch sheet of azure laid *foolscap* writing paper, the lettering first drawn in pencil, then beautifully painted over in brilliant red. Apparently no one thought it unusual that a lunatic or an illiterate or even a prankster would elaborately *paint* a letter that reads:

> *Dear Sir*
>
> *I shall be in Whitechapel on the 20th of this month—And will begin some very delicate work about midnight, in the street where I executed my third examination of the human body.*
>
> *Yours till death*
> *Jack the Ripper*
>
> *Catch Me if you can*
>
> *PS,* [postscript at the top of the page] *I hope you can read what I have written, and will put it* all *in the paper, not leave half out. If you can not see the letters let me know and I* will *write them biger.*

He misspells *bigger* as an illiterate would, and I don't believe the glaring inconsistency in a letter such as this one was an accident. Sickert was playing one of his little games and showing what "fools" the police were. An alert investigator certainly should have questioned why someone would correctly spell "delicate" and "executed" and "examination" and yet misspell the simple word "bigger." But details that seem so obvious to us now have the benefit of hindsight and the analysis of art experts. The only artist looking at those letters then was the artist who created them, and many of his letters are not letters at all, but professional designs and works of art that ought to be framed and hung in a gallery.

Sickert must have thought he had no reason to fear that the police would notice or question the artwork in his taunting, violent, and obscene letters. Or perhaps he assumed that even if a shrewd investigator like Abberline picked up on the uniqueness of some of the letters, the path would never lead northwest to 54 Broadhurst Gardens. After all, the police were "idiots." Most people were stupid and boring, and Sickert often said as much.

Nobody was as brilliant, clever, cunning, or fascinating as Walter Sickert, not even Whistler or Oscar Wilde, neither of whom he enjoyed competing with at dinners and other gatherings. Sickert just might not show up if he wasn't going to be the center of attention. He didn't hesitate to admit that he was a "snob" and divided the world into two classes of people: those who interested him and those who did not. As is typical of psychopaths, Sickert believed that no investigator was his match, and as is also true of these remorseless, scary people, his delusional thinking lured him into leaving far more incriminating clues along his trails than he probably ever imagined.

The distant locations associated with a number of Ripper letters only added to the supposition that most of the letters were hoaxes. The police had no reason to believe that this East End murderer might be in one city one day and in another the next. No one seemed interested in considering that perhaps the Ripper really did move around and that perhaps there might be a link between these cities.

Many were on Henry Irving's theater company's schedule, which was published in the newspapers daily. Every spring and autumn, Irving's company toured major theater cities such as Glasgow, Edinburgh, Manchester, Liverpool, Bradford, Leeds, Nottingham, Newcastle, and Plymouth, to name a few. Often Ellen Terry made the grueling journeys. "I shall be in a railway train from Newcastle to Leeds," she dismally reports in a letter written during one of these tours, and one can almost feel her exhaustion.

Most of these cities also had major racecourses, and several Ripper letters mention horse racing and give the police a few lucky betting tips. Sickert painted pictures of horse racing and was quite knowledgeable about the sport. In the March 19, 1914, *New Age* literary journal, he published an article he titled "A Stone Ginger," which was racing slang for "an absolute certainty," and he tossed in a few other bits of racing slang for good measure: "welsher" and "racecourse thief" and "sporting touts." Racecourses would have been a venue where Sickert could disappear into the crowd, especially if he was wearing one of his disguises and the race was in a city where he wasn't likely to encounter anybody he knew. At the races, prostitutes were plentiful.

Horse racing, gambling in casinos, and boxing were interests of Sickert's, although very little has been written about them in the books and articles I have seen. When the Ripper uses the term "Give up the sponge" in a letter that art experts believe Sickert wrote, is this a peek into Sickert's personality or simply his thoughtless use of a cliché? Is there any meaning to be found in the murky self-portrait that Sickert painted in 1908 that features him in a studio standing behind what is supposed to be a plaster torso of a boxer but looks more like a female who is decapitated, her limbs raggedly severed? Is there any significance in the reference in another Ripper letter to "Bangor Street," an address that doesn't exist in London, but Bangor is the home of a racecourse in Wales?

While I have no evidence that Sickert bet on horse races, I don't have any fact to say he didn't. Gambling may have been a secret addiction. Certainly that would help explain how he managed to go through money so quickly. By the time he and the parsimonious Ellen divorced, she was financially crippled and would never recover. Sickert's organized brain seemed to fail him when it came to finances. He thought nothing of hiring a cab and leaving it waiting all day. He gave away armfuls of paintings—

sometimes to strangers—or let the canvases rot in his studios. He never earned much, but he had access to Ellen's money—even after their divorce—and then to the money of other women who took care of him, including his next two wives.

Sickert was generous to his brother Bernhard, who was a failed artist. He rented numerous rooms at a time, bought painting supplies, read several newspapers daily, must have had quite a wardrobe for his many disguises, was a devotee of the theaters and music halls, and traveled. But most of what he bought and rented was shabby and cheap, and he wasn't likely to go for the best seats in the house or travel first class. I don't know how much he gave away, but after their divorce, Ellen wrote, "To give him money is like giving it to a child to light a fire with."

She believed him to be so financially irresponsible—for reasons she never cited—that after their divorce she conspired with Jacques-Emile Blanche to buy Sickert's paintings. Blanche began purchasing them and she secretly reimbursed him. Sickert "must *never never* suspect that it comes from me," Ellen wrote to Blanche. "I shall tell no one"—not even her sister Janie, in whom she had always confided. Ellen knew what Janie thought of Sickert and his exploitative ways. She also knew that helping her former husband was not really helping him. No matter what he got, it would never be enough. But she could not seem to help herself when it came to helping him.

"He is never out of my mind day or night," Ellen wrote to Blanche in 1899. "You know what he is like—a child where money is concerned. Will you again be as kind as you were before & buy one of Walter's pictures at the right moment to be of most use to him? And will you not forget that this will be of no good unless you insist on arranging how the money is to be spent. He borrowed £600 from his brother in law (who is a poor man) & he ought to pay him interest on the sum. *But I cannot.*"

Addiction to drugs and alcohol ran in Sickert's family. He probably had an addictive predisposition, which would help to explain why he avoided alcohol in his younger years and then abused it later on. It would be risky to say that Sickert had a gambling problem. But money seemed to vanish when he touched it, and while the mention of horse racing and the cities where courses were located in the Ripper letters does not constitute "proof," these details pique our curiosity.

Sickert could have done pretty much whatever he pleased. His career did not require him to keep regular hours. He did not have to account to anyone, especially now that his apprenticeship with Whistler had ended and Sickert was no longer bound to do as the Master demanded. In the autumn of 1888, the Master was on his honeymoon and neither knew nor cared what Sickert did with his days. Ellen and Janie were in Ireland—not that Ellen had to be away when Sickert decided to vanish for a night or a week. Disappearing in Britain was relatively easy, as long as the trains were running. It was no great matter to cross the English Channel in the morning and have dinner in France that evening.

Whatever caused Sickert's chronic "financial muddle," to borrow Ellen's words, it was serious enough to push her to the extraordinary lengths of secretly funneling money his way after she divorced him for adultery and desertion. It was so serious that Sickert died in 1942 with only £135 to his name.

CHAPTER SIXTEEN

STYGIAN BLACKNESS

Five hours after Annie Chapman's body was carried into the Whitechapel mortuary, Dr. George Phillips arrived and found she had been stripped and washed. Furious, he demanded an explanation.

Robert Mann, the mortuary supervisor who had caused so much trouble in Mary Ann Nichols's case, replied that workhouse authorities had instructed two nurses to undress and clean the body. No police officers or doctors had witnessed this, and as the angry Dr. Phillips looked around the mortuary, he noticed Annie's clothing piled on the floor in a corner. His earlier admonition that the body was not to be touched by inmates, nurses, or anyone else unless the police instructed otherwise had had little effect on Mann. The inmate had heard all this before.

The mortuary was nothing more than a cramped, filthy, stinking shed with a scarred wooden table darkened by old blood. In the summer it was stuffy and warm, and in the winter it was so cold Mann could barely bend his fingers. What a job his was, Mann must have thought, and maybe the doctor should have been grateful that two nurses had saved him some trouble. Besides, it didn't take a doctor to see what had killed the poor woman. Her head was barely attached to her neck and she had been gutted like a pig hanging in a butcher's shop. Mann didn't pay much attention as Dr. Phillips continued to vent his disgust, complaining that his working conditions were not only unsuitable but also dangerous to his health.

The doctor's point would be made more fully during the inquest. Coroner Wynne Baxter announced to jurors and the press that it was a travesty that there was no proper mortuary in the East End. If any place in London needed an adequate facility for handling the dead, it was certainly the impoverished East End, where in nearby Wapping, bodies recovered from the Thames had "to be put in boxes" for lack of anywhere else to take them, said Baxter.

There had once been a mortuary in Whitechapel, but it had been destroyed when a new road was built. For one reason or another, London officials hadn't gotten around to building a new facility to take care of the dead, and the problem wasn't one that would soon be addressed. As we used to say when I worked in the medical examiner's office, "Dead people don't vote or pay taxes." Dead paupers don't lobby politicians for funding. Even though death is the great equalizer, it doesn't make all dead people equal.

Dr. Phillips settled down and began his examination of Annie Chapman's body. By now, it was in full rigor mortis, which would have been slower to form because of the cool temperature. Dr. Phillips's estimation that Annie had been dead two or three hours when her body was found may have been relatively within bounds. He was out of bounds, however, when he concluded that the small amount of food in her stomach and the absence of liquid meant she was sober when she died.

Body fluids such as blood, urine, and the vitreous humor of the eye were not routinely tested for alcohol or drugs. Had they been, the doctor would most likely have found that Annie was still under the influence of alcohol when she was murdered. The more impaired she was, the better for her killer.

The cuts to Annie's neck were on the "left side of the spine" and were parallel and separated by approximately one-half an inch. The killer had attempted to separate the bones of the neck, suggesting he had tried to decapitate her. Since the cuts were deepest on the left side and trailed off to the right, he was probably right-handed, assuming he attacked her from behind. Annie's lungs and brain showed signs of advanced disease, and despite her obesity, she was malnourished.

At her inquest, Dr. Phillips gave his assessment of the sequence of events causing Annie Chapman's death: Her breathing was interfered with, and then her heart stopped due to blood loss. Death, he said, was the result of "syncope," or a dramatic drop in blood pressure. Had Virginia's chief medical examiner, Dr. Marcella Fierro, been present at the inquest, I can just imagine what she would have said. A drop in blood pressure was a mechanism, not the cause, of Annie Chapman's death. Blood pressure drops when anyone is dying, and there is no blood pressure when the person is dead.

Breathing stops, the heart stops, digestion stops, brain waves go flat when a person dies. Saying a person died of cardiac or respiratory arrest or syncope is like saying a person's blindness is due to his not being able to see. What Dr. Phillips should have told the jury was that the cause of death was exsanguination due to cutting injuries of the neck. I have never understood the logic of a doctor filling in a death certificate with cardiac or respiratory arrest as the cause of death no matter if the poor person was shot, stabbed, beaten, drowned, run over by a car, or hit by a train.

During Annie Chapman's inquest, a juror interrupted Dr. Phillips to ask if he had taken a photograph of Annie's eyes, in the event her retinas might have captured the image of her killer. Dr. Phillips said he had not. He abruptly concluded his testimony by telling Coroner Baxter that the details given were sufficient to account for the victim's death and to go into further detail would "only be painful to the feelings of the jury and the public." Of course, Dr. Phillips added, "I bow to your decision."

Baxter was not of the same opinion. "However painful it may be," he replied, "it is necessary in the interests of justice" that the details of Annie Chapman's murder be given. Dr. Phillips countered, "When I come to speak of the wounds on the lower part of the body I must again repeat my opinion that it is highly injudicious to make the results of my examination public. These details are fit only for yourself, sir, and the jury, but to make them public would simply be disgusting." Coroner Baxter asked all ladies and boys to leave the crowded room. He added that he had "never before heard of any evidence requested being kept back."

Dr. Phillips did not waver in his demurral, and he repeatedly requested that the coroner spare the public any further details. The doctor's requests were denied, and he was given no choice but to reveal all he knew about the mutilation of Annie Chapman's body and the organs and tissue the killer had taken. He testified that had he been the murderer, he could not possibly have inflicted such injuries upon the victim in less than fifteen minutes. Had he, as a surgeon, inflicted such damage with deliberation and skill, he estimated that it would have taken "the better part of an hour."

The more details Dr. Phillips was forced to divulge, the farther off track he stepped. Not only did he reemphasize the illogical assertion that Mary Ann Nichols's abdomen had been slashed before her throat was, but he went on to say that the motive for Annie Chapman's murder was the taking of the "body parts." He added that the killer must possess anatomical knowledge and was possibly associated with a profession that exposed him to dissection or surgery.

The suggestion of using bloodhounds came up, and Dr. Phillips pointed out that this might not be helpful since the blood belonged to the victim and not the killer. It did not occur to him—and perhaps to no one else at the inquest—that bloodhounds aren't called bloodhounds because they are capable of picking up only the scent of blood.

The conflicting witness statements were not resolved during the inquest and never have been. If Annie was murdered as late at 5:30 A.M., as witness statements to the police would lead one to believe, then according to that day's weather report, she was attacked shortly before the sun began to rise. It would be incredibly risky to grab a victim in a populated area, cut her throat, and disembowel her just before sunrise, especially on a market day when people would be out early.

A plausible scenario was suggested by the foreman of the coroner's jury: When John Richardson sat on the steps to trim his boot, the back door was open and blocked his view of Annie's body two feet below where he sat because the door opened to the left, where the body was. Richardson half agreed with what the foreman suggested, admitting that since he did not go into the yard, he could not say with certainty that the body wasn't there while he was trimming his boot. He didn't think so. But it was still dark when he stopped by his mother's house, and he was interested in the cellar door and his boot, not the space between the back of the house and the fence.

Elisabeth Long's statements are more problematic. She claimed she saw a woman talking with a man at 5:30 A.M. and was certain the woman was Annie Chapman. If this is true, then Annie was murdered and mutilated at dawn and had been dead less than half an hour when her body was discovered. Elisabeth did not get a good look at the man and told police she would not recognize him if she saw him again. She went on to say that he wore a brown deerstalker and perhaps a dark coat and was a "little" taller than Annie, which would have made him quite short since Annie was only five feet tall. He appeared to be a "foreigner," had a "shabby, genteel" appearance, and was more than forty years old.

This is quite a lot of detail for Elisabeth to have observed as she walked past two strangers in the predawn dark. Prostitutes and their clients were not strangers to the area, and more than likely Elisabeth Long knew to mind her own business, so she didn't pause to stare. Besides, if she thought the conversation between the man and woman was friendly, then she might not have been inclined to take much notice anyway. The truth is, we don't know the truth. We have no idea how reliable any of these narrators were. It was a cool, misty morning. London's air was polluted. The sun wasn't up yet. How good was Elisabeth's eyesight? How well did Richardson see? Corrective lenses were luxuries to the poor.

Furthermore, in police investigations it isn't unusual for people to get excited because they witnessed *something* and are eager to help. Frequently, the more often a witness is interviewed, the more detail he or she suddenly remembers, just as the more times a guilty suspect is interrogated, the more embellished and conflicted the lies become.

There are only a few statements I can make with certainty about Annie Chapman's murder: She was not "suffocated" or strangled into unconsciousness, otherwise she would have had noticeable bruises on her neck; she was still wearing the handkerchief when she was murdered, and had her neck been compressed, the handkerchief most likely would have left an imprint or abrasion; her face may have appeared "swollen" because it was fleshy and puffy. If she died with her mouth open, her tongue may have protruded through the gap caused by her missing front teeth.

Coroner Baxter concluded the inquest with his belief that "we are confronted with a murderer of no ordinary character, [whose crimes are] committed not from jealousy, revenge, or robbery, but from motives less adequate than the many which still disgrace our civilization, mar our progress, and blot the pages of our Christianity." The jury returned the verdict of "Wilful Murder against a person or persons unknown."

Three days later, on Tuesday afternoon, a little girl noticed strange "marks" in the yard behind 25 Hanbury Street, two yards away from where Annie Chapman was killed. The girl immediately found a policeman. The marks were dried blood that formed a trail five or six feet long leading toward the back door of another decaying house overcrowded with lodgers. Police concluded that the Ripper left the blood as he passed through or over the fence separating the yards, and that in an attempt to remove some of the blood from his coat, he had taken it off and beaten it against the back wall of number 25, which would explain a bloody smear and a "sprinkle." Police then found a blood-saturated piece of crumpled paper that they believed the Ripper had used to wipe his hands. Jack the Ripper, the police concluded, had fled the crime scene the same way he had entered it.

This conclusion makes sense. In premeditated crimes, the killer carefully plans the entrance and exit, and someone as calculating and meticulous as Sickert would have familiarized himself with a safe escape route. I doubt he left the scene by climbing over the rickety, haphazardly spaced fencing that separated the yards. Had he done so, most likely he would have smeared blood on the boards or even broken a few. It would have been more convenient and sensible for Sickert to escape through the side yard that led to the street.

From there he could have woven in and out of doors and passages of "Stygian blackness, into which no lamp shone," as one reporter described the scene, a place "where a murderer might, if possessed of coolness, easily pass unobserved." Along Hanbury Street, doors were unlocked and weathered fencing enclosed yards and "waste grounds" where houses had been demolished and constables feared to tread. Even if Sickert had been spotted, if he wasn't acting in a way that aroused suspicion, he would have been simply one more shadowy figure, especially if he had dressed to fit the environment. Actor that he was, he may even have bid a stranger good morning.

Sickert may have wrapped Annie Chapman's flesh and organs in paper or cloth. But there would have been blood drips and smears, and modern forensic investigation would have discovered a trail that was much longer than the five or six feet the little girl found. Today's chemicals and alternate light sources could have detected blood easily, but in 1888, it took the eyes of a child to find the strange "marks" in the yard. No blood tests were done, and it can't be said with certainty that the blood was Annie Chapman's.

Sickert may have been in the habit of watching prostitutes with their clients before moving in for the kill. He may have watched Annie in the past and was aware that she and other prostitutes used the unlocked passages and yards of 29 Hanbury Street and neighboring tenements for "immoral" purposes. He may have been watching her the morning he murdered her. "Peeping" at people dressing or undressing or engaging in sex is consistent in a lust murderer's history. Violent psychopaths are voyeurs. They stalk, watch, fantasize, then rape or kill or both.

Watching a prostitute sexually service a client could have been Sickert's foreplay. He might have approached Annie Chapman immediately after her last customer left. He might have solicited sex from her, gotten her to turn her back to him, and then attacked her. Or he might have appeared out of the dark and grabbed her from behind, jerked back her head by her chin, leaving the bruises on her jaw. The cuts to her throat severed her windpipe, rendering her unable to make a sound. Within seconds he could have had her on the ground and yanked up her clothing to slice open her abdomen. It takes no time or skill to disembowel a person. It doesn't take a forensic pathologist or surgeon to find the uterus, ovaries, and other internal organs.

Much has been made of the Ripper's alleged surgical skills. To cut out a uterus and part of the belly wall including the navel, the upper part of the vagina, and the greater part of the bladder does not require surgical precision, and it would be difficult for even a surgeon to "operate" when frenzied and in the dark. But Dr. Phillips was sure that the killer must have had some knowledge of anatomy or surgical procedures and had used a "small amputating knife or a well ground slaughterman's knife, narrow & thin, sharp & blade of six to eight inches in length."

Sickert didn't need exposure to surgery or practice in internal medicine to know a thing or two about the female pelvic organs. The upper end of the vagina is attached to the uterus, and on top of the vagina is the bladder. Assuming the uterus was the trophy Sickert sought, he simply removed it in the dark and took the surrounding tissue with it. This isn't "surgery"; it is expediency, or grab and cut. One can assume he knew the anatomical location of the vagina and that it is close to the uterus. But even if he didn't, there were plenty of surgical books available at the time.

As early as 1872, *Gray's Anatomy* was already in its sixth edition, and had detailed diagrams of the "organs of digestion" and "female organs of generation." For one who had suffered permanent, life-altering debilitation from operations, Sickert was likely to have an interest in anatomy, especially the anatomy of the female genitalia and reproductive organs. I would expect a man of his curiosity, intelligence, and obsessiveness to have looked at *Gray's* or *Bell's Great Operations of Surgery* (1821) with its color plates prepared by Thomas Landseer, the brother of the famous Victorian painter of animals Edwin Landseer, whose work Sickert would have known.

There was Carl Rokitansky's *A Manual of Pathological Anatomy,* volumes I–IV (1849–54), George Viner Ellis's *Illustrations of Dissections* with life-size color plates (1867), and James Hope's *Principles and Illustrations of Morbid Anatomy, with its Complete Series of Coloured Lithographic Drawings* (1834). Had Sickert any doubts as to the location of the uterus or any other organ, he had a number of ways to educate himself without exposure to the medical profession.

Because of the dismal state of forensic science and medicine in 1888, there were a number of misunderstandings about blood. The size and shape of blood spatter and drips meant very little to the Victorian investigator, who believed that a fat person had a significantly greater volume of blood than a thin one. Dr. Phillips would have looked at the yard where Annie Chapman's body was found and focused on whether there was enough blood to indicate she was murdered in that location or elsewhere. Someone with a severed neck should lose most of his or her blood—approximately seven or eight pints. Quite a lot of blood could have soaked into Annie's many layers of dark, thick clothing. Arterial blood would have spurted and could have soaked into the earth some distance away from her.

I suspect the "patches" of closely clustered blood droplets noticed on the wall not far above Annie's head were back spatter from the knife. Each time the Ripper slashed into her body and drew back the knife to slash again, blood flew off the blade. Since we do not know the number, shape, and size of the blood spatters, we can speculate only that they could not have been caused by arterial bleeding unless Annie was already on the ground while her carotid artery or arteries spurted blood. I suspect she was attacked while she was standing, and the deep cuts to her abdomen were made when she was on her back.

Her intestines may have been pulled out and tossed aside as the Ripper groped in the dark for her uterus. Trophies or souvenirs bring back memories. They are a catalyst for fantasies. The taking of them is so typical as to be expected in violent psychopathic crimes. Sickert was far too smart to keep any incriminating souvenir where someone could have found it. But he had secret rooms, and I wonder where he got the inspiration for them. Perhaps there was some experience from his childhood that caused him to be drawn to dreadful places. There is a verse in a poem his father wrote that brings his son's secret rooms to mind:

> What an uncanny/eerie feeling when I am within your walls,
> those high, naked, pale walls, how terrible they are,
> they remind me of the old-fashioned guard rooms . . .
> Does not one, here and there, pile up
> overcoats and caput, long coats, wintercoats
> and does not one carry all kinds of
> garbage into the room . . .

In September 1889, the Ripper writes his return address as "Jack the rippers hole." Sickert could have kept whatever he wanted in his secret places—or "rat holes," as I call them. It is impossible to know what he did with his "garbage," the body parts that would begin to decompose and smell unless he chemically preserved them. In one letter the Ripper writes of cutting off a victim's ear and feeding it to a dog. In another, he mentions frying organs and eating them. Sickert might have been inordinately curious about the female reproductive system that had given birth to his ruined life. He could not study it in the dark. Perhaps he took the organs back to his lair and studied them there.

After Annie Chapman's murder, the relatives who had avoided her in life took care of her in death. They made her funeral arrangements, and at seven o'clock on Friday morning, September 14th, a hearse appeared at the Whitechapel mortuary to take her away clandestinely. Her relatives did not form a procession of coaches for fear of drawing attention to Annie's last journey. She was buried at Manor Park Cemetery, seven miles northeast of where she was slain. The weather had taken a dramatic turn for the better. The temperature was sixty degrees and the sun shone all day.

During the week following Annie's death, businessmen in the East End formed a vigilance committee chaired by George Lusk, a local builder and contractor and member of the Metropolitan Board of Works. Lusk's committee issued the following public statement: "Finding that, in spite of the murders being committed in our midst our police force is inadequate to discover the author or authors of the late atrocities, we the undersigned have formed ourselves into a committee and intend offering a substantial reward to anyone, citizen or otherwise, who shall give such information as will be the means of bringing the murderer or murderers to justice."

A Member of Parliament offered to donate £100 to the reward fund, and other citizens were willing to help. Metropolitan Police documents dated August 31st and those of September 4th note that the response to the citizens' request should be that the practice of offering rewards had been abolished some time ago because rewards encouraged people to "discover" misleading evidence or to manufacture evidence, and "give rise to meddling and gossip without end."

In the East End, resentment and unruly behavior rose to a new high. People caroused at 29 Hanbury Street, gawking, some of them laughing and joking, while the rest of London fell into a "kind of stupor," said *The Times*. The crimes were "beyond the ghastliest efforts of fiction"—even worse than Edgar Allan Poe's *Murders in the Rue Morgue,* and "nothing in fact or fiction equals these outrages at once in their horrible nature and in the effect which they have produced upon the popular imagination."

CHAPTER SEVENTEEN

THE STREETS UNTIL DAWN

Gatti's Hungerford Palace of Varieties was one of the most vulgar music halls in London. It was Sickert's favorite haunt for the first eight months of 1888, and he went there several nights a week.

Built into a 250-foot-wide arch underneath the South Eastern railway near Charing Cross Station, Gatti's could seat six hundred, but on some nights as many as a thousand rowdy spectators crowded in for hours of drinking, smoking, and sexually charged entertainment. The popular Katie Lawrence shocked polite society by dressing in men's breeches or a loose, short frock that exposed more female flesh than was deemed decent at the time. Music-hall stars Kate Harvey and Florence Hayes as "The Patriotic Lady" were regulars when Sickert was making his quick sketches in the flickering lights.

Cleavage and exposed thighs were scandalous, but nobody seemed to worry much about the exploitation of the female child stars prancing about singing the same racy songs as the adults. Girls as young as eight years old dressed in costumes and little frocks and aped sexual awareness that invited pedophilic excitement and became the material for a number of Sickert's paintings. Art historian Dr. Robins explains that "among decadent writers, painters, and poets, there was something of a cult for the supposed sweetness and innocence of child music-hall performers." In her book *Walter Sickert: Drawings,* she provides new insight into Sickert's artistic interpretations of the female performers he watched night after night and followed from music hall to music hall. His sketches are a glimpse into his psyche and how he lived his life. While he did not mind impetuously giving away a painting, he would not part with the on-the-spot drawings he made on postcards and other small pieces of cheap paper.

To look at these faint pencil sketches in the collections at Tate Britain, the University of Reading, the Walker Art Gallery in Liverpool, and Leeds City Art Gallery is to slip inside Sickert's mind and emotions. His hasty artistic strokes capture what he saw as he sat in a music hall, gazing up at the stage. They are snapshots made through the lens of his own fantasies. While other men leered and egged on the half-naked performers, Sickert sketched dismembered female body parts.

One might argue that these drawings were Sickert's attempt at improving his technique. Hands, for example, are difficult, and some of the greatest painters had their struggles with hands. But when Sickert was sitting in his box or several rows back from the stage and making sketches on his little bits of paper, he wasn't perfecting his art. He was drawing a head severed from its neck; arms with no hands; a torso with no arms; plump chopped-off naked thighs; a limbless torso with breasts bulging out of a low-cut costume.

One might also argue that Sickert was thinking about new ways to reposition the body in a manner that wasn't stilted or posed. Perhaps he was trying out new methods. He would have seen Degas's pastel nudes. It could simply be that Sickert was following the lead of his idol, who had moved far beyond the old, static way of using draped models in the studio and was experimenting with more natural human postures and motion. But when Degas drew an arm in isolation, he was practicing technique, and the purpose of that arm was to be used in a painting.

The female body parts Sickert depicted in his music-hall sketches were rarely if ever used in any of his studies, pastels, etchings, or paintings. His penciled-in limbs and torsos seem to have been drawn simply for the sake of drawing them as he sat in the audience watching the scantily dressed Queenie Lawrence in her lily-white lingerie or the nine-year-old Little Flossie perform. Sickert did not depict male figures or male body parts in quite the same way. There is nothing about his sketches of males to suggest the subjects are being victimized, except for a pencil drawing titled *He Killed His Father in a Fight.* In it, a man is hacking to death a figure on a bloody bed.

Sickert's female torsos, severed heads, and limbs are images from a violent imagination. One can look at sketches his artist friend Wilson Steer made at the same time and in some of the same music halls and note a marked difference in Steer's depictions of the human body and facial expressions. He may have drawn a female head, but it does not seem chopped off at the neck. He may have drawn the ankles and feet of a ballerina, but they are obviously alive, poised on toe, the calf muscles bunching. Nothing about Steer's sketches looks dead. Sickert's sketched body parts have none of the tension of life but are limp and disconnected.

His 1888 music-hall sketches and the notes he scribbled on them place him in Gatti's on February 4th through March 24th; May 25th; June 4th through the 7th; July 8th, 30th, and 31st; and August 1st and 4th. Gatti's and other music halls Sickert visited in 1888, such as the Bedford, were by law supposed to end their performances and sales of alcohol no later than half past midnight. If we assume that Sickert stayed until the entertainment ended, he would have been on London's streets on many early mornings. Then he could wander. Apparently Sickert didn't require much sleep.

The artist Marjorie Lilly recalled in her memoir of him that "he only seemed to relax in odd snatches of sleep during the day and was seldom in bed until after midnight, when he might get up again to wander about the streets until dawn." Lilly, who once shared a studio and a house with Sickert, observed that his habit was to wander after the music-hall performances. This peripatetic behavior, she added, continued throughout his life. Whenever "an idea tormented him" he would "thresh round the streets until dawn, lost in meditation."

Lilly knew Sickert well until his death in 1942, and many of the details in her book tell far more about her mentor and friend than she perhaps realized. Consistently, she refers to his wanderings, his nocturnal habits, his secrecy, and his well-known habit of having as many as three or four studios, their locations or purposes unknown. She also has numerous odd recollections of his preference for dark basements. "Huge, eerie, with winding passages and one black dungeon succeeding another like some horror story by Edgar Allan Poe," is how she describes them.

Sickert's private working life "took him to queer places where he improvised studios and workshops," the art dealer Lillian Browse wrote a year after his death. As early as 1888, when he was frequenting the music halls, he obsessively rented secret rooms he could not afford. "I am taking new rooms," he would tell his friends. In 1911 he writes, "I have taken on a tiny, odd, sinister little home at £45 a year close by here." The address was 60 Harrington Street NW, and apparently he planned to use the "little home" as a "studio."

Sickert would accumulate studios and then abandon them after a short while. It was well known among his acquaintances that these hidden rat holes were located on mean streets. His friend and fellow artist William Rothenstein, whom he met in 1889, wrote of Sickert's taste "for the dingy lodging-house atmosphere." Rothenstein said that Sickert was a "genius" at ferreting out the gloomiest and most off-putting rooms to work in, and this predilection was a source of bafflement to others. Rothenstein described Sickert as an "aristocrat by nature" who "had cultivated a strange taste for life below the stairs."

Denys Sutton wrote that "Sickert's restlessness was a dominating feature of his character." It was typical for him to always have "studios elsewhere, for at all times he cherished his freedom." Sutton says that Sickert often dined out alone, and that even after he married Ellen, he would go by himself to the music halls or get up in the middle of a dinner in his own home to head out to a performance. Then he would begin another one of his long walks home. Or perhaps go to one of his secret rooms, somehow meandering into the violent East End, walking the dark streets alone, a small parcel or a Gladstone bag in hand, presumably to hold his art supplies.

According to Sutton, during one of these ambles, Sickert was dressed in a loud checked suit and came upon several girls on Copenhagen Street, about a mile northwest of Shoreditch. The girls scattered in terror, screaming "Jack the Ripper! Jack the Ripper!" In a slightly different but more telling account, Sickert told his friends that it was he who called out, "Jack the Ripper, Jack the Ripper."

"I told her I was Jack the Ripper and I took my hat off," the Ripper wrote in a letter on November 19, 1888. Three days later the Ripper wrote a letter saying he was in Liverpool and "met a young woman in Scotland Road. . . . I smiled at her and she calls out Jack the ripper. She dident know how right she was." About this time, an article appeared in the *Sunday Dispatch* reporting that an elderly woman was sitting in Liverpool's Shiel Park when a "respectable looking man, dressed in a black coat, light trousers, and a soft felt hat," pulled out a long thin knife. He said he planned to kill as many women in Liverpool as he could and send the ears of the first victim to the editor of the city's newspaper.

Sickert made his sketches at Gatti's in an era when there were few inciting props available to psychopathic violent offenders. Today's rapist, pedophile, or murderer has plenty to choose from: photographs, audiotapes, and videotapes of his victims being tortured or killed; and violent pornography found in magazines, films, books, computer software, and on Internet sites. In 1888 there were few visual or audible aids available for a psychopath to fuel violent fantasies. Sickert's props would have been souvenirs or trophies from the victim, paintings and drawings, and the live entertainment of the theater and the music halls. He also could have made dry runs; the terrifying of the old woman in Liverpool could simply have been one of dozens or even hundreds.

Psychopathic killers often try out their modus operandi before going through the plan. Practice makes perfect, and the killer gets a thrill from the near-hit. The pulse picks up. Adrenaline surges. The killer will continue to go through the ritual, each time getting closer to actualizing the violence. Killers who mimic police officers have been known to install emergency lights or attach magnetic dome lights to the roofs of their cars and pull over women drivers many times before actually going through with the abduction and murder.

Jack the Ripper very likely went through dry runs and other rituals before he killed. After a while, dry runs aren't just about practice and instant gratification. They fuel violent fantasies and may involve more than just stalking a victim, especially if the perpetrator is as creative as Walter Sickert. A number of strange events continued to occur in various parts of England. At approximately ten o'clock on the night of September 14th, in London, a man entered the Tower Subway and approached the caretaker. "Have you caught any of the Whitechapel murderers yet?" the man asked as he pulled out a foot-long knife that had a curved blade.

He then fled, yanking off "false whiskers" as he was pursued by the caretaker, who lost sight of him in Tooley Street. The description the caretaker gave the police was of a man five foot three with dark hair, a dark complexion, and a mustache. He was about thirty years old and was wearing a black suit that looked new, a light overcoat, and a dark cloth double-peaked cap.

"I have got a jolly lot of false whiskers & mustaches," the Ripper wrote on November 27th.

After Tower Bridge was completed in 1894, the Tower Subway was closed to pedestrians and turned into a gas main, but in 1888 it was a hellish cast-iron tube seven feet in diameter and four hundred feet long. It began at the south side of Great Tower Hill at the Tower of London, ran under the Thames, and surfaced at Pickle Herring Stairs on the south bank of the river. If what the caretaker told police was accurate, he chased the man through the tunnel to Pickle Herring Stairs, which led to Pickle Herring Street, then to Vine Street, which intersected with Tooley Street. The Tower of London is about half a mile south of Whitechapel, and the subway was sufficiently unpleasant that it is unlikely many people or police officers used it to cross the river, especially if one were claustrophobic or fearful of traveling through a dirty, gloomy tunnel under water.

No doubt the police considered the man with the false whiskers a crank. I found no mention of this incident in any police reports. But this "crank" was rational enough to pick a deserted, poorly lit place for the brazen display of his knife, and it is unlikely he viewed the caretaker as one who could physically overtake him. The man had every intention of causing a stir and no intention of being caught. Friday the 14th was also the day that Annie Chapman was buried.

Three days later, on September 17th, the Metropolitan Police received the first letter signed "Jack the Ripper."

> *Dear Boss,*
>
> *So now they say I am a Yid when will they lern Dear old Boss? You an me know the truth don't we. Lusk can look forever he'll never find me but I am rite under his nose all the time. I watch them looking for me an it gives me fits ha ha. I love my work an I shant stop untill I get buckled and even then watch out for your old pal Jacky*
>
> *Catch me if you can*

The letter came to light only recently because it had never been included in the Metropolitan Police records. Originally, it had been filed at the Home Office.

At ten o'clock at night on September 17th—the same day that the Ripper made his debut in what we know as his first letter—a man appeared at the district police court of Westminster. He said he was an art student from New York, and was in London to "study art" at the National Gallery. A *Times* reporter relayed a dialogue that is so comical and clever it reads like a script.

The "American from New York" said he'd had trouble with his landlady the night before and was seeking advice from the magistrate, a Mr. Biron, who asked what sort of trouble the man meant.

> "A terrible shindy," came the reply.
>
> (Laughter)
>
> The American went on to say he had given the land lady notice that he wanted to leave her premises on Sloane Street, and she had been "annoying" him in every way since. She had pushed him against a wall, and when he inquired about dinner, she almost spat in his face with "the vehemence of her language" and stigmatized him "as a low American."
>
> "Why don't you leave such a land lady and her apartment?" Mr. Biron asked.
>
> "I went there with some furniture, and I was foolish enough to tell her that she might have it and take it out in the rent. Instead she took it out of me."
>
> (Laughter)
>
> "And I could not take it away," the American went on. "I should be positively frightened to try."
>
> (Renewed laughter)
>
> "It seems you have made a very ridiculous bargain," Mr. Biron told him. "You find yourself in an exceedingly embarrassing position."
>
> "I do indeed," the American agreed. "You can have no conception of such a land lady. She threw a pair of scissors at me, lustily screamed

'murder,' and then caught hold of the lappels [sic] of my coat to prevent my escape, really a most absurd situation."

(Laughter)

"Well," said Mr. Biron, "you have brought all the unpleasantness on yourself."

This was the main court story in *The Times,* yet no crime had been committed and no arrest was made. The best the magistrate could offer was perhaps to send an officer to the Sloane Street address to "caution" the landlady that she best behave herself. The American thanked "his worship" and expressed his hope that the caution "would have a salutary result."

The reporter identified the New York art student only as the "Applicant." No name, age, or description was given. There was no follow-up story in days to come. The National Gallery did not have an art school or students. It still doesn't. I find it strange if not unbelievable that an American would use the language the so-called art student did. Would an American use the word *shindy,* which was London street slang for fight or row? Would an American say that the landlady "lustily screamed 'murder' "?

Screaming "murder" could have been a reference to testimony at Ripper victim inquests, and why would the landlady scream "murder" when she was the attacker, not the American? The reporter never mentioned whether the "American" spoke like an American. Sickert was quite capable of faking an American accent. He had spent years with Whistler, who was American.

About this time, a story began to circulate through the news that an American had contacted an assistant curator of a medical school in the hope of buying human uteri for £20 each. The would-be purchaser wanted the organs preserved in glycerine to keep them pliable, and planned to send them out with a journal article he had written. The request was refused. The "American" was not identified, and no further information about him was given. The story gave rise to a new possibility: The East End murderer was killing women to sell their organs, and the stealing of Annie Chapman's rings was a "veil" to hide the real motive, which was to steal her uterus.

The stealing of human organs might seem ridiculous, but it had been barely fifty years since the infamous case of Burke and Hare, the "Resurrectionists"—or body snatchers—who were charged with robbing graves and committing as many as thirty murders to supply doctors and medical schools in Edinburgh with anatomical specimens for dissection. Organ-stealing as a motive for the Ripper's murders continued to be circulated and more confusion eddied around the Ripper crimes.

On September 21st, Ellen Sickert wrote a letter to her brother-in-law, Dick Fisher, and said that Sickert had left England for Normandy to visit "his people," and would be gone for weeks. Sickert may have left, but not necessarily for France. The next night, Saturday, a woman was murdered in Birtley, County Durham. Jane Boatmoor, a twenty-six-year-old mother who was rumored to lead a somewhat less than respectable life, was last seen alive by friends the night before, on Saturday, at eight o'clock. Her body was found the following morning, Sunday, September 23rd, in a gutter near Guston Colliery Railway.

The left side of her neck had been cut through to her vertebrae. A gash on the right side of her face had laid open her lower jaw to the bone, and her bowels protruded from her mutilated abdomen. The similarities between her murder and those in London's East End prompted Scotland Yard to send Dr. George Phillips and an inspector to meet Durham police officials. No helpful evidence was found, and for some reason, it was decided that the killer probably had committed suicide. Local people made extensive searches of mine shafts, but no body was recovered and the crime went unsolved. However, in an anonymous letter to the City of London Police, dated November 20, 1888, the writer offers this suggestion: "Look at the case in County Durham . . . twas made to appear as if it was Jack the Ripper."

The police did not link the murder of Jane Boatmoor to Jack the Ripper. Investigators had no clue that the Ripper liked to manipulate the machinery behind the scenes. His violent appetite had been whetted and he craved "blood, blood, blood," as the Ripper wrote. He craved drama. He had an insatiable appetite for enthralling his audience. As Henry Irving once said to an unresponsive house, "Ladies and gentlemen, if you don't applaud, I can't act!" Perhaps the applause was too faint. Several more events happened in quick succession.

On September 24th, the police received the taunting letter with the killer's "name" and "address" blacked out with heavily inked rectangles and coffins. The next day, Jack the Ripper wrote another letter, but this time he made sure someone paid attention. He sent his missive to the Central News Agency. "Dear Boss, I keep on hearing the police have caught me but they won't fix me just yet," the Ripper wrote in red ink. His spelling and grammar were correct, his writing as neat as a clerk's. The postmark was the East End. The defense would say that the letter couldn't have been from Sickert. He was in France. The prosecutor would reply, "Based on what evidence?" In his biography of Degas, Daniel Halévy mentions that Sickert was in Dieppe at some point during the summer, but there is no evidence I could find that Sickert was in France at the end of September.

Sickert's "people," as Ellen ruefully called them, were his cliquish artist friends in Dieppe. To them, Ellen would always be an outsider. She was not the least bit bohemian or stimulating. It is likely that when she was in Dieppe with her husband, he ignored her. If he wasn't hobnobbing in cafés or in the summer homes of artists such as Jacques-Emile Blanche or George Moore, he was off the radar screen, as usual, wandering about, mingling with fishermen and sailors, or locked away in one of his secret rooms.

What is suspicious about Sickert's alleged plans to visit Normandy at the end of September and part of October is that there is no mention of him in letters exchanged among his friends. One would think if Sickert had been in Dieppe, then Moore or Blanche might have mentioned seeing him—or not seeing him. One might suppose that when Sickert wrote Blanche in August, he might have mentioned that he would be in France next month and hoped to see him—or would be sorry to miss him.

There is no mention in the letters of Degas or Whistler that they saw Sickert in September or October 1888, and no hint that they had a clue he was in France. Letters Sickert wrote to Blanche in the autumn of 1888 appear to have been written in London, because they are written on Sickert's 54 Broadhurst Gardens stationery, which apparently he did not use except when he was actually there. The only indication I could find that he was in France at all during the autumn of 1888 is an undated note to Blanche that Sickert supposedly wrote from the small fishing village Saint-Valery-en-Caux, twenty miles from Dieppe:

"This is a nice little place to sleep & eat in," Sickert writes, "which is what I am most anxious to do now."

The envelope is missing and there is no postmark to prove that Sickert was in Normandy. Nor is there any way to determine where Blanche was. But Sickert very well may have been in Saint-Valery-en-Caux when he wrote the letter. He probably did need rest and nourishment after his frenzied violent activities, and crossing the Channel was not an ordeal. I find it curious if not suspicious that he chose St. Valery when he could have stayed in Dieppe.

In fact, it is curious that he wrote to Blanche at all, because most of the note is about Sickert's "looking for a colorman" so he could send his brother Bernhard "pastel glass paper or sand paper canvass." Sickert said he wanted a "packet of samples" and that he did not know "French measurements." I fail to understand how Sickert, who was fluent in French and had spent so much time in France, did not know where to find samples of papers. "I am a *French* painter," he declared in a letter to Blanche, yet the scientifically and mathematically inclined Sickert says he didn't know French measurements.

Perhaps Sickert's letter from St. Valery was sincere. Perhaps he did want Blanche's advice. Or perhaps the truth is that Sickert was exhausted and paranoid and on the run, and thought it wise to supply himself with an alibi. Apart from this note to Blanche, I could find nothing to suggest that Sickert spent any time at all in France during the late summer, early autumn, or winter of 1888. The bathing season for Normandy was over as well. It began in early July and by the end of September, Sickert's friends closed down their Dieppe homes and studios.

Sickert's salon of artists and prominent friends would have scattered until the following summer. I wonder if it seemed a little strange to Ellen that her husband planned to join "his people" in Normandy for several weeks when nobody was likely to be there. I wonder if she saw her husband much at all, and if she did, did she think he was behaving a bit oddly? In August, Sickert the compulsive letter writer sent a note to Blanche, apologizing for not "writing for so long. I have been very hard at work, and I find it very difficult to find 5 minutes to write a letter."

There is no reason to believe Sickert's "work" was related to the toils of his trade—beyond his going to music halls and seeking inspiration from the streets at all hours of the night. His artistic productivity wasn't at its usual high from August through the rest of the year. Paintings "circa 1888" are few, and there is no guarantee that "circa" didn't mean a year or two earlier or later. I found only one published article from 1888, and that was in the spring. It seems that Sickert avoided his friends for much of that year. There is no indication he summered in Dieppe—which was very unusual. No matter where he went or when, it is clear that Sickert wasn't following his usual routines, if one could call anything Sickert did "routine."

In the late nineteenth century, passports, visas, and other forms of identification were not required to travel on the Continent. (However, by the late summer of 1888, passports were required to enter Germany from France.) There is no mention of Sickert having any form of "picture identification" until World War I, when he and his second wife, Christine, were issued *laissez-passers* to show guards at tunnels, railway crossings, and other strategic places as they traveled about France.

Entering France from England was an easy and friendly transition and remained so during the years Sickert traveled to and fro. Crossing the English Channel in the late 1800s could take as little as four hours in good weather. One could travel by express train and "fast" steamer seven days a week, twice daily, with the trains leaving Victoria Station at 10:30 in the morning or London Bridge at 10:45. The steamer sailed out of Newhaven at 12:45 P.M. and arrived in Dieppe around dinnertime. A single, one-way first-class ticket to Dieppe was twenty-four shillings, second class was seventeen shillings, and part of this Express Tidal Service included trains from Dieppe straight through to Rouen and Paris.

Sickert's mother claimed she never knew when her son would suddenly go to France or suddenly come back. Maybe he hopped back and forth from England to Dieppe while the Ripper crimes were going on in 1888, but if he did, it was probably to cool off. He had been going to Dieppe since childhood and kept several places there. French death and crime statistics for the Victorian era do not seem to have survived, and it was not possible to find records of murders then that might even remotely resemble the Ripper's crimes. But Dieppe was simply too small a town to commit lust-murders and get away with it.

During the days I spent in Dieppe, with its narrow old streets and passageways, its rocky shore and soaring cliffs that sheer off into the Channel, I tried to see that small seaside village as a killing ground for Sickert, but I could not. His work while he was in Dieppe reflects a different spirit. Most of the pictures he painted there are in lovely colors, his depictions of buildings inspiring. There is nothing morbid or violent in most of his Normandy art. It is as if Dieppe brought out the side of Sickert's face that is turned to the light in his Jekyll and Hyde self-portraits.

CHAPTER EIGHTEEN

A SHINY BLACK BAG

The sun did not show itself on Saturday, September 29th, and a persistent, cold rain chilled the night as *Dr. Jekyll and Mr. Hyde* ended its long run at the Lyceum. The newspapers reported that the "great excesses of sunshine were at an end."

Elizabeth Stride only recently had moved out of a lodging house in Dorset Street in Spitalfields, where she had been living with Michael Kidney, a waterside laborer who was in the Army Reserve. Long Liz, as her friends called her, had left Kidney before. She carried her few belongings with her this time, but there was no reason to assume she was gone for good. Kidney would later testify at her inquest that now and then she wanted her freedom and an opportunity to indulge her "drinking habits," but after a spell of wandering off, she always came back.

Elizabeth's maiden name was Gustafsdotter and she would have turned 45 on November 27th, although she had led most people to believe she was about ten years younger than she really was. Elizabeth had led a life of lies, most of them pitiful attempts to weave a brighter, more dramatic tale than the truth of her depressing, desperate life. She was born in Torslanda, near Göteborg, Sweden, the daughter of a farmer. Some said she spoke fluent English without a trace of an accent. Others claimed she did not properly form her words and sounded like a foreigner. Swedish, her native tongue, is a Germanic language closely related to Danish, which is what Sickert's father spoke.

Elizabeth used to tell people she came to London as a young lady to "see the country," but this was just one more fabrication. The earliest record found of her living in London was in the Swedish Church register that listed her name in 1879, with the notation that she had been given a shilling. She was five foot two or four, according to people who went to the mortuary to figure out who she was. Her complexion was "pale." Others described it as "dark." Her hair was "dark brown and curly," or "black," according to someone else. A policeman lifted one of Elizabeth's eyelids in the poorly lit mortuary and decided that her eyes were "gray."

In her black-and-white postmortem photograph, Elizabeth's hair looks darker because it was wet and stringy from having been rinsed. Her face was pale because she was dead and had lost virtually all of the blood in her body. Her eyes may once have been bright blue, but not by the time the policeman lifted a lid to check. After death, the conjunctiva of the eye begins to dry and cloud. Most people who have been dead awhile appear to have gray or grayish-blue eyes unless their eyes were very dark.

After her postmortem examination, Elizabeth was dressed in the dark clothing she was wearing when she was murdered. She was placed in a shell that was stood up against a wall to be photographed. Barely visible in the shadow of her tucked-in chin is the cut made by her killer's knife as it jaggedly trails off inches below the right side of her neck. Her photograph after death may have been the only one taken in her life. She appears to have been thin, with a nicely shaped face and good features, and a mouth that might have been sensuous had she not lost her upper front teeth.

Elizabeth may have been a blonde beauty in her youth. During her inquest, truths about her began to emerge. She had left Sweden to take a "situation" with a gentleman who lived near Hyde Park. It is not known how long that "situation" lasted, but at some point after it ended she lived with a policeman. In 1869, she married a carpenter named John Thomas Stride. Everyone who knew her in the local lodging houses she frequented had heard the tragic tale that her husband had drowned when the *Princess Alice* sank after a steam collier ran it down.

Elizabeth had different versions of this tale. Her husband and two of her nine children had drowned when the *Princess Alice* went down. Or her husband and all of her children drowned. Elizabeth, who would have been quite young when she began bearing children to have produced nine of them by 1878, somehow survived the shipwreck that killed 640 people. While struggling for her life, another panicking passenger kicked her in the mouth, explaining the "deformity" to it.

Elizabeth told everyone that the entire roof of her mouth was gone, but the postmortem examination revealed nothing wrong with her hard or soft palates. The only deformity was her missing front teeth, which must have been a source of shame to her. Records at the Poplar and Stepney Sick Asylum showed that her husband, John Stride, died there on October 24, 1884. He did not drown in a shipwreck, nor did any of their children—if they had children. Perhaps falsehoods about Elizabeth's past made her life more interesting to her, for the truth was painful and humiliating and did nothing but cause trouble.

When the clergy of the Swedish Church she attended discovered that her husband did not die in the shipwreck, they ceased any financial assistance. Perhaps she lied about the death of her husband and their alleged children because a fund had been set aside for the survivors of the *Princess Alice* shipwreck. When it was suspected that no one related to Elizabeth had died in that disaster, the money stopped. One way or another, Elizabeth had to be supported by a man, and when she wasn't, she made what she could from sewing, cleaning, and prostitution.

Of late, she had been spending her nights at a lodging house at 32 Flower and Dean Street, where the deputy, a widow named Elizabeth Tanner, knew her fairly well. During the inquest, Mrs. Tanner testified that she had seen Elizabeth on and off for six years and that until Thursday, September 27th, Elizabeth had been living in another lodging house with a man named Michael Kidney. She had walked out on him with nothing but a few ragged clothes and a hymn book. On that Thursday night and the following Friday night she stayed in Mrs. Tanner's lodging house. On the early evening of Saturday, September 29th, Elizabeth and Mrs. Tanner had a drink at the Queen's Head pub in Commercial Street, and afterward Elizabeth earned sixpence by cleaning two of the lodging-house rooms.

Between ten and eleven, Elizabeth was in the kitchen and handed a piece of velvet to her friend Catherine Lane. "Please keep it safe for me," Elizabeth said, and she added that she was going out for a while. She was dressed for the miserable weather in two petticoats made of a cheap material resembling sacking, a white chemise, white cotton stockings, a black velveteen bodice, a black skirt, a black jacket trimmed with fur, a colorful striped silk handkerchief around her neck, and a small black crêpe bonnet. In her pockets were two handkerchiefs, a skein of black worsted darning yarn, and a brass thimble. Before she left the lodging-house kitchen, she asked Charles Preston, a barber, if she could borrow his clothes brush to tidy up a bit. She did not tell anyone where she was going, but she proudly showed off her six newly earned pennies as she headed out into the dark, wet night.

Berner Street was a narrow thoroughfare of small, crowded dwellings occupied by Polish and German tailors, shoemakers, cigarette makers, and other impoverished people who worked at home. On the street was the clubhouse of the International Working Men's Educational Club, which had approximately eighty-five members, most of them Eastern European Jewish Socialists. The only requirement for joining was to support socialist principles. The IWMC met every Saturday night at 8:30 to discuss various topics.

These meetings always ended with singing and dancing, and it was not unusual for people to linger until one o'clock in the morning. On this particular Saturday night, almost a hundred people had attended a debate in German on why Jews should be socialists. The serious talk was winding down. Most people were heading home by the time Elizabeth Stride set out in that direction.

Her first client of the evening, as far as anyone seems to know, was a man she was observed talking to in Berner Street, very close to where a laborer named William Marshall lived. This was about 11:45 P.M., and Marshall later testified that he did not get a good look at the man's face, but that he was dressed in a small black coat, dark trousers, and what looked like a sailor's cap. He wore no gloves, was clean shaven, and was kissing Elizabeth. Marshall said he overheard the man tease, "You would say anything but your prayers," and Elizabeth laughed. Neither of them appeared intoxicated, Marshall recalled, and they walked off in the direction of the IWMC clubhouse.

An hour later, another local resident named James Brown saw a woman he later identified as Elizabeth Stride leaning against a wall and talking with a man at the corner of Fairclough Street and Berner Street. The man wore a long overcoat and was approximately five foot seven. (It seems that almost every man identified by witnesses in the Ripper cases was approximately five foot seven. In the Victorian era, five foot seven would have been considered an average height for a male. I suppose that height was as good a guess as any.)

The last time Elizabeth Stride was seen alive was by Police Constable William Smith, 452 H Division, whose beat that night included Berner Street. At 12:35 he noticed a woman he later identified as Elizabeth Stride, and it caught his eye that she was wearing a flower on her coat. The man she was with carried a newspaper-wrapped package that was eighteen inches long and six or eight inches wide. He, too, was five foot seven, Smith recalled, and was dressed in a hard felt deerstalker, a dark overcoat, and dark trousers. Smith thought the man seemed respectable enough, and was about twenty-eight years old and clean shaven.

Smith continued his beat, and twenty-five minutes later, at 1:00 A.M., Louis Diemschutz was driving his costermonger's cart to the IWMC building at 40 Berner Street. He was the manager of the socialists' club and lived in the building. He was surprised when he turned into the courtyard to find the gates open, because usually they were closed after 9:00 P.M. As he passed through, his pony suddenly shied to the left. It was too dark to see much, but Diemschutz made out a form on the ground near the wall and poked it with his whip, expecting to find rubbish. He climbed down and struggled to light a match in the wind and was startled by the dimly lit shape of a woman. She was either drunk or dead, and Diemschutz ran into the clubhouse and returned with a candle.

Elizabeth Stride's throat was slashed, and Diemschutz and pony and cart must have interrupted the Ripper. Blood flowed from her neck toward the clubhouse door, and the top buttons of her jacket were undone, revealing her chemise and stays. She was on her left side, her face toward the wall, her dress soaking wet from recent hard rains. In her left hand was a paper packet of cachous, or sweets used to freshen the breath; a corsage of maidenhair fern and a red rose was pinned to her breast. By now, P.C. William Smith's beat had gone full circle, and when he reached 40 Berner Street again he must have been shocked to find that a crowd was gathering outside the clubhouse gates and people were screaming "Police!" and "Murder!"

Smith later testified at the inquest that his patrol had taken no more than a mere twenty-five minutes, and it was during that brief time, while some thirty members of the socialists' club lingered inside, that the killer must have struck. The windows were open and the club members were singing festive songs in Russian and German. No one heard a scream or any other call of distress. But Elizabeth Stride probably didn't make a sound that anyone but her killer could hear.

Police Surgeon Dr. George Phillips arrived at the scene shortly after 1:00 A.M. and decided that since no weapon was present at the scene, the woman had not committed suicide. She must have been murdered, and he deduced that the killer had applied pressure to her shoulders with his hands and lowered her to the ground before cutting her throat from the front. She held the cachous between the thumb and forefinger of her left hand, and when the doctor removed the packet, some of the sweets spilled to the ground. Her left hand must have relaxed after death, Dr. Phillips said, but he could not explain why her right hand was "smeared with blood." This was most strange, he later testified, because her right hand was uninjured and resting on her chest. There was no explanation for the hand being bloody—unless the killer deliberately wiped blood on it. That would seem an odd thing for the killer to do.

Perhaps it did not occur to Dr. Phillips that the reflex of any conscious person who is hemorrhaging is to clutch the wound. When Elizabeth's throat was cut, she would have instantly grabbed her neck. It also made no sense to assume that Elizabeth Stride was pushed to the ground before she was killed. Why didn't she cry out or struggle when the killer grabbed her and forced her down? Nor is it likely that the Ripper cut her throat from the front.

To do that, her killer would have had to force her to the ground, attempting all the while to keep her quiet and under control as he slashed at her neck in the dark, blood spurting all over him. Somehow she still holds on to her packet of cachous. When a throat is cut from the front, there are usually several small incisions because of the awkward angle of attack. When a throat is cut from the rear, the incisions are long and often sufficient to sever major blood vessels and cut through tissue and cartilage all the way to the bone.

Once a killer devises a workable method, he rarely alters it unless something unanticipated occurs, causing the killer to abort his ritual or become more brutal, depending on the circumstances and his reactions. I believe that Jack the Ripper's modus operandi was to attack from the rear. He did not lower his victims to the ground first because he would have risked a struggle and loss of control. These were streetwise, feisty women who would not hesitate to protect themselves should a client get a bit rough or decide not to pay.

I doubt Elizabeth Stride knew what hit her. She may have drifted toward the building in Berner Street because she knew the IMWC members—most of them there without their girlfriends or wives—would begin leaving at around 1:00 A.M. and might be interested in quick sex. The Ripper may have been watching her from the deep shadows as she conducted business with other men, then waited until she was alone. He may have been familiar with the socialists' club and had shown up there before, possibly even earlier that night. The Ripper could have been wearing a false mustache, beard, or some other disguise to insure that he would not be recognized.

Walter Sickert was fluent in German and would have understood the debate that had been going on for hours inside the club the Saturday night of September 29th. Maybe he was in the crowd as the debate went on. It would have been in keeping with his character to participate before slipping out close to one o'clock, just as the singing began. Or maybe he never stepped inside the club at all and had been watching Elizabeth Stride ever since she left the lodging house. Whatever he did, it may not have been as difficult as one might suppose. If a killer is sober, intelligent, and logical; knows several languages; is an actor; has hiding places and does not live in the area, then it really is not so mind-boggling to imagine him getting away with murder in unlit slums. But I think he may have spoken to this victim. There was never an explanation for her single red rose.

The Ripper had ample time to escape when Louis Diemschutz hurried into the building for a candle and members of the socialists' club rushed outside to look. Shortly after the commotion began, a woman living several doors down at 36 Berner Street stepped outside and noticed a young man walking quickly toward Commercial Road. He glanced up at the lighted windows of the clubhouse, and the woman testified later that he was carrying a shiny black Gladstone case—popular in those days and similar in appearance to a medical bag.

Marjorie Lilly recalled in her written recollections of Sickert that he owned a Gladstone bag "to which he was much attached." On one occasion in the winter of 1918 while they were painting in his studio, he suddenly decided they should go to Petticoat Lane and he brought the bag out of the basement. For reasons she failed to comprehend, she wrote, Sickert painted "The Shrubbery, 81 Camden Road," in big white numbers and letters on the bag. She never did understand the "Shrubbery" part of the address, since Sickert had no shrubbery in his patchy front garden. Nor did Sickert ever offer her an explanation for his bizarre behavior. He was fifty-eight years old at the time. He was anything but senile. But he acted strangely sometimes, and Lilly recalled being unnerved when he carried his Gladstone bag out of the door and took her and another woman on a frightening excursion into Whitechapel during a thick, acrid fog.

They ended up in Petticoat Lane, and Ms. Lilly watched in astonishment as Sickert and his black bag disappeared along the mean streets as "the fog exceeded our worst fears" and it was almost as dark as night, she wrote. The women chased Sickert "up and down endless side streets until we were exhausted" as he stared at poor wretches huddled on steps leading into their slums, and joyfully exclaimed, "such a beautiful head! What a beard. A perfect Rembrandt." He could not be dissuaded from his adventure, which had taken him just a few streets away from where the Ripper's victims had been murdered exactly thirty years earlier.

In 1914, when World War I began and London was periodically blacked out, Sickert wrote in a letter, "Such interesting streets lit as they were 20 years ago when everything was Rembrandt." He had just walked home "by bye-ways" through Islington at night, and he added, "I wish the fear of Zeppelins would continue for ever so far as the lighting goes."

I questioned John Lessore about his uncle's Gladstone bag, and he told me he wasn't aware of anyone in the family knowing about a Gladstone bag that might have belonged to Walter Sickert. I tried very hard to find that bag. If it had been used to carry bloody knives, DNA could very well have come up with some interesting findings. Since I am speculating, I may as well add that for Sickert to paint "The Shrubbery" on his bag seems crazy, but then it may not be. During the Ripper murders, the police found a bloody knife in shrubbery close to where Sickert's mother lived. In fact, bloody knives began to turn up in several places, as if left deliberately to excite the police and neighbors.

The Monday night after Elizabeth Stride's murder, Thomas Coram, a coconut dealer, was leaving a friend's house in Whitechapel and noticed a knife at the bottom of steps leading into a laundry. The blade was a foot long with a blunted tip, and the black handle was six inches long and was wrapped in a bloody white handkerchief that had been tied in place with string. Coram did not touch the knife but immediately showed it to a local constable, who later testified that the knife was in the exact spot where he had stood not an hour earlier. He described the knife as "smothered" with dried blood and the sort a baker or chef might use. Sickert was an excellent cook and often dressed as a chef to entertain his friends.

While police were interrogating the members of the socialists' club who were singing inside the building when Elizabeth Stride was murdered, Jack the Ripper was making his way toward Mitre Square, where another prostitute named Catherine Eddows had headed after being released from prison. If the Ripper took the direct route of Commercial Road, followed it west, and turned left into Aldgate High Street to enter the City of London, his next crime scene was only a fifteen-minute walk from his last one.

CHAPTER NINETEEN

THESE CHARACTERS ABOUT

Catherine Eddows spent Friday night in a casual ward north of Whitechapel Road because she did not have fourpence to pay for her half of John Kelly's bed.

It had been seven or eight years now that she had been living with him in the lodging house at 55 Flower and Dean Street in Spitalfields. Before Kelly, she was with Thomas Conway, the father of her children—two boys, of fifteen and twenty, and a daughter named Annie Phillips, of twenty-three, who was married to a lampblack packer.

The sons lived with Conway, who had left Catherine because of her drinking habits. She had not seen him or her children in years, and this was by design. In the past when she would come around, she was always in need of money. Although she and Conway had never been married, he had bought and paid for her, she used to say, and his initials were tattooed in blue ink on her left forearm.

Catherine Eddows was forty-three years old and very thin. Hardship and drink had given her a pinched look, but she may have been attractive once, with her high cheekbones, dark eyes, and black hair. She and Kelly took one day at a time, holding themselves together mostly by hawking cheap items on the streets, and now and then she cleaned houses. They usually left London in the autumn because September was harvest time. They had only just got back on Thursday from weeks of "hopping" with thousands of other people who had fled the city for itinerant work. Catherine and Kelly had spirited themselves away from the East End to roam the farming districts of Kent, gathering hops used in the brewing of beer. The work was grueling, and the couple earned no more than a shilling per bushel, but at least they were far away from the smog and the filth and could feel the sun on their bodies and breathe fresh air. They ate and drank like royalty and slept in barns. When they returned to London, they had not a penny.

On Friday, September 28th, Kelly returned to the lodging house at 55 Flower and Dean Street in Spitalfields, and Catherine stayed without him in a free bed in a casual ward. It is not known what she did that night. Kelly later stated at her inquest that she was not a woman of the streets, nor was he the sort to tolerate her being with another man. Catherine never brought him money in the morning, he added, perhaps to forestall any intimations that she might have picked up a pittance here and there through prostitution. He was adamant that she did not have an addiction to alcohol and was only occasionally "in the habit of slightly drinking to excess."

Catherine and Kelly considered themselves man and wife and were fairly regular in paying the nightly rate of eightpence for their double bed in Flower and Dean Street. It was true they might have a word or two now and then. Some months earlier she had left him for "a few hours," but Kelly swore under oath that he and Catherine had been getting along just fine lately. He said that on Saturday morning she offered to pawn some of her clothing so they could buy food, but he insisted that she pawn his boots instead. She did, for half a crown. That pawn ticket and another one they had bought from a woman while hopping were safely tucked inside one of Catherine's pockets, in the hope that she might be able to reclaim Kelly's boots and other valuables someday soon.

On Saturday morning, September 29th, Catherine met up with Kelly between ten and eleven in the old clothing market in Houndsditch, a healed gash in the earth that in Roman days had been a moat protecting the city wall. Houndsditch ran between Aldgate High Street and Bishopsgate Within, and bordered the northeast side of the City of London. As Catherine and Kelly spent most of his boot money on food and enjoyed what for them was a hearty breakfast, she moved into the outer limits of her life. Within less than fifteen hours, Catherine Eddows would be bloodless and cold.

By early afternoon, she was dressed in what must have been everything she owned: a black jacket with imitation fur around the collar and the cuffs, two outer jackets trimmed in black silk braid and imitation fur, a chintz shirt with a Michaelmas daisy pattern and three flounces, a brown linsey dress bodice with a black velvet collar and brown metal buttons down the front, a gray petticoat, a very old green Alpaca skirt, a very old ragged blue skirt with a red flounce and light twill lining, a white calico chemise, a man's white vest with buttons down the front and two outer pockets, brown ribbed stockings darned at the feet with white thread, a pair of men's lace-up boots (the right boot repaired with red thread), a black straw bonnet trimmed with black beads and green and black velvet, a white apron, and "red gauze silk" and a large white handkerchief tied around her neck.

In her many layers and pockets were another handkerchief, bits and pieces of soap, string, white rag, white coarse linen, blue and white skirting, blue ticking and flannel, two black clay pipes, a red leather cigarette case, a comb, pins and needles, a ball of hemp, a thimble, a table knife, a teaspoon, and two old mustard tins safely securing a precious stash of sugar and tea she had bought with Kelly's boot money. He did not have money for their bed that night, and at 2:00 P.M., Catherine told him she was going to Bermondsey, south of the river. Maybe she could find her daughter, Annie.

Annie used to have a house in King Street, and apparently Catherine didn't know that her daughter had not lived in that house or in Bermondsey for years. Kelly said he wished Catherine wouldn't go anywhere. "Stay here," he said to her. She was insistent, and when Kelly called out to her to be careful of the "Knife"—the street name for the East End murderer—Catherine laughed. Of course she would be careful. She was always careful. She promised to be back in two hours.

Mother and daughter never saw each other that day, and no one seems to know where Catherine went. Perhaps she walked to Bermondsey and was dismayed to find that Annie had moved. Perhaps the neighbors told Catherine that Annie and her husband had left the area at least two years ago. Perhaps no one knew who Catherine was talking about when she said she was looking for her daughter. It's possible Catherine didn't intend to go to Bermondsey at all and just wanted an excuse to earn pennies for gin. She may have been all too aware that no one in her family wanted anything to do with her. Catherine was a drunken, immoral woman who belonged in the dustbin. She was an Unfortunate and a disgrace to her children. She did not return to Kelly by four o'clock, as she had said she would, but got herself locked up at Bishopsgate Police Station for being drunk.

The police station was just north of Houndsditch, where Kelly had seen Catherine last when they were eating and drinking away his boot money. When word reached him that she was in custody for being drunk, he decided she was safe enough and went to bed. At the inquest, he would admit that she had been locked up before. But as was said of the other Ripper victims, Catherine was a "sober, quiet" woman who got merry and liked to sing when she had one drink too many, which, of course, was rare. None of the Ripper's victims were addicted to alcohol, friends swore from the witness box.

In Catherine Eddows's time, alcoholism was not considered a disease. "Habitual drunkenness" afflicted someone "of a weak mind" or "weak intellect" who was destined for the lunatic asylum or prison. Drunkenness was a clear indication that a person was of thin moral fiber, a sinner given to vice, an imbecile in the making. Denial was just as persistent then as it is now and euphemisms were plentiful. People got into the drink. They had a drop to drink. They were known to drink. They were the worse for drink. Catherine Eddows was the worse for drink Saturday night. By eight thirty, she had passed out on a pavement in Aldgate High Street, and Police Constable George Simmons picked her up and moved her off to the side. He leaned her against some shutters, but she could not stay on her feet.

Simmons called for another constable and they got on either side of her to help her to the Bishopsgate Police Station. Catherine was too drunk to say where she lived or whether she knew anyone who might come for her, and when she was asked her name, she mumbled, "Nothing." At close to 9:00 P.M., she was in custody. At quarter past midnight, she was awake and singing to herself. Constable George Hutt testified at the inquest that he had been checking on her the past three or four hours, and when he stopped by her cell at approximately 1:00 A.M., she asked him when he was going to let her go. When she was capable of taking care of herself, he replied.

She told him she was capable of that now, and wanted to know what time it was. Too late for her to get "any more drink," he said. "Well, what time is it?" she persisted. He told her "just on one," and she retorted, "I shall get a damned fine hiding when I get home." P.C. Hutt unlocked her cell and warned her, "And serves you right; you have no right to get drunk." He took her into the office for questioning by the station sergeant, and she gave a false name and address: "Mary Ann Kelly" of "Fashion Street."

P.C. Hutt pushed open swinging doors that led to a passageway, showing her out. "This way, Missus," he said, and told her to make sure to pull the outer door shut behind her. "Good night, ol' Cock," she said, leaving the door open and turning left toward Houndsditch, where she had promised to meet John Kelly nine hours earlier. Probably no one will ever know why Catherine went that way first and then set out to the City, to Mitre Square, which was an eight- or ten-minute walk from Bishopsgate Police Station. Perhaps she planned to earn a few more pennies, and trouble wasn't likely in the City, at least not the kind of trouble Catherine was considering. The wealthy City of London was crowded and thriving during the workday, but most people whose jobs brought them into the Square Mile did not live there. Catherine and John Kelly didn't live there, either.

Their common lodging house in Flower and Dean Street was outside the City, and since Kelly was unaware of her after-hours entrepreneurial activities (or so he claimed after her death), perhaps she concluded that it was wise to stay in the City for a while, and not wander home and get into a row. Perhaps Catherine simply didn't know what she was doing. She had been in a cell for less than four hours. The average person metabolizes approximately one ounce of alcohol—or about one beer—per hour. Catherine must have had quite a lot of alcohol in her to have been "falling down drunk," and it is possible that when P.C. Hutt bade her good night, she was still intoxicated.

At the very least, she was hung over and bleary headed, and maybe suffering from tremors and blank spots in her memory, too. The best cure was a little hair of the dog that bit her. She needed another drink and a bed, and could have neither without money. If her man was going to give her hell, maybe it was best if she earned her pennies and slept somewhere else the rest of the night. Whatever she was thinking, it doesn't appear that returning to Kelly was foremost on her mind when she left the police station. Going to Mitre Square meant walking in the opposite direction from where Kelly was staying in Flower and Dean Street.

Some thirty minutes after Catherine left her cell, Joseph Lawende, a commercial traveler, and his friends Joseph Levy and Harry Harris left the Imperial Club at 16 and 17 Duke Street, in the City. It was raining and Lawende was walking at a slightly faster pace than his companions. At the corner of Duke Street and Church Passage, the street that led to Mitre Square, he noticed a man and a woman together. Lawende would state at the inquest that the man's back was to him, and all he could tell was that the man was taller than the woman and wearing a cap that might have had a peak.

The woman was dressed in a black jacket and a black bonnet, Lawende recalled, and as bad as the lighting conditions were at the time, he was later able to identify these items of clothing at the police station as having belonged to the woman he saw at 1:30 A.M., an exact time he based on the clubhouse clock and his own watch. "I doubt whether I should know him again," Lawende said of the man. "I did not hear a word said. They did not either of them appear to be quarreling. They appeared conversing very quietly—I did not look back to see where they went."

Joseph Levy, a butcher, did not get a good look at the couple, either, but he estimated that the man was perhaps three inches taller than the woman. As he walked along Duke Street, he commented to his friend Harris, "I don't like going home by myself when I see these characters about." When questioned closely by the coroner at the inquest, Levy amended his statement a bit. "There was nothing I saw about the man and woman which caused me to fear them," he said.

City of London officials would assure journalists that Mitre Square was not the sort of place where prostitutes prowled, and that City Police officers routinely were on the lookout for men and women together at late hours. If constables were instructed to take note of men and women in the Square at late hours, perhaps this suggested that questionable activity did go on there. Mitre Square was poorly lit. It was accessible by three long, dark passageways. It was filled with empty buildings, and a policeman's leather heels striking the pavement could be heard from far away and allowed plenty of time to hide.

Because Catherine Eddows was seen with a man just before her murder, it was theorized that before she was locked up, she had made an appointment to meet a client in Mitre Square. Such a suggestion seems unlikely if not absurd. She was with Kelly until 2:00 P.M. She was drunk and in custody until 1:00 A.M. It is hard to believe she promised a customer a late-night rendezvous when quick sex could be bought during the day, too. There were plenty of stairways, tumbledown buildings, and other deserted spots where hidden activities could go on. Even if Catherine had made the "appointment" while she was drunk, there is a good chance she would not have remembered it later. It is simpler to assume that while she may have headed toward the City in search of business, she had no particular client in mind but was looking for the luck of the draw.

The Acting Commissioner of the City of London Police, Henry Smith, who may have been as tenacious as Captain Ahab was in his hunt for the great white whale, probably didn't anticipate that the fiend would surface in his own patch and get away with murder for a hundred years. As usual, Smith was sleeping poorly in his quarters at Cloak Lane Station, built into Southwark Bridge on the north bank of the Thames. A railway depot was in front of the building and vans clanked and rattled at all hours. The furrier's business behind his rooms gave off the stench of curing animal hides, and he had not a single window he could open.

Smith was startled when his telephone rang, and he groped for it in the dark. One of his men told him there had been another murder, this one in the City. Smith dressed and hurried out of the door to a waiting hansom, "an invention of the devil," as he called it, because in the summer he was miserably hot, and in the winter he froze. A hansom was designed to carry two passengers, but on this early morning the one Smith climbed into carried the superintendent and three detectives in addition to himself. "We rolled like a seventy-four [a warship] in a gale," Smith recalled. But "we got to our destination—Mitre Square," where a small group of his officers stood around the mutilated body of Catherine Eddows, whose name they did not yet know.

Mitre Square was a small, open area surrounded by large warehouses, empty houses, and a few shops that were closed after office hours. During the day, fruit vendors, businessmen, and loiterers filled the Square. It was entered by three long passageways, which at night were thick with shadows barely pushed back by gaslights on the walls. The Square itself had only one lamp, and it was some twenty-five yards from the dark spot where Catherine was murdered. A City Police constable and his family lived on the other side of the Square, and heard nothing. James Morris, a watchman stationed inside the Kearley & Tonge Wholesale Grocers warehouse, also in the Square, was awake and working and heard nothing.

It seems that once again, no one heard a sound when the Ripper butchered his victim. If times sworn to can be trusted, Catherine Eddows could have been dead no more than fourteen minutes as P. C. Edward Watkins's beat brought him back into Leadenhall Street and then into Mitre Square. He could walk his beat in twelve to fourteen minutes, he testified at the inquest, and when he passed through the Square last at 1:30 A.M., there wasn't the slightest hint of anything out of the ordinary. When he shone his bull's-eye lantern into a very dark corner at 1:44 A.M., he discovered a woman lying on her back, her face to the left, her arms by her sides with the palms turned up. Her left leg was straight, the other bent, and her clothes were bunched up above her chest, exposing her abdomen, which had been cut open from just below the sternum to her genitals. Her intestines had been pulled out and tossed on the ground above her right shoulder. Watkins ran to the Kearley & Tonge warehouse, knocked on the door, and pushed it open, interrupting the watchman, who happened to be just on the other side, sweeping the steps.

"For God's sake mate, come to my assistance," Watkins said. Watchman Morris stopped sweeping and fetched his lamp as an upset Morris described "another woman cut up to pieces." The two men hurried out to the southwest corner of Mitre Square, where Catherine's body lay in a pool of blood. Morris blew his whistle and ran up to Mitre Street, then to Aldgate, where he "saw no suspicious person about," he recalled at the inquest. He ran and blew his whistle until he found two constables and told them, "Go down to Mitre Square. There has been another terrible murder!"

Dr. Gordon Brown, the police surgeon for the City Police, arrived at the scene not long after two o'clock. He squatted by the body and found next to it three metal buttons, a "common" thimble, and a mustard tin containing two pawn tickets. On the evidence of body warmth, the complete absence of rigor mortis, and other observations, Dr. Brown said that the victim had been dead no longer than half an hour, and he saw no bruises or signs of struggle or evidence of "recent connection," or sexual intercourse.

Dr. Brown was of the opinion that the intestines had been placed where they were "by design." This may be too complicated when one considers the circumstances. In both Annie Chapman's and Catherine Eddows's cases, the Ripper was in a frenzy and could scarcely see what he was doing because it was so dark. He was probably squatting or bent over the lower part of the victim's body when he slashed and tore through clothing and flesh, and it is more likely that he simply tossed the intestines out of the way because it was certain organs he wanted.

Police and newspaper reports vary in their details of what Catherine Eddows's body looked like when it was found. In one description, a two-foot segment of colon had been detached from the rest and was arranged between her right arm and body, but according to *The Daily Telegraph,* the piece of colon had been "twisted into the gaping wound on the right side of the neck." It was fortuitous that City Police Superintendent Foster's son, Frederick William Foster, was an architect. He was immediately summoned to draw sketches of Catherine's body and the area where it was found. These drawings depict a detailed and disturbing sight that is worse than any description at the inquest.

All of Catherine Eddows's clothing was cut and torn open, blatantly displaying a body cavity that could not have been more violated had she already been the subject of a postmortem. The Ripper's cuts opened the chest and abdomen to the upper thighs and genitals. He slashed her vagina and across the tops of the thighs as if he were reflecting back tissue in preparation for dismembering her legs at the hip joints.

The disfigurement to her face was shocking. Peculiar, deep nicks under both eyes were similar to artistic accents Sickert used in some of his paintings, particularly the portrait of a Venetian prostitute he called Giuseppina. The most severe damage to Catherine Eddows's face was to the right side, or the side exposed when the body was discovered, the same side of Giuseppina's face that has disturbing black brush strokes reminiscent of mutilation in a portrait of her titled *Putana a Casa.* A morgue photograph of Catherine Eddows resembles Giuseppina; both had long black hair, high cheekbones, and pointed chins.

Sickert was painting Giuseppina in the years 1903–04. My search through letters and other documentation and my queries to Sickert experts produced no evidence that anyone who might have visited Sickert in Venice had ever actually met or seen the prostitute. Sickert may have painted her in the privacy of his room, but I have yet to find any evidence that Giuseppina existed. Another painting of the same period is titled *Le Journal,* in which a dark-haired woman has her head thrown back, and her mouth open, as she reads a journal that she bizarrely holds high above her stricken face. Around her throat is a tight white necklace.

"What a pretty neklace I gave her," the Ripper writes on September 17, 1888.

Catherine Eddows's "pretty necklace" is a gaping gash in her throat that is shown in one of the few photographs taken before the postmortem and the suturing of the wounds. If one juxtaposes that photograph with the painting *Le Journal,* the similarities are startling. If Sickert saw Catherine Eddows when her throat was laid open and her head lolling back as shown in the photograph, he could not have done so unless he was in the mortuary before the postmortem or was at the crime scene.

Catherine Eddows's body was transported by hand ambulance to the mortuary on Golden Lane, and when she was undressed under close police supervision, her left ear lobe fell out of her clothing.

CHAPTER TWENTY

BEYOND IDENTITY

At two thirty that Sunday afternoon, Dr. Brown and a team of doctors performed the postmortem examination.

Other than one small fresh bruise on Catherine Eddows's left hand, the doctors found no other injuries that might have indicated she fought with her assailant, was struck, yoked, or thrown to the ground. The cause of her death was a six- or seven-inch cut across the neck that began at the left ear lobe—severing it—and terminated about three inches below the right ear. The incision severed the larynx, vocal cords, and all deep structures of the neck, nicking the intervertebral cartilage.

Dr. Brown determined that Catherine Eddows had hemorrhaged from her severed left carotid artery, that death "was immediate," and that the other mutilations were inflicted postmortem. He believed there was only one weapon, probably a knife, and it was pointed. Much more could have been said. The postmortem report indicates that the Ripper cut through Catherine's clothing. Considering the many layers she was wearing, this poses questions and difficulties.

Not just any type of cutting instrument could be used to cut through wool, linen, and cotton, no matter how old and rotten some of the fabrics might have been. I experimented with a variety of nineteenth-century knives, daggers, and cut-throat razors and discovered that cutting through clothing with a blade that is curved or long is tricky, if not treacherous. The blade would have to be very sharp, strong, and pointed. The best choice, I found, was a six-inch dagger with a guard that prevents the hand from slipping down the blade.

I suspect the Ripper didn't actually "cut through" the clothing, but rather stabbed through layers and tore them open, exposing the abdomen and genitals. This is a variation of his method and worth analyzing, because it does not appear that he cut through Mary Ann Nichols's or Annie Chapman's clothing. One simply can't be certain of the details in earlier cases. Records appear to be incomplete and possibly were not meticulously made or kept at the time. Although the City would come no closer to capturing Jack the Ripper, it was better equipped to handle his carnage.

Catherine Eddows's records are surprisingly well preserved and reveal that the examination of her body was very thorough and professional. The City Police had certain advantages, not least of which was learning from recent, much-publicized mistakes. City Police had a substantially smaller, wealthier jurisdiction to control, a suitable mortuary, and access to superb medical men. When Catherine was transported to the mortuary, the City Police assigned an inspector whose only responsibility was to look after the body, clothing, and personal effects. When Dr. Brown performed the postmortem, he was assisted by two other physicians, including the Metropolitan Police surgeon, Dr. George Phillips. If one assumes that Catherine was the first victim whose clothing was "cut off" instead of pushed up, the change of modus operandi shows an escalation in the Ripper's violence and confidence, as well as a heightened contempt and need to shock.

Catherine's body was almost nude, her legs spread, and she was butchered in the middle of a pavement. The blood flowing out of her severed carotid artery seeped under her and left an outline of her body on the ground that was visible to passersby and trodden on the next day. The Ripper struck practically within view of a watchman, a sleeping constable who lived in the Square, and a City officer whose beat took him past the murder scene every twenty-five minutes. The damage the Ripper inflicted on Catherine's body required not so much as a glint of surgical skill. He simply slashed like mad.

The cuts to her face were quick and forceful, the slices to her lips completely dividing them and cutting into the underlying gums. The cut to the bridge of her nose extended down to the angle of her left jaw and laid open her cheek to the bone. The tip of the nose was completely severed, and two other cuts to the cheeks peeled up the skin into triangular flaps. The damage to her abdomen, genitalia, and internal organs was just as brutal. The incisions that laid her open were jagged and were mixed with stabbing injuries. Her left kidney was removed and taken, and half of her uterus was sloppily cut off and taken as well.

She had cuts to her pancreas and spleen, and one in her vagina that extended through her rectum. Hacks to the right thigh were so deep they severed ligaments. There was nothing careful or even purposeful in the damage. The intention was mutilation, and the Ripper was frenzied. He could have done this damage to Catherine Eddows's body in less than ten minutes—maybe as few as five. It was requiring more daring and savagery to achieve the same thrill. The Ripper's "catch me if you can" taunt seemed to be straining to the limit.

The artist, critic, and Sickert supporter D. S. MacColl once wrote in a letter that Walter Sickert "will over calculate himself one day." Sickert didn't, at least not during his lifetime. Law enforcement was not equipped to follow the forensic and psychological traces he left each time he killed. In today's investigations, evidence collection would have been conducted in a way that would have seemed to the Victorians like some fantasy out of Jules Verne. Catherine Eddows's crime scene was a difficult one because it was outdoors in a public place that would have been contaminated by the multitudes. The lighting was terrible, and the sensationalism of the crime would have caused the police to fear further contamination by the curious who were certain to gather—even long after the body had been removed to the City mortuary on Golden Lane.

The most important piece of evidence in any murder is the body. All evidence connected to it must be preserved by any means possible. Today, if Catherine Eddows's body was discovered in Mitre Square, the police would immediately seal off the scene, radio for more officers to secure the area, and contact the pathologist. Lights would be set up, and rescue vehicles would arrive with emergency lights flashing. All streets and passageways leading to the crime scene would be barricaded and guarded by police.

A detective or member of a forensic unit would begin videotaping the scene from the outer perimeter, again aware of bystanders. It is quite possible—in fact, I would bet on it—that Sickert showed up at every crime scene and blended into the crowds. He would not have been able to resist seeing the reaction of his audience. In a painting of his called *The Fair at Night, Dieppe,* the scene he depicts looks very much like what one might expect to see when spectators surrounded the East End locations where the murders took place.

The Fair at Night, Dieppe, circa 1901, shows a mob of people from the rear, as if we are looking through the eyes of an observer who is standing some distance behind the curious crowd. Were it not for what appears to be a carousel tent intruding into the painting from the right, there would be no reason to think the scene has anything to do with a fair. The people don't necessarily seem interested in the carousel, but in the activity occurring in the direction of the tenements or terraced houses.

Sickert painted *The Fair at Night, Dieppe* from a sketch. He drew what he witnessed until he was in his sixties. Then he began to paint from photographs, as if the more his sexual energy waned, the less he felt the compulsion to go out and experience his art. "One can't work at all over 50 like one did at 40," Sickert admitted.

A fair or carnival is exactly what the Ripper's crime scenes became, with boys hawking special editions of newspapers, vendors arriving with carts, and neighbors selling tickets. The International Working Men's Educational Club in Berner Street charged admission to enter the yard where Elizabeth Stride was murdered, thereby raising money to print its socialist tracts. For a penny, one could purchase "A Thrilling Romance" about the Whitechapel Murders that included "all details connected with these Diabolical Crimes, and faithfully pictures the Night Horrors of this portion of the Great City."

In all of the Ripper's murders, no footprints or tracks leading away from the bodies were ever found. It is hard for me to imagine that he didn't step in blood when pints of it were spurting and flowing from the fatal injuries he inflicted on his victims. But these bloody footprints would not have been visible without the aid of alternate light sources and chemicals. Trace evidence would have been missed, and one can be certain that the Ripper left hairs, fibers, and other microscopic particles at the scene and on his victims. He carried trace evidence away with him on his person, footwear, and clothing.

The Ripper's victims would have been a forensic nightmare because of the contamination and mixture of trace evidence—including seminal fluid—from multiple clients, all of it exacerbated by the women's pitiful hygiene. But there would have been some substance, organic or inorganic, worth collecting. Unusual evidence may very well have been discovered. Cosmetics worn by a killer are easily transferred to a victim. Had Sickert applied grease paint to darken his skin, had he temporarily dyed his hair, or had he been wearing adhesives for false mustaches and beards, these substances could be discovered by using a polarized light microscope or chemical analysis or spectrophotofluorometric methods, such as the Omnichrome light, that are available to forensic scientists today.

Some dyes in lipsticks are so easily identifiable by scientific methods that it is possible to determine the brand and trade name of the color. Sickert's grease paints and paints from his studio would not have eluded the scanning electron microscope, the ion microprobe, the x-ray diffractometer, or thin-layer chromatography, to list a few of the resources available now. Tempera paint on a 1920s Sickert painting titled *Broadstairs* lit up a neon blue when we examined it with a nondestructive alternate light source at the Virginia Institute of Forensic Science and Medicine. If Sickert had transferred a microscopic residue of a similar tempera paint from his clothing or hands to a victim, the Omnichrome would have detected it and chemical analysis would have followed.

Finding an artist's paint on a murder victim would have been a significant breakthrough in the investigation. Had it been possible in the Victorian era to detect paints adhering to a victim's blood, the police might not have been so quick to assume Jack the Ripper was a butcher, a lunatic Pole or Russian Jew, or an insane medical student. The presence of residues consistent with cosmetics or adhesives would have raised significant questions as well. Stray knives turning up would have given answers instead of only posing questions.

A preliminary quick-and-easy chemical test could have determined whether the dried reddish material on the blades was blood instead of rust or some other substance. Precipitin tests that react to antibodies would have determined if the blood was human, and finally, DNA would either match a victim's genetic profile or not. It is possible that latent fingerprints could have been found on a knife. It is possible that the killer's DNA could have been determined had Jack the Ripper cut himself or perspired into the handkerchief he wrapped around a knife handle.

Hairs could be compared or analyzed for non-nuclear or mitochondrial DNA. Tool marks imparted by the weapon to cartilage or bone could have been compared to any weapon recovered. These days, all that could be done would be, but what we can't account for is how much Sickert would know were he committing his murders now. He was described by acquaintances as having a scientific mind. His paintings and etchings demonstrate considerable technical skill.

He did some of his drawings in a tradesman's day book that had columns for pounds, shillings, and pence. On the backs of other drawings are mathematical scribbles, perhaps from Sickert's calculating the prices of things. These same sorts of scribbles are on a scrap of lined paper the Ripper wrote a letter on. Apparently he was figuring out the price of coal.

Sickert's art was premeditated and so were his crimes. I strongly suspect he would know about today's forensic science, were he committing his murders now, just as he knew what was available in 1888, which was handwriting comparison, identification by physical features, and "fingermarks." He also would have been keenly aware of sexually transmitted diseases, and it is likely he exposed himself to his victims' body fluids as little as possible. He may have worn gloves when he killed and then removed his bloody clothing as quickly as he could. He may have worn rubber-soled boots that were quiet on the street and easy to clean. He could have carried changes of clothing, disguises, and weapons in a Gladstone bag. He could have wrapped items in newspaper and string.

The day after Mary Ann Nichols's murder, Saturday, September 1st, the *Daily Telegraph* and the *Weekly Dispatch* ran stories about the peculiar experience a dairyman claimed to have had at 11:00 P.M. the night before, or within hours of Mary Ann's murder. The dairyman's shop was in Little Turner Street, off Commercial Road, and he reported to the police that a stranger carrying a shiny black bag came to the door and asked to buy a penny's worth of milk, which he drank in one gulp.

He then asked to borrow the dairyman's shed for a moment, and while the stranger was inside it, the dairyman noticed a flash of white. He went to investigate and caught the stranger covering his trousers with a "pair of white overalls, such as engineers wear." The stranger next snatched out a white jacket and quickly pulled it over his black cutaway as he said, "It's a dreadful murder, isn't it?" He grabbed his black bag and rushed into the street, exclaiming, "I think I have a clue!"

The dairyman described the stranger as about twenty-eight years old with a ruddy complexion, a three days' growth of beard, dark hair and large staring eyes, and as having the general appearance of a "clerk" or "student." The white overalls and jacket—similar to what an "engineer" wore—were also what Sickert used to cover his clothing when he painted in his studios. Three sets of these white overalls were donated by his second wife's family to the Tate Archive.

The dairyman's story takes on even more suspicious shadings when added to it is another account of clothing in the news after Elizabeth Stride's and Catherine Eddows's murders. The day following their murders, Monday, October 1st, at nine o'clock, a Mr. Chinn, who was the landlord of the Nelson Tavern in Kentish Town, discovered a newspaper-wrapped package behind the door of an outbuilding behind the tavern. He ignored the package until he happened to read about Elizabeth Stride's murder and realized that the package in his outbuilding matched the description of the one carried by a man who was seen talking to Elizabeth less than half an hour before her death.

Mr. Chinn went to the police station in Kentish Town Road to report the matter. When a detective arrived at the pub, the package had been kicked into the roadway and had burst open. Inside was a pair of blood-soaked dark trousers. Hair was found adhering to coagulated bloodstains on the newspaper wrapping. No further description of the hair or newspaper wrapping seems to be known, and the trousers were subsequently carried off by a vagrant. I suppose the detective had no further use of them and simply left them in the road.

The description of the man carrying a newspaper-wrapped package whom Police Constable William Smith observed talking to Elizabeth Stride is similar to the description the dairyman gave police: Both men had a dark complexion, were clean-shaven—or at least had no full beard—and were approximately twenty-eight years old. The Nelson Tavern in Kentish Town was about two miles east of where Sickert lived in South Hampstead. He did not have a dark or weathered complexion, but it would have been easy enough for him to create one with makeup. He did not have dark hair. But actors wore wigs and dyed their hair.

It would have been a simple matter to leave wrapped packages or even Gladstone bags in hidden places, and it is doubtful that Sickert would have cared whether the police recovered a pair of bloody trousers. In those days, nothing useful could be learned from them unless they bore some sort of marking that could have been traced back to the owner.

Facial mutilations can be extremely revealing, and a forensic psychologist or profiler would assign great importance to the mutilation of Catherine Eddows's face, which, in Chief Inspector Donald Swanson's words, damaged her "almost beyond identity." The face is the person. To mutilate it is personal. Often this degree of violence occurs when the victim and assailant are known to each other, but not always. Sickert used to slash paintings to tatters when he decided to destroy his work. On one occasion he instructed his wife Ellen to go out and buy two curved, sharp knives that he said were just like ones she used for pruning.

This took place in Paris, according to the story Sickert told the writer Osbert Sitwell. Sickert said he needed the knives to help slash Whistler's paintings. The Master had a habit of being discontented with his work, and when all else failed, he destroyed his art. Burning was one method. Cutting up paintings was another. While Sickert was an apprentice, he probably would have assisted in ripping up canvases, just as he claimed, and perhaps with the very knives he mentioned to Sitwell. Exactly when those knives would have been purchased can't be determined, but it was most likely between 1885 and 1887 or early 1888. Before 1885, Sickert wasn't married. In 1888 Whistler was, and his relationship with Sickert was tapering off and would end entirely less than ten years later.

An artist destroying a painting that he or she has grown to hate is in some measure analogous to a killer destroying the face of a victim. The destruction could be an effort to eradicate an object that causes the artist frustration and rage. Or it could be an attempt to ruin what one can't possess, whether it is artistic perfection or another human being. If one wants sex and can't have it, to destroy the object of lust is to make it no longer desirable.

Night after night, Sickert watched sexually provocative performances at music halls. During much of his career, he would sketch nude female models. He spent time behind locked studio doors, staring at them, even touching them, but never consummating except through a pencil, a brush, a palette knife. If he was capable of sexual desire but completely incapable of gratifying it, his frustration must have been agonizing and enraging. In the early 1920s, he was painting portraits of a young art student named Ciceley Hey, and one day when he was alone with her in the studio, he sat next to her on the sofa and without warning or explanation, started screaming.

One of the portraits he painted of her is *Death and the Maiden.* At some point between the early 1920s and his death in 1942, he gave her *Jack the Ripper's Bedroom.* Where the painting had been since its completion in 1908, no one seems to know. Why he gave it to Ciceley Hey is also a mystery, unless one chooses to suppose that he entertained sexually violent fantasies about her. If she thought there was anything peculiar about Sickert's producing a foreboding piece of work with an equally foreboding title, I am unaware of it.

Perhaps one reason Sickert liked his models ugly is that he preferred to be around flesh he did not desire. Perhaps murder and mutilation were a powerful cathartic for his frustration and rage, and a way to destroy his desire. This is not to say he lusted after prostitutes. But they represented sex. They represented his immoral grandmother, the Irish dancer, whose fault it may have been—in Sickert's twisted psyche—that he was born with a severe deformity. One can offer conjectures that may sound reasonable, but they will never comprise the whole truth. Why any person has such a disregard for life that he or she enjoys destroying it is beyond comprehension.

The theory that each victim's throat was cut while she was lying on the ground remained the predominant one even after the murders of Elizabeth Stride and Catherine Eddows. Physicians and police were convinced that on the evidence of blood patterns, the women could not have been standing when the killer severed their carotid arteries. Possibly what the doctors were assuming was that arterial bleeding would have spurted a certain distance and at a certain height had the victims been on their feet. There may also have been an assumption that the victims lay down to have sex.

Prostitutes weren't likely to lie down on hard pavements or in mud or wet grass, and the doctors were not interpreting blood patterns on the basis of scientific testing. In modern laboratories, blood spatter experts routinely conduct experiments with blood to get a better idea of how it drips, flies, sprays, spurts, and spatters according to the laws of physics. In 1888, no one working on the Ripper cases was spending his time researching how far or how high blood arced when an upright person's carotid artery was cut.

No one knew about the back spatter pattern caused by the repeated swinging or stabbing motions of a weapon. It does not appear that the doctors who attended the death scenes considered that perhaps Jack the Ripper simultaneously cut his victim's throat and pulled her backward to the ground. Investigators didn't seem to contemplate the possibility that the Ripper might have assiduously avoided being bloody in public by quickly getting out of his bloody clothes, overalls, or gloves, and retreating to one of his hovels to clean up.

Sickert was afraid of diseases. He had a fetish about hygiene and was continually washing his hands. He would immediately wash his hair and face if he accidentally put on another person's hat. Sickert would have known about germs, infections, and diseases; he would have known that one didn't have to engage in oral, vaginal, or anal intercourse to contract them. Blood splashed into his face or transferred from his hands to his eyes or mouth or an open wound was enough to cause him a serious problem. Years later, he would go through a time of worry when he thought he had a sexually transmitted disease that turned out to be gout.

CHAPTER TWENTY-ONE

A GREAT JOKE

At 3:00 A.M., September 30th, Metropolitan Police Constable Alfred Long was patrolling Goulston Street in Whitechapel.

H Division wasn't usually his area, but he had been called in because Jack the Ripper had just murdered two more women. Long walked past several dark buildings occupied by Jews, directing his bull's-eye lantern into the darkness and listening for any unusual sounds. His bleary light shone into a foreboding passageway leading inside a building and illuminated a piece of dark-stained cloth on the ground. Written above it in white chalk on the black dado of the wall was

The Juwes are
The men That
Will not
be Blamed
for nothing.

Long picked up the piece of cloth. It was a piece of apron wet with blood, and he immediately searched the staircases of 100–119. He would admit later at Catherine Eddows's inquest, "I did not make any enquiries of the tenements in the buildings. There were six or seven staircases. I searched every one; found no traces of blood or footmarks."

He should have checked all of the tenements. It is possible that whoever dropped the piece of apron might have been going into the building. The Ripper might live there. He might be hiding there. Long got out his notebook and copied down the chalk writing on the wall, and he rushed to Commercial Street Police Station. It was important that he report what he had discovered, and he didn't have a partner with him. He may have been scared.

P.C. Long had passed the same passageway in Goulston Street at 2:20 A.M., and he swore at the inquest that the piece of apron wasn't there then. He would also testify that he couldn't say that the chalk message on the wall was "very recently written." Perhaps the ethnic slur had been there for a while and it was simply a coincidence that the bit of bloody apron had been found right below it. The accepted and sensible point of view has always been that the Ripper wrote those bigoted words right after he murdered Catherine Eddows. It wouldn't make sense for a slur about Jews to have been left for many hours or days in the passageway of a building occupied by Jews.

The writing on the wall has continued to be the source of great controversy in the Ripper case. The message—presumably dashed off by the Ripper—was in a legible hand, and in the Metropolitan Police files at the Public Record Office, I found two versions of it. Long was fastidious. The copies he made in his notebook are almost identical, suggesting they may closely resemble what he saw in chalk. His facsimiles resemble Sickert's handwriting. The uppercase T's appear very similar to ones in the Ripper letter of September 25th. But it is treacherous—and worthless in court—to compare writing that is a "copy," no matter how carefully it was made.

People have always been intent on decoding the writing on the wall. Why was "Jews" spelled "Juwes"? Perhaps the writing on the wall was nothing more than a scribble intended to create the very stir it has. The Ripper liked to write. He made sure his presence was known. So did Sickert, and he also had a habit of scrawling notes in chalk on the dark walls of his studios. There is no photograph of the writing on the wall in Catherine Eddows's case because Charles Warren insisted it was to be removed immediately. The sun would rise soon and the Jewish community would see the chalky slur and all hell would break loose.

What Warren didn't need was another riot. So he made another foolish decision. As his policemen anxiously waited for the cumbersome wooden camera, they sent word to Warren suggesting that the first line, containing the word "Juwes," could be scrubbed off and the rest of the writing left to be photographed for handwriting comparison. Absolutely not, Warren fired back. Rub out the writing *right now.* Day was breaking. People were stirring. The camera had not arrived and the writing was rubbed out.

No one doubted that the piece of apron P.C. Long found had come from the white apron Catherine was wearing over her clothing. Dr. Gordon Brown said he could not possibly know if the blood on it was human—even if St. Bartholomew's, the oldest hospital in London with one of the finest medical schools, was right there in the City. Dr. Brown could have submitted the bloody piece of apron to a microscopist. At least he thought to tie both ends of Catherine's stomach and submit it for chemical analysis in the event narcotics were present. They weren't. The Ripper wasn't drugging his victims first to incapacitate them.

I suspect the question of human blood wasn't important to Dr. Brown or the police. The cut-out piece of bloody cloth seemed to fit the cut-out section of Catherine's apron, and proof that the blood was human may not have been an issue if a suspect went to court. Perhaps not testing the blood was a smart investigative tactic. If the blood had come back as human, one still could not prove it was Catherine's.

The police decided that the killer had cut off the bit of apron so he could wipe blood and fecal matter off his hands. For some reason, he hung on to the soiled fabric as he left the City and retraced his steps back toward Whitechapel. He ducked into the entrance of the building in Goulston Street to write the note on the wall, and then thought to discard the piece of soiled apron—perhaps when he rummaged in a pocket for a piece of chalk, which I suppose he just happened to be carrying around with him.

The bit of bloody apron was not viewed as part of the Ripper's deliberate game, nor was his visit to Goulston Street seen as part of his ongoing mockery of authority. I wonder why police didn't ask why the killer was carrying chalk. Did people of the East End routinely carry chalk or even own it? Perhaps it should have been considered that if the Ripper did bring a stick of chalk with him when he set out that night, he had planned to write the bigoted message—or something like it—on the wall after he committed murder.

For the Ripper to backtrack from Mitre Square to Goulston Street involved his virtually returning to Elizabeth Stride's crime scene. Quite likely, this route took him from the Church Passage out of Mitre Square, and to Houndsditch, Gravel Lane, Stoney Lane—and across Petticoat Lane, where Sickert went on his unnerving sojourn in the fog many years later when he carried his Gladstone bag and took Marjorie Lilly and her friend with him. The police were baffled that the murderer would be this bold. There were constables and detectives all over the place. The law enforcement community would have been better served had it spent more energy analyzing the killer's outrageous backtrack and his piece of chalk instead of getting stuck in the muck of the meaning of "Juwes."

"Togs 8 suits, many hats I wear," the Ripper wrote in an eighty-one-line poem he sent to the "Superintendent of Great Scotland Yard" November 8th a year later. "The man is keen: quick, and leaves no trace—" His objective is to "destroy the filthy hideous whores of the night; Dejected, lost, cast down, ragged, and thin, Frequenters of Theatres, Music-halls and drinkers of Hellish gin."

For Walter Sickert, it would have been another big "ha ha" to return to the scene of Elizabeth Stride's murder and ask a constable what was going on. In the same poem of 1889, the Ripper boasts, "I spoke to a policeman who saw the sight, And informed me it was done by a Knacker in the night. . . . I told the man you should try and catch him; Say another word old Chap I'll run you in.

"One night hard gone I did a policeman meet—Treated and walked with him down High St."

The 1889 poem was "filed with the others." No significant attention was paid to the distinctive form of printing or the relatively clever rhymes, which were not those of an illiterate or deranged person. The reference to theaters and music halls as places where the Ripper spots "whores" should have been a clue. Perhaps an undercover man or two should have begun frequenting such places. Sickert spent many of his nights at theaters and music halls. Lunatics and impoverished butchers and East End ruffians probably did not.

In the 1889 poem, the Ripper admits he reads the "papers" and takes great exception to being called "insane." He says, "I always do my work alone," contradicting the much-publicized theory that the Ripper might have an accomplice. He claims he doesn't "smoke, swill, or touch gin." "Swill" was street slang for excessive drinking, which Sickert certainly did not do at this stage in his life. If he drank at all, he wasn't likely to touch rot-gut gin. He did not smoke cigarettes, although he was fond of cigars and became rather addicted to them in later years.

"Altho, self taught," the Ripper says, "I can write and spell."

The poem is difficult to decipher in places, and "Knacker" might be used twice or might be "Knocker" in one of the lines. "Knacker" was street slang for a horse slaughterer. "Knocker" was street slang for finely or showily dressed. Sickert was no horse slaughterer, but the police publicly theorized that the Ripper might be one.

Sickert's greatest gift was not poetry, but this did not deter him from jotting a rhyme or two in letters or singing silly, original lyrics he set to music-hall tunes. "I have composed a poem to Ethel," he wrote in later years when his friend Ethel Sands was volunteering for the Red Cross:

With your syringe on your shoulder
And your thermometer by your side
You'll be curing some young officer
And making him your pride

In another letter, he includes a verse about the "incessant sopping drizzle" in Normandy:

It can't go on for ever
It would if it could
But there is no use talking
For it couldn't if it would

In a Ripper letter sent in October 1896 to Commercial Street Police Station in Whitechapel, he mocks the police by quoting, " 'The Jewes are people that are blamed for nothing' Ha Ha have you heard this before." The spelling of "Jews" was hotly debated during Catherine Eddows's inquest, and the coroner repeatedly questioned police whether the word on the wall was "Juwes" or "Jewes." Even though the Ripper was supposed to be dead by 1896—according to Chief Constable Melville Macnaghten—the letter of 1896 concerned the police enough to result in a flurry of memorandums:

"I beg to submit attached letter received per post 14th inst. Signed Jack the Ripper stating that writer has just returned from abroad and means to go on again when he gets the chance," Supervisor George Payne wrote in his special report from the Commercial Street Station. "The letter appears similar to those received by police during the series of murders in the district in 1888 and 1889. Police have been instructed to keep a sharp lookout."

A telegram was sent to all divisions, asking police to keep this "sharp look out, but at the same time to keep the information quiet. Writer in sending the letter no doubt considers it a great joke at the expense of the police." On October 18, 1896, a chief inspector wrote in a Central Officer's Special Report that he had compared the recent letter with old Jack the Ripper letters and "failed to find any similarity of handwriting in any of them, with the exception of the two well remembered communications which were sent to the 'Central News' Office; one a letter, dated 25th Sept./88 and the other a post-card, bearing the postmark 1st Oct./88."

What is so blatantly inconsistent in the chief inspector's report is that he first says there are no similarities between the recent letter and the earlier Ripper letters, but then he goes on to cite similarities: "I find many similarities in the formation of letters. For instance the y's, t's and w's are very much the same. Then there are several words which appear in both documents." But in conclusion, the chief inspector decides, "I beg to observe that I do not attach any importance to this communication." CID Superintendent Donald Swanson agreed. "In my opinion," he noted at the end of the inspector's report, "the handwritings are not the same. . . . I beg that the letter may be put with other similar letters. Its circulation is to be regretted."

The letter of 1896 was given no credibility by police and was not published in the newspapers. The Ripper was banished, exorcised. He no longer existed. Maybe he never had existed, but was just some fiend who killed a few prostitutes, and all of those letters were from crackpots. Ironically, Jack the Ripper became a "Mr. Nobody" again, at least to the police, for whom it was most convenient to live in denial.

It has often been asked—and I expect the question will always be asked—if Sickert committed other murders in addition to the ones believed to have been committed by Jack the Ripper. Serial killers don't suddenly start and stop. The Ripper was no exception, and as is true of other serial killers, he did not restrict his murders to one location, especially a heavily policed area where there were thousands of anxious citizens looking for him. It would have been incredibly risky to write letters laying claim to every murder he committed, and I don't think the Ripper did. Sickert thrived on the publicity, on the game. But first and foremost was his need to kill and not be caught.

Eleven months after the Ripper letter of 1896, twenty-year-old Emma Johnson disappeared on the early evening of Wednesday, September 15th, while walking home near Windsor, about twenty miles west of London. The next day, two women picking blackberries close to Maidenhead Road discovered two muddy petticoats, a bloody chemise, and a black coat in a ditch under shrubbery.

On Friday, September 17th, the Berkshire police were notified of Emma's disappearance and organized a search. The clothing was identified as Emma's, and on Sunday, in the same field where the women had been picking berries, a laborer found a skirt, a bodice, a collar, and a pair of cuffs in a ditch. On the banks of a stagnant inlet of the Thames, Emma's mother discovered a pair of her daughter's stays. Near these were the imprint of a woman's boot and scrape marks in the earth apparently made by someone dragging a heavy object toward the murky inlet.

Police dragged the stagnant water, and fifteen feet offshore a muddy, slimy, naked body emerged. It was identified by the Johnsons as their daughter. A doctor examined Emma's body at the family home, and it was his conclusion that she was grabbed by the right arm and received a blow to the head to render her insensible before the killer cut her throat. At some point, her clothing was removed. Then the killer dragged her body to the inlet and shoved or threw it into the water. Maidenhead Road was a well-known spot for romantic couples to frequent at night.

There was no suspect and the murder was never solved. There is no evidence it was committed by Walter Sickert. I do not know where he was in September of 1897, although he was not with Ellen. The couple had separated the year before and were still friendly and occasionally traveled together, but Ellen was in France when Emma Johnson was murdered and had not been in Sickert's company for months. Eighteen ninety-seven was a particularly stressful year for Sickert. An article he had written for the *Saturday Review* the previous year had precipitated the artist Joseph Pennell into suing him for libel.

Sickert had publicly and foolishly claimed that Pennell's prints made by transfer lithography were not true lithography. Whistler used the same lithographic process—as did Sickert—and the Master appeared as a witness in Pennell's case. In an October 1896 letter to Ellen from her sister Janie, Whistler was quoted as saying that he believed Sickert's arrow was really aimed at him, not Pennell. Sickert had a "treacherous side to his character," Whistler told Janie. "Walter will do anything, throw anyone over for the object of the moment." Sickert lost the case, but perhaps the greater sting had already come—when Whistler testified from the witness stand that his former pupil was an unimportant and irresponsible man.

In 1897, Sickert's relationship with Whistler finally came to an end. Sickert was poor. He was publicly humiliated. His marriage was ending. He had resigned from the New English Art Club. The autumn seemed to be a prime time for the Ripper's crimes. It was the time of year when five-year-old Sickert endured his terrible surgery in London. Mid-September was when Ellen decided she wanted a divorce, and it was also the time of year when Sickert usually returned to London from his beloved Dieppe.

CHAPTER TWENTY-TWO

BARREN FIELDS AND SLAG-HEAPS

At the mortuary in Golden Lane, Catherine Eddows's naked body was hung up by a nail on the wall, rather like a painting.

One by one the male jurors and the coroner, Samuel Frederick Langham, filed in to look at her. John Kelly and Catherine's sister had to look at her, too. On October 4, 1888, the jurors returned what was becoming a familiar verdict to the press and the public: "Wilful murder by some person unknown." The public outcry was reaching hysteria. Two women had been slaughtered within an hour of each other, and the police still had no clue.

Letters from the public warned that "the condition of the lowest classes is most fraught with danger to all other classes." Londoners in better neighborhoods were beginning to fear for their lives. Perhaps they ought to raise a fund for the poor to "offer them a chance to forsake their evil lives." An "agency" should be formed. Letters to *The Times* suggested that if the upper class could clean up the lower class, there would be no more of this violence.

Overpopulation and the class system, few people seemed to realize, created problems that could not be remedied by tearing down slums or forming "agencies." The advocacy of birth control was considered blasphemous, and certain types of people were rubbish and always would be. Social problems certainly existed. But class problems were not why prostitutes were dying at the Ripper's hands. Psychopathic murder is not a social disease. People who lived in the East End knew that, even if they didn't know the word "psychopath." The streets of the East End were deserted at night, and scores of plainclothes policemen lurked in the shadows, waiting for the first suspicious male to appear, their disguises and demeanor fooling no one. Some policemen began wearing rubber-soled boots. So did reporters. It was a wonder people didn't terrify each other as they quietly crossed paths in the dark, waiting for the Ripper.

No one knew he had committed yet another murder—this one weeks earlier and never really attributed to him. On Tuesday, October 2nd—two days after the murders of Elizabeth Stride and Catherine Eddows—a decomposing female torso was discovered in the foundations of Scotland Yard's new headquarters, which was under construction on the Embankment near Whitehall.

A severed arm had turned up first on September 11th. No one had got very excited about it except a Mrs. Potter, whose feeble-minded seventeen-year-old daughter had been missing since September 8th, the same morning Annie Chapman was murdered. The police had little power of intervention or interest in the cases of missing teenagers, especially the likes of Emma Potter, who had been in and out of workhouses and infirmaries, and was nothing but a nuisance.

Emma's mother was accustomed to her disappearances and brushes with the law, and was terrified when her daughter took off yet again, and then a dismembered female arm was found as gruesome murders continued in the city. Mrs. Potter's pleas to the police were rewarded by a benevolent fate when a constable found Emma wandering about, alive and well. But had it not been for the hue and cry her mother made and the news stories that followed, it is possible that not much would have been made of a body part. Reporters began to pay attention. Was it possible that the Whitechapel fiend was up to other horrors? But the police said no. Dismemberment was an entirely different modus operandi, and neither Scotland Yard nor its surgeons were inclined to accept the view that a killer changed his pattern.

The arm had been severed at the shoulder and was tied with string. It was discovered on the foreshore of the Thames near the Grosvenor Railway Bridge in Pimlico, less than four miles southwest of Whitechapel and on the same side of the river. Pimlico was about five miles south of 54 Broadhurst Gardens—a short walk for Sickert. "I went [on] such a walk yesterday about 11 kilom.'s," he wrote from Dieppe when he was fifty-four years old. Five miles was no distance at all, not even when he was an old man whose disoriented and bizarre wanderings were a constant worry to his third wife and others who looked after him.

Pimlico was barely a mile east of Whistler's studio in Tite Street, in Chelsea, an area quite familiar to Sickert. Battersea Bridge, which traverses the Thames from Chelsea on the north bank to Battersea on the south, was half a mile from Whistler's studio and approximately a mile from where the arm was found. In 1884, Sickert painted Battersea Park, which was visible from Whistler's studio window. In 1888, Pimlico was a quaint area of neat houses and small gardens where the sewage system was raised lest it overflow into the Thames.

It was laborer Frederick Moore's sorry luck to be working outside the gates of Deal Wharf, near the railway bridge, when he heard excited voices on the shore of the Thames. The tide was low, and several men were talking loudly as they stared at an object in the mud. Since no one seemed inclined to pick up whatever it was, Moore did. The police carried the arm to Sloane Street, where a Dr. Neville examined it and determined it was the right arm of a female. He suggested that the string tied around it was "in order for it to be carried." He said the arm had been in the water two or three days and was amputated after death. Had it been cut off while the person was still alive, Dr. Neville wrongly deduced, the muscles would have been more "contracted."

In the late nineteenth century, the notion persisted that the expression on a dead person's face indicated pain or fear, as did clenched fists or rigidly bent limbs. It was not understood that the body undergoes a variety of changes after death, resulting in clenched teeth and fists due to rigor mortis. The pugilistic position and broken bones of a burned body can be confused with trauma when they are actually due to the shrinking of tissues and fracturing of bones caused by extreme heat, or "cooking."

The arm, Dr. Neville went on to say, had been "cleanly severed" from the body with a "sharp weapon." For a while, the police were inclined to believe the amputated limb was some medical student's doing. It was a prank, police told journalists, a very bad joke. The finding of the torso in the foundations of the new Scotland Yard building was not considered a joke, but maybe it should have been. While the murder wasn't funny, if this was the Ripper's work again, what a huge joke, indeed.

News about this latest development was kept relatively brief. There had been enough bad publicity in August and September, and people were beginning to complain that details printed in the newspapers made matters worse. It was "hurting the work of the police," one person wrote to *The Times*. Publicity adds to the "state of panic," which only helps the killer, someone else wrote.

The police were ignorant and an embarrassment, Londoners began to complain. Scotland Yard could not bring offenders to justice, and in confidential memorandums, police officials worried that "if the perpetrator is not speedily brought to justice, it will not only be humiliating but also an intolerable danger." The amount of correspondence sent to Scotland Yard was overwhelming, and Charles Warren published a letter in newspapers "thanking" citizens for their interest and apologizing that he simply did not have time to answer them. One might expect that a great many letters were also written to newspapers, and to sort out crank mail, *The Times* had a policy that while a person did not have to publish his name and address, the information must be included in the original letter to show good faith.

The policy could not have been an easy one to enforce. The telephone had been patented only twelve years earlier and was not yet a household appliance. I doubt that a member of the newspaper staff got into a hansom or galloped off on a horse to check out the validity of a name and address when the individual wasn't listed in the local directory, and not everybody was. My scan of hundreds of newspapers printed in 1888 and 1889 revealed that anonymous letters were published but not frequently. Most writers allowed their name, address, and even occupation to be published. But as the Ripper crimes began to pick up momentum, there seemed to be an increase in published letters with no attribution beyond initials or cryptic titles, or in some instances, names that strike me, at any rate, as Dickensian or mocking.

Days after Annie Chapman's murder, a letter to *The Times* suggested that the police should check on the whereabouts of all cases of "homicidal mania which may have been discharged as 'cured.' " The letter was signed, "A Country Doctor." A letter published September 13th and signed "J.F.S." stated that the day before, a man had been "robbed at 11:00 A.M. on Hanbury Street" in the East End, and at 5:00 P.M. a seventy-year-old man had been attacked in Chicksand Street, and at 10:00 A.M. that very morning a man ran into a bakery shop and made off with the till. All of this, the anonymous writer said, happened "within 100 yards of each other and midway between the scenes of the last two horrible murders."

What is peculiar about this anonymous letter is that there was no record of any such crimes in the police sections of the newspapers, and one has to wonder how the writer of the letter could possibly have known the details, unless he or she was snooping about the East End or was a police officer. Most letters to the editor were with attribution and offered sincere suggestions. Members of the clergy wanted more police supervision, better lighting, and all slaughterhouses to be moved out of Whitechapel because the violence to animals and the gore in the streets had a bad effect on the "ignorant imagination." Wealthy Londoners should buy up the East End slums and demolish them. The children of wretched parents should be taken away and raised by the government.

On October 15th, a peculiar anonymous letter was published in *The Times*. It reads like a bad short story that is the work of a mocking, manipulative intelligence, and could be viewed as a taunting allusion to Joan Boatmoor's murder in County Durham the previous month:

> *Sir,—I have been a good deal about England of late and have been a witness of the strong interest and widespread excitement which the* WHITE CHAPEL *murders have caused and are causing. Everywhere I have been asked about them; especially by working folk, and most especially by working women. Last week, for instance, in an agricultural county I shared my umbrella during heavy rain with a maid servant, who was going home, "Is it true, Sir," said she, "that they're a-cutting down the feminine seck in London?" And she explained herself to mean that "they was murdering of 'em by ones and twos." This is but one of many examples, and my own main interest in the matter is, that I myself have been taken for the murderer. And if I, why not any other elderly gentleman of quiet habits? It may therefore be well to record the fact by way of warning.*
>
> *Two days ago I was in one of the mining districts, had just called on my friend the parson of the parish, and was walking back in the twilight, alone, across certain lonely, grimy fields among the pits and forges. Suddenly I was approached from behind by a party of seven stout collier lads, each of them about 18 years old, except their leader, who was a stalwart young fellow of 23 or so, more than 6ft high. He*

rudely demanded my name, which, of course, I refused to give. "Then," said he, "You are Jack the Ripper, and you'll come along wi' us to the police at __;" naming the nearest town, two miles off. I inquired what authority he had for proposing this arrangement. He hesitated a moment, and then replied that he was himself a constable, and had a warrant (against me, I suppose), but had left it at home. "And," he added fiercely, "if you don't come quietly at once, I'll draw my revolver and blow your brains out."

"Draw it then," said I, feeling pretty sure that he had no revolver. He did not draw it; and I told him that I should certainly not go with him. All this time I noticed that, though the whole seven stood around me, gesticulating and threatening, no one of them attempted to touch me. And, while I was considering how to accomplish my negative purpose, I saw a forgeman coming across the field from his work. Him I hailed; and, when he came up, I explained that these fellows were insulting me, and that, as the odds were seven to one, he ought to stand by me. He was a dull, quiet man, elderly like myself, and (as he justly remarked) quite ready for his tea.

But, being an honest workman, he agreed to stand by me; and he and I moved away in spite of the leader of the gang, who vowed that he would take my ally in charge as well as me. The enemy, however, were not yet routed. They consulted together, and very soon pursued and overtook us; for we took care not to seem as fugitives. But, meanwhile, I had decided what to do, and had told my friend that I would walk with him as far as our paths lay together, and then I would trouble him to turn aside with me up to the cottage of a certain stout and worthy pitman whom I knew.

Thus, then, we walked on over barren fields and slag-heaps for half a mile, surrounded by the seven colliers, who pressed in upon me, but still never touched me, though their leader continued his threats, and freely observed that, whatever I might do, I should certainly go with him to the town. At last we came into the road at a lonesome and murderous-

looking spot, commanded on all sides by the mountainous shale-hills of disused pits. Up among these ran the path that led to the pitman's dwellings which I was making for. When we reached it, I said to my friend the forgeman, "This is our way," and turned towards the path.

"That's not your way," shouted the tall man, "you'll come along the road with us," and he laid his hand on my collar. I shook him off, and informed him that he had now committed an assault, for which I could myself give him in charge. Perhaps it was only post hoc ergo propter hoc, *but at any rate, he made no further attempt to prevent me and my friend from ascending the byway. He stuck to us, however, he and his mates; swearing that he would follow me all the night, if need were. We were soon on the top of the* col, *if I may so call it, from which the pitmen's cottages, lighted within, were visible in the darkness against a starry sky.*

"That is where I am going," I said aloud. To my surprise, the tall man answered in a somewhat altered tone, "How long shall you be?" "That depends," I replied, "you had better come to the house with me." "No," said he, "I shall wait for you here;" and the forgeman and I walked up to the cottage together. At its door I dismissed my ally with thanks and a grateful coin; and entering in, I told my tale to my friend the stout pitman and his hearty wife, who heard it with indignation. In less than a minute, he and I sallied from his dwelling in search of the fellows who had dogged me. But they had vanished. Seeing me received and welcomed by people whom they knew, they doubtless felt that pursuit was futile and suspicion vain.

Now, I do not object to adventures, even in the decline of life; nor do I much blame my antagonists, whether their motive were righteous indignation, or, as is more likely, the hope of reward. But I think them guilty of a serious and even dangerous error of judgment in not distinguishing between the appearance of Jack the Ripper and that of your obedient servant,

AN ELDERLY GENTLEMAN

There may have been a reason that escapes me for this elderly "gentleman" traveling through the country and Durham's mining area, and omitting his name and the names of the places. I suppose there may have been a reason why a "gentleman" in those very class-conscious days would have friends who were pitmen or forgemen. But I am at a loss when I try to figure out why anyone would assume that Jack the Ripper was an "elderly gentleman," and why a paper as respected as *The Times* would publish such a sophomoric tale, unless its journalists were being infected by Rippermania and were grabbing after any Ripper tidbit they could find.

But there are details in the letter worth noting. The author claims to have been traveling a lot of late, and Ripper letters indicate the same. The "gentleman" mingles with the working class, and Sickert was known for that. The letter reminds readers that the Ripper is feared not just in London, but everywhere, and this would be a self-serving assertion if the "elderly gentleman" were really Walter Sickert. In his role as Jack the Ripper, he wanted to frighten as many people as he could.

"If the people here only new who I was they would shiver in their shoes," the Ripper writes in a letter posted in Clapham on November 22, 1889. And as an additional "ha ha" he uses the return address of "Punch & Judy St." Sickert would have been familiar with Punch and Judy. The puppet plays were wildly popular, and his idol Degas adored Punch and Judy and wrote about the violent puppet plays in his letters.

Granted, acceptable humor in the Victorian era differs from what is acceptable today. Some people find Punch and Judy to be offensive. Punch beats his infant daughter and throws her out of a window. He repeatedly cracks his wife, Judy, on the head, "fairly splitting it in two." He kicks his doctor and says, "There; don't you feel the physic in your bowels? [Punch thrusts the end of the stick into the Doctor's stomach: the Doctor falls down dead, and Punch, as before, tosses away the body with the end of his staff.] He, he, he! [Laughing.]"

In Oswald Sickert's Punch and Judy script, "Murder and Manslaughter or, The Devil Fooled," the puppets' cruel antics go beyond Punch's spending all the household money on "spirits."

Punch dances around with the child.

(*hits the child's head against the railing, the child cries*)

. . . Oh don't . . . be quiet my

boy (*puts him in the corner*).

I will get you something to eat (*exits*).

Punch returns, examines the child very closely.

Have you already fallen? Be quiet, be quiet (*exits, the child continues to cry*)

Punch with porridge and spoon

Son of my quiet love

do not make me stroppy. There, now be quiet.

(*Feeds the child porridge non-stop*) there you go,

there you go. Good heavens! . . . don't you want to be

quiet? Quiet, I say! There you go, there's the rest of the porridge.

(*Turns the bowl upside down into the child's face!*)

Now I have nothing left! (*Shakes it crudely*)

You still won't be quiet?

. . . (*throws the child out of the box*)

Oswald may have been writing and drawing Punch and Judy scripts and illustrations for the magazine *Die Fliegende Blätter,* and Walter eagerly anticipated every copy of the comical magazine the instant it came off the press. I am reasonably certain Walter Sickert would have been familiar with his father's Punch and Judy illustrations and scripts, and several Ripper letters include Punch and Judy–like figures. Consistently, the woman is on her back, the man leaning over her, poised to stab her or strike a blow with his raised long dagger or stick.

The author of the "Elderly Gentleman" letter to *The Times* may have been using the silly notion of an elderly gentleman being mistaken as the Ripper as an allusion to the police and their desperate herding of great masses of "suspects" into police stations for questioning. By now, no East End male was immune from being interrogated. Every residence near the murders had been searched, and adult males of all ages—including men in their sixties—were scrutinized. When a man was taken to a police station, his safety was immediately compromised as angry neighbors looked on. The people of the East End wanted the Ripper. They wanted him badly. They would lynch him themselves if given the chance, and men under suspicion, even briefly, sometimes had to stay inside the police station until it was safe to venture out.

An East End bootmaker named John Pizer—also known as "Leather Apron"—became a hunted man when the police found a wet leather apron in the backyard of 29 Hanbury Street, where Annie Chapman was murdered. The leather apron belonged to John Richardson. His mother had washed it and left it outside to dry. Police should have got their facts straight before word of this latest "evidence" rang out like a gunshot. Pizer may have been an abusive brute, but he was not a lust-murderer. By the time it was clear the leather apron in the yard had nothing to do with the Ripper murders, Pizer dared not leave his room for fear of being torn apart by a mob.

"That joke about Leather apron gave me real fits," the Ripper wrote to the Central News Office on September 25th.

The Ripper was quite amused by many events he followed in the press, and he thrived on the chaos he caused and adored being center stage. He wanted to interact with police and journalists, and he did. He reacted to what they wrote, and they reacted to his reactions until it became virtually impossible to tell who suggested or did what first. He responded to his audience and it responded to him, and Ripper letters began to include more personal touches that could be viewed as an indication of the fantasy relationship the Ripper began to develop with his adversaries.

This sort of delusional thinking is not unusual in violent psychopaths. Not only do they believe they have relationships with the victims they stalk, but they bond in a cat-and-mouse way with the investigators who track them. When these violent offenders are finally apprehended and locked up, they tend to be amenable to interviews by police, psychologists, writers, film producers, and criminal justice students. They would probably talk their incarcerated lives away if their lawyers permitted it.

The problem is, psychopaths don't tell the truth. Every word they say is motivated by the desire to manipulate and by their insatiable egocentric need for attention and admiration. The Ripper wanted to impress his opponents. In his own warped way, he even wanted to be liked. He was brilliant and cunning. Even the police said so. He was amusing. He probably believed the police enjoyed a few laughs at his funny little games. "Catch me if you can," he repeatedly wrote. "I can write 5 hand writings," he boasted in a letter on October 18th. "You can't trace me by this writing," he bragged in another letter on November 10th. He often signed letters "your friend."

If the Ripper was offstage too long, it bothered him. If the police seemed to forget about him, he wrote to the press. On September 11, 1889, the Ripper wrote, "Dear Sir Please will you oblige me by putting this into your paper to let the people of England now [know] that I hum [am] still living and running at larg as yet." He also made numerous references to going "abroad." "I intend finishing my work late in August when I shall sail for abroad," the Ripper wrote in a letter police received July 20, 1889. Later—just how much later we don't know—a bottle washed ashore between Deal and Sandwich, which are across the Straits of Dover from France.

There appears to be no record of who found the bottle and when, or what kind of bottle it was, but inside it was a scrap of lined paper dated September 2, 1889, and written on it was "S.S. Northumbria Castle Left ship. Am on trail again Jack the Ripper." The area of the southeast coast of England where the bottle was found is very close to Ramsgate, Broadstairs, and Folkestone.

At least one Ripper letter was posted from Folkestone. Sickert painted in Ramsgate and may have visited there during 1888 and 1889, as it was a very popular resort and he loved sea air and swimming. There was a steamer from Folkestone to France that Sickert would take on numerous occasions in his life, and there was a service between nearby Dover and Calais. None of this proves Sickert wrote a Ripper note, tucked it inside a bottle, and tossed it overboard or into the sea from a beach. But he was familiar with the Kent coast of England. He liked it enough to live in Broadstairs in the 1930s.

The frustration comes when one tries to trace the Ripper's locations on a map in the hope of following him along his tortuous, murderous path. As usual, he was a master of creating illusions. On November 8, 1888, a Ripper letter posted in the East End boasted, "I am going to France and start my work there." Three days later, on the 11th, the letter from Folkestone arrived, which might hint that the Ripper really was making his way to France. But the problem is, on that same day, November 11th, the Ripper also wrote a letter from Kingston-on-Hull, some two hundred miles north of Folkestone. How could the same person have written both letters during the same twenty-four hours?

A possibility is that the Ripper wrote letters in batches, not only to compare his own handwriting styles and make certain they were different, but also to give them all the same date and post them from different locations or make it appear they were posted from different locations. A letter the Ripper dated November 22, 1888, was written on paper with the A Pirie & Sons watermark. Supposedly, the Ripper mailed it from East London. Another letter on A Pirie & Sons paper, also dated November 22, 1888, claims the Ripper is in Manchester. In two other letters that do not appear to have watermarks (one may have but is too torn to tell) and are also dated November 22nd, he claims to be in North London and in Liverpool.

If one assumes that all of these November 22nd letters were written by the same person—and they bear similarities that make this plausible—then how could the Ripper have sent them from London and Liverpool on the same day? The absence of postmarks precludes knowing with certainty when and where a letter was actually posted, and I do not accept as fact any dates or locations in letters that do not include postmarks. Inside a Ripper envelope with the postmark 1896, for example, was a letter the Ripper dated "1886." This was either a mistake or an attempt to be misleading.

It is within the realm of possibility that the postmarks may have been different from the dates or locations—or both—that the Ripper wrote on some of his letters. Once the police opened the letters, they wrote down the dates and locations in their case books and the envelope was discarded or lost. The actual dates the Ripper wrote on the letters could be inconsistent by a day or maybe two, and who was going to notice or care? But a day or two could make quite a difference to a man on the run who wants to throw off the police by appearing to be in London, Lille, Dublin, Innerleithen, and Birmingham on October 8th.

It would have been possible for a person to be in more than one distant location in a twenty-four-hour period. One could get about fairly rapidly by train. Based on the schedules in an 1887 *Bradshaw's Railway Guide,* Sickert could have left Euston Station in London at 6:00 A.M., arrived in Manchester at 11:20 A.M., changed to another train, and left at noon to arrive in Liverpool forty-five minutes later. From Liverpool he could have gone on to Southport on the coast and arrived in an hour and seven minutes.

In mid-September 1888, the decomposing body of a boy was found in an abandoned house in Southport. At his inquest on the 18th, the jury returned an open verdict. It does not appear that the boy's identity or cause of death were ever known, but the police strongly suspected that he was murdered.

"Any youth I see I will kill," the Ripper wrote on November 26, 1888.

"I will do the murder in an empty house," the Ripper wrote in an undated letter.

Train travel in England was excellent at that time. Sleepers were also available. One could leave London at 6:35 in the evening, have a pleasant dinner and a good night's sleep, and wake up in Aberdeen at five minutes before ten the next morning. One could leave Paddington Station at 9:00 P.M. and wake up in Plymouth at 4:15 A.M., take another train to St. Austell in Cornwall and end up near Lizard Point, the southernmost tip of England. A number of Ripper letters were written from Plymouth or near it. Plymouth was the most convenient main-line station for travellers going to Cornwall by train.

Sickert knew Cornwall. In early 1884, he and Whistler spent quite a lot of time there painting at St. Ives, one of the county's most popular seaside spots for artists. In a late-1887 letter to Whistler, Sickert indicated he was planning on going to Cornwall. He may have visited Cornwall frequently. The southwest part of England has always been attractive to artists because of its majestic cliffs and views of the sea, and its picturesque harbors.

Cornwall would have been a good place for Sickert to tuck himself away when he wanted to rest and "hide." During the Victorian era there was a popular private house called Hill's Hotel—affectionately known as "The Lizard"—at Lizard Point, a narrow peninsula of farmland and steep, rocky cliffs about twenty miles from St. Ives. The sea crashes all around the peninsula. A visit today requires parking into the wind lest it rip off your car door.

CHAPTER TWENTY-THREE

THE GUEST BOOK

In the spring of 2001, award-winning food writer Michael Raffael was working on a *Food & Travel* feature and happened to stay at the Rockland Bed & Breakfast at Lizard Point. The B&B is a modest 1950s farmhouse that can sleep seven, and the woman who owns it is the only living remnant of The Lizard Hotel's distant and illustrious past.

It had been a hard year for Joan Hill, who inherited the Lizard guest books and other records that had been in her husband's family for 125 years. Cornwall had been in the throes of foot-and-mouth disease, and her son is a farmer. Government restrictions reduced his income, and Mrs. Hill, recently widowed, found her business all but gone when quarantine restrictions kept tourists far away from anything with hooves.

Michael Raffael recalled that while he was there, Mrs. Hill began telling him stories about the prosperous days when The Lizard was frequented by artists, writers, MPs, and Lords and Ladies. Scans through the guest books show the introverted scrawl of Henry James and the confident flourish of William Gladstone. Artist and critic George Moore knew The Lizard. Sickert knew James but thought his writing was boring. Sickert was a crony of Moore's and tended to make fun of him. Another artist Fred Hall stayed there, and Sickert couldn't stand him at all.

Food and drink were enjoyed with abandon, the rates were reasonable, and people would travel from as far away as South Africa and the United States to holiday on that desolate spit of land jutting out into the sea. They would forget about their cares for a while as they strolled, cycled, and went sightseeing in the bracing air, or read in front of the fire. Sickert could have mingled with interesting people he did not know, or kept to himself. He could have wandered to the cliffs to sketch—or just wandered, as was his habit. He could have taken excursions by train or horse and carriage to other villages, including St. Ives. Sickert could easily have got away with registering under an assumed name. He could have signed anything he liked in the guest book.

The Lizard had survived two world wars and was a romance from a long-ago past. The Hills sold the three-hundred-year-old farm house in 1950 and opened the small Rockland B&B. Mrs. Hill was telling Michael Raffael all this, and perhaps because he took the time to listen, she was reminded of the old guest book dated from 1877 to July 15, 1888, and dug it out of a cupboard. He "spent maybe thirty minutes flicking through it, mostly by myself," when he came across drawings and the name "Jack the Ripper." "From their position on the page in the book, from the style of handwriting and from the sepia ink I can assure you that the Jack entry was most probably contemporaneous with the book and the other entries around it," he wrote to me after ABC's Diane Sawyer interviewed me about Jack the Ripper on a *Prime Time* special.

I contacted Mrs. Hill, who verified that the guest book existed and had Jack the Ripper entries and some drawings, and I could see it if I liked. Within days I was on a plane to Cornwall.

I arrived with friends, and we were the only guests. The village was virtually deserted and swept by cold winds blowing up from the English Channel. Mrs. Hill is a guileless, shy woman in her early sixties who worries a lot about the happiness of her guests and cooks breakfasts far too big for comfort. She has lived in Cornwall all her life and had never heard of Sickert or Whistler but was remotely familiar with the name "Jack the Ripper."

"I believe I know the name. But I don't know anything about him," she said, except she knew he was a very bad man.

The sketches Raffael was referring to when he alerted me about the guest book are ink drawings of a man and a woman out for a stroll. The man, who is dressed in a cutaway and top hat, and has both monocle and umbrella, has "Jack the Ripper" written in pencil by his very big nose. He is staring at the woman from the rear, and a balloon has been drawn coming out of his mouth. "Aint she a beauty though," he says.

The woman, in feathered hat, bodice, bustle, and flounces, says, "Ain't I lovely." In another balloon underneath is the comment, "only by Jack the Ripper." What was neither noticed nor of much interest, perhaps, was everything else in this remarkable book. An ugly mole has been drawn on a woman's nose, and penciled in under her clothes are her naked breasts and legs. The page is filled in with scribbles and comments and allusions to Shakespeare, most of it crude and snide. I took the book upstairs to my room, and other details I began to notice kept me up until 3:00 A.M., the space heater on high as the wind howled and the water pounded beyond my window.

The annotations and dozens of doodles and drawings and malicious remarks were astonishing and completely unexpected, and I suddenly felt as if Sickert were in my room.

Someone—I am convinced it was Sickert, but I will refer to the person as the "vandal"—went through that book with lead pencil, violet-colored pencil, and pen, and wrote rude, sarcastic, childish, and violent annotations on most of the pages:

bosh! fools, fool, a big fool, wiseass. Hell fool, Ha and *Ha Ha, Dear*

Dear! Funny, O Lord, of girls oh fie (slang when encountering an immoral woman), *garn* (vulgar slang for gal), *donkey* (slang for penis), *Dummkopf* (German for idiot), *ta ra ra boon de á* (refrain of a music-hall song), *henfool* (seventeenth-century slang for a prostitute or mistress), *Ballhead, Bosh! Bosh!! Bosh!!!* or under "Reverend" scrawling "(3 times married)," or after another person's name adding "Became a *Snob*" or altering a guest's name to read "Parchedig*ass.*"

The vandal writes snide ditties on pages filled with cheery comments about what a lovely place Hill's Hotel was, how comfortable it was, how good the food was, and how modest the rates were:

"As I fell out/They all fell in/The rest they ran away."

"Rather a queer sort of place."

If a guest had tried his hand at a verse or two, he thereby set himself up for a blasting, such as a rhyme by F. E. Marshall from Chester:

Misfortune overtook me here
Still had I little cause to fear
Since Hill's kind care cause my every ill
To disappear—*after a pill* [the vandal added]

The vandal drew a cartoon face and remarked, "How Brilliant!!!" After another guest's bad poem the vandal wrote:

A Poet is he? It would be rash
To call one so who wrote such trash.
The moon forsooth in all her glory
Had surely touched his upper storey!!

The vandal corrects the spelling and grammar of guests. This seems to have been a habit of Sickert's. In his copy of Ellen Terry's autobiography, in which she makes no mention of Sickert, he has a good deal to say about her spelling, grammar, and diction. Sickert's copy of the book, which I purchased from his nephew by marriage, John Lessore, is filled with Sickert's annotations and corrections, all in pencil. He changed and added to Terry's accounts of events, as if he knew her life better than she did.

Another bad poem by a guest at Hill's Hotel ends with "Receive all thanks O hostess *fare.*" The vandal makes the correction "fair" and follows it with three exclamation marks. He turns the "O" into a funny little cartoon with arms and legs. Under this, he jots cockney slang, "garn Bill that aint a gal," in response to a guest's mention of having visited the inn with "my wife."

"Why do you leave out your *apostrophe?*" the vandal complains on another page, and includes another cartoon. Turn that page and there is yet another cartoon, this one reminiscent of some of the impish, elfin sketches in the Sickert collection at Islington Public Libraries. The "S"s in the signature of "Sister Helen" and her address of "S. Saviour's Priory London" are turned into dollar signs.

On the bottom of a page, obviously penciled in after that page was already filled, was "Jack the Ripper, Whitechapel." On another page, a guest's London address had been penciled over with "Whitechapel." I noticed drawings of a bearded man in a tailcoat exposing his circumcised penis, and a Punch and Judy–like drawing of a woman striking a child on the head with a long stick. Ink blots had been turned into figures. In some Ripper letters, ink blots were turned into figures.

On two other pages, the vandal signs his name "Baron Ally Sloper." I suppose the "Baron" is ironical—a very Sickert-like snipe at English aristocrats. Sloper was a lowly, sleazy cartoon figure with a big red nose and tattered top hat and a habit of eluding the rent collector. He was very popular with the English lower class and appeared in a periodical and penny dreadfuls between 1867 and 1884, then again in 1916. "Tom Thumb and his wife" signed the book August 1, 1886, even though Tom Thumb (Charles Sherwood Stratton) had died July 15, 1883. There are far too many examples to cite here. The guest book—or "ASSES BOOK," as the vandal called it—is remarkable. After Dr. Anna Gruetzner Robins studied it, she agreed. "Certainly no one could dispute that these drawings match the drawings in the Ripper letters," she said. "These are very skilled pen drawings." One of them, she said, is a caricature of Whistler.

Dr. Robins noticed many details in the guest book that eluded me, including a message in poor German and Italian written over one of the male cartoon figures. Roughly translated, the vandal is saying he is "The Ripper Doctor" and has "cooked up a good meat [or flesh] dish in Italy. News! News!" The play on words and the innuendos, which are difficult to convey in translation, says Dr. Robins, is that the Ripper killed a woman in Italy and cooked her flesh into a tasty meal. Several Ripper letters refer to cooking his victims' organs. Some serial killers do engage in cannibalism. It is possible that Sickert did. It is also possible he cooked up parts of his victims and served them to his guests. Of course, the suggestions of cooking human flesh could be nothing more than taunts meant to disgust and shock.

Dr. Robins believes, as do I, that Sickert's hand is behind the insults, annotations, and most of the drawings in The Lizard guest book. Such names as Annie Besant and Charles Bradlaugh are penciled in and are people Sickert knew or painted. Dr. Robins suspects that male cartoon figures with different hats and beards may be self-portraits of Sickert in Ripper disguises. A drawing of "a local rustic damsel" in the book may suggest that Sickert murdered a woman while he was in Cornwall.

I bought the guest book from Mrs. Hill. It has been studied by many experts, including the forensic paper analyst Peter Bower, who says that nothing about the paper and binding is "out of period." The Lizard guest book is considered so extraordinary by those who have examined it that it is now at the Tate Archive for further study and much-needed conservation.

The Jack the Ripper name did not appear in public until September 17, 1888—two months after The Lizard guest book was filled, on July 15, 1888. My explanation for how the signatures of "Jack the Ripper" could appear in the guest book is fairly simple. Sickert visited The Lizard at some point after the Ripper crimes were committed, and he vandalized the guest book. This may have occurred in October 1889, because in very small writing in pencil, almost in the gutter of the book, there appears to be the monogram "W" on top of an "R," followed by an "S," and the date "October 1889."

While the date is very clear, the monogram is not. It could be a cipher or tease, and I would expect nothing less than that from Sickert. October 1889 would have been a good time for him to flee to the southernmost tip of England. About a month earlier, on September 10th, another female torso was found in the East End, this time under a railway arch off Pinchin Street.

The modus operandi was all too familiar. A constable's beat had taken him past the very spot, and he hadn't noticed anything unusual. Less than thirty minutes later, he passed by again and discovered a bundle just off the pavement. The torso was missing its head and legs, but for some reason the killer had left the arms. The hands were smooth and the nails were certainly not those of someone who led a terribly hard life. The fabric of what was left of her dress was silk, which the police traced to a manufacturer in Bradford. It was a physician's opinion that the victim had been dead several days. Oddly enough, her torso had been found in the place that the London office of the *New York Herald* had been alerted to some days before its discovery.

At midnight on September 8th, a man dressed as a soldier approached a newspaper messenger outside the offices of the *Herald,* and the "soldier" exclaimed that there had been another terrible murder and mutilation. He gave the location as the area off Pinchin Street where the torso was eventually found. The messenger rushed inside the newspaper building and informed the night editors, who rode off in a hansom to find the body. There wasn't one. The "soldier" vanished, and the torso turned up on September 10th. The victim was probably already dead at midnight on September 8th, based on the drying of her tissue. Draped over a fence near her dismembered body was a stained cloth that was the sort women wore during their menstrual periods.

"You had better be carefull How you send those Bloodhounds about the streets because of the single females wearing stained napkins—women smell very strong when they are unwell," the Ripper wrote October 10, 1888.

Once again, the killer had managed to conceal bodies and body parts and carry them in what must have been heavy bundles, which he then dropped virtually at a policeman's feet.

"I had to over come great difficulties in bringing the bodies where I hid them," the Ripper wrote on October 22, 1888.

Twelve days after the woman's torso was found, the *Weekly Dispatch* reprinted a story from the London edition of the *New York Herald,* reporting that a landlord claimed to know the "identification" of Jack the Ripper. The landlord, who is not named in the story, said he was convinced that the Ripper had rented rooms in his house, and that this "lodger" would come in "about four o'clock in the morning," when everybody was asleep. Early one morning, the landlord happened to be up when the lodger came in. He was "excited and incoherent in his talk." He claimed he had been assaulted, his watch stolen, and "he gave the name of a police station," where he had reported the incident.

The landlord checked the information and was told by police that no such report had been filed. The landlord got increasingly suspicious when he found the man's freshly washed shirt and underclothing draped over chairs. The lodger "had the habit of talking about the women of the street, and wrote 'long rigmaroles' " about them in handwriting resembling "that of letters sent to the police purporting to come from Jack the Ripper," according to the news story. The lodger had "eight suits of clothes, eight pairs of boots, and eight hats." He could speak several languages and "when he went out he always carried a black bag." He never wore the same hat two nights in a row.

Shortly after the torso was discovered near Pinchin Street, the lodger told the landlord he was going abroad and left abruptly. When the landlord went into the rooms, he discovered the lodger had left "bows, feathers and flowers, and other articles which had belonged to the lower class of women," and three pairs of leather lace-up boots and three pairs of "galoshes" with India rubber soles and waterproofed uppers that were "bespattered with blood."

The Ripper obviously kept up with the news and was aware of this story as it appeared in the London edition of the *New York Herald,* or perhaps in some other paper such as the *Weekly Dispatch.* In the Ripper's poem of November 8, 1889, he makes clear references to the tale told by the landlord:

"Togs 8 suits, many hats I wear."

He denies he was the peculiar lodger who wrote "rigmaroles" about immoral women:

> Some months hard gone near Finsbury Sqre:
> An eccentric man lived with an unmarried pair—
> The tale is false there never was a lad,
> Who wrote essays on women bad.

It is hard to believe that Walter Sickert would leave boots or any incriminating belongings in rooms he had rented unless he wanted these items to be found. Maybe Sickert had stayed in that lodging house, maybe he never did. But wittingly or not, the Ripper left a wake of suspicion and created more drama. He may even have lurked somewhere behind the curtain of the next act, an account of which was printed right under the story about the "lodger" in the *Weekly Dispatch.*

A "woman" wrote a letter to Leman Street Police Station "stating it has been ascertained that a tall, strong woman has for some time" been working in various slaughterhouses "attired as a man." This story gave rise "to the theory that the East End victims may have been murdered by a woman. It is remarked that in each case there is no evidence of a man being seen in the vicinity at the time of the murder."

The slaughterhouse transvestite was never found, and police searching East End slaughterhouses got no verification at all that a potential "Jill the Ripper" had been in their midst. The letter the "woman" wrote to the Leman Street Police Station does not appear to have survived. Between July 18th (three days after Sickert "resigned" from the *New York Herald)* and October 30th of 1889, thirty-seven Ripper letters were sent to the Metropolitan Police (based on what is in the Public Record Office and Corporation of London files). Seventeen of these letters were written in September. With the exception of three, all were supposedly written from London, which would have placed the Ripper—or Sickert—in London during the time of the "lodger" and the slaughterhouse woman news reports.

Between March and mid-July of 1889, Sickert had written twenty-one articles for the London edition of the *New York Herald.* He was very likely in London on September 8th, because the *Sun* had just interviewed him days earlier at 54 Broadhurst Gardens and published the article on the 8th. The focus of the article was an important Impressionist art exhibition scheduled for December 2nd at the Goupil Gallery in Bond Street, and Sickert's work was to be included in it. The reporter also quizzed Sickert about why he was no longer the art critic for the *New York Herald.*

Sickert's printed reply was evasive and not the whole truth. He claimed he didn't have time to write for the *Herald* anymore. He said that art criticism should be left to people who are not painters. Yet in March 1890, Sickert was at it again, writing articles for the *Scots Observer, Art Weekly,* and *The Whirlwind*—at least sixteen articles for that year. Maybe it is just another one of those Sickert coincidences that the very day his "resignation" from the *New York Herald* was publicized in the *Sun,* the mysterious soldier appeared at the *New York Herald* and announced a murder and mutilation he could not have known about unless he was an accomplice or the killer.

The torso found in September 1889 was never identified. She may not have been a "filthy whore" of doss-houses and the street. She could have been a prostitute higher up the pecking order, such as a music-hall performer. One of these questionable types of women could have disappeared easily enough. They moved about from town to town or country to country. Sickert liked to draw them. He painted the music-hall star Queenie Lawrence's portrait and must have been a bit upset when she refused to accept it as a gift and said she wouldn't even use it as a screen to keep the wind out. Queenie Lawrence seemed to fade from public view in 1889. I have found no record of what became of her. Sickert's models and art students sometimes just slipped away to who knows where.

". . . one of my art students, a darling who drew worse than anyone I have ever seen & has vanished into the country. Her name?" Sickert wrote to his wealthy American friends Ethel Sands and Nan Hudson, probably around 1914.

During Sickert's most intense killing times, he could have been constantly on the move by train. He could have sent letters from all over. Lust murderers tend to move about when they are in the throes of their sexually violent addiction. They go from town to town, from city to city, often killing near rest stops, railway stations, some of their predatory places predetermined, some of them random. Bodies and body parts can be scattered for hundreds of miles. Remains are discovered in rubbish bins and the woods. Some victims are concealed so well that they will always be "missing."

The murderous highs, the risks, the rushes are intoxicating. But these people do not want to be caught, and neither did Sickert. Getting out of London now and then was smart, especially after the double murder of Elizabeth Stride and Catherine Eddows. But if his motive in posting so many letters in so many distant places was to drive the police to distraction and create an uproar, Sickert misfired. In D. S. MacColl's words, he "over-calculated himself." Sickert was so clever that neither the press nor the police believed the letters could be from the murderer. The letters were ignored.

Some of them sent from distant places such as Lille or Lisbon could very well be hoaxes. Or perhaps Sickert got someone else to post the letters for him. He seemed to have a habit of that. In August 1914, while he was in Dieppe, he wrote to Ethel Sands, "I am not always able to nip down to the boat & catch some kind stranger to whom to confide my letters."

CHAPTER TWENTY-FOUR

IN A HORSE-BIN

Early on the frosty morning of October 11, 1888, Sir Charles Warren played the role of felon with Burgho and Barnaby the bloodhounds.

The Commissioner of the Metropolitan Police darted behind trees and shrubbery in Hyde Park, making his getaway, while the magnificent pair of tracking dogs lost his scent and successfully hunted down several strangers who happened to be out strolling. Four other trials on the misty, cold morning ended just as badly. This did not bode well for Warren.

If the hounds couldn't track a man in a relatively deserted park early in the morning, then turning them loose in the crowded, filthy streets and alleyways of the East End probably wasn't such a good idea. Warren's decision to volunteer for the tracking demonstration wasn't such a good idea, either. So much for showing Londoners what a great innovation bloodhounds were and how sure Warren was they would sniff out that

East End fiend at last. Warren's dashing around in the park with his lost hounds was an embarrassment he would never live down.

"Dear Boss I hear you have bloodhounds for me now," the Ripper wrote October 12th and drew a knife on the envelope.

Warren's bad decision may have been precipitated—or at least could not have been helped—by yet another peculiar letter published in *The Times* on October 9th, two days before his romp in the park:

> *Sir—Just now, perhaps, my own personal experiences of what bloodhounds can do in the way of tracking criminals may be of interest. Here, then, is an incident to which I was an eye witness.*
>
> *In 1861 or 1862 (my memory does not enable me to give a more exact date), I was in Dieppe when a little boy was found doubled up in a horse-bin with his throat cut from ear to ear. A couple of bloodhounds were at once put on to the scent. Away they dashed after, for a moment or two, sniffing the ground, hundreds of people, including the keeper and myself, following in their wake.*
>
> *Nor did the highly-trained animals slacken their pace in the least till they had arrived at the other end of town, when they made a dead stop at the door of a low lodging house, and throwing up their noble heads, gave a deep bay. On the place being entered, the culprit—an old woman—was discovered hiding under a bed.*
>
> *Let me add that the instinct of a bloodhound when properly trained, for tracking by scent is so marvelous that no one can say positively what difficulties in following a trail it cannot surmount.*
>
> *Faithfully yours,*
> *Williams* [sic] *Buchanan*
> *11, Burton St., W.C., October 8.*

As is true with the Elderly Gentleman's letter to the editor, the tone does not fit the subject. Mr. Buchanan has the light, cheerful voice of a raconteur as he relays the horrific account of a boy having his throat cut "from ear to ear," his body stuffed into a "horse-bin."

A search through newspaper records in Dieppe turned up no mention of a child having his throat cut or being murdered by similar means in the early 1860s. This isn't necessarily conclusive, because French records from a century ago were poorly kept or lost, or destroyed during two world wars. But if there had been such a murder, the suggestion that Dieppe had at that time trained bloodhounds available "at once" to put on the scent is extremely hard to accept. The huge metropolis of London didn't have trained bloodhounds available in the 1860s, nor even twenty-eight years later, when Charles Warren had to import the dogs into the city and board them with a veterinary surgeon.

In the eighth century, bloodhounds were known as Flemish hounds and were prized for their ability to track bear and other animals and flush them out on hunts. It wasn't until the sixteenth century that it became common to use these deep-throated, long-eared hounds to track human beings. The depiction of them as vicious canines used to hunt down slaves in America's southern states is a terrible falsehood. It is not the nature of bloodhounds to be aggressive or to have physical contact with their quarry. They don't have a mean fold in their sad, floppy faces. Slave-hunting hounds were usually foxhounds or a mixture of foxhound and Cuban mastiff trained to drag a person to the ground or to attack.

Training bloodhounds to track criminals is so specialized and painstaking that few are available to assist police detectives. Not many of the hounds would have been around in 1861 or 1862, when Buchanan claims, in what sounds like a Grimm's fairy tale, that bloodhounds tracked the little boy's murderer straight to the house where an old woman was hiding under a bed.

"Williams"—as *The Times* printed it—Buchanan was not listed in the 1888 post office directory, but the 1889 register of electors for St. Pancras South Parliamentary Borough, District 3 Burton, lists a William

Buchanan as a voting resident of a house at 11 Burton Street. In those days, Burton Street wasn't considered a dreadful part of the city, but it wasn't a good one, either. The house was let for thirty-eight pounds a year with rooms rented by a number of people of various occupations, including an apprentice, a printer's warehouseman, a colorman grinder, a cocoa packer, a French polisher, a chair maker, and a laundress.

William Buchanan wasn't an uncommon name, and no other records could be located to identify him or his occupation. But his letter to the editor shows a literate, creative mind, and he mentions Dieppe, the seaside resort and artists' haven where Sickert would have houses and secret rooms for almost half of his life. Sickert wasn't likely to rent these secret rooms in Dieppe, London, or elsewhere under his own name. In the late 1880s, identification wasn't required. Cash would do. One might wonder how often Sickert used names other than his own, including those that might belong to real people.

Perhaps a person named William Buchanan did write the letter to the editor. Perhaps there was a murdered seven-year-old boy whose body was dumped in a horse bin in Dieppe. I can't say one way or another. But it is a disturbing coincidence that within ten weeks of Buchanan's letter, two boys would be murdered, the mutilated remains of one of them left in a stable.

"I am going to commit 3 more 2 girls and a boy about 7 years old this time I like ripping very much especially women because they don't make a lot of noise," the Ripper wrote in a letter he dated November 14, 1888.

On November 26th, eight-year-old Percy Knight Searle, a "quiet, sharp and inoffensive lad," was murdered in Havant, near Portsmouth, on England's south coast. He was out that evening "between 6 and 7" with another boy named Robert Husband, who later said Percy left him and set off down a road alone. Moments later Robert heard him screaming and saw a "tall man" running away. Robert found Percy on the ground against a fence and barely alive, his throat cut in four places. He died before Robert's eyes.

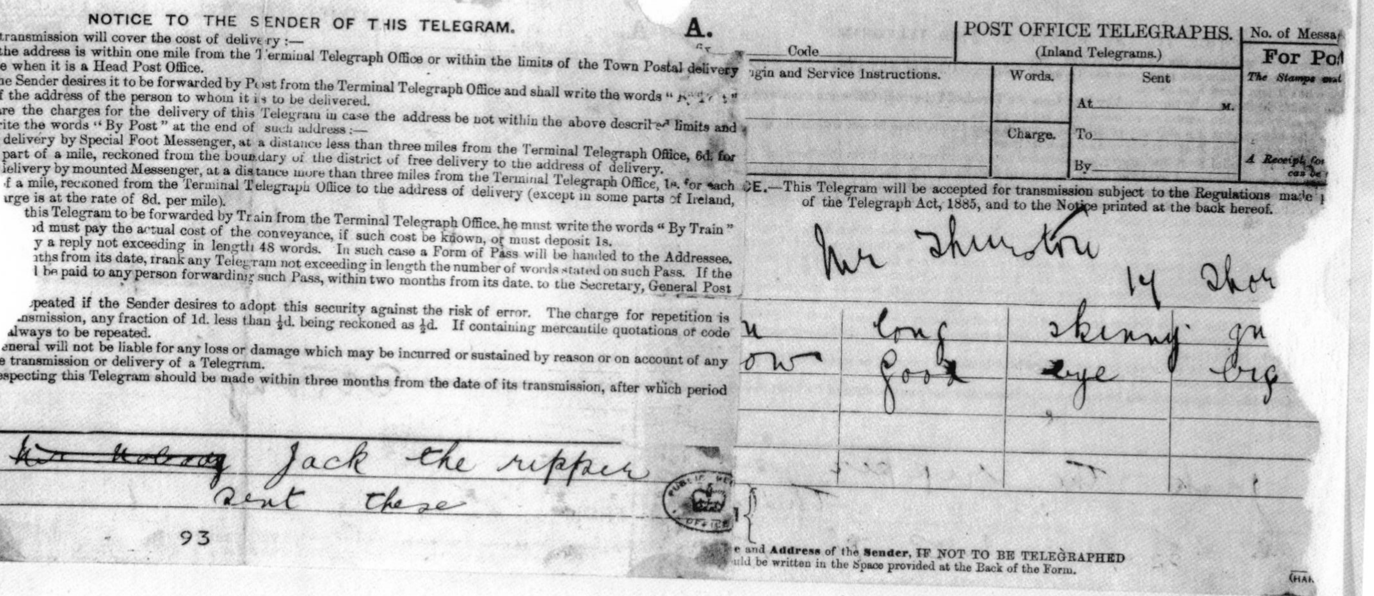

NOTICE TO THE SENDER OF THIS TELEGRAM.

...e for transmission will cover the cost of delivery :—
...) If the address is within one mile from the Terminal Telegraph Office or within the limits of the Town Postal delivery
Office when it is a Head Post Office.
If the Sender desires it to be forwarded by Post from the Terminal Telegraph Office and shall write the words "...
...l of the address of the person to whom it is to be delivered.
are the charges for the delivery of this Telegram in case the address be not within the above described limits and
write the words "By Post" at the end of such address :—
for delivery by Special Foot Messenger, at a distance less than three miles from the Terminal Telegraph Office, 6d. for
or part of a mile, reckoned from the boundary of the district of free delivery to the address of delivery.
...elivery by mounted Messenger, at a distance more than three miles from the Terminal Telegraph Office, 1s. for each
...f a mile, reckoned from the Terminal Telegraph Office to the address of delivery (except in some parts of Ireland,
...arge is at the rate of 8d. per mile).
this Telegram to be forwarded by Train from the Terminal Telegraph Office, he must write the words "By Train"
...d must pay the actual cost of the conveyance, if such cost be known, or must deposit 1s.
...y a reply not exceeding in length 48 words. In such case a Form of Pass will be handed to the Addressee.
...nths from its date, frank any Telegram not exceeding in length the number of words stated on such Pass. If the
...l be paid to any person forwarding such Pass, within two months from its date, to the Secretary, General Post

...peated if the Sender desires to adopt this security against the risk of error. The charge for repetition is
...nsmission, any fraction of 1d. less than ½d. being reckoned as ½d. If containing mercantile quotations of code
...always to be repeated.
...eneral will not be liable for any loss or damage which may be incurred or sustained by reason or on account of any
...e transmission or delivery of a Telegram.
... respecting this Telegram should be made within three months from the date of its transmission, after which period

~~Mr Nobody~~ Jack the ripper
sent these

93

A.

Code

POST OFFICE TELEGRAPHS.
(Inland Telegrams.)

No. of Messa...
For Po...
The Stamps and...

...igin and Service Instructions.

Words. | Charge.

Sent
At ... M.
To
By

A Receipt for ... can be ...

...CE.—This Telegram will be accepted for transmission subject to the Regulations made ...
of the Telegraph Act, 1885, and to the Notice printed at the back hereof.

Mr Thurston
14 Thor...

...n long skinny gr...
...ow good eye bri...

...e and Address of the Sender, IF NOT TO BE TELEGRAPHED
...uld be written in the Space provided at the Back of the Form.

Sickert's stage name when he was an actor was "Mr. Nemo" or "Mr. Nobody." On this Ripper telegraph to the police "Mr. Nobody" is crossed out. © *Public Record Office, London.*

I shall reek content
do what you will
you will never hap

Jack the Ripper

Watch P.C. 60. C. light
moustache shaven chin rather
Stout — he can tell you
almost as much as I can

— ~~J.T.R.~~

7 Place. R. St. W

Ripper letter with "R St. W" initials at the bottom. Sickert sometimes used the initials "W" or "R" or "St." Sometimes he was W. St. (Walter Sickert). Sometimes he was W (Walter), sometimes he was R (Richard). Is this a taunt? © *Public Record Office, London.*

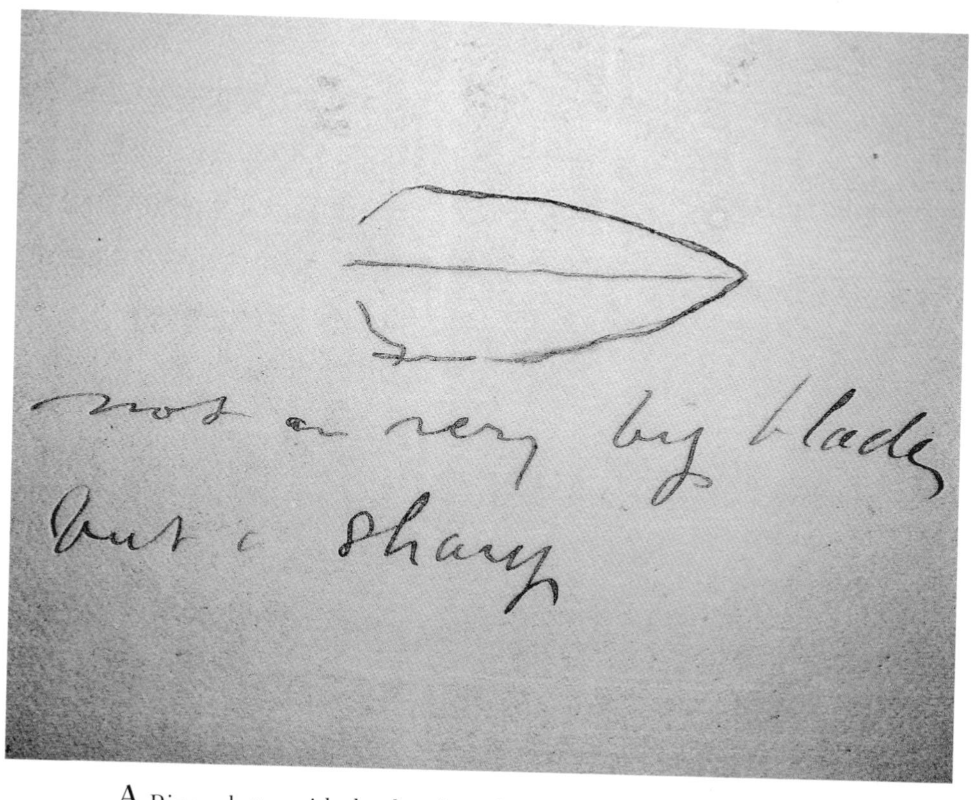

not a very big blade
but a sharp

A Ripper letter with the drawing of a knife blade. Small but sharp.

© Public Record Office, London.

Reasons for Supposing Jack
the ripper a tailor from his letter.
first (Ripper) is a tailors word
(Bukkle) a tailors word

they wont (fix) fix buttons

(proper red stuff) = army cloth
(real fits) — tailors words – good fits or suits
men generally use expressions
borrowed from their trade

Yours truly
Mathematicus

The Ripper displays his facility with Latin in this note, signed "Mathematicus." Sickert was fluent in Latin, too, and known for his mathematical and scientific mind.

(Ha-Ha-Ha) I can see better specimens in garrison town, look out in a day or two yours (not yet) jack the Ripper (Ha-Ha)

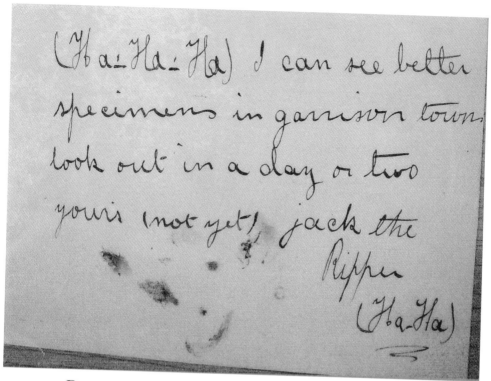

Ripper's notorious "Ha Ha Ha" runs through dozens of his letters.

© Public Record Office, London.

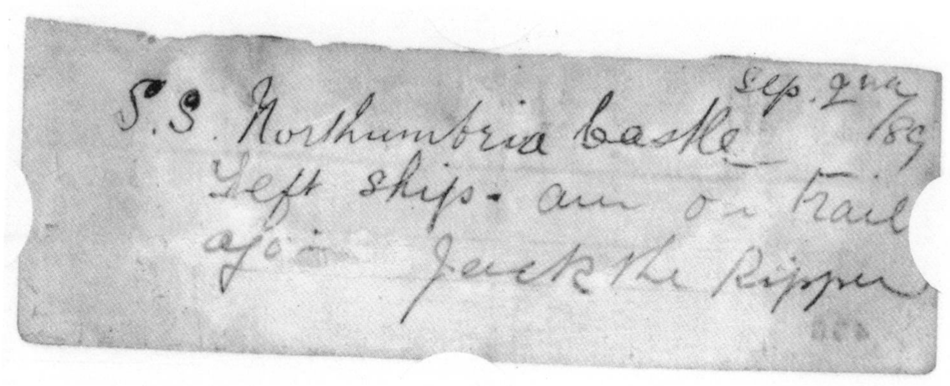

S.S. Northumbria Castle Sep. 2nd /89
Left ships - am on trail agin Jack the Ripper

Note found in a bottle found on the shore between Deal and Sandwich, two towns across the Straits of Dover from Sickert's beloved France. *© Public Record Office, London.*

The Lizard Guest House in Cornwall today. © *Irene Shulgin.*

Annotations and drawings in the old Lizard House guest book are believed to have been done by Sickert, possibly in October 1889. Sickert was quite familiar with Cornwall, and the Lizard was a haven for artists and the London upper class. *Collection of Patricia Cornwell.*

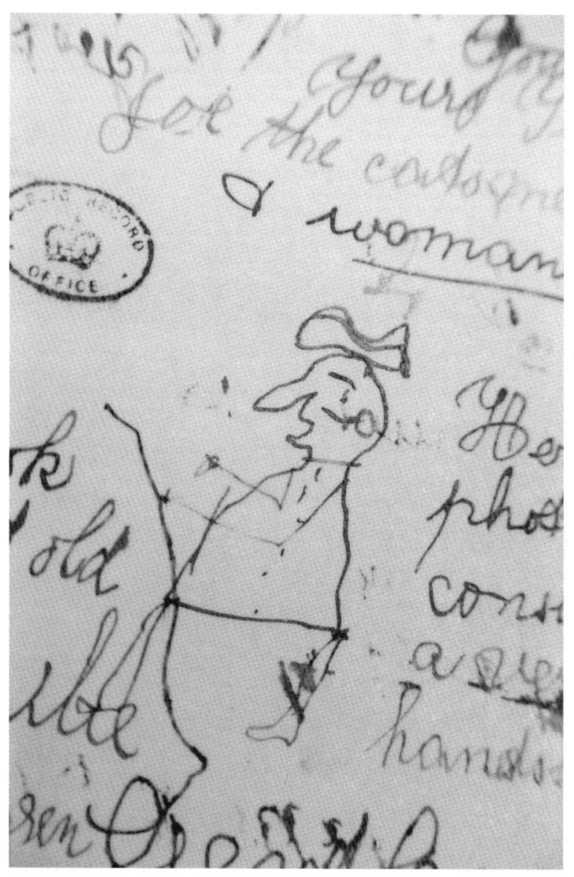

Compare this drawing in a Ripper letter to the drawing in the guest book.
© Public Record Office, London.

Drawing in Lizard guest book believed to be by Sickert.
Collection of Patricia Cornwell.

Drawing of a "Pearly King" from a Ripper letter.

Left: Lizard guest book. Right: a Ripper letter. Some art experts believe the two drawings were done by the same person and hint of Sickert's technique. Sickert doodled, sometimes drawing what appear to be childish cartoons and stick figures. His father did sketches and scripts for Punch and Judy. *Left, Collection of Patricia Cornwell; right, © Public Record Office, London.*

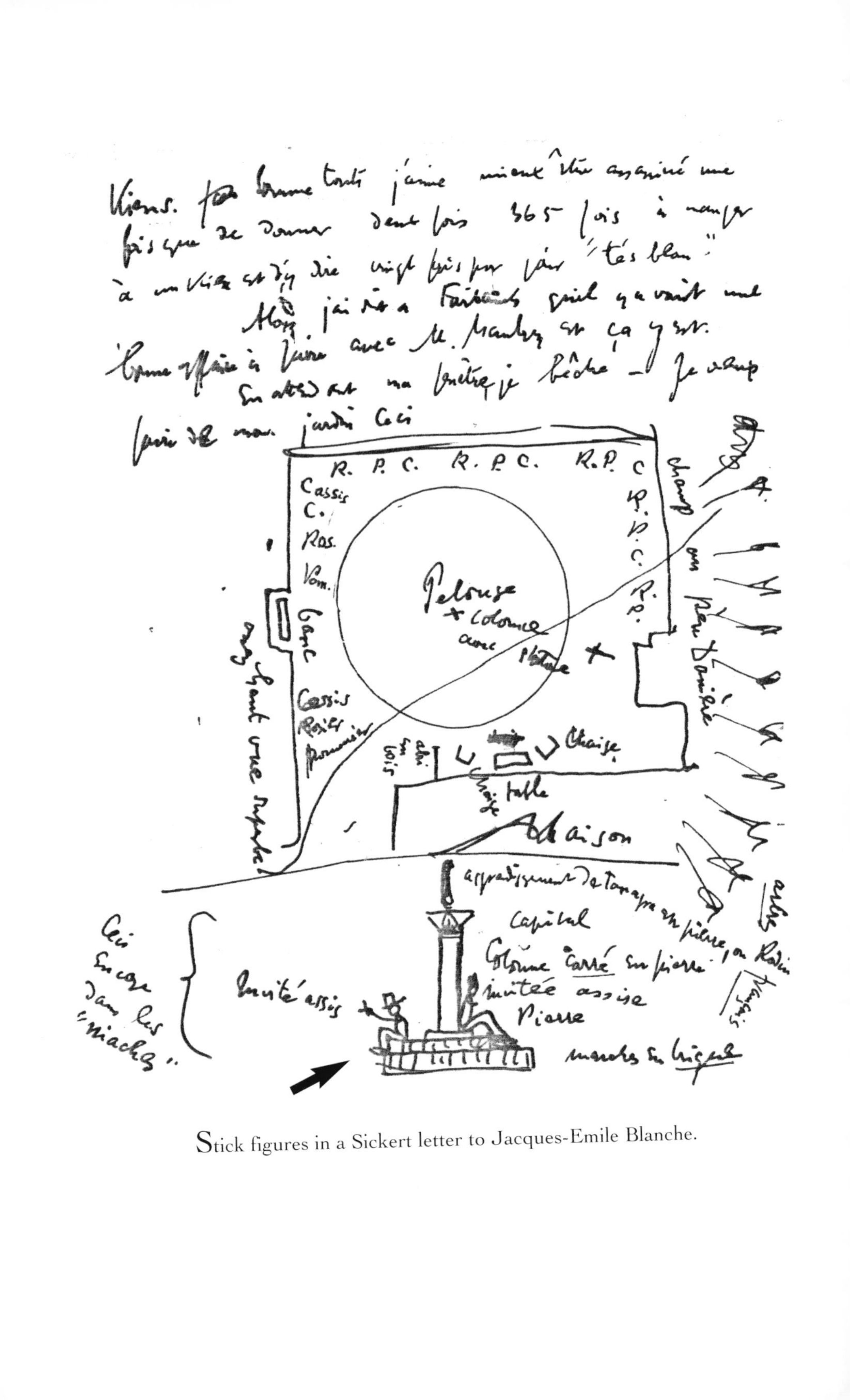

Stick figures in a Sickert letter to Jacques-Emile Blanche.

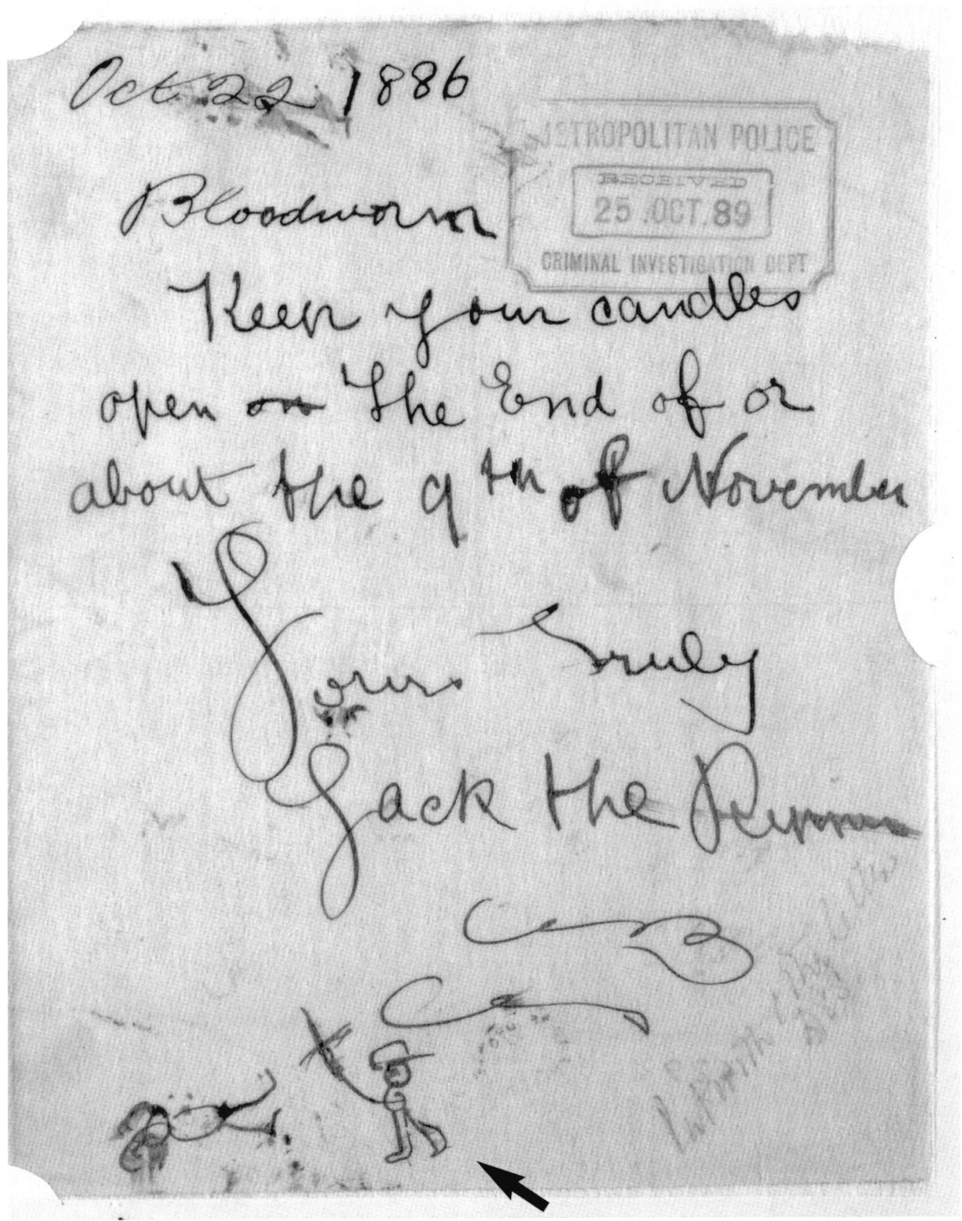

Oct 22 1886

Bloodworm

Keep your candles open on the End of or about the 9th of November

Yours truly

Jack the Ripper

METROPOLITAN POLICE

RECEIVED

25 OCT. 89

CRIMINAL INVESTIGATION DEPT

Stick figures in this Ripper letter are reminiscent of Punch and Judy violence. Another Ripper letter uses the return address of "Punch & Judy St." © *Public Record Office, London.*

The sickly but gentle Christine Angus (middle), a former Sickert art student and his second wife. *Tate Gallery Archive, Photo Collection.*

The Many Faces of Sickert:

Charming and handsome.
Collection of Islington Libraries, London.

A top hat and a shadow.
Collection of Islington Libraries, London.

When the mood struck, he shaved his head.
Collection of Islington Libraries, London.

Sickert with Thérèse Lessore, his third wife, in his paper landfill, the final days.

Tate Gallery Archive, Photograph Collection.

A pocketknife was found nearby, its long blade open and stained with blood. The residents were certain the murder was the work of Jack the Ripper. *The Times* mentions a Dr. Bond at Percy's inquest but does not give a first name. If the doctor was Thomas Bond of Westminster, then Scotland Yard sent him to see if the case might be the work of the Ripper.

Dr. Bond testified at the inquest that the injuries to Percy Searle's neck were consistent with "cuts from a bayonet," and that the boy was killed while standing. A porter at the Havant railway station claimed that a man jumped on the 6:55 train to Brighton without buying a ticket. The porter didn't realize a murder had just occurred and did not pursue the man. Suspicions focused on the boy Robert Husband when it turned out that the "bloody" pocketknife belonged to his brother. Another medical opinion was offered that the four cuts on Percy's neck were clumsy and could have been made by a "boy," and Robert was charged with the crime despite his protests of innocence. Portsmouth, directly across the Channel from LeHavre, is about a three-and-a-half-hour train ride from London.

Nearly a month later, on Thursday, December 20th, another murder occurred, this one in London. Rose Mylett lived in Whitechapel, was about thirty years old, and was described as "pretty" and "well nourished."

She was an Unfortunate and had been out late on Wednesday night, apparently plying her trade, and the next morning at 4:15 a constable discovered her body in Clarke's Yard, Poplar Street, in the East End. He believed she had been dead for only a few minutes. Her clothing was in place, but her hair was in disarray and hanging down, and someone—apparently her killer—had loosely folded a handkerchief around her neck. A postmortem examination revealed she had been garrotted with moderately thick packing string.

There was "nothing in the shape of a clue," *The Times* reported on December 27th, and medical and police officials believe the "deed [was] the work of a skillful hand." A point of medical confusion for the police surgeon was that Rose's mouth was shut when she was found and her tongue was not protruding. Apparently it was not understood that in most cases of garrotting, the ligature—in this case a cord—is pulled tightly around the neck and compresses the carotid arteries or jugular veins, cutting off the blood supply to the brain. Unconsciousness occurs in seconds, followed by death. Unless the larynx, or airway, is compressed, as in murder by manual strangulation, the tongue will not necessarily protrude.

Garrotting is a quick and easy way to control a victim because the person loses consciousness rapidly. Strangulation with the hands, by contrast, causes death by asphyxia, and the victim will most likely put up intense resistance for minutes as he or she panics and fights to breathe. Garrotting bears a similarity to cutting a victim's throat. In both cases, the victim can't utter a sound and becomes quickly incapacitated.

One week after Rose Mylett was murdered, a boy disappeared in Bradford, Yorkshire, a theater city on the Irving company's tour that was four and a half to six hours northwest of London, depending on the number of stops the train made. On Thursday morning, December 27, at 6:40, Mrs. Gill saw her seven-year-old son John hop on the local milk cart for a quick ride. Later, at 8:30, John was playing with other boys, and by some accounts was talking to a man after that. John never came home. The next day, his frantic family put up a poster that read:

> Lost on Thursday morning a boy, John Gill, aged eight. Was last seen sliding near Walmer-Village at 8:30 A.M. Had on navy blue top coat (with brass buttons on), midshipman's cap, plaid knickerbocker suit, laced boots, red and white stocking; complexion fair. Home 41, Thorncliffe Road.

The poster described John as eight because his birthday was a little over a month away. That Friday night at 9:00 P.M., a butcher's assistant named Joseph Buckle was in the vicinity of stables and a coach house very close to the Gills' home. He noticed nothing out of the ordinary. The next morning, Saturday, he was up early to yoke up his employer's horse for a day of work. As was his usual routine, Joseph cleaned out the stable. While he was pitching manure into a pit in the yard, he "saw a heap of something propped up in the corner between the wall and the coach house door." He fetched a light and saw that the heap was a dead body and that an ear had been cut off. He ran to the bakery for help.

John Gill's coat was tied around him with his braces. Several men unwrapped him and found what was left of the boy's body leaning to the right, his severed legs propped on either side of his body and secured with cord. Both ears had been sliced off. A piece of shirting was tied around his neck, and another piece tied around the stumps left of his legs. He had been stabbed a number of times in his chest, his abdomen slashed open, the organs removed and placed on the ground. His heart had been "torn" out of his chest and wedged under his chin.

"I shall do another murder on some young youth such as printing lads who work in the City. I did write you once before but I don't think you had it. I shall do them worse than the women I shall take their hearts," the Ripper had written on November 26th, "and rip them up the same way. . . . I will attack on them when are going home . . . any Youth I see I will kill but you will never kitch me put that in your pipe and smoke it. . . ."

John Gill's boots had been removed and stuffed inside his abdominal cavity, according to one news report. There were other mutilations "too sickening to be described." One might infer these were to the genitals. One of the wrappings found with the body, *The Times* reported, "bears the name of W. Mason, Derby Road, Liverpool." What should have been an incredible lead apparently went nowhere. Liverpool was less than four hours away from London by train, and five weeks earlier the Ripper had written a letter claiming to be in Liverpool, and again on December 19th, or a little more than a week before John Gill's murder, the Ripper sent a letter to *The Times*—allegedly from Liverpool.

"I have come to Liverpool & you will soon hear of me."

Police immediately went after William Barrett, the dairyman who had given John a ride in the milk cart two days earlier, but there was no evidence against him beyond Barrett's keeping his horse and cart at the stables and coach house where John's body was found. Barrett had given John a ride many times in the past and was highly thought of by his neighbors. Police found no bloodstains on John Gill's body or the coat wrapped around it. There was no blood inside the coach house or the stable. The murder had occurred elsewhere. A constable patrolling the area claimed that at 4:30 Saturday morning he had tried the coach house doors to make sure they were secure and had stood on the "very spot" where John Gill's remains were displayed by the killer not three hours later.

Afterward, in an undated, partial letter, the Ripper wrote to the Metropolitan Police, "I riped up little boy in Bradford." A Ripper letter of January 16, 1889, refers to "my trip to Bradford."

There are no known Ripper letters from December 23rd until January 8th. I don't know where Sickert spent his holidays, but I suspect he would have wanted to be in London on the last Saturday of the year, December 29th, when *Hamlet* opened at the Lyceum, starring Henry Irving and Ellen Terry. Sickert's wife may have been with her family in West Sussex, but there are no letters I have found from this period that tell me where either Sickert or Ellen was.

But the month of December could not have been a happy one for Ellen. It is unlikely she saw Sickert much at all, and one has to wonder where she thought he was and what he was doing. She would have been deeply worried and saddened by the critical illness of a dear family friend, the reform politician and orator John Bright. Daily, *The Times* gave reports on his condition, reports that could have evoked bittersweet memories of Ellen's late father, who had been one of Bright's closest friends.

The dairyman arrested in the John Gill case was eventually cleared and the murder would remain unsolved. The murder of Rose Mylett was never solved. The notion that Jack the Ripper might have committed either crime didn't seem plausible and was soon forgotten by the people who mattered. The Ripper didn't mutilate Rose. He didn't cut her throat, and it wasn't his modus operandi to savage a little boy, no matter what was threatened in letters that the police would have considered hoaxes, anyway.

Because of the scarcity of medico-legal facts revealed in the newspapers and the inquest, it is difficult to reconstruct John Gill's case. One of the most important unanswered questions is the identity of the man John was last seen talking to, assuming this reported detail is true. If the man was a stranger, it would seem that quite an effort should have been made to discover who he was and what he was doing in Bradford. Clearly, the boy went off with someone, and this person murdered and mutilated him.

The piece of "shirting" around John's neck is a curious signature on the part of the killer. Every Jack the Ripper victim, as far as I know, was wearing a scarf, a handkerchief, or some other piece of fabric around the neck. When the Ripper cut a victim's throat, he did not cut off the neckerchief, and in Rose Mylett's murder, a folded handkerchief was draped over her neck. Clearly, neckerchiefs or scarves symbolized something to the killer.

Sickert's friend, the artist Marjorie Lilly recalled that he had a favorite red neckerchief. While he was working on his Camden Town murder paintings, and "was reliving the scene he would assume the part of a ruffian, knotting the handkerchief loosely around his neck, pulling a cap over his eyes and lighting his lantern." It was commonly known that if a criminal wore a red neckerchief to his execution, it signaled that he had divulged no truths to anyone, and carried his darkest secrets to the grave. Sickert's red handkerchief was a talisman and not to be touched by anyone, including the housekeeper, who knew to steer clear of it when she saw it "dangling" from the bedpost inside his studio or tied to a doorknob or peg.

The red handkerchief, Lilly wrote, "played a necessary part in the performance of the drawings, spurring him on at crucial moments, becoming so interwoven with the actual working out of his idea that he kept it constantly before his eyes." Sickert began what I call his "Camden Town Murder Period" not long after the actual Camden Town murder of a prostitute in 1907. Lilly said that during this era of his life, "he had two fervent crazes . . . crime and the princes of the Church." Crime was "personified by Jack the Ripper, the Church by Anthony Trollope."

"I hate Christianity!" Sickert once yelled at a Salvation Army band.

He was not a religious man unless he was playing an important Biblical role. *Lazarus Breaks His Fast: Self Portrait* and *The Servant of Abraham: Self Portrait* are two of his later works. When he was almost seventy, he painted his famous *The Raising of Lazarus* by getting a local undertaker to wrap the life-size lay figure once owned by the eighteenth-century artist William Hogarth in a shroud. The heavily bearded Sickert climbed onto a stepladder and assumed the role of Christ raising Lazarus from the dead while Ciceley Hey posed as Lazarus's sister. Sickert painted the huge canvas from a photograph, and in it, Christ is another self-portrait.

Perhaps Sickert's fantasies about having power over life and death were different in his sunset years. He was getting old. He felt unwell much of the time. If only he had the power to give life. He already knew he had the power to take it. Testimony at John Gill's inquest verified that the seven-year-old boy's heart was "plucked," not cut out. The killer reached inside the slashed-open chest and ribs and took the boy's heart in his hand and tore it from the body.

Do unto others as was done unto you. If Walter Sickert murdered John Gill, it was because he could. Sickert had sexual power only when he could dominate and cause death. He may not have felt remorse, but he must have hated what he could not have and could not be. He could not have a woman. He was never a normal boy and could never be a normal man. I don't know of a single instance when Sickert showed physical courage. He victimized people only when he had the advantage.

When he betrayed Whistler in 1896, he did so in the same year that Whistler's wife, Beatrice, died. Her death devastated Whistler. He would never recover from it. In the last life-size self-portrait Whistler painted, his black figure recedes into blackness until the man is hard to find. He was still in the midst of a financially ruinous lawsuit and was perhaps at the lowest point of his life when Sickert covertly went after him in the *Saturday Review*. In the same year Sickert lost the lawsuit, 1897, Oscar Wilde emerged from prison, his once-glorious career in tatters, his body a wreck. Sickert shunned him.

Wilde had been kind to Helena Sickert when she was a girl. From him she received her first book of poetry and encouragement to be whatever she wanted to be in life. When Walter Sickert went to Paris in 1883 to deliver Whistler's portrait of his mother to the annual Salon exhibition, the dashing, famous Wilde entertained the young, wide-eyed artist at the Hôtel Voltaire for a week.

When Sickert's father died in 1885, her mother, Helena wrote, was "nearly mad with grief." Oscar Wilde came to see Mrs. Sickert. She was receiving no company. But of course she will, Wilde said as he bounded up the stairs. It wasn't very long before Mrs. Sickert was laughing—a sound her daughter thought she would never hear again.

CHAPTER TWENTY-FIVE

THREE KEYS

Ellen Cobden Sickert was almost obsessive in her zeal to see that the Cobden role in history would be remembered and cherished. In December 1907, she sent a sealed document to her sister Janie and insisted it was to be locked in a safe. It doesn't appear we'll ever know what was in Ellen's sealed letter, but I doubt it was a will or similar instructions. She wrote all that out later and apparently didn't care who saw it. Those instructions, along with the rest of Ellen's letters and diaries, were donated by the Cobden family to the West Sussex Public Record office.

Ellen sent her sealed letter to Janie three months after the Camden Town murder, which was committed a few streets from Sickert's studios in Camden Town and about a mile from where he had recently settled after returning to London from France. Emily Dimmock was twenty-two years old, of medium height, pale and had dark brown hair. She had been with many men, most of them sailors. According to the Metropolitan

Police, she led "an utterly immoral life," and was "known to every prostitute in Euston Rd." When she was found nude in bed with her throat cut on the morning of September 12, 1907, the police, according to their report, first thought she had taken her own life as "she was a respectable married woman." Respectable women were far more likely to commit suicide than to be murdered, the police apparently believed.

The man Emily lived with was not her husband, but they talked about getting married one day. Bertram John Eugene Shaw was a cook for the Midland Railway. He was paid twenty-seven shillings per six-day week, leaving daily on a 5:42 train for Sheffield, where he would spend the night, then leave the next morning and arrive back at the St. Pancras Station at 10:40. He was almost always home at 11:30 A.M. He later told the police he had no idea that Emily was going out at night and seeing other men.

The police did not believe him. Shaw knew Emily was a prostitute when he met her. She swore to him she had changed her ways, and now she supplemented their income through dressmaking. Emily had been a good woman ever since they had begun to live together. Her days as a prostitute were in the past, he said. He truly may not have known—unless someone had told him—that usually by 8:00 or 8:30 P.M., Emily could be found at the Rising Sun pub on "Euston Road," as witnesses referred to it. The Rising Sun still exists and is really at the corner of Tottenham Court Road and Windmill Street. Tottenham runs into Euston Road. In 1932, Sickert did an oil painting titled *Grover's Island from Richmond Hill,* which has an uncharacteristic Van Gogh–like rising sun so large and bright on the horizon as to dominate the picture. The rising sun is almost identical to the one etched in glass over the front door of the Rising Sun pub.

Letters Sickert wrote in 1907 reveal that he spent part of the summer in Dieppe and was enjoying a "daily bathe before dejeuner. Big breakers that you have to look sharp and dive through." Apparently he was "hard at work" on paintings and drawings. He returned to London earlier than usual and the weather was "chilly" and "miserable." The summer was cool with frequent rains and very little sunshine.

Sickert had art exhibitions coming up in London. The 15th Annual Photographic Salon was opening on September 13th at the Royal Water Color Society's Gallery, and it would not have been unusual for him to want to see that. He was becoming increasingly interested in photography, which "like other branches of art," said *The Times*, "has proceeded in the direction of impressionism." September was a good month to stay in London. The bathing season in Dieppe would soon be ending, and most of Sickert's letters of 1907 were written from London. One of them stands out as weird and inexplicable.

The letter was to his American friend Nan Hudson, and in it Sickert tells the fantastic story of a woman who lived below him at 6 Mornington Crescent suddenly rushing into his room at midnight "with her whole head ablaze like a torch, from a celluloid comb. I put her out by shampooing her with my hands so quickly that I didn't burn myself at all." He said the woman wasn't injured but was now "bald." I fail to see how his story can possibly be true. I find it hard to believe that neither the woman nor Sickert was burned. Why did he mention this traumatic event only to dismiss it quickly and move on to discuss the New English Art Club? As far as I know, he never mentioned his bald-headed neighbor again.

One might begin to wonder whether at age forty-seven Sickert was getting quite eccentric, or perhaps his bizarre story is true. (I don't see how it can be.) I was left to wonder if it might be possible that Sickert fabricated the incident with his neighbor because it might have occurred the same night or early morning of Emily Dimmock's murder, and Sickert was making sure someone knew he was home. The alibi would be a weak one should the police ever check it. It wouldn't be hard to locate a bald downstairs neighbor or find out that she had a full head of hair and no recollection of a horrific encounter with a fiery comb. The alibi may have been for the benefit of Nan Hudson.

She and her companion, Ethel Sands, were very close to Sickert. His most revealing letters are the ones he wrote to them. He shared confidences with them—as much as he was capable of sharing confidences with anyone. The two women were alleged lesbians and, most likely, no threat to him sexually. He used them for money, sympathy, and other favors, manipulated them by mentoring and encouraging them in art, and revealed to them many details about himself that he did not divulge to others. He might suggest they "burn" a letter after they read it, or go to the other extreme and encourage them to save it, in the event he ever got around to writing a book.

It is obvious from other episodes in Sickert's life that he had periods of severe depression and paranoia. He could have had good reason to be paranoid after Emily Dimmock's murder, and if he wanted to make sure that at least somebody believed he was at home in Camden Town the night the prostitute was slain, then he unwittingly placed the time of Emily's murder at around midnight—or when the flaming neighbor rushed into Sickert's bedroom. Emily Dimmock usually took her clients home at half past midnight, when the pubs closed. This is only a theory. Sickert did not date his letters, including the one about his neighbor's flaming hair. Apparently, the envelope with its postmark is gone. I don't know why he felt inclined to tell such a dramatic story to Nan Hudson. But he had a reason. Sickert always had a reason.

He had studios at 18 and 27 Fitzroy Street, which is parallel to Tottenham Court Road and becomes Charlotte Street before passing Windmill Street. He could have walked from either of his studios to the Rising Sun pub in minutes. Mornington Crescent was a mile north of the pub, and Sickert rented the two top floors of the house at number 6. He painted there, usually nudes on a bed in the same setting he used in *Jack the Ripper's Bedroom,* painted from the point of view of someone outside open double doors that lead into a small murky space, where a dark mirror behind an iron bedstead vaguely reflects a man's shape.

Six Mornington Crescent was a twenty-minute walk from the lodging house where Emily Dimmock lived at 29 St. Paul's Road (now Agar Grove). She and Shaw had two rooms on the first floor. One was a sitting room, the second a cramped bedroom behind double doors at the back of the house. After Shaw would leave for St. Pancras Station, Emily might clean and sew or go out. Sometimes she met customers at the Rising Sun, or she might rendezvous with a man at another pub, Euston Station, or perhaps the Middlesex Music-hall (which Sickert painted around 1895), the Holborn Empire (home of music-hall star Bessie Bellwood, whom Sickert sketched many times around 1888), or the Euston Theater of Varieties.

One of Sickert's favorite spots for rendezvous was the statue of his former father-in-law, Richard Cobden, on the square off Mornington Crescent in Camden Town. The statue was presented to the vestry of St. Pancras in 1868 in honor of Cobden's repealing the Corn Laws, and was across from the Mornington Crescent underground station. Even when Sickert was married to Ellen, he had a habit of making sarcastic remarks about the statue as he rode past in a hansom. To use the statue for a rendezvous years after his divorce was perhaps another example of his mockery and contempt for people, especially important ones, especially a man he could never measure up to and had probably heard about all too often from the time he first met Ellen.

Emily Dimmock usually left her lodging house by 8:00 P.M. and did not return while the couple who owned the house, Mr. and Mrs. Stocks, were still awake. They claimed to know nothing about Emily's "irregular" life, and quite a life it was—two, three, four men a night, sometimes standing up in a dark corner of a train station before she might finally bring the last fellow home and sleep with him. Emily was not an Unfortunate like Annie Chapman or Elizabeth Stride. I wouldn't call Emily an Unfortunate at all. She did not live in the slums. She had food, a place to call home, and a man who wanted to marry her.

But she had an insatiable craving for excitement and the attention of men. The police described her as a woman "of lustful habits." I don't know if lust had anything to do with her sexual encounters. More likely her lust was for money. She wanted clothes and pretty little things. She was "greatly charmed" by artwork and collected penny picture postcards to paste in a scrapbook that was precious to her. The last postcard she had added to her collection, as far as anyone knows, was the one artist Robert Wood, employed by London Sand Blast Decorative Glass Works, Gray's Inn Road, had given to her on September 6, inside the Rising Sun. He wrote a note on the back of it, and the postcard became the key piece of evidence when Wood was charged and tried for murdering her. His indictment was based mostly on handwriting comparisons, and after a long, highly publicized trial, he was acquitted.

Emily Dimmock had given venereal disease to so many men that the police had a long list of former clients who had good cause to do her in. She had been threatened numerous times in the past. Enraged men who had contracted the "disorder" harassed her and threatened to "out" or kill her. But nothing stopped her from continuing her trade, no matter how many men she infected. And besides, she remarked to her women friends, it was a man who gave her the disorder in the first place.

Emily was seen with two strangers the week before her murder. One was a man "who had a short leg, or hip trouble of some sort," according to Robert Wood's statement to the police. The other was a Frenchman described by a witness as approximately five foot nine, very dark, with a short cut beard, and dressed in a dark coat and striped trousers. He briefly came into the Rising Sun on the night of September 9th, leaned over and spoke to Emily, then left. In police reports and at the inquest, there is no reference to this man again, nor did there seem to be any interest in him.

Emily Dimmock was last seen alive at a Camden Town pub called the Eagle on the night of September 11th. Earlier in the evening she had been talking to Mrs. Stocks in the kitchen and said she had plans for the evening. Emily had received a postcard from a man who wanted to meet her at the Eagle, near the Camden Road Station. The postcard read, "Meet me at 8 o'clock at the Eagle tonight [Wednesday, September 11th]" and was signed "Bertie," which was Robert Wood's nickname. When she left the house that night in her long housecoat, her hair in curlers, she was "not dressed to go out." She mentioned to acquaintances that she didn't plan to stay at the Eagle long, wasn't eager to go, and that was why she wasn't properly dressed.

She still had the curlers in her hair when she was murdered. Perhaps she was taking extra care to make sure she looked her best the next morning. Shaw's mother was coming to visit from Northampton, and Emily had been cleaning, doing the laundry, and getting the house in order. None of her former clients ever mentioned that Emily wore curlers while giving them pleasure. It would seem a poor business tactic if one was hoping for a generous payment from a client. The curlers could suggest that Emily wasn't expecting the violent visitor who took her life. They might suggest she took her killer home with her and never removed the curlers from her hair.

Her back bedroom on the ground floor was accessible by windows and sturdy cast-iron drainpipes a person could climb up. There is no mention in the police reports that the windows were locked. Only the bedroom double door, the sitting room door, and the front door of the house were locked the next morning when Emily's body was found. Her three keys to those doors were missing when the police and Shaw searched the rooms. It is possible someone climbed into her bedroom while she was asleep, but I don't think it's likely.

When she set out from 29 St. Paul's Road that Wednesday evening, she may not have intended to sell pleasure to anyone, but it could be that while she was on her way home with curlers in her hair, she ran into a man. He said something to her.

"Where are you a goin my pretty little maid?" someone wrote in The Lizard guest book.

If Emily did have an encounter with her killer on her way home or if he was the man she met at the Eagle, he might have told her he didn't mind her curlers in the least. *Will you let me come see you in your room?* It is possible Sickert had noticed Emily Dimmock many times in the past, at railway stations, or just walking about. The Rising Sun was right around the corner from his studios, not far from Maple Street, which he would later sketch as an empty back street late at night with two distant shadowy women lingering on the corner. Emily Dimmock may have noticed Walter Sickert, too. He was a familiar sight along Fitzroy Street, carrying his canvases back and forth from one studio to another.

He was a well-known local artist. He was painting nudes at this time. He had to get his models from somewhere, and he had a penchant for prostitutes. He may have been stalking and watching Emily and her sexual transactions. She was the lowest of the lowest, a filthy diseased whore. Marjorie Lilly writes that once she heard a person defend thieves by telling Sickert, "After all, everyone has a right to exist." He retorted, "Not at all. There are people who have no right to exist!"

"As you can see I have done another good thing for Whitechapel," the Ripper wrote November 12, 1888.

The position of Emily Dimmock's dead body was described as "natural." The doctor who arrived at the scene said he believed that she was asleep when she was killed. She was face-down, her left arm bent at an angle and across her back, the hand bloody. Her right arm was extended in front of her and on the pillow. In fact, her position was not natural or comfortable. Most people do not sleep or even lie down with one of their arms bent at a right angle behind their backs. There was not sufficient space between the headboard and the wall for the killer to attack her from behind. She needed to be face-down, and her unnatural position on the bed can be explained if the killer straddled her as he pulled back her head with his left hand and cut her throat with his right.

Blood on her left hand suggests she grabbed the hemorrhaging left side of her neck, and her assailant may have wrenched her left arm behind her, perhaps pinning it with a knee to keep her from struggling. He had cut her throat to the spine and she could make no sound. He had slashed her neck from left to right, as a right-handed assailant would. He had so little room to work that his violent sweep of the knife cut the mattress ticking and nicked Emily's right elbow. She was on her face, her left carotid squirting her syphilitic blood into the bed and not all over him.

The police did not discover a bloody nightgown at the scene. In the absence of that garment, it might be presumed that Emily was nude when she was murdered—or that her killer took a bloody gown as a trophy. A former client who had slept with Emily three times claimed that on those occasions she wore a nightdress and did not have curlers in her hair. If she had sex on the night of September 11th, especially if she was intoxicated, it is possible that she fell asleep in the nude. Or she may have been with another "client"—her killer—who had her undress and turn over, as if he wanted anal sex or intercourse from the rear. After he cut a six-inch gash in her throat, her killer threw the bedclothes over her. All of this seems to deviate from Sickert's violent modus operandi, with the exception that apparently there was no sign of "connection."

After twenty years, Sickert's patterns, fantasies, needs, and energy would have evolved. Very little is known about his activities after he began spending most of his time in France and Italy during the 1890s. So far, documentation that might reveal unsolved murders with striking similarities to Sickert's crimes doesn't exist or has yet to surface in other countries. I found references to only two cases in France, not in police records but in newspapers. The murders are so unspecific and unverified, I hesitate to mention them: It was reported that in early 1889, at Pont-a-Mousson, a widow named Madame François was found slain, her head nearly severed from her body. About the same time and in the same area, another woman was found with her head nearly severed from her body. The doctor who conducted both postmortem examinations concluded that the murderer was very skillful with a knife.

Around 1906, Sickert returned to England and settled in Camden

Town. He resumed painting music halls—such as the Mogul Tavern (by now called the Old Middlesex Music Hall, on Drury Lane, less than two miles from where he lived in Camden Town). Sickert went out almost every night and was always in his stall at 8:00 P.M. sharp, he wrote in a letter to Jacques-Emile Blanche. Presumably, Sickert stayed until the performances ended at half past midnight.

During his late-night journeys home, it is very possible he could have seen Emily Dimmock out on the streets, perhaps heading to her rooming house with a client. Had Sickert gathered intelligence on her, he could easily have known her patterns, and that she was a notorious prostitute and a walking plague. Periodically she was an outpatient at Lock Hospital in Harrow Road, and most recently had been treated at University College Hospital. When her venereal disease was fulminating, she had eruptions on her face, and she had a few of these at the time of her death. This should have indicated to a street-smart man that she was dangerous to his health.

Sickert would have been foolish to have exposed himself to her body fluids, because by 1907 more was known about contagious diseases. Exposure to blood could be just as dangerous as intercourse, and it would not have been possible for Sickert to disembowel or take organs without subjecting himself to great risk. I believe he would have been shrewd enough to avoid re-creating the twenty-year-old Ripper scare, especially when he was about to begin his most intense period of violent art and produce works that he would not have dared to etch or paint or display in 1888 or 1889. Emily Dimmock's murder was staged to appear to have been motivated by robbery.

Bertram Shaw arrived home from the train station on the morning of September 12th, and discovered that his mother was already there. She was waiting in the hallway because Emily did not answer the door and she could not get into her son's rooms. Shaw tried the outer door and was baffled to find it locked. He wondered if Emily might have gone out to meet his mother at the railway station and the two women had missed each other. He was getting increasingly uneasy, and asked the landlady, Mrs. Stocks, for a key. Shaw unlocked the outer door and found the double doors locked as well. He broke in and flung back the covers from Emily's naked body on the blood-soaked bed.

Drawers had been pulled out of the dresser, the contents rummaged through and scattered on the floor. Emily's scrapbook was open on a chair, and some postcards had been removed from it. The windows and shutters in the bedroom were closed, the windows in the sitting room closed, the shutters slightly open. Shaw ran for the police. Some twenty-five minutes later, Constable Thomas Killion arrived and determined by touching Emily's cold shoulder that she had been dead for hours. He immediately sent for police divisional surgeon Dr. John Thompson, who arrived at the scene around 1:00 P.M. and concluded—based on the coldness of the body and the advanced stage of rigor mortis—that Emily had been dead seven or eight hours.

This would have placed her time of death at 6:00 or 7:00 A.M., which is not likely. The morning was thick with fog, but the sun rose at 5:30. The killer would have been brazen to the point of stupidity had he left Emily's house after the sun was up, no matter how gray and muggy the weather, and by six or seven o'clock, people were stirring, many on their way to work.

Under ordinary conditions, it requires six to twelve hours for a body to be fully rigorous, and cold temperatures can retard this process. Emily's body was under bedclothes that the killer had flung over her, and the windows and doors were shut. Her bedroom would not have been frigid, but on the early morning she died, the low was 47 degrees Fahrenheit. What is not known is how stiff she was, or how advanced her rigor mortis might have been by the time Dr. Thompson began to examine her at some point after 1:00 P.M. She could have been in full rigor mortis—dead a good ten or twelve hours. This would suggest she could have been murdered between midnight and 4:00 A.M.

Dr. Thompson said at the scene that Emily's throat had been cut cleanly with a very sharp instrument. The police found nothing except one of Shaw's cut-throat razors in plain view on top of a dresser, and it would be difficult to use a cut-throat razor to cut forcefully through muscle and cartilage without the blade folding backward and perhaps severely wounding the perpetrator. A bloody petticoat in the hand basin had soaked up all of the water, indicating the killer had cleaned himself before he left. He was careful not to touch anything with bloody hands, the police remarked at the inquest.

The Ripper panic was not suddenly resurrected after Emily's murder, and Sickert's name was never mentioned in connection with the crime. There were no Ripper-type letters to the press or the police, but curiously enough, right after Emily's murder a Harold Ashton, a reporter for the *Morning Leader,* went to the police and showed them photographs of four postcards sent to the editor. It is not clear from the police report who sent these postcards, but the implication is they were signed "A.C.C." Ashton inquired if the police were aware that the writer of the postcards might be a "racing man." The reporter went on to point out the following:

A postmark dated January 2, 1907, London, was the first day of racing after "a spell of wintry weather," and the race that day was at Gatwick.

A second postcard was dated August 9, 1907, Brighton, and the Brighton races were held on the 6th, 7th, and 8th and at Lewes on the 9th and 10th of that month. The reporter said that many people who attended the races at Lewes stayed the weekend in Brighton.

A third postcard was dated August 19, 1907, Windsor, and the Windsor races were held on Friday and Saturday, the 16th and 17th of that month.

The fourth postcard was dated September 9th, two days before Emily's murder, and one day before the Doncaster autumn races. But what was very strange about this card, Ashton pointed out, is that it was a French postcard that appeared to have been purchased in Chantilly, France, where a race had been held the week before the Doncaster autumn races. Ashton said, according to the rather confusing police report, that he believed "the post card may have been purchased in France, possibly at Chantilly, brought over and posted with English stamps at Doncaster"—as if to imply it had been mailed from Doncaster during the races. Had the sender attended the Doncaster autumn races, he could not have been in Camden Town at the time of Emily's September 11th murder. The Doncaster races were held on the 10th, 11th, 12th, and 13th of September.

Ashton was asked to withhold this information from his newspaper, which he did. On September 30th, Inspector A. Hailstone noted on the report that the police thought Ashton was correct about the dates of the races, but the reporter was "quite wrong" about the postmark of the fourth postcard. "It is clearly marked London NW." Apparently, it didn't strike Inspector Hailstone as somewhat odd that a French postcard apparently written two days before Emily Dimmock's murder was for some reason posted in London to a London newspaper. I don't know if "A.C.C." were the initials of an anonymous sender or meant something else, but it seems that the police might have questioned why a "racing man" would have sent these postcards to a newspaper at all.

It might have occurred to Inspector Hailstone that what this racing man had accomplished, whether he intended to or not, was to make it clear he had a habit of attending horse races and was at Doncaster on the date the much-publicized murder of Emily Dimmock occurred. If Sickert was now supplying himself with alibis instead of taunting the police with his "catch me if you can" communications, his actions would make perfect sense. At this stage in his life, his violent psychopathic drive would have lessened. It would be highly unusual for him to continue maniacal killing sprees that required tremendous energy and obsessive focus. If he committed murder, he did not want to be caught. His violent energy had been dissipated—although not eradicated—by age and his career.

When Sickert began his infamous paintings and etchings of nude women sprawled on iron bedsteads—the *Camden Town Murder* and *L'affair de Camden Town,* or *Jack Ashore* or the clothed man in *Despair* who sits on a bed, his face in his hands—he was simply viewed as a respected artist who had chosen the Camden Town murder as a narrative theme in his work. It wouldn't be until many years later that a detail would link him to the Camden Town murder. On November 29, 1937, the *Evening Standard* printed a short article about Sickert's Camden Town murder paintings, and stated, "Sickert, who was living in Camden Town, was permitted to enter the house where the murder was committed and did several sketches of the murdered woman's body."

Supposing this is true, was it another Sickert coincidence that he just happened to be wandering along St. Paul's Road when he noticed a swarm of police officers and wanted to see what all the excitement was about? Emily's body was discovered about 11:30 A.M. Not long after Dr. Thompson examined it at 1:00 P.M., it was removed to the St. Pancras mortuary. There was a relatively short time period of maybe two to three hours for Sickert to have happened to be passing by while Emily's body was still inside the house. If he had no idea when her body would be found, he would have had to case the area for many hours—and risk being noticed—to make sure he didn't miss the show.

A simple solution is suggested by the missing three keys. Sickert might have locked the doors behind him as he left the house—especially the inner and outer doors to Emily's rooms—to make it less likely that her body would be found before Shaw came home at 11:30 in the morning. Had Sickert been stalking Emily, he certainly would have known when Shaw left the house for work and when he returned. While the landlady might not have entered a locked room, Shaw would have, had Emily not responded to his calling out and knocking.

Sickert might have taken the keys as a souvenir. I see no reason for him to need them to make his escape after Emily's murder. It is possible that the three stolen keys could have given him a curtain-up time of approximately

11:30 A.M. So he just happened to show up at the crime scene before the body was removed and innocently ask the police if he might have a look inside and do a few sketches. Sickert was the local artist, a charming fellow. I doubt the police would have refused him his request. They probably told him all about the crime. Many a police officer likes to talk, especially when a major crime is committed on his shift. At the most, the police might have found Sickert's interest eccentric, but not suspicious. I found no mention in police reports that Sickert appeared at the crime scene, or that any artist did. But when I've shown up at crime scenes as a journalist and author, my name has never been entered into reports, either.

Sickert's appearing at the scene also gave him an alibi. Should the police have discovered fingerprints that for some reason or another were ever identified as Walter Richard Sickert's, so what? Sickert had been inside Emily Dimmock's house. He had been inside her bedroom. One would expect him to have left fingerprints and maybe a few hairs or who knows what else while he was busy moving around, sketching, and chatting to the police or to Shaw and his mother.

It was not out of character for Sickert to sketch dead bodies. During World War I, he was obsessed with wounded and dying soldiers and their uniforms and weapons. He collected a pile of them and maintained close relations with people at the Red Cross, asking them to let him know when uniforms might not be needed any longer by ill-fated patients. "I have got a capital fellow," he wrote to Nan Hudson in the fall of 1914. "The ideal noble & somewhat beefy young Briton . . . & I have already drawn him alive & dead."

In several letters she wrote to Janie in 1907, Ellen inquires about "poor young Woods" and wants to know what happened when his case went to trial later that year. Ellen was overseas, and if she was referring to the eventual arrest, indictment, and trial of Robert Wood, accused and later acquitted of being Emily Dimmock's killer, she may have got the name slightly wrong, but the question was an atypical one for her to ask. She did not refer to criminal cases in her correspondence. I have found not a single mention of the Ripper murders or any others. For her to suddenly want to know about "poor young Woods" is perplexing, unless "Woods" is not really Robert Wood, but someone else.

I can't help but wonder if by 1907 Ellen secretly entertained doubts about her former husband, doubts that she dared not articulate and did her best to deny. But now a man was on trial, and should he be found guilty, he would be hanged. Ellen was a moral woman. If the slightest thing disturbed her conscience, she might have felt compelled to write a sealed letter to her sister. Ellen may even have begun to fear for her own life.

After the Camden Town murder, her mental and physical health began to deteriorate, and she spent most of her time away from London. She still saw Sickert now and then and continued to help him as best she could until she severed their relationship for good in 1913. A year later she was dead from cancer of the uterus.

CHAPTER TWENTY-SIX

THE DAUGHTERS OF COBDEN

Ellen Melicent Ashburner Cobden was born on August 18, 1848, in Dunford, the family's old farmhouse near the village of Heyshott, in West Sussex.

At the end of May 1860, when Walter was born in Munich, the eleven-year-old Ellen was spending the spring in Paris. She had saved a sparrow that had fallen out of its nest in the garden. "A dear little tame thing it will eat out of my hand and perch upon my finger," she wrote to a pen pal. Ellen's mother, Kate, was planning a lovely children's party with fifty or sixty guests, and was planning to take Ellen to the circus and to a picnic in an "enormous tree" with a staircase leading to a table on top. Ellen had just learned a special trick of "putting an egg in a wine bottle," and now and then her father wrote special letters just to her.

Life back in England was not so enchanting. In the most recent letter from Richard Cobden, he told his daughter that a violent storm had battered the family estate and torn up thirty-six trees by the roots. A severe cold front destroyed most of the shrubbery on the estate, including the evergreens, and the vegetable garden would be barren come the summer. The report was like a foreshadowing of the evil that had entered the world through a distant city in Germany. Ellen's future husband would soon enough cross the Channel and settle in London, where he would uproot the lives of many people, including hers.

Numerous biographies have been written about Ellen's father, Richard Cobden. He was one of twelve children, and his childhood was a desolate, harsh one. He was sent away from home at the age of ten after his father's disastrous business sense spiraled the family to ruin. Cobden's adolescence was spent working for his uncle, a merchant in London, and attending a school in Yorkshire. This period of his life was physical and emotional torture, and in years to come Cobden could scarcely bear to speak of it.

Suffering bears the fruits of unselfishness and love in some people, and it did with him. There was nothing bitter or unkind about Richard Cobden, not even when he was battered by his most derisive detractors during his polarizing political career. His great passion was people, and he was never far from his pained memories of watching farmers, including his own father, lose everything they owned. Cobden's compassion for people gave him the mission of repealing the Corn Laws, a terrible piece of legislation that kept families poor and hungry.

The Corn Laws were enacted in 1815 when the Napoleonic Wars had left England almost in a state of famine. Bread was precious, and it was illegal for a baker to sell his loaves until after they had been out of the oven for at least twenty-four hours. If bread was stale, people weren't as likely to overeat and would "waste not and want not." The penalty for defying this law was harsh. Bakers were fined as much as five pounds and court costs. As a small boy, Richard Cobden watched the desperate come to Dunford and beg for alms or food that his own family could not afford.

Only well-off farmers and landlords profited, and they were the ones who would make sure that the price of grain remained as high in good times as it had been in bad. The landlords who wanted to keep prices inflated were the majority in Parliament, and the Corn Laws were not hard to pass. The logic was simple: Place impossibly high duties on imported foreign grains, and the supply in England stays low, the prices artificially high. The enactment of the Corn Laws was disastrous for the common worker, and riots broke out in London and other parts of the country. The laws would remain in effect until 1846, when Cobden won his fight to repeal them.

He was greatly respected at home and abroad. On his first trip to America, he was invited to stay in the White House. He gained the admiration and friendship of the author Harriet Beecher Stowe after she came to visit him at Dunford in 1853 and the two of them discussed the importance of "cultivating cotton by free labour." In an essay she wrote a year later, she described him as a slender man of small stature who had "great ease of manner" and "the most frank, fascinating smile." Cobden was a peer to every powerful politician in England, including Sir Robert Peel, the father of the police force that would one day take on Cobden's future son-in-law, Jack the Ripper, and lose.

Richard Cobden was devoted to his family and became the only stability in his daughters' young lives after his only son, Richard Brooks, died at the age of fifteen in 1856. He was in boarding school near Heidelberg, and was healthy, mischievous, and adored. His mother had turned him into her best friend during her husband's frequent absences.

Ellen adored her big brother, too. "I send you a little curl of my hair, that you may sometimes think of one who loves you very much," she wrote to him when he was off at boarding school. "You will write to me very soon and tell me how long it will be before I shall have the pleasure of seeing you." The affection was mutual and unusually sweet. "I shall bring down some presents for you," Richard wrote to her in his boyish scrawl. "I will try to get you a little kitten."

Richard's letters hint at the mature, insightful, and witty man he might have become. He was a practical joker whose April Fools' Day naughtiness included writing "kick me out of the shop" in German and giving the note to a French boy to present as a shopping list at a nearby grocer's. Yet Richard Brooks was tenderhearted enough to be concerned about a family friend's dog, who might need an "extra blanket" during the "east winds."

The boy's letters home were entertaining, and much too full of life to cause anyone to imagine that he would not grow up to be the perfect only son of his famous father. On April 3rd, Richard Brooks wrote a letter to his father from boarding school that would be his last one. He was suddenly stricken with scarlet fever and died on April 6th.

The story is made all the more tragic by an almost unforgivable blunder. The headmaster at Richard's school contacted a Cobden family friend, and each man assumed the other had sent a telegram to Richard Cobden about his son's sudden death. Young Richard Brooks was already buried by the time his father got the news in a most heart-wrenching way. Cobden had just sat down to breakfast in his hotel room in Grosvenor Street, London and was going through his post. He found the April 3rd letter from his son, and eagerly read it first. Moments later, he opened another letter that consoled him over his terrible loss. Stunned and beside himself with grief, Cobden immediately began the five-hour journey to Dunford, anguishing over how to tell his family, especially Kate. She had already lost two children and was unhealthily attached to Richard.

Cobden appeared at Dunford, ashen and drawn, and broke down as he told them what had happened. The shock was more than Kate could bear, and the loss of her beloved son took on the mythical proportions of Icarus flying into the face of the sun. After several days of denial, she fell into an almost catatonic state, sitting "like a statue, neither speaking nor seeming to hear," Cobden wrote. Hour by hour he watched his wife's hair turn white. Seven-year-old Ellen had lost her brother, and now she had lost her mother, too. Kate Cobden would outlive her husband by twelve years, but she was an emotionally stricken woman who, as her husband put it, "stumbles over [Richard's] corpse as she is passing from room to room." She could not recover from her grief and became addicted to opiates. Ellen found herself in a role too overwhelming for any young girl to play. Just as Richard Brooks had become his mother's best friend, Ellen became a replacement helpmeet for her father.

On September 21, 1864, when Ellen was fifteen, her father wrote to her asking her to please look after her younger sisters. "Much will depend on your influence & still more on your example," he wrote. "I wished to have told you how much your Mamma & I looked to your good example," and he expected her to help "bring [your sisters] into a perfect state of discipline." This was an unrealistic expectation for a fifteen-year-old struggling with her own losses. Ellen was never allowed to grieve, and the burden and pain must have become almost unbearable when her father died a year later.

The very smog that helped cloak the peregrinations and violent crimes of Ellen's future husband robbed her father of his life. For years Cobden had been susceptible to respiratory infections that sent him on voyages or to the seaside or the countryside—wherever there was better air than the sooty soup of London. His last trip to London before his death was in March 1865. Ellen was sixteen and accompanied him. They stayed in a lodging house in Suffolk Street reasonably close to the House of Commons. Cobden was immediately laid up with asthma as black smoke gushed from chimneys of nearby houses, and the east wind blew the noxious air into his room.

A week later, he lay in bed praying that the winds would mercifully shift, but his asthma worsened and he developed bronchitis. Cobden sensed the end had come and made out his will. His wife and Ellen were at his bedside when he died on Sunday morning, April 2, 1865, at the age of sixty-one. Ellen was the "one whose attachment to her father seems to have been a passion scarcely equaled among the daughters," said Cobden's lifelong friend and political ally John Bright. She was the last one to let go of her father's coffin as it was lowered into the earth. She never let go of his memory or forgot what he expected of her.

Bright would later tell Cobden's official biographer, John Morley, that Cobden's "was a life of perpetual self-sacrifice. . . . I never knew how much I loved him until I had lost him." On Monday, the day after Cobden's death, Benjamin Disraeli said to the House of Commons, "There is this consolation . . . that these great men are not altogether lost to us." Today, in the Heyshott village church there is a plaque on Cobden's family pew that reads, "In this place Richard Cobden, who loved his fellow men, was accustomed to worship God." Despite Cobden's best intentions, he left an unstable wife to take care of four spirited daughters, and despite the many promises made by influential friends at the funeral, the "daughters of Cobden," as the press called them, were on their own.

In 1898, Janie reminded Ellen how "all those who professed such deep admiration and affection for [our] father during his lifetime forgot the existence of his young daughters, the youngest but 3½ years old. Do you remember Gladstone at father's funeral telling mother that she might always rely on his friendship & her children also—The next time I met him, or spoke to him . . . was more than 20 years later. Such is the way of the world!"

Ellen held the family together, as she had promised her father she would. She handled the family finances while her mother moved numbly through the last few years of her unhappy life. Had it not been for Ellen's dogged cajoling and firm supervision of the family affairs, it is questionable whether bills would have been paid, young Annie would have gone to school, or that the daughters could leave their mother's house and move into a flat at 14 York Place, Baker Street. Ellen's yearly stipend was 250 pounds, or at least this was what she told her mother she would need. It can be conjectured that each daughter received the same amount, insuring them a comfortable existence, as well as a vulnerability to men whose intentions may not have been sterling.

Richard Fisher was engaged to Katie Cobden when her father died, and he rushed her into marriage before the family had stopped writing letters on mourning stationery. Over the years Fisher's greedy demands would prove a constant source of irritation to the Cobdens. In 1880, when Walter Sickert entered the lives of the Cobden daughters, Katie was married, Maggie was too spirited and frivolous to serve an ambitious, manipulative man any useful purpose, and Janie was far too savvy for Sickert to go near. He picked Ellen.

Both her parents were dead. She had no one to advise her or raise objections. I doubt that Sickert would have gained Richard Cobden's approval. Cobden was a wise and insightful man and would not have been fooled by Sickert's acts or enchanted by his charm. Cobden would have detested the absence of compassion in the handsome young man.

"Mrs. Sickert and all her sons were such pagans," Janie would write to Ellen some twenty years later. "How sad that fate has ever brought you into their midst."

The differences between the character of Ellen's father and that of the man she would marry should have been blatantly obvious, but in Ellen's eyes the two men might have appeared to have much in common. Richard Cobden did not have an Oxford or Cambridge education and was in many ways self-taught. He loved Shakespeare, Byron, Irving, and Cooper. He was fluent in French, and as a young man he had fantasized about being a playwright. His love of the visual arts would be a lifelong affair, even if his attempts at writing for the stage were a failure. Cobden too was not adept at handling finances. He might have been canny in business, but he had no interest in money unless he had none.

At one point in his life, his friends had to raise sufficient funds to save the family home. His financial failings were not the result of irresponsibility but were a symptom of his driving sense of mission and idealism. Cobden was not a spendthrift. He simply had loftier matters on his mind, and this may have impressed his daughter Ellen as a noble flaw rather than a blameworthy one. Perhaps it was fortuitous that in 1880, the year Sickert first met Ellen, John Morley's long-awaited two-volume biography of Cobden was published.

If Sickert read Morley's work, he could have known enough about Cobden to script a very persuasive role for himself and easily convince Ellen that he and the famous politician shared some of the same traits: a love of the theater and literature, an attachment to all things French, and a higher calling that was not about money. Sickert might even have convinced Ellen that he was an advocate of women's suffrage.

"I shall reluctantly have to support a bitches suffrage bill," Sickert would complain some thirty-five years later. "But you are to understand I shall not by this become a 'feminist.' "

Richard Cobden believed in the equality of the sexes. He treated his daughters with respect and affection—and never as witless brood mares good for nothing but marriage and childbearing. He would have applauded the political activism of his daughters as they matured. The 1880s were a time of foment for females as they formed purity and political leagues that lobbied for contraception, reforms to help the poor, and the right to vote and to have representation in Parliament. Feminists such as the Cobden daughters wanted to enjoy the same human dignity as men, and that meant quashing entertainment and vices that promoted the enslavement of women, such as prostitution and the lasciviousness of London's many music halls.

Sickert must have sensed that Ellen's life belonged to her father. There was nothing she would do to smear his name. When she and Sickert divorced, Janie's prominent publisher husband, Fisher Unwin, contacted the editors of London's major newspapers and requested that they print "nothing of a personal nature" in their papers. "Certainly," he insisted, "the family name should not appear." Any secret that might have hurt Richard Cobden was safe with Ellen, and we will never know how many secrets she took to her grave. For Richard Cobden, the great protector of the poor, to have a son-in-law who slaughtered the poor was inconceivable. The question may always be whether Ellen knew that Walter had a dark side "From Hell," to quote a phrase the Ripper used in several of his letters.

It is possible that at some point and on some level Ellen suspected the truth about her husband. Despite her liberal stance in regard to women's suffrage, Ellen was weak in body and spirit. Her increasingly friable fabric may have been the result of a genetic trait she shared with her mother, but Ellen might also have been damaged by the torment her well-meaning father put her through because of his own desperate needs. She could not live up to his expectations. In her own eyes, she was a failure long before she and Walter Sickert met.

It was in her nature to blame herself for whatever went wrong in the Cobden family or her marriage. No matter how often Sickert betrayed her, lied to her, abandoned her, made her feel unloved or invisible, she was loyal and would do anything she could for him. His happiness and health mattered to her, even after they were divorced and he married somebody else. Emotionally and financially, Sickert bled Ellen Cobden to death.

Not long before Ellen died, she wrote to Janie, "If only you knew how much I long to go to sleep for good & all. I have been a troublesome sister in many ways. There is a strain of waywardness in my character which has neutralized other qualities which should have helped me thru life."

Janie didn't blame Ellen. She blamed Sickert. She had formed her own silent opinion of him early on, and began to encourage Ellen to go on trips and stay at the family estate in Sussex or at the Unwins' flat at 10 Hereford Square, South Kensington. Janie's biting observations about Sickert would not become blatant until Ellen had finally decided to separate from him in September 1896. Then Janie forcefully spoke her mind. She was infuriated by Sickert's ability to fool other people, particularly his artist friends. They "have quite an exalted idea of his character," she wrote to Ellen on July 24, 1899, days before Ellen and Sickert's divorce was final. "They cannot know what he really is as you do."

The ever-sensible Janie tried to convince her sister of the truth. "I fear to say that W.S. will never change his conduct of life—and with no guiding principles to keep his emotional nature straight he follows every whim that takes his fancy—you have tried so often to trust him, and he has deceived you times without number." But nothing dissuaded Ellen from loving Walter Sickert and believing he would change.

Ellen was a gentle, needy woman. Her childhood letters reveal a "daddy's girl" whose entire existence was about being his daughter. Ellen politicked, said and did the right things, was always appropriate, and carried on her father's missions as much as her limited strength and courage would allow. She could not see a stray or injured animal without trying to rescue it, and even as a small child she could not bear it when the lambs were herded away for slaughter and the mother sheep bleated plaintively in the fields. Ellen had rabbits, dogs, cats, goldfinches, parakeets, ponies, donkeys—whatever came into her kind and sensitive hands.

She deeply cared about the poor and campaigned for free trade and home rule for Ireland almost as tirelessly as Janie did. Over time, Ellen became too worn down to accompany her words with her feet. While Janie would move on to become one of the most prominent women suffragettes, Ellen would drift deeper into depression, illness, and fatigue. Yet in the hundreds of surviving letters Ellen wrote during her relatively short life, she does not lament the social plight of the Unfortunates her husband brought into his studios to sketch and paint. She did nothing to better the lives of those women or their pitiful children.

The suffering remnants of humanity, adult or child, were for Sickert to use or abuse as he pleased. Perhaps his wife did not want to see the music-hall stars who posed for him in the upstairs studio at 54 Broadhurst Gardens or later in Chelsea. Perhaps she could not bear to see any child or childlike person her husband may have been interested in just a bit too much. Sickert watched little girls dance in sexually provocative ways in the music halls. He met them backstage. He painted them. Much later in life, when Sickert became obsessed with the actress Gwen Ffrangcon-Davies, he asked her in a letter if she had any photographs of herself "as a child."

Ellen and Sickert would have no children. There is no real evidence Sickert ever had children, although a story has persisted that he had an illegitimate son by Madame Villain, a French fishwife he stayed with in Dieppe after his separation from Ellen. In a letter, Sickert refers to Madame Villain as a mother figure who took care of him at a low point in his life. This does not mean he did not have sex with her, assuming he could. The supposed illegitimate child's name was Maurice, and Sickert would have nothing to do with him, so the story goes. Madame Villain was said to have had many children by many different men.

In a July 20, 1902, letter from Jacques-Emile Blanche to the novelist André Gide, Blanche says that Sickert's "life more and more defies everyone. . . . This immoralist has ended up living alone in a large house in a working class suburb so that he doesn't have to do anything regarded as normal and can do what ever he likes whenever he likes. He does this without a sou having a legitimate family in England and a fishwife in Dieppe, with a swarm of children of provenances which are not possible to count."

The medical implications of Sickert's early operations would suggest he was unable to father children, but without medical records all one can do is to speculate. He would not have wanted to bother with children, even if he could have fathered them, and Ellen probably wouldn't have wanted them, either. She was almost thirty-seven and he was twenty-five when, after a four-year engagement, they were married at the Marylebone Registry Office on June 10, 1885. He was starting his career and did not want children, says his nephew John Lessore, and Ellen was getting a bit old to have them.

She may also have been an advocate of the Purity League, which encouraged women not to engage in intercourse. Sex was what held women back and victimized them. Ellen and Janie were both ardent feminists, and Janie had no children, either, for reasons not clear. Both women were in agreement with the Malthusians, who used Thomas Malthus's essay on population as the basis for promoting contraception—even if the Reverend Malthus himself was actually opposed to contraception.

Ellen's diaries and correspondence reveal an intelligent, socially sophisticated, decent woman who was idealistic about love. She was also very careful. Or someone was. Over the thirty-four years she knew and loved Walter Sickert, she mentions him very few times. Janie mentions him more often, but not with the frequency one might expect from a thoughtful woman who should have cared about her sister's spouse. Gaps in the some four hundred existing letters and notes the sisters wrote to each other suggest that much of their correspondence has vanished. I found only thirty-odd letters from 1880 to 1889, which is puzzling. During this decade Ellen got engaged to Sickert and they were married.

I found not a single allusion to Ellen's wedding, and based on the list of witnesses on the marriage certificate, no one in her family or Sickert's was present at the Registry Office, a very odd place for a first marriage in those days, especially when the bride was the daughter of Richard Cobden. There does not appear to be a single letter from Ellen when she was on her honeymoon in Europe, and in no archival source did I discover correspondence between Ellen and Sickert or between Ellen and Sickert's family or between Sickert and his family or between Sickert and the Cobden family.

If such letters existed, possibly they were destroyed or have been kept out of public circulation. I find it strange that a husband and wife apparently did not write or send telegrams to each other when they were apart, which was more often than not. I find it significant that the legacy-minded Ellen apparently did not preserve letters from Sickert when she believed in his genius and that he was destined to become an important artist.

"I know how good it is," Ellen writes of Sickert's art. "*I* have always known," she wrote to Blanche.

By 1881, the young, beautiful, blue-eyed Walter had attached himself to a woman whose yearly stipend was as much as 250 pounds—more than what some young physicians earned then. There was no reason why Sickert shouldn't enroll at the prestigious Slade School of Fine Art in London. The 1881 Slade syllabus indicates courses strong in the sciences: antique and life classes, etching, sculpture, archaeology, perspective, chemistry of materials used in painting, and anatomy. On Tuesdays and Thursdays there were lectures that focused on "the bones, joints and muscles."

During Sickert's time at the Slade he became friendly with Whistler, but how they actually met is hazy. One story is that Sickert and Whistler were in the audience at the Lyceum while Ellen Terry was performing. During the curtain call, Sickert hurled roses weighted with lead onto the stage and the fragrant missile almost hit Henry Irving, who was not amused. Whistler's infamous "ha ha!" could be heard in the crowd. As the audience was filing out, Whistler made a point of meeting the audacious young man.

Other accounts suggest that Sickert "ran into" Whistler somewhere or followed him into a shop or met him at a party or through the Cobden daughters. Sickert was never accused of being shy or reticent about whatever it was he wanted at the moment. Whistler supposedly persuaded Sickert to stop wasting his time with art school and come to work in a real studio with him. The young man left the Slade School and became Whistler's apprentice. He worked side by side with the Master, but what his days with Ellen were like is a blank.

Available references to the early years of Ellen and Walter's marriage do not indicate an attraction to each other or the slightest fragrant scent of romance. In Jacques-Emile Blanche's memoirs, he refers to Ellen as so much older than Sickert that she "might have been taken for his elder sister." He thought the couple were well matched "intellectually" and observed that they allowed each other "perfect freedom." During visits to Blanche in Dieppe, Sickert paid little attention to Ellen, but would disappear in the narrow streets and courtyards, and into his rented "mysterious rooms in harbour quarters, sheds from which all were excluded."

The divorce decree cites that Sickert was guilty of "adultery coupled with desertion for the space of 2 years & upwards without reasonable excuse." Yet it was really Ellen who eventually refused to live with Sickert. And there is no evidence he had even one sexual transgression. Ellen's divorce petition states that Sickert deserted her on September 29, 1896, and that on or about April 21, 1898, he committed adultery with a woman whose name was "unknown" to Ellen. This alleged tryst supposedly occurred at the Midland Grand Hotel in London. Then, on May 4, 1899, Sickert supposedly committed adultery again with a woman whose name also was "unknown" to Ellen.

Various biographers explain that the reason the couple separated on September 29th is that on this day Sickert admitted to Ellen that he wasn't faithful to her and never had been. If so, it would appear that his affairs—assuming he had more than the two mentioned in the divorce decree—were with "unknown" women. Nothing I have read would indicate that he was amorous toward women or given to inappropriate touching or invitations—even if he did use vulgar language. His fellow artist Nina Hamnett, a notorious bohemian who rarely turned down a drink or sex, writes in her autobiography that Sickert would walk her home when she was drunk; she stayed with him in France. The kiss-and-tell Nina says not a word about Sickert ever so much as flirting with her.

Ellen may really have believed Sickert was a womanizer, or her claims may have been something of a red herring if the humiliating truth was that they never consummated their marriage. In the late nineteenth century, a woman had no legal grounds to leave her husband unless he was unfaithful and cruel or deserted her. She and Sickert agreed to these claims. He did not fight her. One would assume she knew about his damaged penis, but it is possible the brotherly and sisterly couple never undressed in front of each other or attempted sex.

During their divorce proceedings, Ellen wrote that Sickert promised if she would "give him one more chance he [would] be a different man, that I am the only person he has ever really cared for—that he has no longer those relations with [unknown]." Ellen's lawyer, she wrote, felt certain Sickert was "sincere—but that taking into consideration his previous life—& judging as far as he could of his character from his face & manner he does not believe he is capable of keeping any resolve that he made, and his deliberate advice to me is to go on with the divorce.

"I am dreadfully upset & have hardly done anything but cry ever since," Ellen wrote to Janie. "I see how far from dead is my affection for him."

CHAPTER TWENTY-SEVEN

THE DARKEST NIGHT IN THE DAY

Sickert's roles changed like the light and shadow he painted on his canvases.

A shape should not have lines because nature doesn't, and forms reveal themselves in tones, shades, and the way light holds them. Sickert's life had no lines or boundaries, and his shape changed with every tilt and touch of his enigmatic moods and hidden purposes.

Those who knew him as well as those he brushed past only now and then accepted that *being Sickert* meant being the "chameleon," the "poseur." He was Sickert in the loud check coat walking at all hours through London's foreboding alleyways and streets. He was Sickert the farmer or country squire or tramp or bespectacled masher in the bowler hat or dandy in black tie or the eccentric wearing bedroom slippers to meet the train. He was Jack the Ripper with a cap pulled low over his eyes and a red scarf around his neck, working in the gloom of a studio illuminated by the feeble glow from a bull's-eye lantern.

The Victorian writer and critic Clive Bell's relationship with Sickert was one of mutual love-hate, and Bell quipped that on any given day Sickert might be John Bull, Voltaire, the Archbishop of Canterbury, the Pope, a cook, a dandy, a swell, a bookmaker, a solicitor. Bell believed Sickert wasn't the scholar he was reputed to be and appeared to "know a great deal more than he did," even if he was the greatest British painter since Constable. But one "could never feel sure that their Sickert was Sickert's Sickert, or that Sickert's Sickert corresponded with any ultimate reality." He was a man of "no standards," and in Bell's words, Sickert did not feel "possessively and affectionately about anything which was not part of himself."

Ellen was part of Sickert's self. He had use for her. He could not see her as a separate human being because all people and all things were extensions of Sickert. She was still in Ireland with Janie when Elizabeth Stride and Catherine Eddows were murdered and when George Lusk, the head of the East End Vigilance Committee, received half of a human kidney by post on October 16th. Almost two weeks later, the curator of the pathology museum of the London Hospital, Dr. Thomas Openshaw, received the letter written on A Pirie & Sons watermarked paper and signed "Jack the Ripper."

"Old boss you was rite it was the left kidny . . . I wil be on the job soon and will send you another bit of innerds."

The kidney was suspected of being Catherine Eddows's, and probably was unless the Ripper managed to get half of a human kidney from somewhere else. The organ was anatomically preserved at the Royal London Hospital until it became so disintegrated that the hospital disposed of it in the 1950s—about the time Watson and Crick discovered the double helix structure of DNA.

In centuries past, bodies and body parts were preserved in "spirits" or alcoholic beverages such as wine. Some hospitals during the Ripper's time used glycerine. When a person of high status died aboard ship and required a proper burial, the only way to preserve the body was in mead or whatever spirits were handy. If John Smith, the founding father of Virginia, had died during his voyage to the New World, most likely he would have been returned to London pickled in a keg.

Police reports indicate that the kidney sent to George Lusk was almost two weeks old if it came from Eddows's body, and had been preserved in "spirits," probably wine. Mr. Lusk did not seem horrified or in a frantic hurry to get the kidney to the police. When he received the ghastly gift with a letter that has not survived, he didn't "think much about it." The Victorians were not accustomed to psychopathic killers who took body parts and enclosed them in taunting letters to the authorities.

At first, it was suggested that the kidney was from a dog, but Lusk and the police wisely sought other opinions. The kidney was a hoax, the police agreed as the marinated organ in its box made the rounds. Medical experts, such as the pathologist Dr. Openshaw, believed the kidney was human—although it was a stretch to conclude it was from a "female" who had "Bright's disease." The kidney was turned over to Dr. Openshaw's care at the London Hospital. Had the kidney survived another few decades to be tested, and were Catherine Eddows exhumed for her DNA, there could have been a match. In court that would have hurt Walter Sickert quite a lot—were he still alive to be prosecuted—since the A Pirie & Sons watermark is on his stationery and also on the letter Jack the Ripper wrote to Dr. Openshaw, the stamps on the envelopes of the two letters have a DNA sequence in common, and the Ripper letter is confessional.

If Ellen was keeping up with the news at home, she would have known about the kidney. She would have known about the double murder that happened within a week of her leaving for Ireland. She may have heard of "human bones" wrapped in a parcel in a Peckham gutter, or the parcel containing a decomposing female arm found in the garden of a school for the blind in Lambeth Road, or the boiled leg that turned out to be from a bear.

Ellen should have known about the torso recovered from the foundation of the new Scotland Yard building. The headless, limbless dead woman was transported to the mortuary in Millbank Street, and she had little to say to Dr. Neville or the police, and they could not seem to agree about the arm found in Pimlico on October 11th. It was from the torso, of this Dr. Neville was certain, but its hand was rough, the fingernails unkempt—like those of a woman whose life was hard. When Dr. Thomas Bond was brought in to assist in the examination, he said that the hand was soft with well-shaped nails. The hand would have been dirty, possibly abraded, and the fingernails would have been caked with mud when the arm was found in the muck of low tide. Perhaps when it was cleaned up, it took on a higher social status.

In one report, the dismembered woman had a dark complexion. In another report, she had light skin. Her hair was dark brown, she was twenty-six years old, and five foot seven or eight, the doctor stated. The darkness of her skin could have been due to the discoloration of decomposition. In advanced stages, the skin turns dark greenish-black. Based on the condition of her remains, it may have been just as difficult to determine if her skin was fair.

Discrepancies in descriptions can cause serious problems in identifying the dead. Of course, forensic facial reconstructions—or the sculpting of the face based on the underlying architecture of the bone (assuming the head is found)—were not done in the nineteenth century, but a case some decades ago in Virginia makes my point. An unidentified man's face was reconstructed by using green clay to rebuild his features over his skull. His hair color was based on the racial characteristics of his skeleton, which were those of an African-American, and his orbits were fitted with artificial eyes.

A woman responded to a black-and-white photograph of the facial reconstruction in the newspaper, and appeared at the morgue to see if the missing person might be her son. She took one look at the facial reconstruction and told the medical examiner, "No, that's not him. His face wasn't green." As it turned out, the unidentified murdered young man was the woman's son. (These days, when forensic facial reconstructions or sculptures are done on the unidentified dead, the clay is dyed to approximate the person's color based on race.)

The estimate offered by both Dr. Neville and by Dr. Thomas Bond, that the torso was that of a woman about five foot seven or eight, could have been wrong, and the height they assigned to what was left of the victim could have precluded quite a number of people from coming forward to see if the remains were those of a relative or someone they knew. In that era, five foot seven or eight was quite tall for a woman. Were the doctors' estimate off by as little as two or three inches, it could have been enough to cause the torso never to be identified—and it never was.

I believe the doctors did the best they could, based on what they had to work with. They could not have known about forensic anthropology. The doctors would not have known about today's standard anthropological criteria used to place an individual into age categories, such as *infant* or *15 to 17* or *45-plus*. They may not have known much about epiphyses or growth centers of bone, nor could they have seen them since neither the torso nor recovered limbs were defleshed by boiling them in water. Growth centers are attachments, such as those that connect the ribs to the sternum, and when one is young these attachments are flexible cartilage. With age, they calcify.

In 1888, there were no calibrations and algorithms. There were no late-twentieth-century gadgets such the Single Photon Absorptiometer or scintillation detectors to estimate height based on the length of the humerus, radius, ulna, femur, tibia, and fibula—the long bones of the arms and legs. The changes in density or mineral concentrations of bones are age-dependent. For example, a decrease in bone density usually correlates with an older age.

It could not accurately be claimed that the dismembered woman was exactly twenty-six years old, although it could have been said that her remains appeared to be those of a post-prepubescent female who probably was in her late teens or twenties, and that she had dark brown hair in her axillae, or armpits. The estimate that the woman had died five weeks earlier was also a guess. Doctors simply did not have the scientific means to judge time of death by decomposition. They knew nothing about entomology—the interpretation of insect development as a marker for time of death—and maggots teemed over the torso when it was found in the new Scotland Yard building's foundation.

The postmortem revealed pale, bloodless organs that indicated hemorrhage and would have been consistent with the woman's throat having been cut before she was dismembered. At her inquest, Dr. Thomas Bond testified that the remains were those of a "well nourished" woman with "breasts that were large and prominent" and who at some point had suffered from severe pleurisy in one lung. Her uterus was missing, and her pelvis and legs had been sawn off at the fourth lumbar. The arms had been removed at the shoulder joints by several oblique cuts, and she had been decapitated by several incisions below the larynx. Dr. Bond said that the torso had been skillfully wrapped, and the flesh bore "clearly defined marks" where it had been bound with string. These marks left by string are noteworthy. Experiments conducted in the early– and mid–nineteenth century revealed that ligature marks are not formed on bodies that have been dead for a while, indicating that the string was tied around the dismembered woman either while she was alive, or more likely, not long—perhaps only hours—after her death.

The severing of the pelvis from the torso is quite unusual in dismemberments, but neither the doctors nor the police seemed to have given this detail much thought, or even offered opinions about it. No other body parts of the woman turned up, except what was believed to be her left leg, which had been severed just below the knee. The partial limb had been buried several yards from where the torso had been found. Dr. Bond described the foot and leg as "exquisitely molded." The foot was well cared for, the toenails neatly trimmed. There were no corns or bunions that might indicate that the victim had been a "poor woman."

The police and physicians were of the opinion that the dismemberment was an attempt to conceal the victim's identity. This conclusion is inconsistent with the killer severing the pelvis at the fourth lumbar and at the hip joints—or essentially removing the victim's sexual organs and genitalia. One might wonder if there is a similarity between such a mutilation and what the Ripper did when he slashed open the abdomen of his victim and took her uterus and part of her vagina.

When the torso was found on the site of Scotland Yard's new headquarters, it was bound in old cloth and "a lot of old string of different sorts tied all around in each direction," said Frederick Wildore, the carpenter who noticed a mysterious shape at six o'clock in the morning on October 2nd, when he reached inside a dark recess of the foundations, looking for his basket of tools. He dragged out the bundle and cut open the string and for a moment did not know what he was looking at. "I thought it was old bacon or something like that," he said at the inquest. The foundation was a labyrinth of recesses and trenches, and the bundle could not have been hidden there unless the person knew his way, Wildore claimed. It was "always as dark as the darkest night in the day."

Adhering to the remains were bits of newspapers that were fragments from an old *Daily Chronicle,* and a blood-saturated six-inch-long, four-inch-wide section of the August 24, 1888, edition of the *Echo,* a daily paper that cost a halfpenny. Sickert was a news addict. A photograph of him in later life shows a studio that is a landfill of newspapers. The *Echo* was a liberal publication that published numerous articles about Sickert throughout his life. In the August 24, 1888, edition, on page 4 is the "Notes & Queries" section with its instructions that all queries and answers must be written on postcards, and one is to refer to the query he is answering by using the number of that query as assigned by the newspaper. Advertising in disguise, the *Echo* warns, "is inadmissible."

Of eighteen "Answers" on August 24, 1888, five of them were signed "W. S." They are as follows:

Answer One (3580): OSTEND.—I would not advise "W. B." to choose Ostend for a fortnight's holiday; he will be tired of it in two days. It is a show place for dresses, &c., and very expensive. The country around is flat and uninteresting; besides, the roads are all paved with granite. To an English tourist I can recommend the "Yellow House" or "Maison Jaune," which is kept by an Englishman, close by the railway station or steamboat pier; also the Hotel du Nord. Both are reasonable, but avoid grand hotels. The sands are lovely. No knowledge of French is required.—W.S.

(Ostend was a seaport and resort in Belgium accessible from Dover, and a place Sickert had visited.)

Answer Two (3686): POPULAR OPERAS.—The popularity of *Trovatore* is naturally due to the sweetness of the music and the taking airs. It is not generally accepted as a "high class" music—indeed, I have frequently heard "professional" musicians call it not music at all. For myself, I prefer it to any other opera, except *Don Juan.*—W.S.

Answer Three (3612): PASSPORTS.—I am afraid "An Unfortunate Pole" will have to confine his attention to those countries where no passports are required of which latter there are plenty, and are, besides more pleasant to travel in. I once met a countryman of his who traveled with a borrowed passport; he was caught at it and sent to quod [street slang for prison], where he remained some time.—W.S.

Answer Four (3623): CHANGE OF NAME.—All "Jones" has to do is to take a paint brush, obliterate "Jones" and substitute "Brown." Of course this will not relieve him from any liabilities as "Jones." He will simply be "Jones" trading under the name of "Brown."—W.S.

Answer Five (3627): LETTERS OF NATURALISATION.—In order to obtain these, a foreigner must have resided either five consecutive years, or at least five within the last eight years, in the United Kingdom; and he must also make a declaration that he intends to reside permanently therein. Strict proofs of this will be required from four British-born householders.—W.S.

To offer answers by using the original query number implies the writer was familiar with the *Echo* and was probably an avid reader of it. To send in five answers is compulsive and in keeping with Sickert's prolific writing and the stunning number of Ripper letters received by the police and the press. Newsprint is a leitmotif that shows up repeatedly in Sickert's life and in the Ripper's game playing. A Ripper letter to a police magistrate is written in an exquisite calligraphy on a section of the *Star* newspaper, dated December 4th. The torn-out section of paper includes the notice of an etching exhibition, and on the back of the paper is a subheadline "Nobody's Child."

Walter Sickert was never sure who he was or where he was from. He was "No Englishman," to quote the signatory of another Ripper letter. His stage name was "Mr. Nemo" (or Mr. Nobody), and in a telegram the Ripper sent to the police (no date, but possibly the late autumn of 1888) the Ripper crosses out "Mr. Nobody" as the sender and writes in "Jack the Ripper" instead. Sickert wasn't French but considered himself a French painter. He once wrote that he intended to become a French citizen—which he never did. In another letter he states that in his heart he will always be German.

Most Ripper letters posted between October 20th and November 10th, 1888 were postmarked London, and it is a certainty Sickert was in London prior to October 22nd to attend an early showing of the "First Pastel Exhibition" that opened at the Grosvenor Gallery. In letters that Sickert wrote to Blanche, references to the New English Art Club's election of new members indicate that Sickert was based in London or at least was in England during the autumn, and most likely into November and possibly until the end of the year.

When Ellen returned home to 54 Broadhurst Gardens at the end of October, she came down with a terrible case of the flu that lingered and sapped her health well into November. I could find no record of her spending time with her husband or whether she knew where he was from one day to the next. I don't know if she was frightened by the violent atrocities happening a mere six miles from her home, but it is hard to imagine she wasn't. The whole of London was terrorized, but the worst was yet to come.

Mary Kelly was twenty-four years old and very pretty with a fresh complexion, dark hair, and youthful figure. She was better educated than the other Unfortunates who trolled the area where she lived at 26 Dorset Street. The house was rented by John McCarthy, who owned a chandler's shop and let out all the rooms at 26 Dorset Street to the very poor. Mary's ground-floor room, number 13, was twelve feet square and separated from another room by a partition that was flush against her wooden bedstead. Her door and two large windows opened onto Miller's Court, and some time ago—she wasn't sure when—she had lost her key.

This hadn't caused a huge problem. Not so long ago, she had a bit too much to drink and got into a row with her man, Joseph Barnett, a coal porter. She couldn't remember, but she must have broken a windowpane then. She and Barnett would reach through the jagged hole in the glass to release the spring lock of the door. They never bothered to repair the glass or replace the key, and probably didn't think either was a wise expenditure of what little money they had.

Mary Kelly and Joseph Barnett's last big row was ten days earlier. They exchanged blows, the cause of the fight being a woman named Maria Harvey. Mary had begun sleeping with her on Monday and Tuesday nights, and Barnett wouldn't put up with it. He moved out, leaving Mary to somehow pay off the £1 9s. owed in rent. Barnett and Mary patched up their relationship a bit, and he dropped by occasionally and gave her a little money.

Maria Harvey last saw Mary on the Thursday afternoon of November 8th, when Maria visited Mary in her room. Maria was a laundress and asked if it would be all right to leave some dirty laundry: two men's shirts, a little boy's shirt, a black overcoat, a black crêpe bonnet with black satin strings, a pawn ticket for a gray shawl, and a little girl's white petticoat. She promised to retrieve the garments later, and was still in the room when Barnett showed up unexpectedly for a visit.

"Well, Mary Jane," Maria said on her way out, "I shall not see you this evening again." She would never see Mary again.

Mary Kelly was born in Limerick, the daughter of John Kelly, an Irish iron worker. Mary had six brothers who lived at home, a brother in the Army, and a sister who worked in the markets. The family had moved to Caernarvonshire in Wales when Mary was young, and at sixteen she married a collier named Davis. Two or three years later, he was killed in an explosion, and Mary left for Cardiff to live with a cousin. It was at this time that she began to drift into drink and prostitution, and for eight months she was in an infirmary to be treated for venereal disease.

She moved to England in 1884, and continued to have no trouble attracting business. There are no photographs I've found that show what she looked like, except after the Ripper completely destroyed her body. But contemporary sketches depict her as a very handsome woman with the hourglass figure coveted in that era. Her dress and manner were a remnant of a better world than the wretched one she tried to forget through alcohol.

Mary was a prostitute in the West End for a while, and met gentlemen who knew how to reward a pretty woman for her favors. A man took her to France, but she stayed only ten days and returned to London. Life in France, she told friends, did not suit her. She lived with a man on Ratcliff Highway, then with another man on Pennington Street, then with a plasterer in Bethnal Green. Joseph Barnett was not certain how many men she had lived with or for how long, he testified at the inquest.

One Friday night in Spitalfields, the pretty Mary Kelly caught Joseph Barnett's eye and he treated her to a drink. Days later they decided to live together; this was eight months before he rented Room 13 at 26 Dorset Street. Now and then Mary got letters from her mother in Ireland, and unlike many Unfortunates, she was literate. But when the East End murders began, she got Barnett to read accounts of them to her. Perhaps the news of the slayings was too unnerving for her to take in alone and in the quiet of her own imagination. She may not have known the victims, but there is a good chance she had seen them on the street or in a public house at some point.

Mary's life with Joseph Barnett wasn't a bad one, he testified at her inquest, and the only reason he left her was "because she had a person who was a prostitute whom she took in and I objected to her doing so, that was the only reason, not because I was out of work. I left her on the 30th October between 5&6 P.M." Barnett said he and Mary remained on "friendly terms" and the last time he saw her alive was on Thursday night between 7:30 and 7:45, when he dropped in and discovered Maria in the room. Maria left, and Barnett stayed with Mary briefly. He told her he was sorry but he had no money to give her, and "We did not drink together," he testified. "She was quite sober, she was as long as she was with me of sober habits" and only got drunk now and then.

Mary Kelly was vividly aware of the monstrous murders happening not far from her lodging house, but she continued walking the streets at night after Barnett moved out. She had no other way to earn money. She needed her drink, and she was about to get evicted with no prospect of another decent man to take her in. She was becoming desperate. Not so long ago she was a better class of prostitute who frequented the finer establishments of the West End. But recently, she had been sliding down deeper into the bottomless pit of poverty, alcoholism, and despair. Soon enough she would lose her looks. It probably did not occur to her that she might lose her life.

Few facts are known about Mary Kelly, but a number of rumors circulated at the time. It was said that she had a seven-year-old son and that she would rather kill herself than see him starve to death. If this son existed, there is no mention of him in the police reports and inquest testimony. On the last night of her life, she supposedly ran into a friend at the corner of Dorset Street whom she told she had no money. "If she could not get any," the friend later told police, "she would never go out any more but would do away with herself."

Mary was quite noisy when she was drunk, and she had been drinking on Thursday night, November 8th. The weather had been wretched the entire month, with days of hard rain and fierce winds from the southeast. Temperatures were dipping into the low forties and mist and fog enveloped the city like gauze. Mary was spotted several times that Thursday night, apparently heading off to the nearest pub not long after Joseph Barnett left her room. She was spotted in Commercial Street, quite drunk, and then at 10:00 P.M. in Dorset Street. Times cited are not to be trusted, and there is no certainty that when a person saw "Mary Kelly" it was really Mary Kelly. The streets were very dark. Many people were intoxicated, and after the Ripper's recent murderous spree, witnesses seemed to spring up from everywhere and their stories were not always to be trusted.

One of Mary's neighbors, a prostitute named Mary Ann Cox who lived in room 5 of Miller's Court, testified at the inquest that she saw Mary Kelly intoxicated at midnight. She wore a dark, shabby skirt, a red jacket, and no hat, and was accompanied by a short, stout man who had a blotchy complexion and a thick carroty mustache and who was dressed in dark clothing and a hard, black billycock hat. He carried a pot of beer as he walked Mary Kelly toward her door. Mary Ann was walking several steps behind them and bid Mary Kelly good night. "I'm going to have a song," Mary Kelly replied as the man shut the door to Room 13.

For more than an hour, Mary was heard singing the poignant Irish song "Sweet Violets."

"A violet I plucked from my mother's grave when a boy," she sang, and the light of a candle could be seen through her curtains.

Mary Ann Cox worked the streets, periodically stopping by her room to warm her hands before going out again in search of clients. At 3:00 A.M., she came in for the night and Mary Kelly's room was dark and silent. Mary Ann went to bed with her clothes on. A hard, cold rain was slapping the courtyard and streets. She did not sleep. She heard men come in and out of the building as late as a quarter of six. Another neighbor, Elizabeth Prater in room 20 directly above Mary Kelly, said at the inquest that at close to 1:30 A.M., she could see a "glimmer" of light through the "partition" that separated Mary Kelly's room from hers.

I assume by "partition" Elizabeth was referring to cracks in the floor. Elizabeth Prater secured her door for the night by wedging two tables against it and went to bed. She'd had something to drink, she testified, and slept soundly until a kitten began restlessly walking over her at approximately 4:00 A.M., waking her up. By now, the room below her was dark, Elizabeth testified. Suddenly, she said, "I heard a cry of 'oh! Murder!' as the cat came on me and I pushed her down." She said the voice was faint and from close by and that she did not hear it a second time. Elizabeth went back to sleep and woke up again at 5:00 A.M. Men were harnessing horses in Dorset Street as she walked to the Ten Bells pub for an eye-opener of rum.

John McCarthy was working hard in his chandler's shop by midmorning. He was also trying to figure out what to do about room 13 in the lodging house he leased at 26 Dorset Street. As he worked on that foggy, cold Friday morning, he was forced to ponder the inevitable. Joseph Barnett had moved out more than two weeks ago and Mary Kelly was £1 9s behind with the rent. McCarthy had been patient with Mary Kelly, but this simply could not continue.

"Go to number 13 and try and get some rent," he told his assistant, Thomas Bowyer. It was close to eleven when Bowyer walked over to Mary Kelly's room and knocked on the door. He got no response. He tugged on the handle, but the door was locked. He pushed the curtains aside and looked through the broken window and saw Mary Kelly naked on the bed, covered with blood. He ran back to his employer, and both he and McCarthy hurried to Mary's room and looked in. Bowyer ran to find the police.

An H Division inspector hurried to get to the scene, and he sent immediately for Police Surgeon Dr. George Phillips and dispatched a telegram to Scotland Yard about the latest Ripper murder. Within half an hour, the crime scene was crowded with inspectors, including Frederick Abberline, who ordered that no one in the courtyard was allowed to leave, and no one could enter without police authorization.

Charles Warren was also sent a telegram. Abberline inquired if the commissioner would like the bloodhounds to respond. The seasoned investigator probably knew full well what a waste of time that would be. But he was following orders. The order was countermanded and the dogs never came. By the end of the day, the press would learn that Warren had resigned.

There was no rush to get inside Mary Kelly's room. As Dr. Phillips said at the inquest, he looked through "the lower broken pane and satisfied myself that the mutilated corpse lying on the bed was not in need of any immediate attention from me." The police removed a window from Mary Kelly's room and Dr. Phillips began to take photographs through the opening. At 1:30 P.M., police officers used a pickaxe to pry open the door, and it banged against a table on the left of the bedstead. Police investigators and Dr. Phillips entered the room and what they saw was unlike any travesty the men had ever encountered in their entire careers.

"It looked more like the work of a devil than a man," McCarthy would later recount at the inquest. "I had heard about the Whitechapel murders but I swear to God I had never expected to see such a sight as this."

Mary Kelly's body was two-thirds of the way across the bed, almost against the door. Crime-scene photographs reveal remains so mutilated that she may as well have been run over by a train. The Ripper hacked off her ears and nose and slashed and defleshed her face down to the skull. She had no features left, only her dark hair, still neatly styled, probably because she never struggled with the Ripper. There wasn't room to attack her from behind the bed, so he attacked her from the front.

Unlike the Camden Town murder, Mary was face-up when a strong, sharp blade severed her right carotid artery. Blood soaked through the bed and pooled on the floor.

Abberline, who was in charge of the case, searched the room. He found burned clothing in the fireplace and surmised that the killer continued to feed the fire while he worked so he would have enough light to see, "as there was only one piece of candle in the room," Abberline testified. The heat was so intense that it melted the spout of a kettle. One might wonder how a fire could burn so brightly and not have been noticed in the courtyard, even through drawn curtains. Someone might have worried that the room was on fire, unless the fire was a low, hot, steady one. As usual, people were minding their own affairs. Maybe the Ripper worked by the tiny light of the single candle in the room. Sickert didn't mind the dark. The "pitch dark," he said in a letter, "is lovely."

Except for a coat, all of Maria's dirty laundry had been burned. Mary Kelly's clothing was found neatly folded by the side of the bed, as if she had willingly undressed down to her chemise. Her killer ripped and cut and hacked into her body, laying it wide open, mutilating her genitalia to a pulp. He amputated her breasts and arranged them next to her liver on the side of the bed. He heaped her entrails on top of the bedside table. Every organ except her brain was removed, and her right leg was flayed open to the knee, exposing a completely defleshed, gleaming white femur.

Plainly visible on the left arm are curved cutting injuries, and a dark line encircling her right leg just below the knee suggests the Ripper may have been in the process of dismemberment when, for some reason, he stopped. Perhaps the fire had burned down or the candle was about to go out. Maybe it was getting late and time for him to make his escape. Dr. Thomas Bond arrived at the scene at 2:00 P.M., and in his report he said that rigor mortis had set in and increased during the course of his examination. He admitted he could not give an exact time of death, but the body was cold at 2:00 P.M. Based on that, and on rigor mortis and the presence of partially digested food in her ripped-open stomach and scattered over her intestines, he estimated she had been dead twelve hours by the time he reached the scene.

If Dr. Bond was correct in saying that rigor mortis was still in the process of forming when he began to examine the body at the scene by 2:00 P.M., then it is possible that Mary had not been dead as long as twelve hours. Her body would have been cold long before that. It was drained of blood, she was slender, her body cavity was exposed, and she was covered by nothing but a chemise in a room in which the fire had gone out. Also, if witnesses are to be believed, Mary Kelly was still alive at 1:30. Times given to the police and at the inquest were based on local church clocks that rang the half hour and the hour, on changes of light, and on when the East End was silent or beginning to stir.

It may be that the most reliable witness to time of death in Mary Kelly's murder is the kitten that began walking over Elizabeth Prater at around 4:00 A.M. Cats have extraordinarily good hearing and the kitten may have been disturbed by sounds directly below. It may have sensed the pheromones secreted by people who are terrified and panicking. About the time the kitten woke up Elizabeth, she said she heard from nearby someone cry, "Murder!"

Mary Kelly would have seen what was coming. She was undressed and on the bed. She was face-up. She might have seen him pull out the knife. Even if the Ripper threw a sheet over her face before cutting her throat, she knew she was about to die. She would have lived for minutes as she hemorrhaged and he began slashing her. We can't assume the Ripper's victims felt no pain and were already unconscious when he began mutilating them. It isn't possible to know in Mary Kelly's case if the Ripper started on her belly or her face.

If the Ripper hated Mary Kelly's sexually alluring, pretty face, he might have started there. Or it may have been her abdomen. She may have felt the cuts as the loss of blood quickly caused her to shiver. Her teeth might have begun to chatter, but not for long as she grew faint, went into shock, and died. She may have drowned as blood gushing out of her carotid artery was inhaled through the cut in her windpipe and filled her lungs.

"The air passage was cut through at the lower part of the larynx through the cricoid cartilage," reads page 16 of the original postmortem report.

She could not have screamed or uttered a sound.

"Both breasts were removed by more or less circular incisions, the muscles down to the ribs being attached to the breasts."

This would require a sharp, strong knife with a blade that was not so long as to make the weapon unwieldy. A dissecting knife has a four- to six-inch blade and a handle with a good grip. But a common killing knife available to the Ripper would have been the kukri, with its unique blade that sweeps into a forward bend. The blade lengths can vary, and the knives are sturdy enough for chopping vines, branches, or even small trees. When Queen Victoria was the Empress of India, many British soldiers wore kukris, and the knives would have found their way into the English market.

Jack the Ripper wrote in a letter dated October 19th that he "felt rather down hearted over my knife which I lost comming [sic] here must get one tonight." Two days later, on the Sunday night of October 21st, a constable discovered a bloody knife in the shrubbery not far from where Sickert's mother lived. The knife was a kukri. Such a knife could have been used on Mary Kelly. The kukri was used in battle to cut throats and sever limbs, but because of its curved blade, it is not a stabbing knife.

"The skin & tissues of the abdomen . . . were removed in three large places. . . . The right thigh was denuded in point to the bone. . . . The lower part of the [right] lung was broken and torn away. . . . The Pericardium was open below & the heart absent."

These details come from pages 16 and 18 of the original postmortem report and seem to be the only pages from any of the postmortems to have survived. The loss of these reports is truly a calamity. The medical details that would tell us the most about what the killer did to his victim are not as clearly defined in the inquests as they would be in postmortem reports. It was not mentioned in Mary Kelly's inquest that her heart was taken. That was a detail the police, the doctors, and the coroner thought the public didn't need to know.

Mary Kelly's postmortem examination was held at Shoreditch mortuary and lasted six and a half hours. The most experienced forensic medical men were present: Dr. Thomas Bond of Westminster, Dr. Gordon Brown of the City, a Dr. Duke from Spitalfields, and Dr. George Phillips and an assistant. Accounts say that the men would not complete their examination until every organ had been accounted for. Some reports suggest no organs were missing, but that isn't true. The Ripper took Mary Kelly's heart and possibly portions of her genitals and uterus.

The inquest began and ended on November 11th. Dr. Phillips had barely described the crime scene when Dr. Roderick McDonald, the coroner for Northeast Middlesex, said that it would not be necessary for the doctor to go into any further particulars at that time. The jurors—all of whom had viewed Mary Kelly's remains at the mortuary—could reconvene and hear more later, unless they were prepared to reach a verdict now. They were. They had heard quite enough. "Wilful murder against some person unknown."

Immediately, the press fell silent. It was as if the Ripper case was closed. Scans through days and weeks and months of newspapers after Mary Kelly's inquest and burial reveal few mentions of the Ripper. His letters continued to arrive and they were filed "with the others." They were not printed in respectable newspapers. Any subsequent crimes that might have brought up the question of the Ripper were eventually dismissed as not being the work of the Whitechapel fiend.

In June 1889, dismembered female remains were found in London. They were never identified.

On July 16, 1889, an Unfortunate named Alice McKenzie, known to "be the worse for drink" now and then, went out to the Cambridge

Music-hall in the East End and was overheard by a blind boy to ask a man to treat her to a drink. At close to 1:00 A.M., her body was found in Castle Alley, Whitechapel, her throat cut, and her clothing pushed up to display severe mutilation to her abdomen. Dr. Thomas Bond performed her postmortem and wrote, "I am of the opinion that the murder was performed by the same person who committed the former series of Whitechapel murders." The case was never solved. Little public mention was made of the Ripper.

On August 6, 1889, an eight-year-old girl named Caroline Winter was murdered in Seaham Harbour, south of Newcastle-upon-Tyne. Her skull was bashed in, her body "bearing other terrible injuries," and she was dumped in a pool of water near a sewer. She was last seen playing with a friend who told the police that Caroline was talking to a man with black hair, a black mustache, and dressed in a shabby gray suit. He offered Caroline a shilling to come with him, and she did.

The female torso found in the railway arch off Pinchin Street on September 10th showed no sign of mutilation, except for dismemberment, and there was no evidence her death was caused by a cut throat, even if she had been decapitated. An incision down the front of the torso could not have been the work of the Ripper, according to the official report. "The inner coating of the bowel is hardly touched and the termination of the cut towards the vagina looks almost as if the knife had slipped, and as if this portion of the wound had been accidental. Had this been the work of the previous frenzied murderer we may be tolerably sure that he would have continued his hideous work in the way which he previously adopted." The case was never solved.

On December 13, 1889, at Middlesbrough docks, just south of Seaham Harbour, decomposing human remains were found, including a woman's right hand that was missing two joints of the little finger.

"I am trying my hand at disjointing," the Ripper wrote December 4, 1888, "and if can manage it will send you a finger."

On February 13, 1891, a prostitute named Francis Coles was found with her throat cut in Swallow Gardens, Whitechapel. She was approximately twenty-six years old, and "of drunken habits," according to police reports. Dr. George Phillips performed the postmortem examination and was of the opinion that the body wasn't mutilated and he did "not connect this with the series of previous murders." The case was never solved.

A case involving dismembered female body parts found in London in June 1902 was never solved.

Serial killers keep killing. Sickert kept killing. His body count could have been fifteen, twenty, forty before he died peacefully in his bed in Bathampton, January 22, 1942, at the age of 81. After the butchery of Mary Kelly, Jack the Ripper faded into a nightmare from the past. He was probably that sexually insane young doctor who was really a barrister and who threw himself into the Thames. He could have been a lunatic barber or a lunatic Jew who was safely locked up in an asylum. He could be dead. What a relief to make such assumptions.

After 1896, it seems the Ripper letters stopped. His name wasn't connected to current crimes anymore, and his case files were sealed for a century. In 1903, James McNeill Whistler died and Walter Sickert gracefully assumed center stage. Their styles and themes were quite different—Whistler didn't paint murdered prostitutes and his work was beginning to be worth a fortune—but Sickert was coming into his own. He was evolving into a cult figure as an artist and a "character." By the time he was an old man, he was the greatest living artist in England. Had he ever confessed to being Jack the Ripper, I don't think anybody would have believed him.

CHAPTER TWENTY-EIGHT

FURTHER FROM THE GRAVE

Sickert's fractured pieces and personas seemed to go AWOL in 1899, and he withdrew across the English Channel to live very much like the paupers he terrorized.

"I arise from dreams & go in my nightshirt & wipe up the floor for fear of the ceilings & shift a mattress I have put there 'to catch the drips,' " he wrote to Blanche.

In between killings and spurts of work, he had drifted about, mostly in Dieppe and Venice, his living conditions described by friends as shockingly appalling. He subsisted in filth and chaos. He was a slob and he stank. He was paranoid and told Blanche he believed Ellen and Whistler had conspired to ruin his life. He feared someone might poison him. He became increasingly reclusive, depressed, and morbid.

"Do you suppose we only find anything that is past so touching and interesting because it was further from the grave?" he ponders in a letter.

Psychopathic killers can sink into morbid depression after murderous sprees, and for one who had exercised seemingly perfect control, Sickert may have found himself completely out of control and with nothing left of his life. During his most virile, productive years, he had been on a slaughter binge. He had ignored and avoided his friends. He would disappear from society without warning or reason. He had no caretaker, no home, and was financially destitute. His psychopathic obsession had completely dominated his life. "I am not well—don't know what is the matter with me," he wrote to Nan Hudson in 1910. "My nerves are shaken." By the time Sickert was fifty, he had begun to self-destruct like an overloaded circuit without a breaker.

When Ted Bundy decompensated, his crimes had escalated from spree killings to the orgy of the crazed multiple butcheries he committed in a Florida sorority house. He was completely haywire and he did not live in a world that would let him get away with it. Sickert lived in a world that would. He was not pitted against sophisticated police investigators and forensic science. He traversed the surface of life as a respectable, intellectual gentleman. He was an artist on his way to becoming a Master, and artists are forgiven for not having a structured or "normal" way of going about their affairs. They are forgiven for being a little odd or eccentric, or a bit deranged.

Sickert's fractured psyche threw him into constant battles with his many selves. He was suffering. He understood pain as long as it was his own. He felt nothing for anyone, including Ellen, who was hurt far more than Sickert because she loved him and always would. The stigma of divorce was worse for her than it was for him, her shame and sense of failure greater. She would punish herself for the rest of her life for tarnishing the Cobden name, betraying her late father, and proving a burden to those she loved. She had no peace, but Sickert did because he saw nothing wrong with anything he had done. Psychopaths don't accept consequences. They don't feel sorry—except for the misfortune they bring upon themselves and blame on others.

Sickert's letters to Blanche are masterly works of machination and give us a peek into the dark recesses of a psychopathic mind. Sickert first wrote, "Divorce granted yesterday, thank God!" To this he added, "[T]he first emotion when a thumb screw is removed is a sense of relief that makes one light-headed." He did not feel grief over the loss of Ellen. He was relieved to have one set of complications out of his life, and he felt more fragmented than before.

Ellen gave him a sense of identity. The marriage gave him a safe base in the endless game of tag he played. He always had her to run back to, and she always gave him what she could—and would continue to do so, even if it was secretly purchasing his paintings through Blanche. Sickert the showman didn't do well without an audience or a supporting cast. He was alone backstage in a dark, cold place, and he didn't like it. He did not miss Ellen the way she missed him, and the ultimate tragedy of Sickert is that he was damned to a life that would not allow physical or emotional intimacy. "At least you *feel!*" he once wrote to Blanche.

Sickert's genetic aberrations and childhood traumas had found his fissures and chiseled him to pieces. One piece of him would give painting lessons to Winston Churchill, while another piece wrote a letter to the press in 1937 praising Adolf Hitler's art. One piece of Sickert was kind to his drug-addicted, weak brother Bernhard, while another piece thought nothing of appearing at the Red Cross hospital to sketch soldiers suffering and dying, and then ask for their uniforms since they wouldn't be needing them anymore.

One piece of Sickert could praise a fledgling artist and be very generous with his time and instruction, while another piece trashed Masters such as Cézanne and Van Gogh and wrote a lie in the *Saturday Review* with the intention of defaming the careers of Joseph Pennell and Whistler. One piece of Sickert fooled friends into thinking he was a lady's man, while another piece of him called women "bitches"—or in Ripper letters, "cunts"—and wrote them off as a lower order of life, and murdered and mutilated them and further degraded and violated them in his art. The complexities of Sickert may very well be endless, but one fact about him is clearly etched: He did not marry for love.

But in 1911, he decided it was time to marry again. It was a decision he may have premeditated less than his crimes. His courtship was a blitz on one of his young art students who was described by Robert Emmons, Sickert's first biographer, as lovely and having a "swan neck." She apparently suffered great misgivings and jilted Sickert at the altar, deciding to marry someone better suited to her station in life.

"Marriage off. Too sore to come," Sickert said in a telegram to Ethel Sands and Nan Hudson on July 3, 1911.

Immediately, he turned his attention to another one of his art students, Christine Drummond Angus, the daughter of John Angus, a Scottish leather merchant who was sure Sickert was after his money. Money was a very good commodity but not the only need in Sickert's life. He had no one to take care of him. Christine was eighteen years younger than Sickert, and a pretty woman with a childlike figure. She was sickly and rather lame, having spent much of her life suffering from neuritis and chilblains—or inflammation of the nerves and painful, itchy swelling. She was intelligent and capable of museum-quality embroidery, and a very competent artist, but she did not know Walter Sickert personally.

They had never socialized outside the classroom when he decided to marry her. He overwhelmed her with telegrams and letters many times a day until the unexpected and excessive attention from her art teacher made her very ill and her family sent her away to rest in Chagford, Devon. Sickert was not invited to join her but got on the train and did just that. Within days, they were engaged, much against her father's wishes.

Mr. Angus conceded to the engagement when he learned that the penniless artist had suddenly sold a large portrait to an anonymous buyer. Maybe Christine wasn't making such a bad decision after all. Sickert's anonymous buyer was Florence Pash, a patron and friend of

Sickert's who wanted to help him out. "Marrying Saturday a certain Christine Angus," Sickert said in a telegram to Nan Hudson and Ethel Sands on July 26, 1911. But, he added his bad news, the jeweler "would not take the wedding ring back" that Sickert had bought for the first art student he had pursued.

Christine and Sickert were married at the Paddington Registry Office, and began spending much of their time in Dieppe and ten miles away, in Envermeu, where they rented a house. When World War I broke out in 1914, they returned to London. Artistically, these were productive years for Sickert. He wrote numerous articles. His paintings reflect tension between couples that is enigmatic and powerful and made him famous.

During the early years of his marriage to Christine, he produced his masterpiece *Ennui,* he painted battle scenes, then returned to the music halls, going to the New Bedford "every bloody night." There were also those other works that show his sexually violent side. In *Jack Ashore,* a clothed man approaches a nude on a bed. In *The Prevaricator,* a clothed man leans over the foot of a wooden bedstead that is similar to Mary Kelly's and a rare departure from Sickert's typical iron bedstead. A form is in the bed, but we can't make it out clearly.

Christine's health continued to cause inconvenience for Sickert, and he wrote manipulative letters to his helpful lady friends. He claimed he was so pleased that he was "contributing to make one creature happier than she would otherwise have been." If only he could make more money, he adds, because he needed two servants to take care of his sick wife. "I can't leave my work & I can't afford to take her away to the country." He wished Nan Hudson would let Christine come and stay with her for a while.

After the war, the Sickerts moved to France, and in 1919 he took a fancy to a disused gendarmerie, or police station, on Rue de Douvrend in Envermeu. Christine paid 31,000 francs for the run-down barracks with its upstairs bedroom that had formerly been jail cells all on one side. Her new husband's responsibility was to restore Maison Mouton, as it is still called, and get it ready for her while she stayed in London to settle certain matters and ship their furniture across the Channel. Intermittently, she collapsed in bed when her neuritis flared up, at one point so ill she was kept awake "for 45 nights . . . with drugs and infections, and even when the acute pain is gone, one can hardly move."

It appears Sickert could hardly move, either, at least not in a way that was remotely helpful to his frail wife. In the summer of 1920, Christine wrote to her family that Maison Mouton was "uninhabitable." A photograph of Sickert he sent to Christine showed he had not cleaned his shoes since she saw him last, almost four months earlier. "I am afraid he has spent all the money I had reserved for the kitchen floor and sink." He told her he had bought "a loggia overlooking the river and a 15th century life-size carved and painted Christ," which was to "preside over our fortunes."

By the end of the summer of 1920, Christine had not seen Sickert in so long that she wrote in what may have been her last letter to him, "Mon Petit—I suppose it is the last time I shall write letters at the window looking into Camden Road. It will be wonderful to see you again, but very strange." Soon after, Christine arrived with the furniture to move into her new home in Envermeu and discovered there was no lighting and no running water—only tubs to gather rain. Inside the well was a dead cat that one of Christine's sisters said "had been drowned." Lame and weak, Christine had to walk to the back of the garden and along a flint path and down steep stairs to get to the "earth closets." Her family would indignantly remark after her death that it was "no wonder poor Christine gave up the ghost."

Christine had not been well during the summer, but then she improved somewhat, only to take a dramatic turn for the worse at Envermeu in the autumn. On October 12th Sickert sent a telegram to her sister Andrina Schweder that Christine was dying painlessly, and that she was sleeping a lot. Her spinal fluid had tested positive for "Koch's tubercle bacillus." Sickert promised to wire again "when death takes place," and said

Christine would be cremated in Rouen and buried in the small churchyard in Envermeu.

Her sister and father set out immediately and arrived at Maison Mouton the following day to find Sickert cheerfully waving a handkerchief at them from a window. They were taken aback when he greeted them at the door in a black velvet jacket, his head shaved, his face very white, as if he were wearing makeup. He was pleased to tell them that Christine was alive, though barely. He took them up to her room, where she was unconscious. She was not in the master bedroom. That was downstairs behind the kitchen and had the only big fireplace in the house.

Andrina sat with Christine while their father went downstairs and was so entertained by Sickert's stories and singing that Angus later felt guilty for enjoying himself. The doctor arrived and gave Christine an injection. Her family left, and soon afterward she died. They did not find out until the next day, the 14th. Sickert sketched his wife's dead body while it was still upstairs in bed. He sent for a caster to make a plaster cast of her head, then met with an agent who was interested in buying paintings. Sickert asked Angus if he would mind sending a telegram to *The Times* about her death, only to become irritated that Angus had described Christine as the "wife of Walter Sickert" and not the "wife of Walter Richard Sickert." Sickert's friends gathered about him, and the artist Thérèse Lessore moved in and took care of him. His grief was apparent—and apparently as false as most everything about him, his sentiments about his "dear departed," as D. D. Angus bitterly described it, "completely bogus." Sickert, wrote Angus, "lost no time getting his Therese [sic]." In 1926, he and Thérèse would marry.

"You must miss her," Marjorie Lilly consoled Sickert not long after Christine's death.

"It's not that," he replied. "My grief is, that she *no longer exists*."

In the early months of 1921, when Christine's ashes had been in her grave not even half a year, Sickert wrote obsequious, morbid letters to his father-in-law, the point of them clearly being that he wanted his share of Christine's estate prior to the probate of her will. He needed money now to pay the workmen who were continuing to restore Maison Mouton. It was so "unpleasant" not to pay one's bills on time, and since Mr. Angus was on his way to South Africa, Sickert certainly could use an advance to make sure Christine's wishes about the Maison were respected. John Angus sent Sickert an advance of £500.

Sickert—one of the first people in Envermeu to own a motor car—spent £60 on building a garage with a deep brick mechanic's pit. It "will make my house a good motoring centre," he wrote to Angus. "Christine always had that idea." Sickert's many letters to Christine's family after her death were so obviously self-serving and manipulative that her siblings passed them around and found them "entertaining."

He continued to worry about dying intestate, as if this could happen at any moment. He needed the services of Mr. Bonus, the Angus family lawyer, to draft a will right away. Mr. Bonus lived up to his name. By using him, Sickert didn't have to pay legal fees. "I am in no hurry for probate," Sickert assured Angus. "My only anxiety is not to die intestate. I have given Bonus directions about my will."

Finally, the seventy-year-old Angus wrote the sixty-year-old Sickert that his relentless "anxiety" about dying "intestate, may be summarily dismissed, as surely it won't take Bonus years and years and years to draw up your will." Christine's estate was valued at about £18,000. Sickert wanted his money, and used the excuse that all legal matters needed to be settled immediately lest he suddenly die, perhaps in a motoring accident. Should the worst happen, Sickert's wishes were to be cremated "wherever convenient, and my ashes (without box or casket)" were to be poured into Christine's grave. He generously added that everything Christine had left him was to revert back "unconditionally" to the Angus family. "If I live a few years," Sickert promised, he would make arrangements to insure that Marie, his housekeeper, had an annual annuity upon his death of 1,000 francs.

In 1990, when Christine's private papers were donated to the Tate

Archive, a member of her family (her father's grandson, it would seem) wrote that Sickert's " 'intentions' to leave it all to the Angus Trust was completely bogus! Not a penny came our way."

In a letter to them about ten days after the burial, Sickert describes the sad affair as a grand occasion. The "entire village" showed up and he greeted each one at the cemetery gate. His dear late wife was buried "just under a little wood which was our favorite walk." It had a "lovely view of the whole valley." As soon as the earth settled, Sickert planned on buying a slab of marble or granite and having it carved with Christine's name and dates. He never did. For seventy years, her green marble headstone was carved with her name and "made in Dieppe," "but not," according to Angus, "the dates he promised." They were finally added by her family.

Marie Françoise Hinfray, the daughter of the family that bought Maison Mouton from Sickert, was kind enough to give me a tour of the former gendarmerie where Sickert lived, and Christine died. It is now occupied by the Hinfrays, who are undertakers. Madame Hinfray said that when her parents bought the house from Walter Sickert, the walls were painted in very somber shades, all "dark and unhappy with low ceilings." It was filled with abandoned paintings, and when the outside latrine was dug up, workmen discovered rusted pieces of a small-caliber six-shot revolver dating back to the turn of the century. It was not the sort of gun used by the gendarmes.

Madame Hinfray showed me the revolver. It had been soldered back together and painted black, and she was very proud of it. She showed me the master bedroom and said that Sickert used to keep the curtains open to the dark street and build such big fires that the neighbors could see in. Madame Hinfray sleeps there now, and the generous space is filled with plants and pretty colors. I had her take me upstairs last, to the room where Christine died, a former jail cell with a small wood-burning stove.

I stood there alone looking around, listening. I knew that had Sickert been downstairs, or out in the garden or garage, he could not have heard

Christine call him if the stove needed stoking or she wanted a glass of water or was hungry. He didn't need to hear her because she probably couldn't make a sound. She probably did not wake up very often, or if she did, she dozed. Morphine would have kept her floating in painless slumber.

There is no record of the entire village gathering at Christine's funeral. It seems most of the crowd was Sickert's people, as Ellen used to call them, and Christine's father was there. He later recalled being "shocked" by Sickert's "sangfroid," or complete indifference. It was raining when I visited the old graveyard surrounded by a brick wall. Christine's modest headstone was hard to find. I saw no "little wood" or "favorite walk," and from where I stood, there was no "lovely view of the whole valley."

The day of Christine's funeral was blustery and cold, and the procession was late. Sickert did not pour her ashes into her grave. He dug his hands inside the urn and flung them into the wind, which blew them onto the coats and into the faces of his friends.

MY TEAM

Without the help of many people and archival and academic resources, I could not have conducted this investigation nor written the account of it.

There would be no story of Walter Sickert—no resolution to the vicious crimes he committed under the alias of Jack the Ripper—had history not been preserved in a way that really is no longer possible because of the rapidly vanishing arts of letter-writing and diary-keeping. I could not have followed Sickert's century-old tracks had I not been aided by tenacious and courageous experts.

I am indebted to the Virginia Institute of Forensic Science and Medicine—especially co-directors Dr. Paul Ferrara and Dr. Marcella Fierro and forensic scientists Lisa Schiermeier, Chuck Pruitt, and Wally Forst; The Bode Technology Group; Sickert curator and researcher Vada Hart; art historian and Sickert expert Dr. Anna Gruetzner Robins; paper historian and forensic paper expert Peter Bower; letterer Sally Bower; paper conservator Anne Kennett; FBI profiler and law enforcement instructor Edward Sulzbach; Assistant New York District Attorney Linda Fairstein; rare documents and antiquarian book researcher Joe Jameson.

I thank artist John Lessore for his kind and gentle conversations and generosity.

I am grateful to members of my relentless and patient staff who have facilitated my work in every way possible and demonstrated admirable talents and investigative and technical skills of their own: Irene Shulgin, Alex Shulgin, and Viki Everly.

I fear I cannot remember everyone I have met along this grueling and often painful and depressing journey, and I hope any person or institution I might have overlooked will be forgiving and understanding.

I could not have carried on without the following galleries, museums, and archival sources and their staffs: Paul Johnson, Hugh Alexander, Kate Herst, Clea Relly, and David Humphries of the Public Record Office, Kew; R. J. Childs, Peter Wilkinson, and Timothy McCann at the West Sussex Record Office; Hugh Jaques and the Dorset Record Office; Sue Newman at Christchurch Local History Society; Ashmolean Museum; Dr. Rosalind Moad at Cambridge University, King's College Modern Archives Centre; Professor Nigel Thorp and Andrew Hale at Glasgow University Library, Special Collections Department.

Jenny Cooksey at Leeds City Art Gallery; Sir Nicholas Serota, director, Tate Gallery; Robert Upstone, Adrian Glew, and Julia Creed at the Tate Gallery Archive, London; Julian Treuherz at the Walker Art Gallery, Liverpool; Vada Hart and Martin Banham of Islington Central Libraries, Islington Archives, London; Institut Bibliotheque de L'Institut de France, Paris; James Sewell, Juliet Banks, and Jessica Newton of the Corporation of London Records Office; University of Reading Department of History of Art.

The Fine Art Society, London; St. Mark's Hospital; St. Bartholomew's Hospital; Julia Sheppard at the Wellcome Library for the History and Understanding of Medicine, London; Bodleian Library, Oxford University, M.S. English History; Jonathan Evans at the Royal London Hospital Archives and Museum; Dr. Stella Butler and John Hodgson at the University of Manchester, the John Rylands Library and History of Art Department; Howard Smith, Manchester City Galleries; Reese Griffith at the London Metropolitan Archives; Ray Seal and Steve Earl at Metropolitan Police Historical Museum; Metropolitan Police Archives.

John Ross at the Metropolitan Police Crime Museum; Christine Penny of Birmingham University Information Services; Dr. Alice Prochaska at the British Library Manuscripts Collection; National Register of Archives, Scotland; Mark Pomeroy of the Royal Academy of Arts, London; Iain MacIver of the National Library of Scotland; Sussex University Library Special Collections; New York Public Library; British Newspaper Library; rare books, autographs, and manuscripts dealer Clive Farahar and Sophie Dupre; Denison Beach of Harvard University's Houghton Library.

Registrar Births, Deaths and Marriage Certificates, London; Aberdeen University Library, Special Libraries and Archives, Kings College (business records of Alexander Pirie & Sons); House of Lords Records Office, London; National Registrar Family Records Center; London Bureau of Camden; Marylebone Registry Office.

Since I do not speak French, I would have been quite helpless in all things French were it not for my publisher, Nina Salter, who mined the following sources: Professor Dominique Lecomte, Director of the Paris Institute for Forensic Medicine; Records of Department of the Seine-Maritime; Archives of the French National Gendarmerie; Archives of the Central Police Station in Rouen; the archives of the Town Council, Rouen; the archives of the prefecture in Rouen; the Rouen Morgue; Reports of the Central Police in Rouen; Records of the Sectors of Dieppe, Neuchâtel, and Rouen; Records of the French regional press; the National Archives in Paris; Appeal Courts 1895–1898; Dieppe Historical Collection; Appeal Courts of Paris and Rouen.

Of course, my respectful, humble thanks to Scotland Yard, which may have been young and inexperienced in days of old, but is now an enlightened force against injustice. First, my gratitude to the remarkable Deputy Assistant Commissioner John D. Grieve; and to my British partner in crime fighting, Detective Inspector Howard Gosling; to Maggie Bird; Professor Betsy Stanko; and Detective Sergeant David Field. I thank the people of the Home Office and the Metropolitan Police Department. All of you were nothing but cooperative, courteous, and encouraging. No one tried to get in my way or cast the slightest shadow of egotism, or—no matter how cold the case—to be an obstruction to long-overdue justice.

My warmest gratitude, as always, to my masterful editor, Dr. Charles Cornwell; to my empowering agent, Esther Newberg; to my British publisher, Hilary Hale; to David Highfill and all the fine people at my American publisher, Putnam; and to my special publishing advisor and mentor, Phyllis Grann.

I honor those who have gone before me and dedicated their efforts to catching Jack the Ripper. He is caught. We have done it together.

Patricia Cornwell

BIBLIOGRAPHY

There is already in print an abundance of information, misinformation, and speculation about the identity and crimes of Jack the Ripper. For factual details and the spelling of names, I have relied altogether on my primary sources and my newspaper of record, *The Times*.

Title page quotation: H. M., *'Twixt Aldgate Pump and Pope: The Story of Fifty Years Adventure in East London,* The Epworth Press, London, 1935. (Note: H. M. was a missionary to the East End and in all of his publications remains anonymous.)

PRIMARY SOURCES

Abberline, Frederick. Inspector Abberline's Press Cutting Book (private, unpublished diary kept by Frederick Abberline from 1878 to 1892). Courtesy of Scotland Yard.

Alexander Pirie & Sons Ltd., Paper Manufacturers, Aberdeen, Scotland, Records and Papers: University of Aberdeen Historic Collections, Special Libraries and Archives.

Bird, Maggie, Inspecting Officer of the Records Management Branch of Scotland Yard. Interview, London, March 4, 2002.

Christchurch Times, January 12, 1889 (obituary of Montague Druitt).

Cobden Papers: Ellen Cobden Sickert, Jane Cobden Unwin, Richard Cobden, Jr., and Richard Cobden. West Sussex County Library.

Cobden, Ellen. Letter to her father, Richard Cobden, July 30, 1860. West Sussex Record Office, Cobden Papers, #38E.

———. Letters of Ellen Melicent Cobden Sickert, West Sussex Record Office, Ref. Cobden 965.

Cobden, Ellen and Richard Brook Cobden. Letters undated (circa late 1840s), West Sussex Record Office, Ref. Add Ms 6036.

Cobden, Ellen Melicent. *A Portrait,* Richard Cobden-Sanderson, 17 Thavies Inn, 1920. (One of 50 copies printed for private circulation by Woods & Sons, Islington).

Corporation of London Records Office, Whitechapel Murder Files. These files include some three hundred letters pertaining to the Ripper crimes.

Daily Telegraph, The, London, articles of September 1–28, and October 1, 3, 4, 6, and 7, 1888.

Dobson, James. Letter to his wife, February 13, 1787, the day before he was hanged before the Debtors Door of Newgate Prison. Author's collection.

"Double Duty." *The Police Review and Parade Gossip,* April 17, 1893, and August 18, 1905.

Druitt Collection. West Sussex Record Office.

Druitt, Montague. Material at Christchurch Library, Dorset; Dorset Record Office; Greenwich Local History Library; and Lewisham Local History and Archives.

Eastern Mercury newspaper, articles of October 12, 1888, August 6, 1889, September 10, 1889, September 17, 1889, September 24, 1889, October 15, 1889, December 17, 1889, February 12, 1889.

Ffrangcon-Davies, Gwen. Letters, Tate Gallery Archive.

Friel, Lisa, Esq. Assistant District Attorney, *The People of the State of New York against John Royster.* Transcript of her summation for the prosecution, Supreme Court of the State of New York, County of New York.

Hill's Hotel guest book, 1877–1888, Lizard Point, Cornwall, England. Author's collection.

Home Office Records. Public Record Office, Kew, HO 144/220/A49301 through HO 144/221/A49301K.

Hudson, Nan. Letters, Tate Gallery Archive.

Illustrated Police News, The: Law Courts and Weekly Record, London, September–December, 1888.

Institut Bibliothèque de L'Institut de France, Paris. Jacques-Emile Blanche—Walter

Sickert Correspondence, Document Numbers 128, 132, 136, 137, 139, 148, 150–155, 168, 169, 183–186, 171, 179, 180.

Irving, Henry. Private correspondence (collection of letters that show the various cities where he and his company performed). Author's collection.

King Edward VII. Letter to Professor Ihre (Prince Albert Victor's German tutor), July 12, 1884. Author's collection.

Lessore, John. Conversation with Lessore at his studio in Peckham, spring 2001.

Llewellyn, Dr. Rees Ralph. Information regarding Dr. Llewellyn and fees charged by doctors called upon by coroners and police: Royal London Hospital Archives and Medical Directories at the Wellcome Medical Library.

Macnaghten, Melville. Memorandum, February 23, 1894, courtesy of Scotland Yard.

Metropolitan Police: Special reports of Martha Tabran's murder, August 10–October 19, Public Record Office, Kew.

Metropolitan Police Museum, archives of: details of police hand ambulances, buildings, salaries, uniforms, and equipment.

Metropolitan Police Records, MEPO 2/22, MEPO 3/140–41, MEPO 3/3153–57, MEPO 3/182, Public Record Office, Kew.

Metropolitan Police, records of, Metropolitan Police Crime Museum.

Metropolitan Police, records of, Metropolitan Police Historical Museum, Metropolitan Police Archives.

Norwich, Julius, grandson of Dr. Alfred Duff Cooper. Telephone interview, spring 2001.

Pall-Mall Gazette, articles of September 3, 6, 7, 8, 10, 14, 21, 24, 25, 27, 28, October 1, 2, 1888.

Pash, Florence. Material in the Sickert Collection, Islington Public Libraries.

Pritchard, Eleanor. "The Daughters of Cobden [part 2]," West Sussex Public Record Office, Ref. West Sussex History Journal, No. 26, September 1983.

Rhind, Neil. Transcript of talk on November 21, 1988, Lewisham Local History and Archives.

St. Mark's Hospital. Interview with recordkeepers, 2001. I was told that any old patients' records would be at St. Bartholomew's Hospital, and a check of the record books there revealed nothing prior to 1900.

Sands, Ethel. Letters, Tate Gallery Archive.

Sickert, Walter. Collected papers, Islington Public Libraries. This collection of Walter Sickert's private papers includes some writings of his father, Oswald Sickert, and more than a hundred sketches on scraplike paper that have no titles, dates, or signatures. While one suspects that the sophistication of many of the drawings indicates they were done by Oswald, it is reasonable to attribute a number of the works to Walter, due to what appears to be a fledgling artist's early attempts at drawing in addition to a familiarity of style that is seen in his mature art. Sickert scholar Dr. Anna Robins, who looked at the sketches, verified that some of them were most likely done by Walter as a boy and possibly as late as 1880 or 1881 when he was in art school.

———. Letter to Ciceley Hey, circa August 1923, Islington Public Libraries.

———. "The New Age," May 14, 1914, Islington Public Libraries, Sickert Collection.

———. Letter to Bram Stoker, Feb. 1, 1887, Leeds University Brotherton Library, Department of Manuscripts and Special Collections.

———. Letter to Jacques-Emile Blanche (circa 1906), Institut Bibliotheque de L'Institut de France, Paris. Jacques-Emile Blanche—Walter Sickert Correspondence, Document Number 182.

———. Letter to Jacques-Emile Blanche (1906), Institut Bibliotheque de L'Institut de France, Paris. Jacques-Emile Blanche—Walter Sickert Correspondence, Document Numbers 183–186.

———. Letters to Virginia Woolf, New York Public Library.

———. Letter to unknown recipient, return address Frith's Studio, 15 Fitzroy Street (circa 1915). Author's collection.

———. Letters and edited drafts of his published articles. Author's collection.

———. Letters of, William Rothenstein Collection, Harvard University.

———. Sketches & Painting of, Ashmolean Museum.

———. Sketches of, Islington Central Library, Islington Archives, London.

———. Sketches of, Leeds City Art Gallery.

———. Sketches of, Tate Gallery Archive.

———. Sketches of, University of Manchester, John Rylands Library and History of Art Dept.

———. Sketches of, University of Reading Department of History of Art.

———. Sketches of, Walker Art Gallery, Liverpool.

Stage, The, "Death of Sir Henry Irving," October 19, 1905.

Stowe, Harriet Beecher. "Sunny Memories of Foreign Lands" (her essay on a breakfast with Richard Cobden), 1854. Papers of Richard Cobden, West Sussex Record Office, Ref. Cobden 272.

Sunday Dispatch, London, articles of September 2, 9, 16, 23, and 30, 1888.

Sunday Weekly Dispatch, London. Annotated scrapbook of articles, original owner unknown, August 12, 1888, through December 30, 1888. Author's collection.

Swanwick, Helena Sickert. Correspondence, Bodleian Library, Oxford University, M.S. English History.

———. Letter, National Art Gallery, Victoria and Albert Museum.

Terry, Ellen. Letter to a Mr. Collier, March 24 (no further date, possibly early 1900s). Author's collection.

———. Private correspondence (letters that show the various cities where she and Irving's theater company performed). Author's collection.

———. *The story of my Life,* Hutchinson & Co., London, 1908. Sickert's personal copy, fully annotated by him. Author's collection.

Sphere, The. "Sir Henry Irving, An Appreciation," October 21, 1905.

The Times of London. These original newspapers exclude the Sunday editions, and were bound for me in volumes that I reviewed in their entirety for the years 1888, 1889, 1890, 1891. All references to *Times* articles are taken from these original articles.

———. Articles of September 13, 14, 17, 21, October 1, 7, 8, 15, 16, 22, 23, 29, 1907.

University of Manchester, History of Art Department. Collection of Sickert sketches.

Victor, Prince Albert, the Duke of Clarence. Letters to his barrister George Lewis (December 17, 1890, and January 15, 1891). Author's collection.

SECONDARY SOURCES

Ackroyd, Peter. *London: The Biography,* Chatto & Windus, London, 2000.

Adam, Hargrave L. *The Police Encyclopaedia,* Vol. I, The Blackfriars Publishing Co., London; date unknown (circa 1908).

Amber, Miles (Ellen Cobden Sickert). *Wistons: A Story in Three Parts,* Charles Scribner's Sons, New York, 1902.

American Psychiatric Association, *Diagnostic and Statistical Manual of Mental Disorders,* third edition, revised, Washington, D.C., 1987.

Aronson, Theo. *Prince Eddy and the Homosexual Underworld,* John Murray, 1994.

Artists of The Yellow Book & the Circle of Oscar Wilde, The Clarendon & Parkin Galleries, October 5–November 4, 1983, Clarendon Gallery, London.

Ashworth, Henry. *Recollections of Richard Cobden, M.P., and the Anti-Corn League,* Cassell, Petter & Galpin, London (circa 1876).

Bacon, Francis. *Proficience of Learning, or the Partitions of Sciences,* Rob Yound & Ed Forest, Oxford, 1640.

Baedeker, Karl. *London and its Environs,* Karl Baedeker, Publisher, London, 1908.

Baron, Wendy. *Sickert,* Phaidon Press, Ltd., London, 1973.

Baron, Wendy, and Richard Shone. *Sickert: Paintings,* Yale University Press, New Haven and London, 1992.

Barrere, Albert, and Charles G. Leland. *A Dictionary of Slang, Jargon & Cant,* Vol. I and II, The Ballantyne Press, 1890.

Baynes, C. R. *Hints on Medical Jurisprudence,* Madras, Messrs. Pharoah & Co., Mount Road, 1854.

Bell, Clive. *Old Friends,* Chatto & Windus, London, 1956.

Bell, Quentin. *Victorian Artists,* Routledge and Kegan Paul, London, 1967.

———. *Some Memories of Sickert,* Chatto & Windus, London (circa 1950).

Bertram, Anthony, ed. *Sickert,* World's Masters New Series, London, The Studio Publications, 1955.

Besant, Annie. *An Autobiography,* T. Fisher Unwin, London, 1893.

Besant, Walter. *East London,* Chatto & Windus, London, 1912.

Bingham, Madeleine. *Henry Irving and the Victorian Theatre: The Early Doors,* George Allen & Unwin, London, 1978.

Blair, R. J. R. "Neurocognitive Models of Aggression, the Antisocial Personality Disorders, and Psychopathy," *Journal of Neurology, Neurosurgery and Psychiatry,* December 2001.

Blake, P. Y., J. H. Pincus, and C. Buckner. "Neurologic Abnormalities in Murderers," Department of Neurology, Georgetown University Medical Center, Washington, D.C., 20007, *Neurology,* Vol. 45 9, American Academy of Neurology, 1995.

Booth, General William. *In Darkest England and The Way Out,* International Headquarters of the Salvation Army, London, 1890.

Bower, Peter. *Turner's Later Papers: A Study of the Manufacture, Selection and Use of his Drawing Papers 1820–1851,* Tate Gallery Publishing, Oak Knoll Press, London, 1999.

Brimblecombe, Peter. *The Big Smoke,* Methuen, London and New York, 1987.

Bromberg, Ruth. *Walter Sickert: Prints,* Paul Mellon Centre Studies in British Art, Yale University Press, New Haven and London, 2000.

Brough, Edwin. *The Bloodhound and its Use in Tracking Criminals.* The Illustrated "Kennell News" Co., Ltd., 56 Ludgate Hill, London, undated (circa early 1900s).

Brower, M. C., and B. H. Price. "Neuropsychiatry of Frontal Lobe Dysfunction in Violent and Criminal Behavior: A Critical Review," *Journal of Neurology, Neurosurgery and Psychiatry,* December 2001.

Browne, Douglas G., and E. V. Tullett. *The Scalpel of Scotland Yard: The Life of Sir Bernard Spilsbury,* E. P. Dutton and Company, Inc., New York, 1952.

Browse, Lillian. *Sickert,* Rupert Hart-Davis, Soho Square, London, 1960.

———. *Sickert,* Faber and Faber, Ltd., London, 1943. When I purchased this book,

I was pleasantly surprised to discover that the previous owner was Dorothy Sayers.

Carter, E. C. *Notes on Whitechapel,* Cassell and Company, Ludgate Hill, London (date unknown, circa early 1900s).

Casanova, John N. *Physiology and Medical Jurisprudence,* Headland & Co., London, 1865.

Casper, Johann Ludwig. *A Handbook of the Practice of Forensic Medicine: Based Upon Personal Experience,* Vol. I, The New Sydenham Society, London, 1861.

———. *A Handbook of the Practice of Forensic Medicine: Based Upon Personal Experience,* Vol. III, The New Sydenham Society, London, 1864.

Cassell's Saturday Journal. London, February 15, 1890.

Chambers, E. *Cyclopaedia: of an Universal Dictionary of Arts and Sciences,* vols. I and II, fifth edition, D. Midwinter, London, 1741.

Cooper, Alfred, F.R.C.S. *Diseases of the Rectum and Anus,* J. & A. Churchill, London, 1892.

———. *A Practical Treatise on the Diseases of the Rectum,* H.K. Lewis, London, 1887.

Cotran, Ramzi S., Vinay Kumar, and Stanley Robbins. *Robbins Pathologic Basis of Disease,* fifth edition, W.B. Saunders Company, Philadelphia, 1994.

Cruikshank, George. *Punch and Judy. Accompanied by the Dialogue of the Puppet-Show, an Account of its Origin, and of Puppet-plays in England,* S. Prowett, London, 1828.

Darwin, Charles. *The Expression of the Emotions: In Man and Animals,* John Murray, London, 1872.

DeForest, Peter R., R. E. Gaensslen, and Henry C. Lee. *Forensic Science: An Introduction to Criminalistics,* McGraw-Hill, Inc., New York, 1983.

Di Maio, Dominick J., and Vincent J. M. Di Maio. *Forensic Pathology,* CRC Press, New York, 1993.

Dictionary of Modern Slang, Cant, and Vulgar Words, by a London Antiquary, John Camden Hotten, Piccadilly, 1860.

Dilnot, George. *The Story of Scotland Yard,* Houghton Mifflin Co., New York, 1927.

Dorries, Christopher. *Coroner's Courts: A Guide to Law and Practice,* John Wiley & Sons, New York, 1999.

Douglas, John, and Mark Olshaker. *The Anatomy of Motive,* Scribner, New York, 1999.

Douglas, John E., Ann W. Burgess, Allen G. Burgess, and Robert Ressler. *Crime Classification Manual,* Lexington Books, New York, 1992.

Edsall, Nicholas C. *Richard Cobden, Independent Radical,* Harvard University Press, Cambridge, Massachusetts, 1986.

Ellman, Richard. *Oscar Wilde,* Hamish Hamilton, London, 1988.

Emmons, Robert. *The Life and Opinions of Walter Richard Sickert,* Faber and Faber Ltd., London, 1941.

Evans, Stewart P., and Keith Skinner. *Jack the Ripper: Letters from Hell,* Sutton Publishing, Ltd., Stroud, UK, 2001.

———. *The Ultimate Jack the Ripper Sourcebook,* Constable & Robinson, Ltd., London, 2000.

Evelyn, John. *Fumifugium, Or the Inconvenience of the Aer and Smoake of London Dissipated,* National Smoke Abatement Society, reprint of 1661 edition, 1933.

Fairstein, Linda A. *Sexual Violence,* William Morrow and Company, New York, 1993.

Farr, Samuel. *Elements of Medical Jurisprudence,* J. Callow, London, 1814.

Fisher, Kathleen. *Conversations with Sylvia,* edited by Eileen Vera Smith, Charles Skilton, 1975.

Fishman, William J. *East End 1888,* Hanbury, London, 2001.

Frith, Henry. *How to Read Character in Handwriting,* Ward, Lock, Bowden and Co., New York, 1890.

Furniss, Harold, ed., *Famous Crimes,* Fleet Street, London, editions of September–November, 1888.

Galton, Sir Francis. *Fingerprint Directories,* Macmillan & Co., London, 1895.

———. *Inquiries into Human Faculty and its Development,* Macmillan & Co., London, 1883.

Gilberth, Vernon J. *Practical Homicide Investigation,* second edition, CRC Press, Boca Raton, FL, 1993.

Granshaw, Lindsay. *St. Mark's Hospital, London,* King Edward's Hospital Fund for London, 1985.

Griffith, Maj. Arthur. *The World's Famous Prisons: An Account of the State of Prisons from the Earliest Times to the Present Day, With the History of Celebrated Cases,* undated (circa 1905).

Guerin, Marcel, and Bruno Cassirer, eds. *Degas Letters,* Oxford, undated (circa mid 1900s).

Guy, William Augustus, and David Ferrier. *Principles of Forensic Medicine,* Henry Renshaw, London, 1875.

Hamnett, Nina. *Laughing Torso,* Constable & Co. Ltd., London, 1921.

Hampstead Artists' Council, Camden Town Group. Hampstead Festival Exhibition Catalogue, 1965.

Harrison, Michael. *Clarence: Was He Jack the Ripper?* Drake Publishers, Inc., New York, 1972.

Heywoode, Thomas. *Gynaikeion: or, Nine Bookes of Various History Concerning Women; Inscribed by the names of the Nine Muses,* Adam Islip, London, 1624.

Hinde, Wendy. *Richard Cobden: A Victorian Outsider,* Yale University Press, New Haven and London, 1987.

Hone, Joseph. *The Life of Henry Tonks,* William Heinemann, Ltd., London, 1939.

———. *The Life of George Moore,* Victor Gollancz, Ltd., London, 1936.

Hooke, Robert. *Micrographia: Or Some Physiological Descriptions of Minute Bodies Made by Magnifying Glasses. With Observation and Inquiries Thereupon,* Jo. Martyn and Ja. Allestry, Printers to the Royal Society, London, 1665.

House, Madeline, and Graham Storey, eds. *The Letters of Charles Dickens,* Vol. II, 1840–41, Clarendon Press, Oxford, 1969.

Howard, John. *The State of the Prisons in England and Wales, with Preliminary Observations, and an Account of Some Foreign Prisons and Hospitals,* William Eyres, London, 1784.

Howship, John. *Disease of the Lower Intestines, and Anus,* Longman, Hurst, Rees, Orme, and Brown, London, 1821.

Jervis, John. *A Practical Treatise on the Office and Duties of Coroners: with Forms and Precedents,* S. Sweet, W. Maxwell, and Stevens & Norton, Law Booksellers and Publishers, London, 1854.

Johnson, Samuel. *A Dictionary of the English Language,* vols. I and II, second edition, W. Strahan, London, 1756.

———. *A Dictionary of the English Language,* Vol. II, London, 1810.

Kersey, John. *Dictionarium Anglo-Britannicum,* J. Wilde, London, 1708.

Krill, John. *English Artists' Paper: Renaissance to Regency,* Winterthur Gallery, Oak Knoll Press, London, 2002.

Kuhne, Frederick. *The Finger Print Instructor,* Munn & Company, Inc., New York, 1916.

Larson, J. A. *Single Fingerprint System,* D. Appleton and Company, New York, 1924. (A bit of interesting trivia: On September 3, 1938, the author gave this book to a colleague and wrote, "With deepest appreciation in memory of hours spent in the search for truth." Under the inscription, Mr. Larson left his inked left thumbprint.)

Laski, Harold J., and Sidney and Beatrice Webb. *The Socialist Review* (circa 1929).

Lattes, Leone. *Individuality of the Blood: In Biology and in Clinical and Forensic Medicine,* Oxford University Press, London, 1932. (I was fascinated to discover after purchasing this book that it was once owned by Dr. Bernard Spilsbury, and it would appear that certain key forensic passages were underlined by him. Spilsbury was perhaps the most famous forensic pathologist in England's history. He was called "the incomparable witness" and is believed to have performed more than 25,000 postmortem examinations in his career.)

Laughton, Bruce. *Philip Wilson Steer, 1860–1942.* Clarendon Press, Oxford, 1971.

Laver, James. *Whistler,* Faber & Faber, London, 1930.

Leeson, Ex-Det. Sergeant B. *Lost London: The Memoirs of an East End Detective,* Stanley Paul & Co., Ltd., London (no date, circa early 1900s).

Lilly, Marjorie. *Sickert: The Painter and His Circle,* Elek Books Ltd., London, 1971; Noyes Press, New Jersey, 1973.

London, Jack. *The People of the Abyss,* The Macmillan Company, New York, 1903.

Luckes, Eva, C. E. *Matron, The London Hospital 1880–1919,* the London Hospital League of Nurses (no date).

MacDonald, Arthur. *Criminology,* Funk & Wagnalls Co., London, 1893.

MacGregor, George. *The History of Burke and Hare,* Thomas D. Morison, Glasgow, 1884.

Macnaghten, Sir Melville. *Days of My Years,* Edward Arnold, London, 1914.

Magnus, Philip. *King Edward the Seventh,* John Murray, London, 1964.

Maile, George Edward. *Elements of Juridical of Forensic Medicine: For the Use of Medical Men, Coroners and Barristers,* E. Cox and Son, London, 1818.

Malthus, Thomas Robert. *An Essay on the Principle of Population, As It Affects the Future Improvement of Society,* J. Johnson, London, 1798.

Marsh, Arnold. *Smoke: The Problem of Coal and the Atmosphere,* Faber and Faber, Ltd., London, undated (circa 1947).

Martin, Theodore. *The Life of His Royal Highness The Prince Consort,* Smith, Elder & Co., London, 1880.

Mellow, J. E. M. *Hints on the First Stages in the Training of a Bloodhound Puppy to Hunt Man,* privately published, Cambridge, 1934.

Morley, John. *The Life of Richard Cobden,* vols. I and II, Chapman and Hall, 1881.

Moyland, J. F. *Scotland Yard and The Metropolitan Police,* G. P. Putnam's Sons, London, 1929.

Oliver, Thomas. *Disease of Occupation,* Methuen & Co., Ltd., 1916.

Pennell, J., and E. R. Pennell. *The Whistler Journal,* J.B. Lippincott Co., Philadelphia, 1921.

———. *The Life of James McNeill Whistler,* Volume II, William Heinemann, London, 1908.

Petroski, Henry. *The Pencil: A History of Design and Circumstance,* Alfred Knopf, New York, 2000.

Pickavance, Ronald. *Sickert,* The Masters 86 (originally published in Italy, 1963), Knowledge Publications (Purnell & Sons Ltd.), London, 1967.

Poore, G. V. *London (Ancient and Modern). From a Sanitary and Medical Point of View,* Cassell & Co., London, 1889.

Powell, George. *The Victorian Theatre, A Survey,* Geoffrey Cumerlege, Oxford University Press, London, 1956.

Prothero, Margaret. *The History of the Criminal Investigation Department at Scotland Yard,* Herbert Jenkins Ltd., London, 1931.

Robins, Anna Gruetzner. *Walter Sickert: The Complete Writings on Art,* Oxford University Press, Oxford, 2000.

———. *Walter Sickert: Drawings,* Scolar Press, Gower House, 1996.

———. "Sickert 'Painter-in-Ordinary' to the Music-Hall" in *Sickert Paintings,* Wendy Baron and Richard Shone, eds., Yale University Press, New Haven and London, 1992.

Rodwell, G. F., ed. *A Dictionary of Science,* E. Moxon, Son and Co., London, 1871.

Rogers, Jean Scott. *Cobden and His Kate: The Story of a Marriage,* Historical Publications, London, 1990.

Rothenstein, John. *Modern English Painters: Sickert to Smith,* Eyre & Spottiswoode, London, 1952.

Rothenstein, William. *Men and Memories,* vols. I–III, Faber & Faber, London, 1931–39.

Sabbatini, Renato M. E. "The Psychopath's Brain," *Brain & Mind Magazine,* September/November 1998.

Saferstein, Richard. *Criminalistics: An Introduction to Forensic Science,* seventh edition, Prentice Hall, New Jersey, 2001.

St. John, Christopher, ed. *Ellen Terry and Bernard Shaw,* The Fountain Press, New York, 1931.

Sanger, William W. *The History of Prostitution: Its Extent, Causes, and Effects Throughout the World, Report to the Board of Alms-House Governors of the City of New York,* Harper & Brothers, New York, 1859.

Scott, Harold. *The Early Doors: Origins of the Music Hall,* Nicholson & Watson Ltd., London, 1946.

Sickert, Walter. "The Thickest Painters in London," *The New Age,* June 18, 1914.

———. unpublished draft of "The Perfect Modern," *The New Age,* April 9, 1914.

———. "The Old Ladies of Etching-Needle Street," *The English Review,* January, 1912.

———. "The International Society," *The English Review,* May 1912.

———. "The Royal Academy," *The English Review,* July 1912.

———. "The Aesthete and the Plain Man," *Art News,* May 5, 1910.

———. "Idealism," *Art News,* May 12, 1910.

———. "The Spirit of the Hive," *The New Age,* May 26, 1910.

———. "Impressionism," *The New Age,* June 30, 1910.

———. draft of article, "Exhibits," undated.

Sickert, The Fine Art Society, Ltd., 148 New Bond St., London, May 21–June 8, 1973.

Sickert, Walter Richard. *Drawings and Paintings, 1890–1942,* catalogue, Tate Gallery, Liverpool.

Sickert, Walter. *Centenary Exhibition of Etchings & Drawings,* March 15–April 14, Thomas Agnew & Sons, Ltd., London, 1960.

Sickert, Bernhard. *Whistler,* Duckworth & Co., London, undated.

Sims, George R., ed. *Living London,* vol. I, Cassell and Company, Ltd., London, 1902.

Sinclair, Robert. *East London,* Robert Hale Ltd., 1950.

Sitwell, Osbert. *Noble Essences,* Macmillan & Co., Ltd., London, 1950.

———. *A Free House! Or the Artist as Craftsman, Being the writings of Walter Richard Sickert,* Macmillan & Co., London, 1947.

Slang Dictionary, The: Etymological, Historical, and Anecdotal, Chatto and Windus, London, undated (circa 1878).

Smith, Thomas, and William J. Walsham. *A Manual of Operative Surgery on the Dead Body,* Longmans, Green, and Co., London, 1876.

Smith, Lieut.-Col. Sir Henry. *From Constable to Commissioner,* Chatto & Windus, London, 1910.

Stevenson, Robert Louis. *The Strange Case of Dr. Jekyll and Mr. Hyde,* Longmans, Green and Co., London, 1886.

Stoker, Bram. *Personal reminiscences of Henry Irving,* vols. I and II, William Heinemann, London, 1906.

Sutton, Denys. *Walter Sickert: A Biography,* Michael Joseph Ltd., London, 1976.

Swanwick, H. M. *I Have Been Young,* Victor Gollancz Ltd., London, 1935.

Taylor, Alfred Swaine. *The Principles and Practice of Medical Jurisprudence,* John Churchill & Sons, London, 1865.

World's Famous Prisons, The, vol. II, The Grolier Society, London, undated (circa 1900).

Thompson, Sir. H. *Modern Cremation,* Smith, Elder & Co., London, 1899.

Treves, Sir Frederick. *The Elephant Man, and Other Reminiscences,* Cassell & Co., London, 1923.

Troyen, Aimee. *Sickert as Printmaker,* Yale Center for British Art, February 21, 1979.

Tumblety, Dr. Francis. *The Indian Herb Doctor: Including His Experience in the Old Capitol Prison,* Cincinnati (published by the author, 1866).

Walford, Edward. *Old and New London,* vol. III, Cassell, Petter, Galpin & Co., London (date unknown, circa late nineteenth century).

Webb, Beatrice. *My Apprenticeship,* Longmans, Green and Co., London, 1926.

Welch, Denton. "Sickert at St. Peter's," in *Late Sickert, Paintings 1927–1942,* Arts Council of Great Britain, 1981.

Wheatley, H. B. *Reliques of Old London Suburbs, North of the Thames,* drawn in lithography by T. R. Way, George Bell and Sons, London, 1898.

Whistler, James McNeill. *The Baronet & the Butterfly: Eden Versus Whistler,* Louis-Henry May, Paris, February 10, 1899. (This particular volume was owned by one of Sickert's own circle, artist and writer William Rothenstein.)

———. *Mr. Whistler's Ten O'Clock,* London, 1888.

Whistler: The International Society of Sculptors, Painters & Gravers, Catalogue of Paintings, Drawings, Etchings and Lithographs, William Heinemann, London (circa 1905).

Wilde, Oscar. *The Trial of Oscar Wilde.* From the Shorthand Reports, privately printed, Paris, 1906.

Wollstonecraft, Mary. *Equality for Women Within the Law,* J. Johnson, London, 1792.

Wray, J. Jackson. *Will it Lift? The Story of a London Fog,* James Nisbet & Co., London, undated (possibly circa 1900).

INDEX

22
Adjoining 8 Sheet
23
24
J
K
L
M
N
Adjoining 15 Sheet
CITY ROAD
CITY ROAD BASIN
WENLOCK BASIN
NEW NORTH ROAD
GOSWELL ROAD
ST. JOHN STREET ROAD
NORTHAMPTON SQUARE
KING SQUARE
ST. LUKES
CLERKENWELL
OLD STREET
ST. Lukes Hospital
Bunhill Fields
Bur.l Ground
(Closed)
ARTILLERY GROUND
FINSBURY SQUARE
GREAT EASTERN STREET
OLD STREET
KINGSLAND ROAD
HIGH STREET SHOREDITCH
GREAT EASTERN RAILWAY STATION
ALDERSGATE STREET
ALDERSGATE ST. STATION
MOORGATE ST.
FINSBURY CIRCUS
BISHOPSGATE STREET WITHOUT
METROPOLITAN MEAT MARKET
POULTRY MARKET
HOLBORN VIADUCT
FARRINGDON STREET
NEWGATE STREET
L O N D O N
CHEAPSIDE
ST. PAULS CATHEDRAL
NEW BRIDGE STREET
CANNON STREET
QUEEN VICTORIA STREET
FENCHURCH STREET RAILWAY TERMINUS
MONUMENT
CUSTOM HOUSE
LONDON BRIDGE
SOUTHWARK BRIDGE ROAD
Barclay's Brewery
SOUTHWARK
T H A M E S
G.W. Bacon, F.R.G.S. 127 Strand, London. Copyright
22
Adjoining 24 Sheet
SCALE
1 Mile